THE GREAT
AMERICAN
DESERT

THE GREAT AMERICAN DESERT

THE LIFE, HISTORY AND LANDSCAPE
OF THE AMERICAN SOUTHWEST

JON MANCHIP WHITE

London

GEORGE ALLEN & UNWIN LTD

RUSKIN HOUSE   MUSEUM STREET

Maps by Donald T. Pitcher

Except where otherwise noted, all photographs are from the Arizona State Museum at the University of Arizona and the author wishes to thank the museum and Helga Teiwes, L. F. H. Lowe, E. B. Sayles and B. L. Fontana, photographers.

First published in Great Britain in 1977

© Jon Manchip White 1975

ISBN 0 04 917007 4

Printed in the U.S.A.

Permission is gratefully acknowledged to Alfred A. Knopf, Inc., and to Laurence Pollinger Ltd. and the Estate of the late Mrs. Frieda Lawrence for permission to quote a passage from D. H. Lawrence's *Mornings in Mexico,* copyright 1927 by D. H. Lawrence and renewed 1955 by Frieda Lawrence Ravagli; to Alfred A. Knopf, Inc., for permission to quote passages from Willa Cather's *The Professor's House,* copyright 1925 and renewed 1953 by Edith Lewis and The City Bank Farmers Trust Co., and from *Death Comes for the Archbishop,* copyright 1927 and renewed 1955 by Edith Lewis and The City Bank Farmers Trust Co.; to Harper & Row, Publishers, Inc., and to Chatto & Windus Ltd. for permission to quote from Aldous Huxley's *Brave New World,* copyright 1932, 1960 by Aldous Huxley; to Random House, Inc., for permission to quote four lines from Robinson Jeffers' "A Redeemer" in *The Selected Poetry of Robinson Jeffers,* copyright 1928 and renewed 1956 by Robinson Jeffers.

By the Author

For

CYNTHIA VARTAN

Europe-Africa-America

LIST OF MAPS

"Do you know everything—?"
"Everything?"
"In Europe?"
"Oh, yes," I laughed, "and one or two things even in America."

HENRY JAMES, *Europe*

"Who ever goes to America and Egypt? The English—that's how
God made them—and besides, there's no room for them at
home . . ."

IVAN GONCHAROV, *Oblomov*

Through my acquaintance with many Americans, and my trips
to and in America, I have obtained an enormous amount of insight into the European character; it has always seemed to me that
there can be nothing more useful for a European than some time
or another to look out at Europe from the top of a skyscraper.

C. G. JUNG, *Memories, Dreams, Reflections*

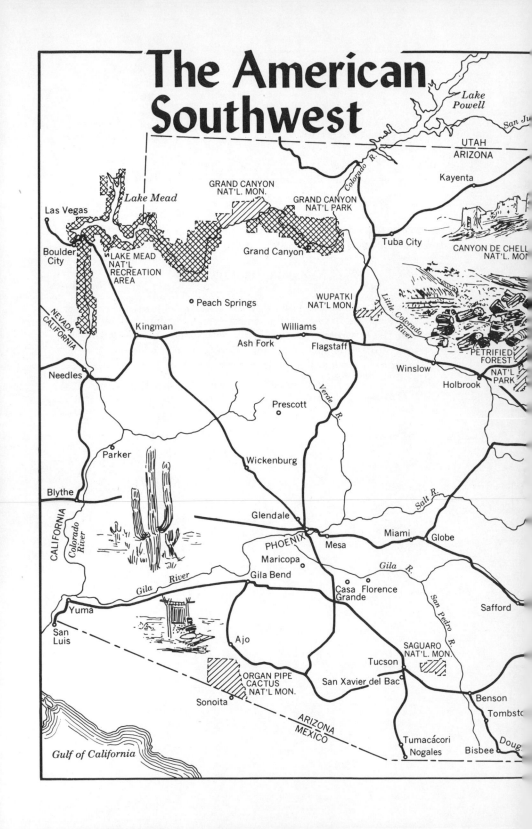

The American Southwest

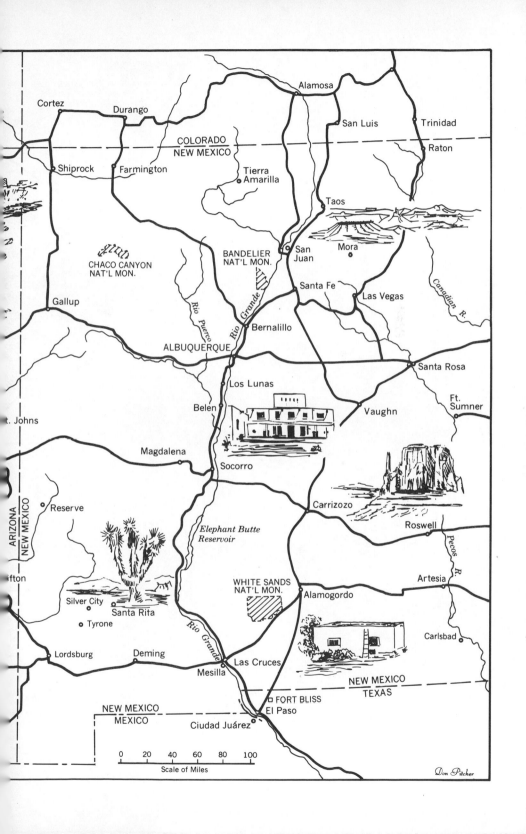

Cortez
Durango
Alamosa
San Luis
Trinidad

COLORADO
NEW MEXICO
Raton

Shiprock
Farmington
Tierra
Amarilla

Taos

CHACO CANYON
NAT'L MON.

BANDELIER
NAT'L MON.
San
Juan
Mora

Santa Fe

Gallup
Las Vegas

Canadian R.

Rio Puerco
Rio Grande
Bernalillo

ALBUQUERQUE

Santa Rosa

Los Lunas

Ft.
Sumner

Belen
Vaughn

Magdalena

Socorro

Reserve

Carrizozo

Roswell

Elephant Butte
Reservoir

Pecos R.

WHITE SANDS
NAT'L MON.
Alamogordo
Artesia

Silver City
Santa Rita

Tyrone

Carlsbad

Lordsburg
Deming
Rio Grande
Las Cruces
Mesilla

NEW MEXICO
TEXAS

St. Johns

ARIZONA
NEW MEXICO

Clifton

NEW MEXICO
MEXICO

FORT BLISS
El Paso
Ciudad Juárez

0   20   40   60   80   100
Scale of Miles

Don Pitcher

THE GREAT
AMERICAN
DESERT

ONE

WHEN I WAS LAST in England, my dear Rex, you and my other friends kept expressing your astonishment that I should have removed myself so far and so drastically from Europe. What terrible thing could have happened, you asked, that I had gone to settle in a place inhabited only by savages and wild animals, and by "men whose heads do grow beneath their shoulders"?

I tried to explain that Texas, even West Texas, is no longer exactly classified as *terra incognita,* and that I was very unlikely to drop off the edge of the world. I don't think I had much success. All of you were familiar, of course, with the spectacle of English writers leaving England to live in France, Italy, Spain or Greece. But Texas? Wasn't that carrying the motto of one of the great expatriates, James Joyce, "Silence, Exile and Cunning," to ridiculous lengths?

Over many a glass of good English ale I struggled to convince you of the beauty, strangeness, and amenity of this far-off place. But I could tell, from your elaborate politeness, that you honestly believed that I had taken leave of my senses. The Frenchmen of the *grand siècle* felt Poussin and Claude had gone utterly mad to prefer living in Rome to Paris. So what could have possessed me, of all people, a man so rooted in England, to take such a step? I know that you, Rex, were convinced that I must have hit on this lonely spot so that I could work undisturbed, beyond the reach of telephones, telegrams, and runners with messages in cleft sticks. That, after all, had been Descartes's solution, hadn't it, when he had settled in Amsterdam, a city where he was such a total stranger that nobody paid him any attention, and there was nothing to interrupt his reveries?

I was conscious that it was you, Rex, more than the rest, whom I wanted to convince of the rightness of the decision that I had taken six years before. I wanted to convince you not only because you were one of my oldest friends, from Cambridge days, or because I was amused by your air of insular superiority, but because for ten years, since your accident, you have been blind. You could not even see the photographs and color slides that the others were murmuring politely about. So, in the pages that follow, what I am struggling to do, before everything else, is to make you, Rex, *see*. I want you to appreciate something at least of the grandeur and fascination of the American Southwest. I want to try to bring it to life for you, to try to impress it on your inner eye. I think that even you may then begin to comprehend something of its true scope and scale.

Time and chance, as you know, have on the whole been very kind to me. My lines have fallen in pleasant places. You will remember your visits to St. John's Wood and to Gloucestershire, before you lost your sight. And here, in West Texas, I can assure you, my luck has not deserted me. You need not fear that fate has landed me in one of Graham Greene's Banana Republics.

Nevertheless I was naturally uneasy, as you can guess, as I set out from Europe, at the age of forty-three, to transport myself five thousand miles to a totally different environment. You may recall that I increased the bizarre nature of my leave-taking by driving aboard the *France* in my thirty-year-old Mercedes 320, in which I meant to make the six-day journey to the Southwest. I remember how you loved that car. It was sybaritically roomy and comfortable, and though you were unable to see the soft green countryside, during our drives around the West Country, I recall how you were pleased and soothed by the sweet strong hum of the engine.

That black-and-yellow monster, which I found in Madrid when I was living and working there, was originally in such poor condition, you will remember, that I had to drive it backwards across the Pyrenees on my final return to England. Now I was using it to make the two-thousand-mile trek to the Pecos. Each night I tended and watered it, like a knight of old attending to his horse. (. . . *Ames de chevaliers, revenez-vous encore?* . . .) On the seats around me were piled my suitcases and my miscellaneous belongings. I rolled down through Philadelphia, Baltimore, Washington, crossed the Appalachians, then took the Blue Ridge Parkway toward the South.

Bowling along with the hood down, through the August sunshine, smoking the Upmanns I had smuggled through the New York customs, I had plenty of leisure to consider that question that still exercises you and my other friends. Why in fact had I forsaken the fat and petted fields of Gloucestershire to embrace the tawny vistas of the West? It was not an easy thing to answer. My reasons for leaving, I decided, could ultimately be reduced to six.

First of all, I might mention the fact that three years earlier I had paid an extended visit to southern Africa. In past years I had spent some time in north Africa and in Egypt—but the enormous perspectives of southern Africa came as a shock to me. Before then, I had been in a similar position to people like you, Rex, who express such well-bred and lukewarm interest when I talk about Arizona or New Mexico. One is aware that such immense landscapes must exist—but until one views them for oneself it is impossible to grasp their impressiveness, or experience their liberating quality. Until I went to South Africa and to Southwest Africa, I was like a man who has been staring all his life through the wrong end of a telescope. Some sort of internal shift took place, and when I returned to the cozy proportions of Europe I was unable to settle down again. Something inside me was pinned to the coloring and expanse of the deserts and parched mountains. Well, the Southwestern United States, where I now am, happens to bear an extraordinarily close resemblance to Southwest Africa. Was there, perhaps, some compass needle buried in my heart, swinging naturally in the direction of southwest? Do we have some kind of *querencia,* some mysterious place that we all instinctively head for, like the bull in the bullring?

A second reason, also personal, stemmed from the fact that twenty years before, at the university, I had taken my degrees in archaeology and anthropology. It was on raw, rainy mornings in the lecture rooms in Downing Street that I first heard of the tombs and temples of the Mayas, of the Aztecs and Toltecs, the Mixtecs and Zapotecs. Now, by traveling to my new place of residence on the Mexican border, I would soon be able to see these marvels for myself. And as a student I had also become familiar, without dreaming that one day I might actually see them, with the Indian tribes and pueblos of the Rio Grande. At Cambridge the names of Ruth Benedict, Ruth Bunzel, Franz Boas, Clark Wissler, Clyde Kluckhohn, and other American anthropologists had been as familiar to me as those of the Elizabethan and metaphysical poets. You too, Rex, have a profound and abiding passion for history. Many are the evenings I have seen you sit, motionless and attentive, your head tilted up, as I read to you from Geoffrey of Monmouth, or Gibbon, or Ranke, or about Charlemagne or Frederick of Hohenstaufen. I do not think I shall find it too difficult to convince you of the absorbing character of a part of the world where no less than five separate cultures, the oldest reaching back more than a millennium, are superimposed in a visible, living way upon one another (figure 1).

And then, of course, for me there was also the bonus of being about to find myself once more in a Spanish-speaking *ambiente.* The landscape of the Southwest not only reminded me of southern Africa—it was a broader version

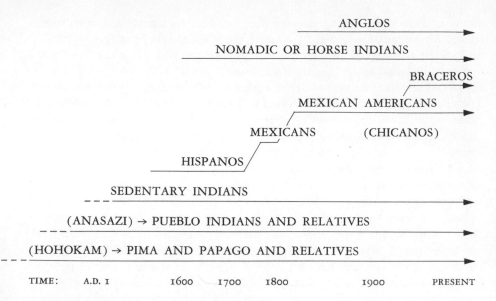

FIGURE 1. The people of the Southwest.

of the sun-baked landscape of Castile, where I had spent four memorable years. I had learned Spanish as a boy at school; I had written the biographies of two celebrated Spaniards: and now I would be settling down in a city where every day I would hear the tongue of Lope de Vega and Cervantes spoken, with many of the forms and inflections it once possessed, centuries ago, in the cradle of *la raza*. Moreover, as a *lagniappe,* or extra titbit, as they say in New Orleans, one of the largest *plazas de toros* in the Western hemisphere would be only a fifteen-minute drive away.

What else? Well, Rex, then there was the weather. I was born in a part of the British Isles where it rains for two hundred days in the year, and I was coming to a place where there is sunshine for three hundred days in the year. West Texas has one of the finest climates in the world. But, I hear you ask (a little wistfully perhaps?), don't you ever miss the rain? No, Rex, *never*. I *never* miss the rain. I wouldn't be sorry if I didn't face another drop of the stuff all the rest of my life. In Europe—apart from the pleasures of a good storm—I came to loathe the rain. I walked through it glumly, as if the skies were dripping acid. In West Texas there are no umbrellas. I can never get too much of the sun. England has made me a sun-fanatic. I never tire of waking up to another sun-drenched day. Oh no, Rex, I don't miss the slush or the sleet. Oh no, I don't miss the marrow-piercing cold.

But more important than the rain or the cold, Rex, I think that what I had been unconsciously seeking, finally, was the wildness and the isolation, the sense of a land unravaged and numinous. Apart from its awful climate, Britain has become too crowded, even by the standards of Europe. One is almost never out of sight of a house, or a car, or another human being. More than fifty million Britons are packed into an island that could be tucked three or four times into Texas, or California, or several other American states. Texas, of course, as Texans are happy to tell you, is larger than any European country except western Russia. It is seven hundred miles across and seven hundred miles deep, yet it contains only eleven million people. Moreover, four of those eleven million are concentrated in only nine urban centers. Blessed Texas! League after league of forest and desert, mountain and scrub. Mile after mile of delicious damn-all—an emptiness where one can get away from the human race and consider first and last things—a healing nothingness.

Don't you think that the overpopulation, together with the bad climate, must be largely responsible for the malaise of modern England? I am sure you know about those experiments where the rats go mad when they are herded too closely together. Freud believed that the pressures exerted by modern living breed neurosis. Jung has written of the "dissociated society," cut off by its artificial character from its nourishing roots, condemned to distemper and despair. The England I left was a discontented place. As Admiral Beatty remarked to his flag-captain at the Battle of Jutland, "something is wrong with our bloody ships today." In a poll conducted in 1967, thirty-eight out of every one hundred persons stated that they would like to emigrate if they were given the opportunity—double the number in ten other countries polled, and more than treble the American figure. Well, I was one of the 38 percent lucky enough to be able to go abroad.

When I boarded the *France,* England was being governed by the most wretched administration to hold office during my lifetime. I had the misfortune to be born in the year that Ramsey Macdonald became Britain's first Labour Prime Minister. Since then, the decline has been swift—from second to seventeenth place in the standard-of-living league table in only a quarter of a century. The Labour Party is succeeding in turning a self-reliant country into a servile one. It is foisting on a robust people its mean, paltry, dog-in-the-manger creed, based mainly on envy, the silliest and most corrosive of human emotions.

I will dwell no further on my disenchantment with British politics. The wiser and most graceful course, when one is disaffected, is not to waste one's energy in snarling and grousing, but to remove oneself to less oppressive surroundings. I did not wish to remain at home, slowly encrusting myself, as Cyril Connolly once put it, with the gentlemanly protection of English selfishness. I was willing and eager to work elsewhere. Then why stay in England and endure the stale rhetoric and heavy-handed bullying of Socialist zealots I believe with all my heart what Flaubert once wrote: "I loathe everything compulsory, all laws, government and regulations. What is society, that it should *force* me to do anything at all? What God made it my master? See how it falls back into the old injustices of the past. It will no longer be despots that oppress the individual, but the masses, the public safety, the state that is always right, the universal catchword, Robespierre's maxim. I prefer the desert, and I shall return to the Bedouin, who are free."

The Jacobins—or what an earlier generation called the Fanatiques—have prevailed. They are not now to be deterred. Britain is a socialist, collectivist country, with the harassment, torpor, and inefficiency such a condition creates. I will only say that I found it painful to watch the spectacle of the Socialists rooting in the entrails of what, when I was young, was still, in spite of the First World War, a vigorous and independent country. I do not like the New Totalitarians, as a Swedish writer calls them, in a book about his own Social Democrats. I shall merely quote, in conclusion, what Lord Macaulay wrote about the Gradgrinds 130 years ago: "It is not by the intermeddling of their idol, the omniscient and omnipotent State, but by the prudence and energy of the people that England has hitherto been carried forward in civilization. Our rulers will best promote the improvement of the nation by strictly confining themselves to their own legitimate duties, by leaving capital to find its most lucrative course, commodities their fair price, industry and intelligence their natural reward, idleness and folly their natural punishment, by observing strict economy in every department of the State. Let the Government do this: the People will assuredly do the rest."

No, the strike-ridden winters and the nasal exhortations of my Socialist masters were altogether too much to put up with.

I wanted to rediscover the nourishing roots.

"I prefer the desert, and will return to the Bedouin, who are free."

TWO

I AM PRETTY SURE that I could convey to you, Rex, something of the effect made by the western sky in such a way as to make you see it with your mind's eye. Yet I wonder if I could recreate for you anything of the intangible element that bestows on it its special charm and quality—I mean the quality of the sunlight. For this western sunlight has a radiance that equals that of Provence or the Campagna. It is brilliant, constant, with an airy sheen, a silvery sparkle. It is the fine-spun straw of a Vouvray, a Sancerre, a Quincy. The secret is in the sunlight, Rex, and I wish I could make you see it.

It was through this sun-stroked, honey-soaked landscape that I began to make my long drives, once I had settled down. I did not make them, of course, in the Mercedes; grand as it was, its cruising speed of 58 mph was too sedate for the immense distances involved. I made them in a Mustang, a model with a special chassis made for Central and South American roads, that I bought from a Mexican dealer in Juárez. With its eight cylinders thrumming in front of me, I enjoyed the pleasures of old-fashioned motoring. Here in the West it is still possible to get behind the wheel and go—to drive and drive all day, at high speed, through unmatchable scenery. In fact, I was taking advantage of what may turn out to have been the last classic age of motoring. Those were the days when the gasoline companies urged you on radio and television to burn up gas, and gave you gifts and trading stamps. Now the introduction of ration cards may sooner or later lie ahead, or at least feelings of social guilt whenever one undertakes a lengthy trip. But until recently it has been possible to reel off six or seven hundred miles a day in pursuit of enjoyment, the excitement of traveling swiftly and smoothly through incomparable surroundings. Can you grasp it, Rex?—six or seven hundred miles a day?—without the least fatigue? Land's End to John O'Groats in a single day, instead of three?—and almost entirely without compulsory stops or traffic lights? What is the average distance in England, I wonder, between traffic lights?—a couple of hundred yards? Out here in the West, outside the main towns, they are curiosities. One is actually grateful to them, as an interruption that brings one back to reality. It is four hundred miles from where I am writing these lines to Santa Fe, and in that distance there are three traffic lights—three—I have counted them. And between here and Austin, a distance of six hundred miles, there are seven. One can drive for hour after hour at an uninterrupted seventy or eighty—faster, if one feels like it, when one is safely beyond the beat of the local sheriff. What is the point of owning a sports car if, as in England, the Mrs. Grundys prevent you from driving it at the speed for which it was designed? There is a stretch of Interstate 10 between Ozona and Sonora where you can easily work up to a hundred and sixty. The signs whirl past . . . Sutton County, Devil's River, Crockett County . . . There is a swishing sound like the sea as the car surges beneath the underpasses . . .

The impressions of the long drives fuse together in a bright melting dream. Red tips of the ocotillo . . . soft emerald of the pecan orchards . . . burnt orange and brown tassels of the corn . . . tender sulphur of the cotton flowers . . . crimson skeins of chile drying on adobe walls . . . flash floods and dust devils . . . monarch butterflies and dusky swallowtails . . . the smell of verbena and creosote bushes after the rain . . . sun-spun . . . sun-struck . . . a dream. . . .

To drive through such landscapes, to walk or ride a horse through them, is a healing process. You regain contact with nature as we knew it before individuation sundered us and the divorce occurred. This is what it was like in the Garden of Eden, before we knew self-consciousness and ceased to exist in a simple harmony with our surroundings. To live in the West is to be given a glimpse of our aboriginal bliss. "O how I long to travel back, and tread again that ancient track! . . ."

We have been warned by twentieth century philosophers, particularly the Existentialists, not to indulge in the pathetic fallacy. Sartre, Robbe-Grillet, and others have been severe in condemning the habit of speaking of oceans or mountains as "mighty," "majestic" or "noble." Such a tendency, they assert, is atavistic, a return to primitive and prescientific modes of thought. An ocean or a mountain is not "mighty," "majestic" or "noble": it is a vast indifferent sheet of water, or a great indifferent pile of rock. It is foolish, they hold, to seek to humanize and personalize them by ascribing human emotions to them; to cherish such fantasies is to falsify one's capacity to face the truth, to see existence as it really is; we enjoy no cozy relationship with oceans and mountains; they know nothing of us. Only Camus, among the Existentialists, forbore to preach so bleak a message: but he was a man of a more humane and poetic temper, reared beneath the bright sun of the Mediterranean, on the warm beaches of Algeria. The awesome facts of nature are not to be dismissed as easily in North Africa as they are on the curbed banks of the Seine.

Yet more than a century ago the cautionary modern note, the note of alienated man, had already been struck. Darwin, in 1859, wrote a hymn to "the great Tree of Life." He accepted as a Christian the idea of a Creator who had originally "breathed life into a few forms or into one," so that "from so simple a beginning endless forms most beautiful and most wonderful have been, and are being evolved." Yet he spoke also of the difficulty of avoiding "personifying the word Nature," stating that by "Nature" he only meant "the aggregate action and product of many natural laws, and by laws the sequence of events as ascertained by us." This was already a significant narrowing of the role of Nature as it was understood by Wordsworth, or as Tennyson represented it in *In Memoriam*. With the rationalist ethos introduced by the French Revolution, and Nietzsche's notion of "the death of God," the universe had begun to grow cold, to become a lonely place. Nature was no longer consoling, no longer revealed the handiwork of the Almighty; it seemed in a scientific age to be empty; in its sprawling indifference it seemed actually hostile.

There is a passage in *The Education of Henry Adams* where the author is summoned from England to Italy to the bedside of his sister, who has suffered "a miserable cab-accident that had bruised her foot." Tetanus set in. "Hour by hour the muscles grew rigid while the mind remained bright, until after ten days of fiendish torture she died in convulsions." The experience proved "the last lesson—the sum and term of education. He had passed through thirty years of rather varied experience without having once felt the shell of custom broken. He had never seen Nature—only her surface—the sugar-coating that she shows to youth. Flung suddenly in his face, with the harsh brutality of chance, the terror of the blow stayed by him henceforth for life, until repetition made it more than the will could struggle with; more than he could call on himself to bear. The first serious consciousness of Nature's gesture—her attitude towards life—took form as a phantasm, a nightmare, an insanity of force. For the first time, the stage-scenery of the senses collapsed. Society became fantastic, a vision of pantomime with a mechanical motion. With nerves strained for the first time beyond their power of tension, he slowly travelled northwards with his friends, and stopped for a few days at Ouchy to recover his balance in a new world. For the first time in his life, Mont Blanc for a moment looked to him what it was—a chaos of anarchic and purposeless forces."

The Existentialists expected this *néant* of nature, its very blankness, to appear bracing in its own mournful way. It is certainly possible to derive a joy from nature's stoniness, for it is by lifting our eyes to the hills that we put our puny problems in perspective. We are finite; nature is infinite. "I change, but cannot die." However small and sordid our individual existences, we have the consolation of projecting them against a dignified setting; however squalid the drama, it is played out in a grand amphitheater. Here, in the spaces of the American West, you can run across men and women, or the members of entire small communities, whose faces are marked by the thoughtfulness and resignation that comes from the knowledge of playing such a humble part on such a great stage. There is a quietness, a reverence in their faces, as if they were aware of the proscenium arch of eternity. When you have seen the buttes, the canyons, the mesas, you learn the scale of the backdrop. You learn, too, that human strain and hysteria belong to the cities, that you can leave them behind, shed them like irritating garments. There is a time to dwell in cities and a time to depart from them. The people who live their lives in the shadow of high buildings often never realize, in the words of Shakespeare's Coriolanus, that there is "a world elsewhere." Wandering across America, across the West, you recognize with genuine relief that the population could double, treble, quadruple, yet the major portion of the landscape would still remain empty. They can never saturate it. They can never bury it beneath Coca-Cola bottles, chewing-gum wrappers, used-car dumps. They can never totally disfigure it with billboards and fried-chicken stands. It will swallow them up. One half of the United States, the whole western half of the country, is technically a desert: and a desert it will remain, to desert it will return. Nature, like God, is not mocked. Men can pollute her oceans, poison her rivers, rummage in her guts—she will survive. She *must* survive. She is the frame of things. Her wounds must heal. (Forgive me, you Existentialists, for the slide into personification.) There is a consolation in our inability to damage nature or permanently insult her. To live in the West is to appreciate, as you cannot do in cities or in teeming Europe, the bedrock realities. They teach you that there is no need to be horrified by the stupendous vacancies of heaven. and earth. Viewed from one angle, they render you insignificant; viewed from another, they lend you stature and a kind of immortality. The West teaches you your place: but in that process it bestows on you a sense of peace and acquiescence. You know where ultimately you belong.

I am selfishly pleased that human beings are by nature gregarious. Huddled in their urban congeries, building upward and upward rather than outward and outward, they thereby avoid clogging up the entire landscape. Fortunately, the desire to seek a close relationship with nature is not shared by the majority of men and women, or the majority of Americans. In the minds of most Americans she is still the great antagonist. Americans have inherited their fear of her from their pioneer ancestors. They assault her frantically; they rip and hack at her; they shoot and slaughter her birds and animals. America came into being and achieved prosperity by raping nature, not appeasing her. It is interesting to drive through the West with American passengers. They seldom utter exclamations of delight at the sight of some magnificent prospect; instead they hunch down and glower at it. They relax when they catch sight of some garish billboard smeared along the roadside; they smile when the car begins to enter the tacky outskirts of a town. To them, as for the pioneers, nature is intimidating and oppressive.

And I must confess that on my initial visit to the first of the natural features I must describe in this chapter—the Grand Canyon—I experienced a sensation of dismay that resembled the feelings of my American passengers.

The Grand Canyon is on the northern perimeter of the American Southwest. The Southwest is a loose term, differently defined by different authors. For the purposes of this book it comprises the state of Texas west of the Pecos River ("To the east of the Pecos there is no law, to the west of the Pecos there is no God"); the states of New Mexico and Arizona; and the southern portions of the states of Nevada, Utah, and Colorado. The Grand Canyon is in Arizona, and is a long haul from where I write in West Texas: but I have journeyed there twice, to view it from both its Northern and Southern Rims. It is so vast that to travel from one rim to the other entails a journey of two hundred miles; therefore two separate journeys are usually indicated.

Driving there, after you have lived for some time in the West, you imagine you are more or less acclimated to it. You are not. It is easy to appreciate what emotions the Spaniard Don García López de Cárdenas must have felt when, detached from Coronado's expedition, he and his party reached it in 1540. They were the first Europeans to set eyes on it. García López was badly injured. His little band of cavalrymen were suffering from extremes of hunger and thirst. The Canyon must have seemed to them, during their brave but futile attempt to find their El Dorado, the ultimate obstacle, the final discouragement. Still, it was not easy to discourage the Spaniards of the *Siglo de Oro*. Just as Cortés, on his march from Veracruz to Mexico City, ordered his liveliest lieutenant to climb Popocatépetl, so García López sent a party to explore the Canyon. They went in search of water from the Colorado River, snaking through its granite groove far below. Since, as their leader put it, the Canyon was deeper than the height of the Cathedral of Seville, it was not surprising that in their weakened condition they failed to reach it and were forced to turn back.

Believe it or not, Rex, the Canyon is a mile deep. At places it is nineteen miles wide. Two separate ecological systems flourish on the opposing sides. The South Rim displays the flora and fauna of the Lower Sonoran, Upper Sonoran, and Transition Zones; the North Rim, fifteen hundred feet higher, extends into the colder Canadian and Hudsonian Zones. Both rims afford stunning views: Havasupai, Mohave, Hopi, Yaki, Grandview, Moran, Lipan and Navajo Points on the South Rim; Point Imperial, Cape Royal, Bright Angel and Point Sublime on the North. The South Rim offers the more impressive lateral view, the North the more profound horizontal one. I happen to favor the latter, since the lip of the South Rim is perpetually encrusted with a scurf of tourists and their campgrounds, cabins, trailer villages, garages, "group areas," hotels, motels, and souvenir shops. The North Rim is harder to reach and relatively deserted. It contains only one hotel, a small inn, and a modest campground. It possesses three promontories that jut like piers into the Canyon—the well-named Walhalla Plateau, Bright Angel Point, and the dirt road that leads you to Point Sublime. They present unparalleled prospects, particularly at dawn and sunset. Although the road is closed in winter, in summer and autumn you can enjoy the delicious coolness and remoteness of its blue spruces, white firs, and quaking aspens.

You must not expect the beauties of the Canyon to register immediately. For most people the first sensation is of shock, of fear and paralysis. Curiously, this fear is absent when you fly above the Canyon, for flying is a disembodied business and breeds detachment. You need to be anchored physically to the earth to appreciate its full effect; you have to feel it sensually, through the soles of the feet. Peering into the Canyon from the edge is a hundred times more pulse-quickening than staring down at it from overhead. You feel an appalling sense of shrinkage, psychological as well as physical. It is like the feeling that seized Alice when she swallowed the potion and began to grow smaller and smaller. You shrivel to the scale and perspective of your earliest infancy, when the world was monstrous and gigantic, when you felt helpless at being confronted with it. There is a strange sense of being turned somehow inside out—as if you were contemplating an interior rather than an exterior landscape—an "inscape," as Gerard Manley Hopkins called it. "O the mind/Mind has mountains, cliffs of fall/Frightful, sheer, no-man-fathomed . . ." Aldous Huxley has noted the phenomenon in his *Heaven and Hell*. "The revelation of the wilderness, living its own life according to the laws of its own being, transports the mind towards its antipodes; for primeval Nature bears a strange resemblance to that inner world where no account is taken of our personal wishes or even of the enduring concerns of man in general." The sight of the voids and ranges of Nature suddenly give us a glimpse of the voids and ranges within us. "The Mind, that Ocean where each kind/Does straight its own resemblance find." Such moments awaken a primitive terror. To look at the Grand Canyon is to look at eternity and death. Few people desire to dwell on those entities. Even the strongest regard them tangentially, in the way we regard another disturbing presence, the sun. To march up to the lip of that terrible gash in mother earth and rake it with a glance is not something most visitors do. You would have to be very stoical or very insensitive to do that. Most people hesitate, brace themselves, take a deep breath, then walk hesitantly to the edge. They grip the handrail hard. Below them stretches that Nothingness so dear to the Existentialists.

Why do we feel an urge to throw ourselves into such cruel vacancies? The intensity and irrationality of our feelings frightens us. One is reminded

The Grand Canyon, Arizona. (BRUCE COLE COLLECTION, ARIZONA STATE MUSEUM)

of those flying dreams that are so common in childhood. One is tempted to leap, if not to death, at least into that beckoning emptiness, to twist and dive and soar among the cliffs and crags. Was Ferenczi right when he speculated that such dreams are a residual memory of the aeons when we dwelt in the ocean, aeons which have left their mark on our bodies in the shape of our breathing system, residual gill slits, the salinity of our blood? Or are those other psychologists correct, who affirm that they derive from a later level of our experience, when for a hundred million years we swung through the trees as cousins of the lemurs and the lorises?

I have spoken of my conviction that nature is consoling. But perhaps the Grand Canyon is too stark for that. You can cultivate the pathetic fallacy in connection with most mountains, rivers, and forests, to which it can be comfortable to relate. But the Canyon is what I called it—an atrocious wound in the body of the earth. You can see deep down into her viscera. It is a compulsive yet embarrassing privilege, like watching an operation on your mother from the gallery of an operating theater. Layer after layer of epidermis and flesh have been stripped away and you can see clear to the bottom of the incision where the river gnaws like a green worm in the bowel.

No, it is not comforting, this clinical, geological view. The canyon is only —(*only!*)—nine million years old. Yet it reveals a complete section of earth's history reaching back three billion years, to the time when there was no life on the planet, not even in the form of algae, bacteria, or protozoa. Nothing, no continents or mountains, only the shifting wind and drifting rain, the meandering rivers and vague seas. Probably you, Rex, in your blindness, can grasp that condition of chaos and old night more vividly than I. As Tennyson wrote:

> The hills are shadows, and they flow
> From form to form, and nothing stands;
> They melt like mist, the solid lands,
> Like clouds they shape themselves and go . . .

I have been haunted all my life by the long vistas of time. *Fugit, jam fugit, irreperabile tempus.* It may be my Welsh blood, a Celtic predisposition. The Celts, unlike the Saxons, are a time-ridden breed; their apprehension of its ruinous processes is bound up with their sense of tragedy, defeat, and loss. The Grand Canyon is the physical incarnation of the geological history of the world, displayed with a brutality from which not even a Celt could derive a gloomy enjoyment. It is not pleasant to stare down at three billion years. When you stand on the rim of the Canyon, on the Coconino Plateau, you are already standing on a formation of the Permian period that was laid down more than two hundred million years ago, before there were trees, or birds, or reptiles, or mammals, or flowering plants. And thence you can see down, down, down, past the shales, past the limestones, past the sandstones, five hundred million, a billion years, past the extinct amphibians, past the fossilized fish, to the Precambrian granites—at the bottom of the gorge. As a schoolboy, I always took a patriotic pride in the fact that these oldest rocks of earth were named after my own country, after Cambria, after Wales; it seemed to add to Wales's antiquity and renown. Now, contemplating those reeling depths, I am not sure that the Victorian archaeologists paid Wales a compliment.

Three billion years. And man has been in existence, in some sort of recognizable shape, for only a million. On the cusp between Miocene and Pliocene, he was still the uncouth hand-axe-maker whose clumsy relics have been uncovered in the gravels of Kenya. A quarter of a million years ago, he was a pathetic Pithecanthropoid and Neanderthaloid. For no more than a paltry few hundred thousand years has he been the prancing, preening biped who boasts such a conceit of himself. *Man, man, Caliban: get yourself a new man.* The black rocks at the foot of the slot are three thousand million times older than mankind. I use the American term for a billion, a thousand million, which Britons call a milliard; in England the billion is reckoned as a million

million, which Americans call a trillion. But a thousand million, or a million million, does it matter, standing on that ledge and staring down into the well of Time? When you look into the Grand Canyon, you are seeing earth as it once was, and will be again. You are witnessing the frightening blind force of nature, that can thrust up a mountain or lop off its summit as easily as you can slice the top off an egg. Is not a certain shiver of hopelessness pardonable? "I have a sin of fear, that when I've spun/My last thread, I shall perish on the shore . . ." Stepping away from those falls of stone, you can only trust in Teilhard's belief that that blunt and twisted chaos down there is our Alpha point, that God in His own good time (which is not *our* time) will raise us to the Omega point where everything will meet again in Him. There are moments at the Grand Canyon when I am gripped by the thought that the instant of death might be like this. The Canyon might be as close as we can come while living to the sensation of sinking into eternity, being carried to heaven by an Archangel, or being hauled into Paradise by our hair, like a Muhammadan . . .

There are, fortunately, other canyons in the Southwest that produce a less desolating effect (Figure 2). The somber strata of the Grand Canyon stretch away and away, rigid and uncompromising; whereas the appeal of the lesser canyons is their warm coloration and the novelty of their forms. The great canyons of southwest Utah—Zion National Park, Bryce Canyon, Cedar Breaks —are splashed with salmons and scarlets, ochres and yellows. Zion spreads itself over two hundred and thirty square miles, its crimson gorges slashing down to the Virgin River through the Mesozoic rocks of the Kolob Plateau, while Bryce and Cedar Breaks are gouged from the Wasatch limestones of the Paunsaugunt Plateau. These limestones, hollowed into a string of massive amphitheaters, soar skyward in the shape of the fantastic Pink Cliffs. Whimsical as a landscape by Tanguy, frizzled with Engelmann spruce and juniper, they are furnished with what look from above like real villages, with real inhabitants, but which are houses and people of stone. It is as though nature was making amends for the terrors of the Grand Canyon, showing a wittier side to her character. At sunset she puts on a superbly vulgar display, the sun flaring through the clear air behind the fretted crests. It is the sort of thing that prompted Whistler to say, "I see that Nature is trying to creep up on Art again . . ."

Whistler was echoed, as a matter of course, by Wilde. "The more we study Art, the less we care for Nature. What Art reveals to us is Nature's lack of design, her extraordinary monotony, her absolutely unfinished condition. Nature has good intentions, but, as Aristotle once said, she cannot carry them out." So, at the Canyon de Chelly, Oak Creek, and Glen Canyon, man has lent poor old nature a helping hand. The Canyon de Chelly, with its tributary, the

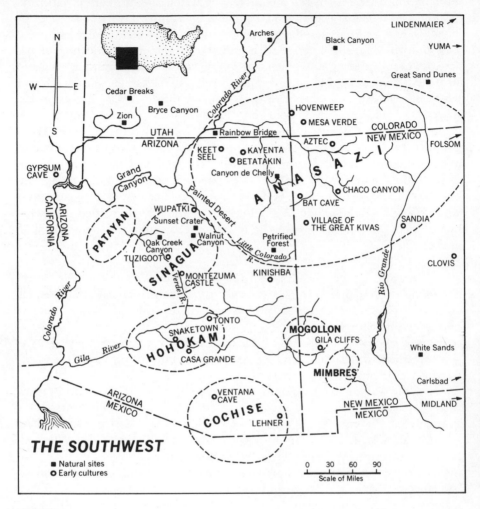

FIGURE 2

Canyon del Muerto, have been for a thousand years the home of Pueblo farmers and Navajos. Oak Creek, southwest of Flagstaff, is a ten-mile lava-tipped furrow in the earth, with fields and orchards clustered around the busy little stream at its heart. It was there, at Sedona, that Max Ernst settled in 1946, having first seen Arizona in 1943. He lived there for fifteen years. It is easy to guess from his geological fantasies of the 1930s how such a landscape must have impressed him. In such canvases as *Vox Angelica,* and the celebrated *L'oeil du silence,* the presence of Arizona is palpable. Their images express the indwelling spirit of nature—mysterious, inexplicable, neither to be questioned nor ever rendering an answer.

Glen Canyon, too, is softened by the presence of water. A dam, 500 feet deep and 180 river-miles long, represents another determined attempt by man to improve on nature's imperfections. "Well done, water, by God!," Turner exclaimed when he saw the fountains of Tivoli. The cobalt expanse of Lake Powell is named after the one-armed Civil War veteran who first sailed down the Green and Colorado rivers in 1869 and 1871. Indeed, nature herself seems to view the efforts of man at Glen Canyon with indulgence, for she has added a few fiorite of her own in the shape of willows, tamarisks, and cottonwoods. Already, however, a dozen "recreation centers" are under construction, and an official brochure tells us that "these will provide campgrounds, boat ramps, picnic areas, ranger stations, and concessionary-operated facilities such as restaurants, motels, trailer villages, boat services, etc." One of the less admirable characteristics of Americans is their compulsion to carry out almost every activity in the mass. They would not appreciate the appeal, particularly to those who seek to align themselves with nature, of Cicero's *Numquam minus solus quam cum solus,* "I am never less alone than when I am alone."

Can Glen Canyon escape the fate of Lake Havasu, three hundred miles

The Mittens: Monument Valley, Utah.

lower down the Colorado? There an entrepreneur has been allowed to turn the eastern shore of the man-made lake into a disaster area. Tatty trailer parks and shoddy bungalows extend for mile after mile, like the mindless ribbon development of England in the 1930s. With luck, the speculation will fail, as other plywood developments in Arizona and New Mexico have done, though not before thousands of small investors were gulled by preposterous sales talk.

When I was at Lake Havasu, in 1971, the only object of any quality to be seen was old London Bridge. It is an extraordinary object to encounter in that dazzling waste. That compact, elegant, gray granite artifact, like a queer handle or staple fastened on the yellow desert, produces the effect of an hallucination. It is what the surrealists call an *objet troublant*—an object standing in a place where it has no call to be. It stands up to the wilderness wonderfully well. In isolation, one can appreciate the graceful lines of Barry's conception, the craftsmanship of the masons who shaped and cut the blocks in the reign of William IV. It seems a sort of betrayal that the Lord Mayor of London should have traveled five thousand miles, with his gold chain of office, his beaver hat and scarlet robes, to perform an "opening ceremony" staged by the chain-saw tycoon who is the founder of Havasu City—if such a shabby litter can be called a city. By such actions England can claim her share of the "collective mediocrity" which Toqueville regarded as the main hazard of democratic government, and of which Havasu City is such a melancholy example.

No matter. One day the chain-saw millionaires will all be dead. New forests will spring up to replace the ones they destroyed. The eyesores they perpetrated will disappear. The sun will shine, the wind will blow. The detritus of Havasu City will disintegrate. The only human relic will be London Bridge, a black rib of rock, a hunk of Aberdeen granite mysteriously transported to Arizona.

"God," said Plato, "is always doing geometry." Nor does He (She? It?) confine his activities to scratching canyons in the topsoil. He is also capable of scooping huge holes beneath it. At the Crystal Cave and the Colossal Cave, both in Arizona, or at the Cave of the Winds in Colorado, you can visit some of the cave systems with which the Southwest is riddled. They remind you that the kingdom of Pluto is as grand and extensive as the realm of Jove. There are caverns at Sonora, in Texas, on the eastern edge of the Southwest, which contain marvelously subtle formations, and which always merit a stopover: but the most notable of all nature's cellars or basements in the United States are the renowned Carlsbad Caverns, in the southwestern corner of New Mexico.

The Caverns were discovered by accident, just as the French boys and their dog stumbled on the caves of Lascaux, or the little Spanish girl found the caves of Altamira. The arid foothills of the Guadalupe Mountains were not penetrated by white men until less than a century ago; and it was not until 1901 that a cowboy called Jim White broke through into a cave in whose entrance he was digging bat manure. He wandered with his feeble oil lamp along gallery after gallery, each loftier and more intricate than the one before. In 1923 the Caverns were declared a national monument, and in 1930 the whole area, consisting of over seventy square miles, became a national park. Even today they have not been completely plumbed; but one can descend to the accessible parts at the 750 to 800 foot level and make a circuit of three miles through the linked congeries of caverns. The walk lasts four hours, along narrow, twisting, damp paths, in a temperature of 56 degrees. Again, as at the Grand Canyon, you receive a foretaste of death and dissolution. It is as motionless and timeless down below as at the bottom of the ocean—which it once was. If the lights failed, you would know the horror Poe felt at the prospect of being buried alive, or the moment in Verne's *A Journey to the Centre of the Earth* when the party's "Ruhmkorff apparatus" went out.

In most places the lights are arranged with taste and skill; in others, they render effects that are pure visual kitsch. Similarly, most of the names given to the main rooms are dignified and appropriate—Queen's Room, King's Room, Green Lake Room, even at a pinch the Big Room, since it covers fourteen acres; but some, like the lights, tend to be unfortunate. "The Baby Hippo" or "The Papoose Room" underline the Walt Disneyish tendency in the American psyche, the instinct to pretend that nature is not a tiger but a pussycat. Such cloying labels give the pathetic fallacy a bad name. The parking lots, restaurants, curio-shops, and the well-drilled guides are all part of the American policy of sitting firmly on nature.

An enjoyable feature of a trip to the Caverns during the summer, even if one has to witness it in the company of a thousand other people, is the nightly flight of the Mexican free-tailed bats. At dusk they come twittering and corkscrewing out of Jim White's old entrance to the caves in a dense black cloud, like wraiths of smoke or a giant soft scarf waving in the darkening sky. They circle around—always, for some reason unknown to man, in an anticlockwise direction—then all at once dart southward toward the distant valleys of the Black and Pecos rivers. There they will gorge all night on the river insects before returning in the dim light of dawn, like a million little Draculas. Mysterious creatures. When the cold creeps on they will describe a last broad brushstroke on the sunset and wing their way to Yucatán, Chiapas, Guatemala, or Honduras.

How long have those rich and fetid swarms occupied their cavern? Since before mankind trod upon the soil of the Americas, reckoning from the thickness of their droppings. How long will they remain? Perhaps until mankind has moved on or passed away. And when they themselves have ceased to gibber in their indigo depths, then the caves will return to their original silence. No sound will be heard; there will be nothing, no one, to hear it. Through the nothingness will echo the muffled tap of a drop of water as it detaches itself gently—so gently—from the spongy roof. Two hundred million years ago

Petrified Forest National Park, Arizona. (PHOTO BY AUTHOR)

these caves were part of a barrier reef at the mouth of an inland ocean. How many years will wear away, in English or American reckoning, before the waves inch back to claim their own?

> There rolls the deep where grew the tree,
> O earth, what changes hast thou seen!
> There where the long street roars hath been
> The stillness of the central sea . . .

To vary the basic elements of her design, as represented by caves and canyons, nature has added a number of bold embellishments. One of them which particularly catches the imagination is the so-called Petrified Forest, midway between Gallup and Flagstaff. Alas, what you see today are not towering groves of giant, fernlike Triassic pines but their shattered remains, their fallen trunks. They were smothered in sediment and volcanic ash, and thus prevented from rotting by the deprivation of oxygen. At this period Arizona was an inland sea, whose floodplain was to produce the Carlsbad Caverns. The logs became stuffed with silica, which in the process of one of time's leisurely conjuring tricks was transformed into quartz. Later still, as a result of a volcanic action that raised the mountains and repulsed the ocean, the stone logs were heated until they cracked into more or less regular segments. Now they sprawl on the desert like stunned heavyweights, or the Giants who, after piling Pelion on Ossa, attacked Olympus and were only slaughtered by Zeus and his fellows after a savage battle.

At the core of the wood are amethystine crystals, much sought after by gem hunters in earlier days. When the Atlantic and Pacific (later Santa Fe) Railway reached northern Arizona in 1883, until the area became a National Park in 1958, it was common practice for commercial collectors to blast open the logs to reach the treasures hidden in their heart. Some sections of fossil wood can be given a polish more exquisite than amethyst, taking on a soft rainbow texture. In the Park Center is a tabletop, originally intended for the Czar of Russia, in which the iron and manganese oxides have created a flurry of violet and lavender, lilac and rose, that reminds us that nature can work not only on a Brobdingnagian scale but also with the touch of a Fabergé.

A hundred miles west of the Petrified Forest, as you drive along the famous old east-coast-to-west-coast Highway 66, now better known as Interstate 40, is another of nature's *fioritura*. Even in a region lavishly supplied with volcanoes, buttes, mesas, gorges, and canyons, Sunset Peak merits a detour. It was visited and named by John Wesley Powell in 1879, as he was making his way to the Grand Canyon, sixty miles to the north. He was impressed by the hectic lemon-and-crimson splashes round the rim of the thousand-foot-high crater of the extinct volcano; they reminded him of the colors of sunset.

This great iridescent bulge is what volcanologists, those most arcane of scientists, call a cinder cone. A cinder cone, unlike a shield or composite volcano, spouts out flames and ash from its summit while molten lava floods out through rifts and fissures at its base. Miniature volcanoes known as fumaroles explode from the lava in their turn, released by the violent escape of the imprisoned gases. Sunset Peak or Sunset Crater is only one of three hundred extinct cinder cones in the area, grouped round Mount Humphrey, the highest point of the San Francisco Mountains.

The eruption of the San Francisco volcano field occurred only nine hundred years ago, but it affected an area of some eight hundred square miles. The volcanic ash spread out so far and provided such a thick black mulch on the arid soil that ten thousand prehistoric farmers headed for the region. There they sowed seed in the ash, in the fashion that in Southeast Asia is known as *djuming*. They subsisted contentedly for over three centuries, until winds had blown the ash away. Today the basalt blocks of the great lava fields look as fresh, thanks to the dry atmosphere of the West, as when they were laid down. The principal citadel of the primitive farmers is strikingly well preserved, suggesting that their standard of living compared very favorably with that of their Saxon counterparts, who at that exact moment were awaiting the descent of the Normans.

The Southwest is so rich in extinct volcanoes, lava fields, and volcanic *malpais*—whose literal translation gave the word *badlands* to the language— that even Sunset Crater is not unique. If you are a connoisseur of volcanoes you should go south and drive the road from Mexico City to Veracruz, where you will pass Ixtaccíhuatl and Popocatépetl, puffing away with the same treacherous innocence as when Cortés rode between them four hundred and fifty years ago.

Unique to the Southwest, on the other hand, are the famous White Sands of southern New Mexico. Internal sand dunes are not, of course, rare in the world, and occur on every continent. Even in the Southwest the White Sands are not the only dunelike area: there are the sixty-mile-square Great Sand Dunes, in the San Luis Valley in central Colorado, a national monument of outstanding beauty; and a smaller expanse west of Yuma, in southern California. The latter have the true Saharan aspect, which is why Hollywood makes its Foreign Legion and other North African horse operas there. Many are the Beau Gestes who, at the end of a gritty week's shooting, have driven to San Diego to "chuck a couple behind the collar," as the Legionnaires used to say.

What gives the White Sands their individuality is not so much their size —they stretch out for more than a hundred miles—as the fact that they are composed of pure gypsum of the creamiest consistency. They are situated in the Tularosa Basin, a few miles west of the featureless but famous town of Alamogordo, where the physicists from Oak Ridge and Los Alamos assembled to detonate the first atom bomb. "Fat Man," as the original atom bomb was named, with the *Galgenhumor* characteristic of scientists, was exploded at 5:30 A.M. on July 16, 1945. Three weeks later, a second bomb was "successfully" exploded over Hiroshima, killing 75,000 people. A third, three days afterwards, was dropped on Nagasaki, this time killing a mere 39,000. Today you can visit the place where the gross god of modern science made his appearance on earth. The spot stands between two outcroppings of lava between Carrizozo to the east and Truth or Consequences to the west, almost exactly at the halfway mark between Albuquerque and El Paso. Robert Oppenheimer gave the point another callous and facetious name—the Trinity Site—because the blast fused the virginal sands around into a green glassy substance called trinitite. What Trinity could Dr. Oppenheimer and his colleagues have considered they were invoking? I keep a fragment of trinitite on my desk, to remind me of what the distilled essence of evil looks like. The Spaniards used to call this waterless and Apache-infested stretch of the great *Camino real* that linked Mexico City to Santa Fe the *Jornada del Muerto,* the Journey of the Dead Man. They had hit upon a name more prophetic than they knew. Today, nothing is to be seen of the Trinity Site but the remains of the tower and a twelve-foot obelisk of lava blocks raised to commemorate the event by a proud commander of the White Sands Missile Range. The bronze plaque on the

The White Sands, Alamogordo, New Mexico. (NEW MEXICO STATE TOURIST BUREAU)

obelisk is scribbled over by picnickers and their children—for it is here, of all spots in this accursed valley, that the Alamogordo Chamber of Commerce chooses for its annual outing. Here they come by the hundreds, with their cameras and packed lunches, and their kids clamber on the obelisk while they drink their coffee and Coca-Cola. It is like cracking a bottle of champagne in the cemetery at Verdun.

Drive quickly to the southward, lest you too, *hypocrite lecteur,* be turned to a pillar of trinitite. Here, fifty miles away, is the area which the Parks Service calls the Heart of Sands. Here you can walk upon the healing, innocent dunes that render the Western sky a burning blue. You can drive for sixteen miles on a road like hard-packed salt. The dunes tower as much as thirty feet high, and beyond their pure crests spread the dark reaches of the Sacramento Mountains to the east, and the San Andres Mountains to the west. The dunes are actually not sand at all, but hills of gypsum. Although they reach such stately heights, their base is shallow, and the blowing of the prevailing north-easterly wind causes them to "walk" steadily forward at the rate of a few

Yucca in bloom.

inches a year. Nature, we have constantly to remind ourselves, is by no means the static, passive entity we take it for: in terms of its own time scale, it is restless, flighty, and ever-changing.

Oddly, plants and animals flourish in this pallid world, paler than Proserpine's garden. Certain types of mouse and lizard have adapted themselves to this peculiar environment, and over the course of the centuries have evolved an albino coloration to mask them from predators. In the center of the dunes plant life is scarce; you are in the middle of an immaculate and crystalline landscape; yet even here such plants as squawbush, rabbit brush and saltbush manage to survive. An unforgettable sight is the occasional tall and regal yucca, its bell-like flower whiter than the wind-stroked sand beyond.

This indeed is the particular quality of the West: that every object should stand out with such a clarity and purity upon the bare expanse of the landscape. One sees each rock or plant in glowing isolation, as if it were the *Ding an sich*. What could Wilde have meant by the "absolutely unfinished condition" of nature? He had never seen the yucca in the Heart of Sands. Walking down Piccadilly, "with a poppy or a lily in his mediaeval hand," did he never glance at it to notice how finished—finished *ad unguem*—the work of nature can be? Nature has her (its? his?) gothic fancies, but as often as not would seem to favor a taste for symmetry, sometimes fearful but sometimes mild. The branches and twigs of Darwin's great Tree may actually grow with a grace and orderliness that is simply too vast for us to be able to see.

White Sands, Sunset Crater, Carlsbad Caverns—even the dizzying gulf of the Grand Canyon—these are the arabesques with which nature has adorned the scroll of the Southwest. But the scroll itself is the fulvous and unmitigated desert—or deserts, for there is more than one of them.

The whole guts of the Southwest is an immense twin desert system: the Chihuahua Desert on the east, the Sonora Desert on the west. They are divided from each other by the vertical cleft of the Colorado Plateau and by the intrusive tongue of the Rockies. Although they possess different indicators with regard to flora and fauna, they share the same origin. They both owe their existence to the Rockies and the Sierra Nevada, mountain systems that suck the rain from the clouds and rob the surrounding area of moisture. Moreover, looking at the larger picture, the Chihuahua and Sonora deserts are only two of a series of interlinked deserts that together make up the awesome Great American Desert. W. Eugene Hollon, in his book of that name (1966), agreed with Walter Prescott Webb and other earlier authorities that the Great American Desert extends in its entirety over no less than sixteen states. It runs from the Mexican to the Canadian border, spreading over a million square miles, or 30 percent of the continental United States. Some writers, such as Odie B. Faulk in his *Land of Many Frontiers* (1968), would go so far as to include the whole western half of Texas within the boundaries of the Southwest, since it can be argued that it is an integral part of the Great American Desert. He would have that Desert embrace central Texas, the Texas and Oklahoma panhandles, and the southwestern corner of Kansas. However its frontiers be defined, the Great American Desert encompasses the Painted Desert, the Mojave Desert, the Oregon Desert, and the Great Basin Desert, the latter sprawling across most of Utah, Oregon, and northern California (Figure 3).

The Rockies are the backbone of our southwestern deserts. They continue from the United States down into Mexico, where they change their name to the Sierra Madre Occidental. Finally, after reaching as far as Durango, they join hands with the Sierra Madre del Sur to form virtually a single chain from the Yukon to Panama. The Sonora Desert, west of the Rockies, occupies half of southern California, most of Baja California, and much of the Mexican state of Sonora. To the east, the Chihuahua Desert begins just south of Albuquerque in New Mexico and thence descends through Central Mexico until— believe it or not—it touches Mexico City.

I wish you could see, Rex, the royal deserts and mountains of this South-

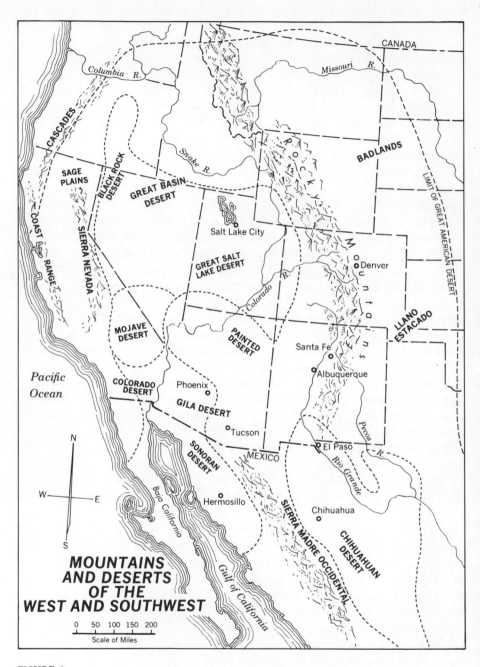

CANADA

Columbia R.

Missouri R.

CASCADES

Snake R.

BADLANDS

SAGE
PLAINS

BLACK ROCK
DESERT

GREAT BASIN
DESERT

COAST RANGE

SIERRA NEVADA

Salt Lake City

GREAT SALT
LAKE DESERT

R O C K Y

Denver

Colorado R.

LIMIT OF GREAT AMERICAN DESERT

Pacific
Ocean

MOJAVE
DESERT

PAINTED
DESERT

Santa Fe

Albuquerque

M o u n t a i n s

LLANO
ESTACADO

COLORADO
DESERT

Phoenix

GILA DESERT

Tucson

SONORAN
DESERT

MEXICO

El Paso

Pecos R.

Rio Grande

N

W   E

S

Baja California

Hermosillo

Chihuahua

SIERRA MADRE OCCIDENTAL

CHIHUAHUAN
DESERT

**MOUNTAINS
AND DESERTS
OF THE
WEST AND SOUTHWEST**

Gulf of California

0   50   100 150 200

Scale of Miles

FIGURE 3

west. I wish you could see the rivers that are associated with them. Those rivers are substantial, but are fearfully punished by the landscape through which they run. Heat causes evaporation; the sandy soil drains them dry except during the flood season; their beds are too shallow and intermittent to support navigation. In places even the formidable Colorado, fifth longest river in America, loses heart and creeps underground; and I can recall how disappointed I was when I first drove my Mercedes across the Rio Grande, which at that season ran as weak and weedy as the Manzanares below Madrid. In fact, although the Colorado flows more than seven hundred miles, much of its majesty has been engineered by man; while the Rio Grande, rambling nineteen hundred miles from the San Juan Mountains of Colorado to the Gulf of Mexico, carving its way through impressive gorges, is often as meager as a town ditch.

Water, the source and the support of life, is a very scarce commodity in the Southwest. Droughts are distressingly common. Throughout the region there is not a single natural lake of respectable proportions; only a few brackish marshes and salt pans. The Great Salt Lake in Utah is a stern reminder of what the desert does to water. In the cosmic duel between wet and dry, in the Southwest the dry has won one of its most crushing victories.

As Dodge and Zim note, in their useful little guide to the Southwest (1955), "Aridity is its principal overall characteristic." They add that the region nonetheless offers "amazing contrasts and diversity of climate, geography and people. Its 464,000 square miles include such superlatives as the lowest land, the biggest canyon, the highest mountain, the driest deserts, the hottest valley, the richest mines, and the oldest towns in the United States." Certainly the variation in temperature is among the most striking of these contrasts. In places the thermometer can climb to 130 degrees; in others it will drop as low as minus 50. Such extremes require, as at White Sands, not only plant and animal but special human adaptation. And there are such additional hazards as "dusters" or dust storms, and also the erratic patterns of the rainfall. In the Southwest either the rain fails to fall at all for years together, or crashes from the sky in blinding sheets which produce flash floods. One locality can have twenty inches of rain a year, in the form of monsoons, while another close by will have less than five inches. Thus the rivers never wind along smooth and deep, but hurtle down in swollen torment or else their beds are as dry as bone. On the other hand, there are certain spots and cities in the Southwest with a superbly equable climate. Where I am writing in El Paso, for example, the temperature ranges mainly between 50 and 90 degrees, and there is an average of 345 days of sunshine a year.

The principal and ceaseless struggle in the Southwest is first to find, then to conserve, water. There are reptiles and animals so well adapted to the desert environment that they seldom need to take in water by drinking nor lose it by excreting. Others store water in extra stomachs, or additional lengths of intestine, or can subsist on the water in their tissues for an extraordinary time. All desert animals can browse on shrubs and plants that appear totally dry and which bristle with ferocious defenses. Men too develop remarkable skills in finding water and provender, although the scarcity of the latter defeats almost all men in the end; even the hardiest Apache were finally driven out of the desert to surrender at last. It is probable that hunger and dehydration have slain fully as many men as knives and bullets.

The most artful organisms in the Southwest are those plants of unearthly appearance at which travelers gape. Their weird shapes are determined by the battle to entrap and retain fluid. Yuccas, agaves, lechuguillas, sotols, saguaros, chollas, Judas trees, and the innumerable varieties of cacti, are all designed with this in mind. These desert plants are mostly xerophytes, or "dry plants"; they possess extensive lateral or horizontal root systems, and a capacity to store moisture almost indefinitely. Alternatively, they can enter a dead-looking sleep in which no moisture is required. They know tricks to avoid exposing their leaves to the scorching rays of the sun as it pours down its rays ceaselessly overhead; they curl them up or turn them away; or else they actually discard leaves as luxuries, or coat them if they exist with a fine film of wax to repel the heat and conserve moisture.

Yet it would be misleading to convey the impression that even the spikiest of desert plants is gray and grim in appearance. The celebrated saguaro of Arizona and Sonora is positively genial, standing around on the desert in little Henry Moore families. The ocotillo, ferociously armored as it is, deserving its nickname of "Devil's Coachwhip," develops rich crimson tips after a bout of rain and spatters the desert with sharp drops like blood. The most unpromising and heavily armored of the cacti, barrel, fishhook, beaver tail or hedgehog, will put forth a bright and limpid blossom. The flower of a desert plant must be preternaturally brilliant if it is to attract and seduce the fertilizing insect.

Along the washes, where the water runs once or twice a year and moisture remains trapped not far below the surface, there are florid and abundant growths. Few of the pampered plants in a city park can rival the springtime exuberance of the honey mesquite, the blue or yellow paloverde, the bird-of-paradise flower, the smokethorn, the tamarisk. Such feathery shrubs, dormant and sticklike for most of the year, burst into bloom in late March and April and daub the desert with slabs of color—pink, violet, indigo, chrome, emerald, Venetian red. One of the choicest and most spectacular of all the desert plants does not bloom by day. This is the night-blooming cereus, *Peniocereus greggii,* a cactus native to the Chihuahua Desert. Called by the Mexicans *La Reina de la Noche,* between dusk and dawn in midsummer its thorny coils bear masses of large pale creamy yellow flowers that fill the air with fragrance and wilt with the coming of the light. To see and smell it is to experience a small peculiar thrill, as if one were enjoying a moment-out-of-time. It

Papago woman gathering saguaro fruit, Saguaro National
Monument, Arizona.

seems a flower from another world, a flower of the mind or the imagination,
a distillation of the warm star-sprinkled darkness.

The deserts of the Southwest are vast and lonely—but one must not picture them as dreary and sterile. It is true, of course, that they do not yield up
their secrets without a search. Desert birds and animals are rarely seen; the
surface of the desert and the sky above seems immobile and impassive. Yet
scores of mammals and many varieties of bird exist, and with patience can be
detected and watched.

Among these shy inhabitants may be numbered mountain sheep and
Mexican antelope, two species of deer—the Mule and Fantail—the gray and
kit fox, and the bobcat. Most animals are small, averaging two feet in length
or less. The exceptions are the mountain lion and the coyote. The former, a
splendid beast, is called in Spanish *el león,* but actually resembles a house cat
who has decided not to stop growing until he has reached a size of between
six and eight feet. He is encountered throughout Central and South America,
and once roamed all North America as far as the east coast; now he is found

only in New Mexico and the Florida Everglades. The coyote, on the other hand, resembles a dog—a yellow dog with a bushy tail, five feet long, and weighing up to fifty pounds. His nightly wailing can still be heard on the outskirts of the big cities, and his smashed body can be seen on the roads around them.

The other animals are small. They include the noble badger, four types of skunks, two types of jackrabbits, the engaging little ringtail or cacomistle, and an extraordinary array of squirrels, chipmunks, gophers, rats, and mice. All these creatures, even the mountain lion, are harmless. Many of them are nocturnal—though neither their harmlessness nor their nocturnal habits can save them. Most of them are being steadily trapped, shot, and poisoned. There are said to be less than two hundred mountain lions surviving in the whole of the huge state of New Mexico, yet it is still legal at certain times of the year to hunt them. Their main enemy, and the enemy of most of animal creation in the American West, is the sheepman. Sheepmen, even more than cattlemen, are a mercenary breed, with paranoid ideas about their environment. They regard it as almost as much of a personal insult if a small animal walks over their land as if a human being does. To live and let live is not the motto of the American rancher. If you want to see what these original owners of the desert looked like, you should visit the Desert Museum at Tucson, an enterprising establishment where the desert fauna is displayed against a natural background. It might be your last chance to look at some of them. A few years ago, in Lincoln, New Mexico, I saw a hunter return at dawn and, with every expression of satisfaction, string up a beautiful raccoon on the clothesline in his back yard. What purposeless cruelty and vanity could have motivated that man? What possible damage could a raccoon or a mountain lion do to a town or a farm that could justify slaughtering it? Then you recall the Trinity Site and the green glass, and such pieces of the human puzzle drop into place.

The birds that have habituated themselves to the desert outnumber the animals, and are too numerous to mention in detail. They range from the larger eagles, the vultures and hawks—particularly the handsome red-tailed hawks—to the tiny elf owls and diminutive cactus wrens, each only an inch or two long. The cactus wrens are responsible for pecking the holes in the saguaros and building their nests there. A bird of special interest is the roadrunner, which looks, as one authority puts it, like an underfed pheasant, but is actually related to the cuckoo. This grotesque but endearing bird is big, sometimes over two feet long; it is long-legged, long-tailed, and long-necked, with a high scrubby crest, and would rather run than fly. It relieves the monotony of an unbroken stretch of desert as it scoots across the road ten feet in front of your front wheels. Often it will have a snake or lizard drooping from its beak, for clownish though it looks, it is a capable and fearless forager. You will come across dried snake and lizard skins draped over the limbs of the ocotillos, which serve as its own private larder; it prefers its meat gamy and well hung.

It is fortunate in being the state bird of New Mexico, otherwise it would probably be destroyed, like most of the larger species, or such smaller ones as the desert quail and ringdove, both mercilessly pursued. In Montana, in 1971, pits were discovered in which the bodies of up to two hundred golden eagles had been concealed. The local sheepmen excused themselves for the slaughter by asserting that eagles have a habit of seizing young lambs and flying off with them. In the whole of recorded history it is doubtful if any man has ever seen an eagle stoop and carry off a lamb; it is pure mythology. Yet this was the pretext the sheepmen used to try and exterminate them. Some of them shot the birds from helicopters. One pilot told how the eagles had sometimes turned on the helicopters and directly attacked them before they were shot out of the sky. Peerless creatures. Looking into those pits must have been the aquiline equivalent of looking into the mass graves of Buchenwald or Katyn. Two hundred golden eagles. In Hemingway's *The Short Happy Life of Francis Macomber,* the professional hunter tells his client: "You don't shoot them from cars." In Montana, they do.

Many of the reptiles, whose occupation of the desert is more ancient than that of bird and animal, suffer similarly at the hands of man. It has been calculated that your chance of being killed by lightning is greater than being killed by a rattlesnake; nonetheless the creature is tracked down with a hysterical passion. There is also a trade in rattlesnake skins that resembles in a small way the African trade in crocodile skins; thus the Great White Hunter can not only slake his thirst for dealing death but can make a profit as well. Rattlesnakes are more frightened of humans than humans are of them. Once, in the Black Range, I was walking with someone who stepped on one as it was snoozing on a sunny rock. Man and snake jumped yards from each other, regarding each other in mutual terror, the snake rattling, the human quaking. We all then went quietly about our business. If you do not stir southwestern snakes up, they will not trouble you. Few of the world's snakes, I am told, are actively aggressive. Prudent behavior, of course, when walking or camping, is always called for, and it always gives me a thrilling little tingle when I put my snakebite outfit into my haversack; but there seems little need to contribute to the decimation of bull snakes, whipsnakes, black-headed snakes, lyre snakes, king snakes, long-nosed snakes, patch-nosed snakes, or the beautiful Arizona mountain-king snake, all of which are inoffensive to man. Even the pretty coral snake, which I have not seen in the wild, and which possesses a potent venom, is said to have a timid disposition, and although a member of the cobra family, it can be handled by experienced persons. It is so small, and its jaws are so tiny, that it is doubtful if it could get a child's finger in its mouth. In seven years in the Southwest, I have yet to hear of a death from snakebite, though they do occasionally occur. I do not expect to be using my snakebite kit any time soon.

The reptiles, after all, have a better claim to occupy the desert than we have. It seems ungracious to enter a house and attack your host. There are, of course, creatures you would not want to fool around with. These include the Gila Monster—if you can call something which is barely two feet long a monster. But this spectacular brown-and-yellow lizard, the only (moderately) poisonous lizard in North America, is rarely encountered, and reacts only if provoked. Most of the other lizards, lilliputian in size, are benign. The chuckwalla, the gecko, and the zebra-tailed lizard will play amusing tricks with you; while the horned lizard or "toad," despite its disconcerting ability to shoot blood out of its eyes when threatened, makes an amiable pet and has been a toy of Indian children for centuries.

Scorpions, admittedly, fall into a different category. One would not wish to "mess," as they say, with scorpions, admirable though their parental habits are said to be, or with their cousins the giant millipedes. Again, however, many scorpions, such as the vinegaroon or whip scorpion, and the very strange solpugid, or Child of the Earth, are innocuous. The noxious kinds are the *Centruroides sculpturatus* and the rarer *Centruroides gertschi*. Both are barely two inches long, from their front claws to their curved segmented tail, but they can give you a painful sting. They are encountered not only when camping in the desert, when it is advisable to shake out your bedroll and clothing in the morning, but also in the outskirts of the big cities. In the desert they are attracted by the campfire, in cities by central heating. In the winter months they creep into new apartment buildings on the desert fringes, and they cause their occupants some heart-stopping moments. Stings occur only if they are stepped on—but these can be excruciating. The treatment is an immediate cold compress or ice bag. I captured one from the ceiling of my house and put it in a jar to see how long it would take before it weakened from lack of air, food, and water. I imagined it would be a matter of twenty-four hours or so. Six weeks later, the little creature was still trying to climb the smooth walls. Whenever I lifted the jar, it darted at my hand and tried to attack me. Awed and humbled, I took it out on to the desert and shook it free. It scuttled furiously away.

The spiders, as integral to the desert drama as the snakes and scorpions, enjoy an equally bad reputation, most of it also unfounded. The tarantula, for instance, fearsome as it looks, is a very tame creature. Like the praying mantis, it is a useful adjunct to one's garden, devouring the grubs and larvae. The tarantula too has been adopted as a pet by enterprising children, though this is not recommended, since it does bite fairly sharply. However, there is no need to run a mile when you see one. On the other hand, have no truck with the little spider with a reddish-brown hourglass on its abdomen. This is the so-called Black Widow which, together with the innocent-looking Brown Spider, can inflict a superlatively wicked bite if it somehow becomes trapped against the human body. Fortunately they are seldom encountered.

There is little call to be apprehensive about the wild creatures of the desert. After all, even here in the remote Southwest, the world is in greater peril from politicians, real estate developers, or the vast army of idiots carrying guns.

Such, then, is the desert: a great brown patch on the skin of the American continent. It is belied by its name. The desert is not flat. It is pinched and folded into mountains and mesas, buttes and canyons. The desert is not drab. Its tawny hide, lit up by the quintessential daylight, is spattered with violet and purple and burnt orange. The desert is not featureless. It sports a thousand distinct and individual growths. The desert is not silent. It continually sings, murmurs, skirls, or whispers.

And such is the place, Rex, of my supposed exile. I hope that you and my friends are beginning to agree that I may have chosen well? . . .

Often, out here, there come back to me some lines of Li Po, from Mahler's *Das Lied von der Erde,* which you and I used to hum when we were out hiking or climbing in Europe in the old Cambridge days. Remember? . . .

> *Wohin ich geh'? Ich geh', ich wand're in die Berge,*
> *Ich suche Rube für mein einsam Herz,*
> *Ich wandle nach der Heimat, meiner Stätte.*

Where am I bound? I go. I wander among the mountains.
    I seek rest for my lonely heart.
I am wandering towards my home, my native place . . .

THREE

SINCE COMING TO AMERICA I have been astonished not so much by the typical American's ignorance of world history, as by his shamefaced assumption that America itself has no history to speak of. This is an *idée reçue* among Americans.

History, except for American history, is a subject that tends to be spottily taught in American schools; and in many schools geography is scarcely taught at all. Americans live so much in the present, and America itself is so enormous, that it is easy for Americans practically to ignore the existence of foreign countries, and to be only vaguely aware of their location and culture. There are many Americans, even prosperous ones, who have never visited New York or Los Angeles, and who promise themselves only in a desultory way to fly over one day and take a look at Paris or Rome. America seems self-sufficient.

On the other hand, much of the defensiveness and unease of Americans, many of the mistakes they have made in their brief period as a leading power, stem from their unfamiliarity with the great world, with the larger processes in which their own processes are subsumed. The point has been cogently put by Dr. Daniel Boorstin, the eminent—and eminently readable—historian and former director of the National Museum of History and Technology at the Smithsonian. In an article which he contributed to a symposium devoted to the social upheavals of the late 1960s, he wrote: "Our inventive, up-to-the-minute, wealthy democracy makes new tests of the human spirit. Our very instruments of education, of information and of 'progress' make it harder every day for us to keep our bearings in the larger universe, in the stream of history and the whole world of peoples who feel strong ties to their past. A new price of our American standard of living is our imprisonment in the present. We think we are the beginning and the end of the world. And as a result we get our nation and our lives, our strengths and our ailments, quite out of focus. In a word, we have lost our sense of history. In our schools, the story of our nation has been displaced by 'social studies.' In our churches the effort to see man *sub specie aeternitatis* has been displaced by the 'social gospel.' Our book publishers and literary reviewers no longer seek the timeless and the durable, but spend most of their efforts in fruitless search for *à la mode* 'social commentary.' Without the materials of historical comparison, having lost our traditional respect for the wisdom of ancestors and the culture of kindred nations, we are left with nothing but abstractions, nothing but baseless utopias to compare ourselves with. For we have wandered out of history . . ."

"Wandered out of history." The phrase helps to indicate why so many Americans, and those the thoughtful ones, sometimes feel a chronic sense of being lost and helpless; the acceleration of their culture has cut them adrift from the past, and they have no guide, no compass. It also indicates why those nations who, in Dr. Boorstin's words, possess strong ties to their pasts, feel a distrust for a country which, to change the metaphor, has sheered away and become a maverick—the old western word for a steer that breaks away from its fellows.

May not such a situation, however, actually possess its advantages as well as its drawbacks? Many commentators, of whom one of the most recent is Jean-François Revel in his *Without Marx or Jesus,* have pointed out that Americans have an instinct for existing in a state of negative capability that staid and hidebound Europeans might envy. In this age in which, as Conrad put it in *Victory,* we are "camped like bewildered travellers in a garish, unrestful hotel," American society is protean, open-ended, subject to continuous change. Not bound by conventional norms, it can adapt to novel situations in a flexible way. America may be favorably placed to absorb those shocks of acceleration which, while they are more evident in America than elsewhere, are the outstanding feature of our era.

It was Goethe who, in a short poem, declared that America was happier than Europe because it had no antique statues and ruined castles, because it had "a present life" unburdened by useless memories and pointless strife. There is still truth in this, despite the fact that with the passage of time, the devourer, the *edax rerum,* the innocence of America is being eaten away; like other nations, she is acquiring her memories, amassing her victories and defeats. It is in this respect that her lack of an historical perspective might become a hindrance. For she may come to know the sour truth of the adage that those who are ignorant of history are compelled to live it over again. Americans, as Dr. Boorstin indicated, have an endearing tendency, because they lack standards of comparison, to believe that whatever they think, experience, or invent has never before been thought, experienced, or invented in the whole history of the world. They lack the real if melancholy consolation of history, which teaches one that, above the level of mere gadgetry, there is no new thing under the sun.

Certainly there is little that seems new under the equable sun of the Southwest. If Americans were only more aware of it, it is here in the Southwest that their yearning for a pedigree could be assuaged. For the record of history in the Southwest stretches back—believe it or not—for 30,000 years. This is a very respectable antiquity. The culture of the United States is every bit as "old" as the culture of Europe, but this fact has not yet penetrated the consciousness of many people on both sides of the Atlantic. The United States is not a "young" country except in a very narrow sense.

Europe itself is "young," of course, if you compare it with Africa, China, or Southeast Asia. There is an abundance of early fossil material from South Africa, Botswana, and Tanzania, while later but still early material has been found in Java, Peking, Algeria, and, again, in Tanzania. The only remains of comparable date in Europe are the Heidelberg jaw and the recently discovered Vertesszöllös cranium, and man only emerges significantly in Europe as a contemporary of the Neanderthaler of the Upper Pleistocene. In the division of the Upper Pleistocene called the Late Paleolithic, which began about 40,000 years ago, *Homo sapiens* finally came into his own—and it was at this period, in a guise exactly similar to the Cro-Magnon hunters of Europe, that the first tribesmen began crossing the Bering Straits between Siberia and Alaska and started to trickle down into the vast spaces of the New World.

Unfortunately, human fossil material from the Americas is hard to find and hard to date. The best-attested would seem to be Midland Man, discovered near the town of that name in West Texas in 1933. Probably the bones of a young woman, they can be given a fairly convincing age of 10,000 to 15,000 years. Tepexpán Man, unearthed in 1947 in Mexico City, is possibly of the same age; and much more dubious and debatable is the skull found forty years ago in Laguna, California, which may possibly—but only possibly—be between 16,000 to 19,000 years old. After knocking about in museums for four decades, it was accepted as the most ancient of North American fossils by the great African palaeontologist Louis Leakey. Leakey then investigated prehistoric "workshop areas" in the Calico Mountains in San Bernardino County, California, and declared them to be genuine, thereby tentatively pushing the dawn of American history back another 20,000 years. Other experts did not view Leakey's "hand-axes and scrapers" with his own eye of faith, regarding them as naturally chipped and eroded pebbles. However, the inspired predictions of Leakey concerning the Olduvai Gorge in Tanzania have been triumphantly vindicated; so Europeans may one day have to accept that the human history of America commences at more or less the same point and at the same level as their own. In any case, what does the short start enjoyed by Europe signify, in terms of those three billion years represented by the Grand Canyon? . . .

It is logical to look for such early tools and fossils in California. When the first huntsmen crossed the Bering land bridge, they appear to have filtered southward along two main routes—down the West Coast, and along the eastern flanks of the Rockies. Some authorities still do not agree that the *terminus ante quem* for the populating of America occurred much more than 10,000 years ago; but certainly at that time groups of people of Mongoloid stock were traversing the thousand miles of tundra—harsh, windswept, but dry—that then linked Asia with North America, instead of the sixty miles of water that separate them today. The fourth and final onset of the Great Ice Age had squeezed the Arctic Ocean in such a way that near the ice caps the water level was lowered two hundred feet and an isthmus was created. This isthmus, formed 50,000 years ago, disappeared 8,000 years ago; so it is putatively between those two dates that the main waves of immigrants made their journey from Asia.

Geological and climactic conditions to the south of Alaska were also very different from today. Even before the fourth and final retreat of the glaciers, when North America as far south as the Great Lakes lay beneath a sheet of ice, Southwest America was a lush, steamy, marshy hunting ground. The process of desiccation only set in, as it did in North Africa, 5,000 years ago. The onset of the ice had driven the bulk of the animals southward, toward the warmth and the sun. Thither our early ancestors followed them, in America as in Europe. And striking animals they were. They included not only animals familiar to us, such as the caribou, moose, elk, deer, and peccary, but the last survivors of a legendary age, the mammoth, mastodon, camel, the tapir, the weird and ungainly giant sloth, who walked on the backs of his hands, the musk-ox, and the huge long-horned bison. They also included the horse—for the horse existed and either died out or was killed off by early American hunters long before the arrival of Cortés. Some of these animals clung to the fringes of the ice, others inhabited the greener lands to the south. All were sought out by the nomadic hunters who depended on their flesh for food and their hides for clothing and tents. This diet of meat they eked out with whatever roots and berries they could pluck and grub up along the way.

The Southwest was certainly a principal hunting ground and cultural heartland of these people. Evidence of their activities is plentiful. Oldest of all may have been the people who inhabited the Sandia Cave in the sweeping curve of mountains that guards the Rio Grande below Albuquerque. Their stone tools were first identified in 1936, after a difficult and dusty excavation, and consist chiefly of elongated, leaf-shaped, rather roughly worked flint spearpoints. The tribesman who took refuge in the Sandia Cave may not be as old as were first supposed, but they seem to have antedated the Folsom people, first identified eleven years earlier at an open site near the town of that name in northeast New Mexico. The Folsom spearpoints were also leaf shaped, but of finer workmanship. In subsequent years Folsom artifacts have turned up in many places, notably at the great Lindenmeier site on the northern border of Colorado, and as far south as the Burnet Cave in southern New Mexico; and their tools were also discovered overlying those of the Sandia people in Sandia Cave itself.

Allied to the Folsom people, and perhaps even predating them, may have been the Clovis people, named from another town in eastern New Mexico, who later wandered·over into southern Arizona. The Clovis spearpoints are exceptionally beautiful, elegant and tapering. They are as satisfying to finger and fondle as the Aurignacian points of the Cro-Magnon hunters who were their contemporaries in Europe, and who led much the same sort of existence. Even more beautiful are the so-called parallel-point flakes of the nearby Yuma culture in Colorado; while yet another hunting people, makers of smaller but equally delicate tools, left traces of their passage at the Gypsum Cave in southeast Nevada, which was occupied continuously from 10,000 B.C. right down to modern times.

Sandia-Folsom-Clovis. Such would appear to be the chronological succession. But the story is necessarily hazy, and these groups of hunters may have been enemies who extinguished each other rather than brothers who helped one another—just as in Europe it is impossible to tell if the Cro-Magnon people intermarried with the Neanderthalers, or else ruthlessly exterminated them, or a mixture of both. However, it is possible to state that about 10,000 years ago they were certainly roaming over the same ranges with spear and spear-thrower. They were probably a more numerous folk than we imagine, for in the course of time they fanned out from their southwestern ranges across the whole of North America. Clovis and Folsom points have been found as far afield as the northern Great Plains and the northeastern woodlands of America, and as far south as the Chile-Argentine border. Disconcertingly, not a scrap of adequate fossil material survives to show us what they looked like; nor did they bequeath us any magnificent works of art, as the Cro-Magnon hunters of the Magdalenian period did at Altamira in Spain and Lascaux in the Dordogne. But it is not entirely fanciful or romantic to view them as a lost race of mighty hunters. They endured for 10,000 years, and with their slender flint blades and sharpened stakes brought low many a gigantic beast. They were a hardy, resourceful breed, and when their physical remains are eventually found they will probably indicate that, given certain differences in racial stock, they resembled the European Cro-Magnons in appearance: tall, long-legged, muscular, with broad well-modeled features. When we are eating our corn-fed steaks, we ought to devote an occasional thought to these half a million rangy hunters who wandered through North and Central America, slaying the ferocious mammoth practically with their bare hands. Unfortunately, their hunting methods, no doubt backed up by such methods as trapping, driving the herds into water or stampeding them over cliffs, may have become only too efficient. We are accustomed to thinking of "prehistoric" animals such as the mammoth as dying out by natural means countless ages ago; but many of them seem to have been cropping the grasses of America until only two or three thousand years before the birth of Christ. There is some evidence from excavations, such as those of the Clovis mammoth "kills" in Arizona, that their disappearance was hastened by intemperate slaughter. They may have been exterminated as brutally as the buffalo a century ago. If so, at least the men responsible for it were men committed to a hunting life for their existence. They were in a different category from the fearless coon hunters of Lincoln County, or the intrepid eagle killers of Montana. We have by no means reached the stage where we have conquered nature; but surely we are living on rather better terms with her than our fathers did? Should we not behave toward her with a decent tact and forbearance?

The first steps of mankind, like those of children, were the hardest. Those early Americans deserve our respect. They had no cars, washing machines, fluoride toothpaste, or underarm deodorants. All they had were craft and courage. It might help us, especially in the bad times, to remember them.

The French assure us that *les absents ont toujours tort*. The dead, too, always seem to be in the wrong. By dying, they lose their right to be taken seriously. In a civilization like the American, where an advertisement for an insurance company proclaims that "the future is now," the past is deemed to have no value. It is wraithlike and nerveless. Americans do not see history, in Spengler's phrase, "not as things-become but as things-becoming"; they are not placed to draw nourishment from it, whether it is their own or someone else's.

Yet, as I have indicated, American history begins not with the Pilgrim Fathers in 1620, or with Coronado's *entrada* into the Southwest eighty years before, but fully two-and-a-half millennia earlier. Incredibly, in the Southwest, American history can be studied as a living, continuous process extending from prehistoric times to the present day. There, in a unique anthropological museum, four distinct branches of the tree of man can be seen existing side by side. First come the surviving descendants of the distant huntsmen and food gatherers; then the Navajo, the Apache, and the other tribes who later invaded their homelands; then the stock of the Spaniards and Mexicans who once held the territory; and finally the sons and daughters of the American pioneers. These four peoples occupy the Southwest together, carrying on the diverse traditions of their forebears. They provide a deeply interesting and exciting spectacle. Where in Europe, except perhaps in Lapland, can one view a cross section of human culture that embraces the Stone Age on the one hand and our own Steel Age on the other? Even in Africa or Asia, there seldom exist those intermediate stages and gradations which make the Southwest such a fascinating living laboratory. It would be eccentric to search for the descendants of Cro-Magnon Man among the inhabitants of southern France—but here, in Southwest America, in the persons of the Pima, the Papago, and the pueblo dwellers along the Rio Grande, one can visit the aboriginal societies of America still thriving and in a viable condition. There is here enough history—and to spare—for even the most history-deprived American. And to become curious about the early inhabitants of the Southwest is not at all an academic or antiquarian pursuit. It is to understand a little of what has made many Americans what they are today.

It is not possible, of course, to do more than guess at the ways in which most of the Sandia-Folsom-Clovis peoples died out, dispersed, or became absorbed into later cultures. Yet there are two large and well-defined groups of people in the southwestern heartland who clearly owe their origins to them. One group came to occupy the area to the south, the other the area to the north. The southerners seem to have been the older established, and to demonstrate the closer link with the earliest cultures. Thus it seems logical to describe it first (Figure 4).

This southerly group came into existence on almost the exact spot on the Arizona-Mexican border where the Clovis communities had carried out their mammoth kills. It has been given the overall name of the Hohokam Culture, a word from the language of the present-day Pima Indians, who are its direct descendants. The word means "Those Who Have Gone Before." It appears very probable that the Hohokam Culture grew out of an earlier and more primitive culture known as the Cochise Culture, named after the county of southern Arizona called after the Apache chieftain who made his presence felt there only a century ago.

The Cochise people, whose remains have been found near the town of Douglas, flourished over a period of not less than 10,000 years, from some time before 10,000 B.C. to approximately 500 B.C. Their culture has been divided into three periods—Sulphur Springs, Chiricahua, and San Pedro. During the two earlier phases, when the climate was still damp and fertile, hunting and domestic activities were carried out by means of a tool kit of crude stone-points, choppers, and scrapers, and the diet was supplemented by means of roots, tubers, nuts, and berries. Later, as the climate grew drier and desert conditions came to prevail, the quality of the tools progressively improved; they began to be manufactured from more exotic materials, such as quartz and obsidian. During the third phase pottery appeared, probably under the influence of people to the south, and shells and mica for ornaments and vessels were traded with tribes on the west coast. At the Ventana Cave, on the present Papago Indian reservation, important excavations were begun in 1941 that revealed the history of the Cochise folk in all three stages. Folsom tools lay in

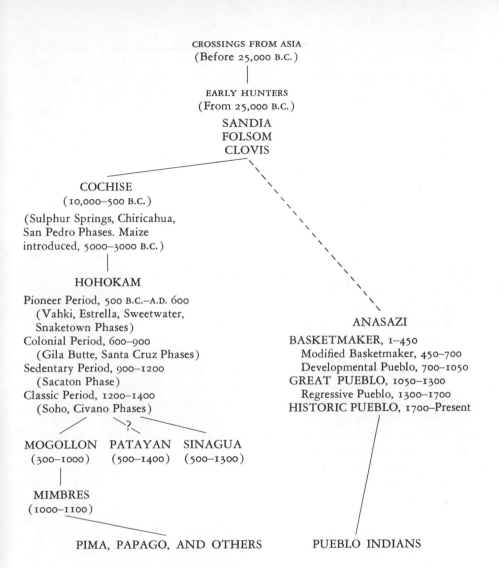

CROSSINGS FROM ASIA
(Before 25,000 B.C.)

EARLY HUNTERS
(From 25,000 B.C.)
SANDIA
FOLSOM
CLOVIS

COCHISE
(10,000–500 B.C.)
(Sulphur Springs, Chiricahua,
San Pedro Phases. Maize
introduced, 5000–3000 B.C.)

HOHOKAM
Pioneer Period, 500 B.C.–A.D. 600
(Vahki, Estrella, Sweetwater,
Snaketown Phases)
Colonial Period, 600–900
(Gila Butte, Santa Cruz Phases)
Sedentary Period, 900–1200
(Sacaton Phase)
Classic Period, 1200–1400
(Soho, Civano Phases)

ANASAZI
BASKETMAKER, 1–450
Modified Basketmaker, 450–700
Developmental Pueblo, 700–1050
GREAT PUEBLO, 1050–1300
Regressive Pueblo, 1300–1700
HISTORIC PUEBLO, 1700–Present

MOGOLLON   PATAYAN   SINAGUA
(300–1000)   (500–1400)   (500–1300)

MIMBRES
(1000–1100)

PIMA, PAPAGO, AND OTHERS   PUEBLO INDIANS

FIGURE 4. Early cultures of the Southwest.

the bottom stratum, and after the Cochise sections there came other strata which brought the story of the cave's occupation by successive Indian tribesmen to about A.D. 1800—a record of almost continuous occupation for 15,000–25,000 years. Any European archaeologist would be delighted with such a sequence.

It was at the third or San Pedro level in the Ventana Cave that ears of wild corn were found, yielding evidence of the early consumption of maize, the great staple food in the Americas. The Ventana wild corn was not, however, as ancient as that found in 1948 in the Bat Cave, near the town of Magdalena in western New Mexico; there the husks could be dated to 3000 B.C., and in upper layers evidence was found that the corn had been subsequently carefully cultivated. And in 1949, in the valley of Tehuacán in northern Mexico, investigation of five cave sites elicited the fact that the forerunners of the modern Mexicans were familiar with corn in the wild state as long ago as 5000 B.C. and were the first people thus far known in the Americas to breed and develop it. Like the art of pottery, the art of raising crops appears to have arisen in Mexico and to have been introduced retroactively into America.

Once acquired, both these arts flourished notably in southern Arizona. The Hohokam people, who are almost certainly the lineal descendants of the Cochise people, did not leave behind them as many grand monuments as the other great group in the north which I shall be dealing with shortly; but they were wonderfully capable farmers. It is quite possible that they actually hailed from as far afield as southern Mexico, trekking north and settling down with all appearances of amity with the Cochise people. Ultimately they spread out until they constituted a series of interlinked settlements along the Gila and Salt rivers, and four distinct phases of their culture have been distinguished. The original, formative era has been called the Pioneer Period, beginning after the termination of Cochise and lasting from about 500 B.C. to about A.D. 600. Then came the Colonial Period (600–900), the Sedentary Phase (900–1200), and the Classic Phase (1200–1400), the latter bearing the resounding title of "the Golden Age of Southern Arizona."

"Those Who Have Gone Before" were a numerous and industrious folk. They seem to have possessed the predominantly peaceful and pastoral character of the modern Pima, Papago, and Maricopa, in whose veins their blood now flows. In spite of their Mexican origin or influence, they developed an individual personality of their own. They were the only people in the Southwest who cremated their dead, pounding up the bones and inserting them first in pits and later in urns. They also had the ritual habit of smashing up their funerary objects, which makes it difficult to form an accurate picture of their way of life. Their surviving pottery is of excellent quality, decorated with sophisticated red and buff patterns. In addition, they made intriguing clay figurines, together with a remarkable array of personal ornaments in such varied materials as shell, steatite, turquoise, and argillite, enhanced by beautiful little carvings of birds, animals, and reptiles. The shells they used include such specimens as the cardium, conus, glycimeris, and olivella, all of which must have been obtained by barter from the fishermen of the Gulf of California. Their inventiveness and artistry is further shown in their stone palettes, their mosaic plaques or mirrors inlaid with thin pieces of iron pyrites, and by their celebrated etched shells. The intricate etching on these shells was produced by covering the raised parts of the design with pitch or resin, then soaking away the exposed parts in some kind of acid, probably obtained from the fermented juice of the saguaro. The first European to see the artistic possibilities of etching was Dürer, who took it from the Nuremberg armorers; so the Hohokam people were employing the technique a full three centuries earlier.

Their houses were simple rectangular structures with rounded corners, the roof consisting of two stout poles and a ridgepole, the walls of reeds. Cooking was done in the typical fire pit you can still watch being employed on the Pima reservation. Their settlements were less remarkable for ambitious architecture than for the size they attained, particularly in the Sedentary Period; the Snaketown settlement on the Gila River Indian reservation near Chandler may have numbered five thousand houses at its peak. The only grandiose feature was the ball courts, which were constructed as early as 700–800, in the Colonial Period. Some of these were two hundred feet long, and their earth walls may have been twenty feet high. No less than eighty of them have been identified in Arizona. These ball courts are indisputably a Mexican feature, and I shall be noting some of the Mexican examples in a later chapter; some form of ball games were certainly played as early as 700 B.C. in the Valley of Mexico. The Toltec colonists at the pretty, out-of-the-way site at La Quemada, in Zacatecas, who have provided a hypothetical connection between the Toltec and Hohokam cultures, built themselves a ball court; and once, when I spent a day there, I played a game of handball with the ghosts, with a tennis ball, for old times' sake. This strange game, part sport and part ritual, became a passion throughout Central America, and at one time was played from Hohokam mud villages in northern Arizona to the august Mayan temples of Guatemala. The Hohokam examples are very humble affairs; but in 1937 an authentic rubber ball, dated to about 1100, was found on a Hohokam site, inside a pottery jar. Other specifically Mexican traits are the platform mounds on which temple huts were built; the shape of some of the pottery; and small copper bells which could only have been produced by the copper-working peoples to the south.

The Hohokam were farmers. As farmers always do, they lavished their labors on their fields rather than their dwellings. As agriculturalists, they were altogether outstanding. They devised a system of irrigation canals of extraordinary complexity to bring the water from the Salt and the Gila. In the valley of the Salt, the canals stretch for an aggregate length of 150 miles, and in places are up to 30 feet wide and 10 feet deep. Like the Egyptians and other canal-building peoples, their efforts must have been carried out with great self-discipline and close attention to the public good. The creation and maintenance of a network of canals, where the farmer downstream is dependent on the farmer upstream, demands a high standard of order and civic responsibility. So well, in fact, did the Hohokam carry out their work, that in modern times the Pima and Papago needed merely to clean out and maintain the Hohokam canals in order to cultivate the same crops as their prehistoric ancestors —squash, maize, tobacco, beans, pumpkins, and cotton.

Only the so-called Classic or final Period of Hohokam produced a remarkable piece of architecture. The Casa Grande, in the Gila valley, is situated fifty miles from the junction of the Gila and the Salt rivers, south of modern Phoenix. It was first given its Spanish name of "Great House" in 1694, by the incomparable and indefatigable Father Kino, to whom I shall be paying tribute at a later stage. It was then in the territory occupied by the Sobaipuri, a branch of the Pima. It now seems clear that this impressive landmark was not constructed so much by the Hohokam as by an intrusive people, who had penetrated the region and been accepted peaceably by them. These folk have been given the name of the Salado people, and their presence as a distinctive enclave in Hohokam country might not have taken place in Classic Hohokam times (1200–1400) but as early as 700. There is a debate as to whether they were an offshoot of the Anasazi people to the north, or whether they were once again of Mexican origin, as the ball court, temple mound, and polychrome pottery at Casa Grande seem to suggest. Once more, a connection appears likely with the Chalchihuites people of distant Zacatecas, who were in turn a shattered remnant of the Toltec empire. A noteworthy difference between the Salado and Hohokam was that the former inhumed instead of cremating their dead.

Today the Casa Grande presents a weird appearance. It is the only ancient monument that I have visited that is protected by a huge steel canopy. The canopy, designed to prevent erosion of the mud or caliche walls by rain and sunshine, began as a simple sheet of corrugated iron in 1902, and was replaced by a more substantial structure in 1932. At some future date the Parks Service plans to enclose it in a huge bubble of plastic, an idea which could well be extended to other important and friable archaeological remains. Approached across the flat, sun-struck Sonora landscape, studded with squat, ragged salt bushes, the steel canopy gives it the appearance of hovering on the desert like some gleaming Venusian spaceship.

The Casa Grande was one of the main buildings of an ancient Hohokam-Salado township. From its summit can be seen the traces of no less than five surrounding townships. Father Kino called it a castle, and it is possible that it was some sort of citadel or ceremonial building. It has also been suggested that it was a prehistoric grain elevator, or even a prehistoric apartment house. Its dimensions are a modest forty by sixty feet and it comprises only eleven rooms, but after six hundred years it still stands four stories high and its stiff mud walls are four feet thick. The Salado people seem to have specialized in such multistory buildings. At Los Muertos, a few miles to the north, was a settlement dominated by a structure larger than the Casa Grande; it was destroyed by nineteenth century farmers. Los Muertos is additionally interest-

Casa Grande National Monument, Arizona.

ing because there the Hohokam and Salado peoples appear to have lived in the same town, burying or cremating their dead according to their individual rites and making their personal styles of pottery side by side with one another.

To visit a site like Casa Grande is on the face of it hardly like visiting the Step Pyramid, or the Parthenon, or the Colosseum, or even Stonehenge or Hadrian's Wall. It struck me as odd, then, that when looking at this and similar monuments of the Southwest, I should have been seized by the same mood which seized me when, as an undergraduate, I was helping with Bronze Age, Iron Age, Roman, or Anglo-Saxon excavations in Britain, or when I first set eyes on the monuments of the Egyptians, Greeks, Romans, or Mayas. I felt the same flavor of mystery, the sense of the closeness of death and destiny, of regret at the passing away of an industrious and inventive people, at the demise of an attractive way of life. These humbler sites cannot induce the hypnotic awe of the Acropolis, or the plateau of Gizeh: but they are not to be viewed as an inferior substitute, either. The more blinkered European or Asian archaeologist—and there are not many such—need not think that in touring the Southwest he is doing a backward area a big favor. These stone, adobe, or caliche ruins are testimony to an impressive episode in human history. However, it is less important to convince the non-American of that fact than it is to stamp it on the minds of Americans themselves. Few Americans, alas, have yet begun to register the existence and achievements of their distant forerunners. It could be several generations before they realize that the civilization they assume to be aching with newness is actually a graft on a very ancient stock.

A final word about the Hohokam. Over the course of so many centuries there was bound to be, as in the instance of the Salado, a considerable diffusion or commingling of traits between neighboring peoples. One main development appears to have been that a sizable group went east from the densely populated Gila-Salt homeland, while another went to seek their fortune in the northwest. Neither group wandered out of the southwestern orbit, and both settled down within 150 miles of their point of origin.

The older and larger of the two groups was that of the Mogollon culture. Their villages have been found on the San Francisco River, and are extensive enough to have provided the Mogollon with four tentative phases, beginning about 300 and ending about 1000. Some authorities think they may not be an offshoot of the Hohokam, although they may have sprung from the same Cochise stock; others believe they belong with the nearby Anasazi culture. Their pottery shows an influence from both those major cultures, and they cremated as well as inhumed their dead. Other writers hold that they were so distinctive as to constitute a third basal culture in the region. About 1000 the Mogollon people appear to have given rise in turn to a brilliant minor culture, seventy-five miles further toward the southeast. This was the Mimbres culture, from the river of that name, which produced the most vivid pottery ever to be found in the whole of the Southwest. The polychrome and black-on-white wares of the Mimbres people are masterly in manufacture, in form, and in decoration. Their makers excelled both in abstract geometric and in naturalistic designs. The latter include not only birds, fish, animals and insects, but men and women, who are shown in vignettes that provide valuable information about their dress, customs, and daily occupations. The valley in which they lived was unusually sheltered and fertile; nevertheless, after only a century they seem to have moved on, probably into the Mexican state of Chihuahua, whence some bands of the Salado people seem to have made their way at much the same time.

The second group pushed up from the Salt-Gila on to the Colorado perhaps as early as 500, but did not really become significant for several centuries. These were the Sinagua and the Patayan peoples. Again, their origins are much debated. The Sinagua people were those who were described in the last chapter as the peasants who took advantage of the favorable agricultural conditions created by the eruption of Sunset Crater in 1066. The Patayan people, about whom not much is yet known, pushed higher upstream toward the Grand Canyon. Both were probably among the ancestors of the present-day Hopi. The Sinagua, borrowing Anasazi traits, built themselves a truly spectacular five-story cliff dwelling known as Montezuma Castle, in the Verde Valley. In the same valley they constructed a massive gray hilltop city called Tuzigoot; and at Wupatki, near Sunset Crater, they erected a walled village which is one of the most beguiling of all southwestern sites. It lies in rolling open country on the edge of the rose-and-amber expanse of the Painted Desert, and is constructed of neat small slabs of warm brown stone. The houses, plazas, and the ball court are all judiciously laid out—and one feels, strolling there, that life on that sunny escarpment, littered with over eight hundred prehistoric farmhouses, must have been a friendly place to live a thousand years ago. It has a homely and businesslike air.

Today the descendants of the Hohokam or their cognate peoples—the Pima and Papago in the Gila-Salt area, the Maricopa, Walapai, Yavapai and Havasupai in the Sinagua-Patayan area—are still mild-mannered farmers. So are the descendants of the equally great and more northerly group, the Anasazi. However, the physical presence of the latter was more arresting than the Hohokam, both in antiquity, when they built huge communal centers and cliff dwellings, and in modern times. Today they live in the adobe pueblos along the Rio Grande to which they moved five hundred years ago, when their earlier dwellings were abandoned. The people of the pueblos thus exemplify a way of life that came into being at about the time of Christ. It is amazing to encounter them, with their tenacious traditions, their *gravitas,* their sense of the holiness and mystery of things, in the middle of the brittle, hurried, makeshift culture of twentieth century America.

The archaeological term Anasazi is derived from a Navajo word, signifying "The Old Ones." The Navajo have no connection whatever with any of the older peoples of the Southwest; they only drifted down from the north into the Southwest after the Anasazi-Pueblo people had already departed, three centuries earlier, for the banks of the Rio Grande. On reaching the Southwest, the Navajo stumbled upon the splendid deserted townships of the Anasazi, and were as awed and stirred by them as we modern visitors are today.

"The Old Ones" was a word with reverential overtones. The Anasazi were not one of the ambitious, conquering nations of mankind; they did not manifest a taste for aggression; they were no Assyrians or Aztecs. Throughout their two-thousand-year history, although they have manifested occasional bursts of rage, and have never been loathe to defend themselves, the Anasazi-Pueblo people have been almost consistently shy, elusive, and withdrawn. They were stay-at-homes, scrupulous minders of their own business. Their ancient remains possess a quiet charm that communicates itself to the passerby like a faint, lost perfume.

The Hohokam, if we accept their Cochise derivation, may perhaps claim a slightly older ancestry, though they were establishing themselves on the Gila-Salt at more or less the same date—round about the beginning of our era —that the Anasazi were establishing a similar home on the San Juan River and its numerous tributaries. This was a full 350 miles to the northeast, mainly in the Four Corners region, where Arizona, New Mexico, Colorado, and Utah all come together. In time, if they did not become a more numerous people than the highly concentrated Hohokam, they spread out over a wider area. Their settlements finally extended along the San Juan as far as its junction with the Colorado to the west, the upper Rio Grande to the east, and southward on to the Little Colorado, where they came into close contact with the Hohokam, Sinagua, Mogollon, and Mimbres peoples.

Their prehistoric period, like that of the Hohokam, is divided by modern archaeologists into four periods—although it must be borne in mind that such periods and their accompanying dates and nomenclature are always liable to revision. I find it strange to look over the notes I made as an archaeology student at Cambridge, only a quarter of a century ago, and see how radically the picture has changed in almost every part of the world.

The Anasazi time-divisions are usefully assumed to fall into two sections, called Basketmaker and Pueblo. The initial period, known simply as Basketmaker, lasted from about A.D. 1 to about 450; then came Modified Basketmaker, from 450 to 700; Developmental Pueblo, 700 to 1050; and Great Pueblo, from 1050 to 1300. However, since the history of the Anasazi did not terminate with the economic or other disasters which were to strike them at the end of the thirteenth century, and since "The Old Ones" have so obviously become "The New Ones," it has been necessary to tack on two further phases to bring the story up to date. These are the so-called Regressive Pueblo, 1300–1700, and Historic Pueblo, running from 1700 to the present time.

The Basketmaker-Pueblo people seem to have been addicted, right from the start, to caves and rock shelters. They clung to the faces of cliffs as though for psychological as much as for physical protection, while their preference for living in the cold clefts of the Rockies or in inaccessible canyons indicates their love of solitude. Even their houses, when they were eventually driven away from their overhangs and rock shelters, possessed features that resembled caves. The earliest Basketmaker dwellings were nothing more than deep holes in the ground, usually circular, entered by a ladder through a round aperture in the roof. They were the prototypes of the subterranean kivas I shall be describing in a moment. Today, entering the adobe rooms of a modern pueblo, there is still the same atmosphere of the lair, the burrow, the earth-refuge. They also employed caves for burying their dead, in twos or threes, or sometimes in regular cemeteries of twenty or more. The burials unveil for us a wealth of information about early Basketmaker times, since at that crisp altitude the bodies in their dry, shallow, rock-protected graves were perfectly preserved and mummified. These were natural mummies, remarkably like the mummies produced by the hot sands of Egypt during the Egyptian predynastic period, four thousand years earlier. As in Egypt, the natural juices leaked away, leaving behind the dehydrated flesh, bones, nails, hair, and skin; and, as in Egypt, the body had been flexed soon after death, while it was still pliable, with the knees drawn up to the chin, in the fetal position, awaiting the moment of rebirth into eternity. The same tightly flexed position was practiced in the European Old Stone Age: and it is probable that both there and in the American Southwest there was the same desire not just to give the departed a good send-off, but to cripple him so he could not leave his grave and walk abroad. Most primitive peoples are frightened of the spirits of the dead.

The mummies reveal that the Basketmakers were a small, slender, reddish-skinned people, with thick coarse black hair, dark eyes, and little facial or body hair. The men wore their hair in three braids, and though the long tresses of the women were sheared off after death, to yield materials for weaving, it appears from their cactus combs that they too paid great attention to the business of hairdressing. If the hair of their modern descendants is an indication, their hair styles must have been elaborate indeed. Hair ornaments of bone and feather were a principal part of their dress, which, apart from multiple strings of bone, shell, and stone beads, was scanty, considering the rigor of the mountain climate. It consisted only of a flimsy wool fiber apron round the loins. Probably the Basketmakers went naked, relying for warmth on the fur blanket that, after death, was wrapped tenderly around their remains. These cloaks were made of bear and rabbit skins, sometimes of the tanned hides of deer, and occasionally they were entirely woven of hair and fiber. The Basketmakers were cunning weavers, utilizing their own hair and the stringy portions of such plants as the milkweed, topping off their work with elegant toggles, cords, and fringes. Perhaps the best testimony to their weaving skill is not their cloaks, but their sandals, a brand new pair of which was always placed ceremoniously with the dead, to help them tread the paths of the Beyond. I have looked at scores of these sandals in museums in the Southwest, and have never seen two pairs that were alike. The decoration of these square-toed sandals, with their loops at toes and heels, essential equipment for that ungrateful terrain, is extraordinarily inventive. It would have been equally apt to have called them the Sandalmaker people.

They were, indeed, a people with a marked artistic bent, as we know from the paintings on the walls of their caves. Often they utilized the simple techniques used by cave painters all over the world, such as placing a hand on the surface, splaying the fingers, and daubing around it with a brush or blowing paint from the mouth. But much of the work is more advanced, depicting Basketmaker men and women at work and play. They were also excellent carvers of wood, from which they made their clubs, spears, and spear throwers. With these weapons they hunted game—not merely the larger game, but also gophers, rabbits, prairie dogs, even rats and mice, with which the primitive hunters before them had supplemented their larder. In their hunting activities they were aided by their dogs, of whom they possessed several breeds. We have the mummies of many of the favorite dogs which they took with them into the next world. They were also expert at making snares and traps; a net from the White Dog Cave on the Black Mesa was 240 feet long, 3 feet wide, weighed 28 pounds, and contained nearly 4 miles of knotted string.

Their pottery was crude stuff, not fired but sun baked, and was not an important item in their economy; by the time they began making it, the Hohokam had already been practiced potters for five centuries and more. The Basketmakers actually had no great need of pottery, for they relied on the most magnificent baskets that have ever issued from the hand of man, splendid artifacts that are still made today in the Southwest. (I started a collection of them five years ago—but alas, like Indian jewelry, they are becoming fashionable and damnably expensive; a fine Papago basket can cost $150 to $200.)

The ancient baskets were made in all sizes and consistencies, varying from soft and flexible bags and carrying baskets to huge baskets for storage and for holding water. The latter were woven with a tight mesh, their insides caulked with pitch or resin. They also served for cooking food, as on the Pacific seaboard; the soup or gruel was brought to the boil by dropping in heated stones. Special straps were attached to the baskets, either for slinging or for fastening as a tumpline round the forehead. Everyday utensils though they were, they were often sumptuously decorated by the men who fashioned them. In the storage baskets were kept the corn, squash, beans, cotton, acorns, nuts, seeds, and berries of all kinds which the women and children cultivated or gathered. Turkeys were domesticated at a later stage, though whether man domesticated the turkey or the latter, like the dog, attached itself to man, is not known.

In the Modified Basketmaker period, a rough pottery and rudimentary clay figurines began to be made. More important, the spear thrower that had served the huntsmen of the Southwest for 15,000 to 20,000 years was gradually superseded by the bow and arrow. Basketmaker bows and arrows are among the earliest found in America, but it is almost certain that they were not indigenous to the Southwest but brought in from the outside. Indeed, between 700 to 1050, the period known as Developmental Pueblo, the Basketmaker-Pueblo people were in close contact with other peoples as far afield as Nevada and southwestern Texas, and ideas were being exchanged with the Hohokam groups to the south. It may even have been an influx of new settlers who induced or inspired the tremendous upsurge of cultural energy that was to result in the triumphs of the Great Pueblo Period.

About 750, the Basketmaker people started to transform their rock shelters, makeshift huts, and pithouses into a type of dwelling which, in the space of three to four centuries, became increasingly imposing. In most respects their material culture remained the same, although great improvements took place in the realm of the applied arts. However, at the same time that the Hohokam people were beginning to concentrate their population, in their Sedentary Period, the Basketmakers also began to coalesce into the closely knit communities that gave rise to the modern pueblos. The transition can be seen most clearly in the fertile hideaway known as the Chaco Canyon, in northwestern New Mexico. There they left their primitive hutments strung out along a tributary of the Chaco River and came together in clusters of substantial stone-and-earth houses called by archaeologists clan or unit houses. Incorporated into them were pious copies of the old subterranean pithouse, which in the course of time developed into the gigantic stone community townships of the Great Pueblo Period.

To reach Chaco Canyon you have to drive sixty miles over dirt or gravel roads from the town of Aztec in northwestern New Mexico. It is worth the effort. At first you drive across a featureless plateau splattered with scrub, until at length you reach a region of scarps and gullies which broadens out into the valley of the Chaco. And there, over a stretch of nine miles, you encounter several clusters of ancient buildings. Coming immediately after the wood-and-earth hogans of the modern Navajo, strung along the rugged road from Aztec, the huge high-rise dwellings of the Anasazi come as a stunning surprise.

Pride of place among the structures in the canyon is the so-called Pueblo Bonito, which appears to have occupied the central position in a society that once numbered at least 5,000 people. Pueblo Bonito, in its somber brown stony setting, is somehow reminiscent of the Bronze or Iron Age villages of Celtic Britain, though on a much larger scale. The resemblance is fortuitous, as the Anasazi had no knowledge of any metal whatever, except for the small copper bells which, together with parrot feathers, were brought to them by the merchants who operated the great caravan routes down through central Mexico, ancestors of the adventurous traders of Aztec times. Pueblo Bonito is a huge free-standing structure, although by instinct its builders placed it with its back against a gigantic cliff. At its peak, it occupied an area of three acres, had 800 rooms, and housed up to 1,200 people. It was semicircular, with an outer wall that could be barricaded and defended when necessary, and the rooms were arranged in tiers, five stories high. Access everywhere was by means of ladders. The most striking feature of the building is the beauty and precision with which the sandstone slabs were squared and laid around the rubble core. In places there are thin layers of darker stone placed between the layers of sandstone, and the appearance of the stonework is everywhere exquisite. It is possible that the entire surface of the outer walls may once have been covered with paintings executed on smooth adobe plaster; it would be consistent with the imagination and originality which these people brought to every aspect of their existence.

The excavation of Pueblo Bonito was carried out over a span of thirty years, from 1896 to 1927. The rooms were small and rectangular, giving on to each other, so that each family had to traverse the rooms of another to reach its own quarters. The preferred rooms were those facing the huge sunny courtyard, while the gloomier rooms at the rear, shadowed by the cliff, were used for storage or lived in only sporadically. The ceiling of one room constituted the floor of the room above, and was stoutly and ingeniously constructed. First came a layer of large timbers of ponderosa pine, carefully smoothed; then a layer of peeled willows; and finally a layer of split juniper and juniper bark. On top of the juniper was a four-inch thickness of hard-packed earth, wetted from time to time to lay the dust and keep it firm. A few house-proud families provided themselves with floors of hewn planks or flagstones.

There was no furniture. Families slept on grass, reed, or yucca mats, or on padded quilts, like Mexican *campesinos* on their *petates*. Probably the rooms were only used at night, while the work of the pueblo was carried on in the sunshine of the courtyard, or on the flat roofs and terraces. Here the baskets, pottery, weapons, and agricultural implements were made. Here the women ground the corn which the men brought in from the fields that extended the length of the valley and were irrigated by an intricate system of ditches. The corn was placed on a massive block of sandstone, called a *metate,* and rolled out by means of a *mano;* it is the way in which cornmeal is still prepared in primitive communities throughout the Americas. Some of the rooms were used for burial purposes, or at least as ossuaries, and in one of them the remains of twenty-four individuals were discovered.

It was a simple but, if we can judge from its survival after a thousand years, a satisfying life. It was not free from sickness, fear, or anxiety about the weather and the crops; and although, like the Hohokam, the Anasazi appear to have found the secret of a protracted peace, yet in the nature of things there must have been clan rivalries and perhaps more serious clashes. Yet one detects a certain fundamental composure and sobriety, perhaps akin to the passivity and sense of acceptance which one finds among the Indians of Mexico, their modern relatives. They may have combined, as the Mexicans do, a love of gay and garish color with a basically somber and fatalistic view of life.

A central feature of Anasazi culture, which immediately impresses the visitor to Chaco Canyon, is the presence of dozens of kivas—large or small, simple or elaborate. In Pueblo Bonito alone there are thirty-two. The kiva is a circular subterranean or semisubterranean structure which grew out of the original pithouse. Gradually it came to lose its domestic associations, and served as the center for religious ceremonies and as a place for tribal debate. In addition, it was used as a clubhouse, or a warm retreat in cold weather. Like

A kiva in the Pueblo del Arroyo, Chaco Canyon, New Mexico.

the London club, it seems to have been a male preserve, into which women were invited only on special occasions. There are three Great Kivas in the interior courtyard of Pueblo Bonito, another a mile away at a site called Chetro Kettle, and a particularly fine one facing Pueblo Bonito, on the other side of the valley, in a pueblo called the Casa Rinconada, or the House Without Corners. The kiva at the Casa Rinconada was the focal point of a village of forty-five rooms, which had five smaller kivas. It was built on a rocky bluff, was sixty-four feet in diameter, and constructed of a uniform dark stone. Four great postholes held the timbers that once supported the roof, and there were the customary fire pits, stone benches, storage areas, sweat-baths, and niches in the walls for the sacred objects and images.

Even more remarkable than the magnificent kivas at Chaco Canyon is the Great Kiva at Aztec, sixty miles to the north. Aztec, of course, has nothing at all to do with the Aztec Empire, which came into existence two to three hundred years after the Anasazi sites had been deserted. Another Anasazi site I shall mention is called Montezuma Castle, and there is a town in the neighborhood called Cortez. These names reflect the romantic influence of W. H. Prescott's *History of the Conquest of Mexico,* published in 1843. This splendid book bestowed enormous glamour on the Aztecs, their tragic Emperor, and the heroic Spaniard who subdued them, and for a half-century thereafter every substantial ruin in Central or North America was deemed to be the work of the Aztec nation.

The first man to study the ruins at Chaco Canyon and Aztec seriously was Lewis Henry Morgan, whose *Ancient Society, or Researches in the Lines of Human Progress from Savagery, through Barbarism, to Civilization,* published in 1877, is a seminal work in the field of anthropology, and one of the most original works of the nineteenth century. Morgan journeyed about the area in a covered wagon, composing lucid accounts of his researches and embellishing them with careful drawings. He found much of the ancient pueblo at Aztec relatively undamaged; but during the course of the next half-century, until excavation began in 1916, the ruins were plundered and gutted by the pioneers who had begun to settle in the Southwest. Fortunately, the main excavations, intensively pursued over the next two decades, were carried out with exceptional skill and devotion. A visit to Aztec, situated in a pretty green valley, more hospitable in appearance than Chaco Canyon, with its stern gray overhangs, is an instructive and memorable experience.

Aztec was an enclosed, self-contained community, like Pueblo Bonito, and was patently an offshoot or ally of the Chaco Canyon culture. The remains of 352 rooms, almost twenty of them intact, have been traced, and the main building rose at least four stories high. The first period of activity lasted from 1110 to 1130. Then, for some reason, the site was completely abandoned for ninety years, until a new wave of settlers arrived in 1220. The newcomers worked energetically until 1250, before vanishing mysteriously in their turn. We do not know what droughts, epidemics, or sudden attacks of fear or wanderlust overwhelmed these "Old Ones." As at Pueblo Bonito, the standard of the stonework is so smooth and neat that one runs a hand over it with a sensual satisfaction. Some of the walls are enhanced with a highly effective contrasting motif, consisting of three to five bands of thin black stone.

The glory of Aztec is its kiva. Originally it was no more if no less impressive than the kiva at Casa Rinconada, and its dimensions were slightly smaller; but it was brilliantly restored by Earl Morris, the original excavator, and is now one of the principal attractions of southwestern archaeology. Except for the kiva at the Coronado National Monument, it is the only kiva, ancient or modern, which an outsider can enter. As restored by Morris, the exterior is a drum-shaped structure with multiple light wells; it is twelve feet high and has a square boxlike entrance at one end. It possesses the compactness and symmetry associated with all Anasazi buildings. You approach it over the flinty, hard-packed ground, with lofty cottonwoods flickering overhead, and descend

The Great Kiva at Aztec ruin, New Mexico.

fourteen steps into the underground temple. Four square, massive, smoothly plastered pillars sustain the thick beams of the roof. As in all kivas, a dim light reveals a bench running the entire distance around the inner wall, wide-curbed pits, baths, and storage areas. Here, in this sophisticated edifice with its subtle warm brown hues, the ancient inhabitants of the Southwest felt themselves close to those chthonic deities whose existence was so intimately bound up with their own. Here the shamans and rainmakers danced round the sacred fire in their horned headdresses. The flames sent forth their scented fumes, while the men on one side and women on the other sang, chanted, and shook their gourds and rattles, their bodies oiled and glistening in the crimson glow.

The pueblo at Aztec, built by farmers stemming from the Chaco Canyon tradition, possesses additional historic interest, since its second wave of inhabitants represented another aspect of Anasazi culture during the Great Pueblo Period. This wave belonged to the people whose characteristics are most strikingly demonstrated at Mesa Verde, thirty miles northwest of Aztec. Aztec is therefore intermediate between what might be termed the "Under-the-Cliff Dwellings" of Chaco Canyon, and the true "Cliff Dwellings" of Mesa Verde.

The cliff dwellers spread out in a half circle north of Chaco Canyon, a half circle of which the latter was the hub. The Chaco Canyon and Mesa Verde peoples appear to have risen and declined at much the same time, but the former were rather the more advanced technologically and may indeed have been the parents, or at least the elder brothers, of Mesa Verde. In point of architecture, on the other hand, Mesa Verde yields nothing to its relative. If anything, it is even more original. Seldom in the history of the world has a single prehistoric culture given birth to two such beautiful and contrasting architectural styles.

The Basketmakers had been drawn toward caves and cliffs; the Chaco Canyon people had moved a little way away from them; and the Mesa Verde people retired once again to the cliffs. The Chapin Mesa at Mesa Verde, which contains the largest and most accessible group of cliff dwellings, makes an ineffaceable first impression on all who see it. There are actually forty cliff communities implanted in the walls of the various canyons surrounding Chapin Mesa, besides numerous pithouses and pueblo ruins. The larger cliff dwellings, such as the Spruce Tree House, the Square Tower House, the Sun Temple, the Cliff Palace, the Balcony House, are spread out over an area of a square mile and are truly spectacular. Jacquetta Hawkes, in *Journey down a Rainbow,* a book on Texas and the Southwest which she wrote with her husband, J. B. Priestley, has a chapter on Mesa Verde in which she recreates the tingling impact that the first glimpse of the Cliff Palace made on her. "With the suddenness of most delight it was there before us. We were at the edge of a deep canyon—the earth opened before us. The upper parts were vertical walls of sandstone, banded buff and brown; lower down, these broke into steep slopes dark with vegetation. This natural grandeur so suddenly revealed was marvellous enough, but there, opposite to us on the far side of the canyon, was a hanging city, a little pale gold city of towers and climbing houses filling a vast oval hollow in the rock. The dark points of the pines rose up to its foot, the immense black shadow of the cave roofed it with a single span, but the fronts of houses and towers were in bright sunlight, all their angles revealed

The Cliff Palace at Mesa Verde National Monument, Colorado.

and the doors and windows showing us jet-black squares. It was like an intaglio sharp-cut in an oval bezel. The limestone rose sheer about it to meet the forest and then the unbounded blue. It looked so infinitely remote, there across the gulf, so remote and serene in its rock setting, that it seemed like some dream or mirage of an eternal city."

Another distinguished writer, Willa Cather, has described the same scene in an episode named "Tom Outland's Story" which she inserted in her novel *The Professor's House,* published in 1925. At that time, before the Parks Service had tidied the site to cope with tourism, Mesa Verde was still isolated and wild. It was the tower that stands like a buttress in the center of the Cliff Palace that caught Willa Cather's eye. She speaks with the voice of the young pioneer, Outland, as he comes accidentally upon the ruins of the Anasazi.

"It was such rough scrambling that I was soon in a warm sweat under my clothes. In stopping to take breath, I happened to glance up at the canyon wall. I wish I could tell you what I saw there, just as I saw it, on that first morning, through a veil of lightly falling snow. Far up above me, a thousand feet or so, set in a great cavern in the face of the cliff, I saw a little city of stone, asleep. It was as still as sculpture—and something like that. It all hung together, seemed to have a kind of composition: pale little houses of stone nestling close to one another, perched on top of each other, with flat roofs, narrow windows, straight walls, and in the middle of the group, a round tower.

"It was beautifully proportioned, that tower, swelling out to a larger girth a little above the base, then growing slender again. There was something symmetrical and powerful about the swell of the masonry. The tower was the fine thing that held all the jumble of houses together and made them mean something. It was red in color, even on that gray day. In sunlight it was the color of winter oakleaves. A fringe of cedars grew along the edge of the cavern, like a garden. They were the only living things. Such silence and stillness and repose—immortal repose. That village sat looking down into the canyon with the calmness of eternity. The falling snow-flakes, sprinkling the piñons, gave it a special kind of solemnity. I can't describe it. It was more like sculpture than anything else. I knew at once that I had come upon the city of some extinct civilization, preserved in the dry air and almost perpetual sunlight like a fly in amber, guarded by the cliffs and the river and the desert."

I have been fortunate to visit several of these cliff dwellings at the same time of year as Outland, when they were not crawling with visitors. Mesa Verde is busy all year round: but there are smaller, remoter sites where one can still experience the sense of wonder and closeness to the past that Outland felt when he came panting up the slope. One of them is the Canyon de Chelly, in the northeast corner of Arizona, forty miles from Gallup. Like.Mesa Verde, the Canyon de Chelly is actually a network of interconnecting canyons. Here, too, there are cliff dwellings scattered in caverns on the rock faces—in Jacquetta Hawkes' expressive phrase, "like an intaglio sharp-cut in an oval bezel." The most impressive are the White House, the Antelope House, and the Mummy Cave Ruin. The Mummy Cave contains a three-story house in the shape of a tower, and it was these multilevel buildings that led Willa Cather to speak of "towers" almost in a military sense. Actually, they had no such significance, and were not even watchtowers. The lookout posts were small buildings standing at strategic points on the cliffs above. It seems unlikely, in fact, that any of the Anasazi peoples were notably aggressive, and the Mesa Verde people appear to have lived in holes in the rock for shelter rather than for military defense. True, entrance could only be effected by ladders of rope or wood, which could be pulled up behind them, leaving them perched inviolably in midair; but ladders were their normal mode of access to their quarters, in any case. They were so remote that their enemies were much more likely to be wild animals than humans. Unlike herdsmen, whose wandering life leads almost automatically to warlike activity, the Anasazi had no domestic animals; they were agriculturalists, normally a peaceful type of folk. Excavation has not revealed that they were any more pugnacious than their cousins the Hohokam, whose generally amiable character has been noted.

The Canyon de Chelly was occupied by the Anasazi for a thousand years, from the Basketmakers of 350 to the end of Great Pueblo of 1300. They were more cramped for space than their Chaco Canyon relatives, and lacked a readily available supply of stone; but what space they had they used with extraordinary ingenuity, each family finding room even in such narrow quarters for its indispensable kiva. The stone is white and glistening, which enhances the magical effect, like a scene in Rider Haggard. In the case of the White House in the Canyon de Chelly, a vast pale comb of rock soars hundreds of feet above the cliff dwelling tucked into its base, enhancing its dreamlike appearance. The high sweep of rock is stained with delicate natural streaks, like giant brushstrokes, as if a huge stone curtain had been suspended from the canyon far above. It is curious to stand on the opposite rim of the canyon, contemplating these tiny, delicate white townships of the original Americans, and suddenly see, rounding a stony outcrop on the green floor, half a mile below, a jeep carrying a Navajo farmer to his fields somewhere in the recesses of Black Rock Canyon. The Navajo occupied this abandoned outpost of the Basketmaker-Pueblo people four hundred years after the original inhabitants had departed, and during the past three centuries have made it their own. They did not take over the original dwellings, because of their superstitious fear of the dead; but on the walls of some of the houses they have painted fantastic murals. As we shall see, the Canyon de Chelly was to hold a terrible and tragic experience in store for the Navajo people.

Much more modest in scale than the Canyon de Chelly or Mesa Verde, but more evocative, because so lonely, are the cliff dwellings in the Gila Wilderness. To reach them entails a hard but satisfying forty-mile drive along a winding road from Silver City, in southern New Mexico. The Wilderness is well named. It is splendid country for hiking and camping, and one can walk for days in the woods and along the river without setting eyes on another human being. Here, one brisk, biting late autumn afternoon, I went up to the cliff dwellings, situated above a small clear trout stream that runs into a tributary of the majestic Gila. To the scent of piñon and ponderosa was added the dry straw smell of the yellowing grass. The sunlight was straw colored; the leaves were gold and copper; a late brood of tortoiseshells dipped and darted on the rocky apron outside the mouth of the principal cavern. One of them alighted on my sleeve. I felt a sensation of complete isolation and tranquillity. I had a glimpse of the peaceful pace of life as those distant people must have felt it on another such afternoon of sharp October sunshine. I sat on a ledge, 150 feet above the creek, watching the butterflies, listening to the redstarts, sipping Chablis, and it was as if I were on another planet, or were the last man on earth.

These Gila folk had been primarily of Hohokam-Mogollon stock, but had moved into the cultural orbit of the cliff dwellers to the north. Later, after they, too, had suddenly abandoned the homes they had constructed with such care, bands of Apaches had usurped their empty places.

There are, of course, other examples of Great Pueblo that are more impressive than the little Gila settlement. Keet Seel and Betatakin, for example, were among the most northwesterly of the cliff dwellings, and among the last to remain occupied. There the style of life developed along slightly different lines, and the handicrafts were of a somewhat lesser quality. Instead of kivas, square ceremonial rooms were built above the ground, and it is interesting to note that the relatively dense population of this west San Juan area constructed both cliff dwellings and free-standing pueblos. Thus the two forms of living were not mutually exclusive.

Keet Seel, Betatakin, Tuzigoot, Hovenweep, Kayenta, Kinishba, the "Village of the Great Kivas" near modern Zuni—the list of widely scattered cliff dwellings is long. Tom Outland, looking at the gemlike city in the canyon above him, rightly said that he felt that "only a strong and aspiring people could have built it, and a people with a feeling for design." And he went on: "A people who had the hardihood to build there, and who lived day after day looking down upon such grandeur, who came and went by those hazardous trails, must have been a fine people. But what had become of them? What catastrophe had overwhelmed them?"

Unanswerable questions. Between 1200 and 1350, not only the cliff dwellers in the northern part of the Anasazi area but the pueblo dwellers to the south left their homes and departed for the Rio Grande and other regions. The manner of their leaving remains mysterious and unaccountable.

What happened? It appears certain that they were not physically driven out by people covetous of their lands and goods. There is little evidence of fighting, or destruction, or the usurpation by strangers of their dwellings. There are no large mass burials, suggesting the aftermath of battles, nor extensive signs of fire and slaughter. One possibility is that there was an outbreak of some devastating pestilence. Such visitations must have been common even before the Spaniards introduced unknown diseases into the New World. It is a fact established by Spanish census that between 1538 and 1580 the population of Mexico fell from 6,300,000 to 1,900,000. The big killers were smallpox, chickenpox, tuberculosis, the common cold, and malaria, all imported from Europe. At the present time the average life expectancy of the pueblo Indian in New Mexico is about forty-four, and it would have been even shorter in protohistoric times. Living crowded together in small dark rooms, epidemics were no doubt regular occurrences.

However, a more likely explanation is that the Anasazi were driven away by the appalling drought that struck the Southwest in 1276. It lasted for twenty-three years, ending only in 1299. Its existence and duration is attested by dendrochronology, the technique of dating the past by the study of tree rings. This brilliant technique was devised by an astronomer, Dr. A. E. Douglass, who pioneered it in the Southwest. In that equable climate, the pine trees utilized in house building in prehistoric times showed a remarkably consistent pattern throughout the whole area. The period of drought detected by Douglass in his tree ring sequence was later confirmed by independent astronomers, who found that the world's periods of wet and dry weather are determined by the behavior of sunspots.

Probably the fields of the Hohokam and Anasazi were largely leached out some time before the great drought struck. Since they were purely agriculturalists, and kept no animals, they had no supply of natural fertilizer. They could, of course, have used their own excrement—which, in turn, would be a potent source of pestilence. In all probability they knew nothing of rotating crops, in order to spare the land. Moreover, the land itself seems to have been growing increasingly desiccated. The streams that fed the canals were dwindling, the topsoil was drifting away, the earth was cracking. The high density of the population in the Gila-Salt and San Juan areas can only have compounded their difficulties. The Hohokam appear to have held on to their settlements up to a century longer than the Anasazi; nor did they stray so far away or alter their way of life so radically. It was the Anasazi who felt the harsher blow and were forced to retreat farther. Indeed, some of the Anasazi took up their abode among the Hohokam, seemingly coming as luckless refugees rather than as bellicose intruders.

Have I, then, forgotten Egypt and Persia, Greece and Rome—*real* civilizations, that had passed into history by the time the wretched troglodytes of the Southwest had started to hack their holes in the cliffs? Byzantium, the Ommayads and Abbasids, Asoka and Akbar, the Han Dynasty? Have I forgotten that in Central America a score of elaborate civilizations had run their course? Or that in South America the Tiahuanacans and Incans were moving toward their peak? And in the face of all that, have I really devoted an entire chapter to talking about a pack of miserable rabbit trappers and pumpkin eaters, scratching about on the fringes of some God-forsaken desert? . . .

The Hohokam and Anasazi were no Vikings or Golden Horde. They were mute inglorious Miltons, village Hampdens. But does human history only consist of its gorgeous, gilded pages? And is it not appropriate that the forerunners of this American democracy should have been not Caesars and Alexanders, but quiet and unassuming farmers? They were plain pastoral people, who pioneered the wilderness. Many Americans of the twentieth century might give a great deal to be able to recapture their simple virtues. They possessed, after all, what Nietzsche, in *The Birth of Tragedy,* called "That harmony with Nature, which we late-comers regard with such nostalgia."

FOUR

THE ANASAZI packed up their traps and moved downhill toward the river.

Water, now as then, is the obsession—human, plant and animal—of the Southwest. It is lack of water that has limited the population of Arizona and New Mexico, which between them occupy 235,000 square miles, to less than three million people, most of them squeezed into a dozen towns. I have mentioned already the travails of the Colorado and the Rio Grande as they labor across the Sonora and Chihuahua deserts.

Rivers, of course, have always served as the cradles of civilization. That is why it is ingratitude, even more than simple economic folly, to pollute them. As T. S. Eliot observed, our rivers sweat oil and tar, "empty bottles, sandwich papers, silk handkerchiefs, cardboard boxes, cigarette ends, or other testimony of summer nights." He declared that he "did not know much about gods," but thought that a river "was a strong brown god." I feel that he may have been thinking not so much of the Thames, as of that mighty American river beside which he had grown up as a boy, when he had lived in Locust Street, St. Louis.

The Rio Grande was never as robust, even in its formative years, as Eliot and Twain's Mississippi. At the time when the land was drying out, it ran more thinly than it does today. However, to the Anasazi it was evidently more inviting than the streams that trickled fitfully through the upland canyons and washes, and the soil beside its banks was fertile.

Many civilizations have come into existence because of the creeping desiccation of the land around them. I have agreed not to indulge in the *folie de grandeur* of comparing the New Mexican pueblos with the old high civilizations. Indeed, by the time they settled on the Rio Grande, the most original and exalted days of the Anasazi were over. It seems safe to say that the life of the modern pueblo I am now going to describe is merely an impoverished version of the life that prevailed at Pueblo Bonito or Mesa Verde. The ancient ways had a sparkle and comeliness that is lacking in the modern pueblo, where daily existence is a dour business, relieved only by an occasional brave ritual. Yet, for all that, I shall argue that the inhabitant of the modern pueblo has an elusive beauty in his life that makes much of the allegedly more advanced life around him appear petty and pointless. The same is true of the descendants of the Hohokam, the Pima and the Papago, whom I shall come to in a later chapter.

Naturally, the old Anasazi style of living did not suffer an immediate and total breakup. Those who did not elect to migrate to Mexico, or to move like the Hopi toward the northeast, descended to the plains in reasonably good order. The term "Regressive Pueblo," given to the period between 1300 and 1700, by which time the outlines of modern pueblo society had been firmly established for more than a century, is misleading, for it suggests a condition of degeneration which did not actually exist. During this period the Pueblo people built a number of sites that compare favorably with Pueblo Bonito or Mesa Verde, and are far superior to the hotchpotch character of most of the modern pueblos.

The two most impressive sites of this epoch are the Coronado National Monument, near Albuquerque, and Tyuonyi, in the Bandelier National Monument. Unfortunately, we do not know what most of these ancient sites were called by their original preliterate inhabitants, so the names are purely notional. Coronado is called after the Spanish explorer and conquistador, who is supposed to have spent the winter of 1540–41 at the pueblo, on his march to the fabled land of Cíbola. It is possible, however, that the pueblo was originally called Kuaua, a word from the Tiwan or Keresan languages spoken in the surrounding pueblos.

The situation of Kuaua-Coronado is sublime. It stands on a broad reach of the Rio Grande, directly opposite the Sandia Mountains where, almost 30,000 years before, the early hunters had squatted in their cave. Except for the "Sky City" of Acoma, it enjoyed the most spectacular position of any pueblo of the prehistoric period. In its prime it was a spacious township, comprising at least twelve hundred rooms, grouped around three plazas, two of which had their own rectangular kivas, while the third had two rectangular kivas and two circular ones. Founded about 1300, the pueblo flourished for some three centuries, existing well into the Spanish era. Of special interest to the modern visitor is the "Painted Kiva" in the main plaza, which can be entered by means of a ladder in the roof. It is tiny compared with the great restored kiva at Aztec, but it possesses carefully executed copies of the murals that once covered

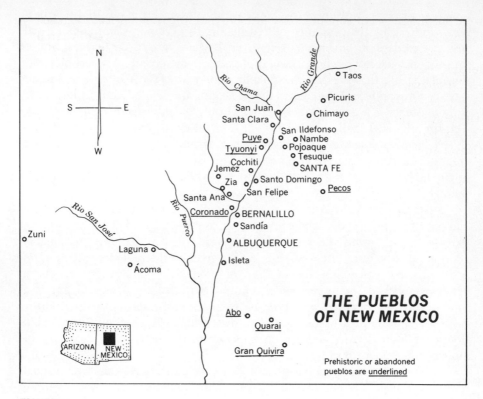

FIGURE 5

its plaster walls. Once again, without wanting to exaggerate, I must say that going down into this kiva reminds me of entering one of the smaller tombs of the nobles in the Valley of the Kings. Its birds, animals, and agricultural scenes have much of the immediacy and innocence of their Egyptian counterparts; they both reflect an easygoing agricultural society, living in partnership with nature. There is a concordance, too, as I indicated in my opening chapter, between the silver glitter of the New Mexico sunlight and that of Egypt, while the leonine landscapes of the Nile and the Rio Grande both flow between the rocky ranges of the sprawling desert.

Whenever I drive northward in the summer, on the way to Santa Fe for the opera, I turn off at Bernalillo to visit Coronado. It is one of the most accessible and attractive of the ancient monuments of the area, and it is pleasant to eat one's sandwiches beneath a straw-roofed *ramada* beside the fast-flowing shallows of the Rio Grande. There is usually something new to see, for although the main excavations were undertaken in the 1930s, restoration work is constantly in progress. Last time I was there, a group of workmen were making bricks of sun-dried clay in a big multiple frame. I have watched the process in Africa, and it is always a satisfying sight. This primal material is still widely employed throughout the Southwest, and a fine material it is—reliable, durable, cool in summer, warm in winter.

Tyuonyi, another important "Regressive" site, is also situated on the west bank of the Rio Grande, though in a canyon two miles above the river. The canyon is called Frijoles or Beans Canyon, and is one of a complex of canyons that cut down to where the Rio Grande flows through White Rock Canyon in the Bandelier National Monument. The Monument abuts the Santa Fe National Forest to the west, and the property reserved for the Atomic Energy Commission to the north. One wonders what Adolf Bandelier, who had such a zest, such a feeling for the high color of life, would have made of the mournful atmosphere of Los Alamos. The town epitomizes the reinforced-concrete ethos of the 1930s and 1940s; its gray crumbling houses and hutments bear an ironic resemblance to the *Wolfsschanze,* or the Berlin bunker. They are anomalous, dumped down beside what may be the loveliest of all the national parks in the Southwest. Bandelier is a paradise where you can spend whole days botanizing. Within a single acre you can identify literally a hundred different wild flowers. It is only right that Bandelier should have had named after him one of the most fragrant spots in a region to which he devoted six years of his hyperactive life.

It was about Tyuonyi, which he discovered in 1886, that he wove the plot of his novel, *The Delight Makers.* The book paints a vivid portrait of the life of these vanished people. Jacquetta Hawkes, another novelist, was also struck by the radiant character of Tyuonyi. The main ruin in the enchanted valley, filled with flowers, birds, and butterflies, is a semicircular communal house, containing a triple row of rooms. It was once two stories high, and within its central courtyard were three kivas. It is possible that this impressive structure was not a free-standing living site, like Pueblo Bonito, but a religious center, and that the domestic dwellings were those that exist in the cliffs nearby. In fact the canyons within a six-mile radius are sprinkled with houses large and small, some built on the tops of bluffs, others cut into the rock in true Mesa Verde style. They have all been dated within the century 1420–1520. Nearby is a cluster of cliff dwellings and houses atop the mesa on the Puye Cliffs, which were no doubt a fraternal outlier of Tyuonyi. The Puye site is owned by the modern pueblo of Santa Clara, a pueblo of medium size but with wealthy land holdings and excellent work opportunities in the neighboring towns of Los Alamos and Española. Enterprising folk, the Santa Clarans have organized an annual fiesta on the hilltop, among the ruins, in which they have invited other Tewa-speaking pueblos to participate. The ceremonials and tribal dances are not authentic, and have been got up for the benefit of the visitor; but the tribal costumes are exquisite, the girls beautiful, the children enchanting, the pottery and handicrafts passable, the homemade bread and

Tyuonyi ruin in Frijoles Canyon, Bandelier National Monument, New Mexico.

cakes delicious, and altogether in that elevated spot beneath the broad blue heavens the mood is gay and carefree. A delight-making way to spend an August afternoon.

Larger than Tyuonyi and Puye, larger even than Coronado, was the protohistoric pueblo at Pecos, situated on the opposite bank of the river, thirty-five miles away, twenty miles south of Santa Fe. It is one of the few sites I have not visited, but it bulks large in the archaeological literature because it once housed many thousands of people, and because it was excavated during the course of three decades by the doyen of southwestern archaeology, the great A. V. Kidder. Kidder unearthed a complete cross section of pueblo life extending over five hundred years, for Pecos was founded as early as 1300, and continued in use until as late as 1883. In that year, a pitiful remnant crossed the river and were given refuge by their blood relations at Jemez. Jemez itself, though at present it houses 1,000 people, is an isolated pueblo with a declining, problem-ridden population; in the 1950s alone it lost a third of its inhabitants. So it would seem that the Towa dialect which was spoken at Pecos, and is now spoken only at Jemez, might be on its way, after many thousand years, to extinction.

At Pecos, you can observe the actual transition between the "Old Ones" and the "New Ones." For here in the Southwest, within the feverish boundaries of modern America, is incapsulated a stubborn and sharply defined tradition that can be traced back with fair certainty to those Stone Age hunters who were coeval with the prehistoric hunters of Europe, Asia, and Africa. (I ask again—who says the United States has no history?) It would have been extraordinary if this incapsulation had occurred within the body of any modern industrialized society, let alone America. It is as if a number of prehistoric villages had survived into present-day Britain. When you walk into a Rio Grande pueblo, it is the equivalent of walking into an Icenian hamlet in the days of Boadicea.

When they left their homelands, five hundred years ago, fanning out and then regrouping, the pueblo peoples were already differentiated into six linguistic strains. Tiwan, Tewan, and Towan, which are interrelated, and belong to the Tanoan family, are of Uto-Aztecan stock. Keresan, which is quite distinct, is perhaps the original tongue of the ancient Anasazi. As for the distant Zuni, their language seems to be derived from Penutian stock, and may be basically related to Tanoan. And lastly, there is a Shoshonean dialect of Tanoan, spoken in the farthest-flung group of pueblos by the Hopi. The 4,000 Hopi occupy eleven villages, on three mesas, spread out over a distance of thirty miles in northern Arizona, seventy-five miles northeast of Flagstaff. They are thus over 150 miles away from the Rio Grande pueblos: and yet the Hopi, part of the Uto-Aztecan family, are obviously of the same blood and origin as their cousins in New Mexico (Figure 6).

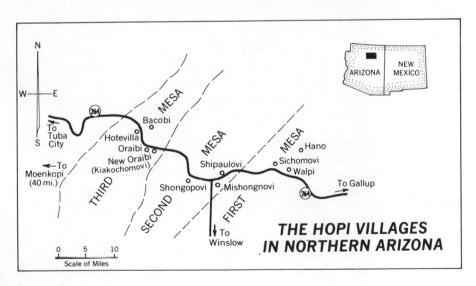

THE HOPI VILLAGES IN NORTHERN ARIZONA

FIGURE 6

NAME AND POPULATION (1970)	LANGUAGE	NATIVE NAME	MEANING
ACOMA (2,500)	Keresan	*Ako,* from *Akóme*	People of the White Rock
COCHITI (700)	Keresan	*Kotyete*	(Unknown)
HOPI (5,500)	Shoshonean	*Hópituh*	The Peaceful Ones
ISLETA (2,500)	Tiwan	*Tuei*	Town (*Isleta,* Spanish, Island)
JEMEZ (1,600)	Towan	*Walatowa*	People in the Canyon
LAGUNA (5,000)	Keresan	*Kawaik*	(Unknown) (*Laguna,* Spanish, Lake)
NAMBE (250)	Tewan	*Nambe*	People of the Earthen Mound
PICURIS (300)	Tiwan	*Piwwetha*	Pass in the Mountains
POJOAQUE (100)	Tewan	*Posunwage*	Drink-Water Place
SANDIA (250)	Tiwan	*Nafiat*	Sandy Place (*Sandia,* Spanish, Watermelon)
SAN FELIPE (1,500)	Keresan	*Katishtya*	(Unknown)
SAN ILDEFONSO (300)	Tewan	*Pokwoge*	Where the Water Cuts Through
SAN JUAN (1,250)	Tewan	*Oke*	(Unknown)
SANTA ANA (450)	Keresan	*Tamaya*	(Unknown)
SANTA CLARA (800)	Tewan	*Kápo*	(Unknown)
SANTO DOMINGO (2,000)	Keresan	*Kiuwa*	(Unknown)
TAOS (1,500)	Tiwan	*Tua*	Houses or Village
TESUQUE (250)	Tewan	*Tatunge*	Dry-Spotted Place
ZIA (500)	Keresan	*Tseja*	(Unknown)
ZUNI (5,000)	Penutian	*Ashiwi*	The Flesh

FIGURE 7. Modern pueblos of the Southwest.

Figure 7 gives the distribution and affinities of the twenty pueblos that exist in the Southwest today. Nowadays the names of the pueblos are either Spanish or have been Hispanicized; but the original Indian names of most of the pueblos founded in the early part of the Regressive Period have come down to us. We have seen that the original name of the Coronado National Monument was probably Kuaua; later it seems to have been one of a group of pueblos known at Tiguex. To take a few other examples, Pecos in its original tongue was Cicúique, Taos was Braba, Isleta was Tutahaco, Santo Domingo was Quirix, Acoma was Acucu. The names of other pueblos, such as Chía or Xemes, slid naturally into Spanish as Zía and Jemez. Today the inhabitants of the pueblos customarily use the Spanish names for their pueblos: but most of them still speak their ancient language among themselves, and learn and use English only as a second tongue. Needless to say, the American government and Americans at large regard this as a fearful and unnecessary "handicap," just as the English, out of their deep concern for the Welsh, consider that their persistence in talking their own language is ridiculous. It is always hard to explain to the possessors of an imperial tongue that a particular language, even the obscure language of a small people, somehow fits the curve of its mind better than the language of its neighbors. The loss of one of the world's minor languages is a little death for humanity.

The people of the Rio Grande and the Hopi have shown an admirable tenacity in clinging not only to their language but to the other elements of their ancient inheritance. They are living on the lands where their ancestors lived before them, and have refused to embrace the alien concept of life-as-a-permanent-flux adopted out of necessity by the whites around them. The latter were immigrants; they had left their own countries behind them; and it was a part of the original American compact that they should endorse the idea of the melting pot. Their European idiosyncrasies might have made them more individually interesting, but would have prevented the country as a whole from becoming what it desperately wanted to be: a homogeneous people. The Americans came together on an entirely different basis from the other peoples of the world, and are entitled to conduct their national life in a different way. On the whole, the melting pot concept has been successful—perhaps, indeed, rather too successful. Strangely enough, as I shall mention later, the only large American minorities that refuse to be melted down are these very peoples of the Southwest whom I am successively describing: the Indians of the pueblos; the Spanish-Americans; the Mexican-Americans or *Chicanos;* and the tribal Indians, three-quarters of whom live in Arizona and New Mexico. They pose the rest of the Americans a vexing problem. Are these people breaking the specific American contract, which stipulates that after a decent interval all the citizens of America must shed their former ethnic identity and become "Americans"? Or have these non-Anglo, nonimmigrant southwesterners the right, as each of them say they have, to remain aloof? May they not be, each in their own way, unassimilable—but do the assimilated Americans yet feel strong enough, and secure enough, to agree that a special situation may exist in these particular cases? Furthermore, is not "standard America" itself now so monolithic that a little cultural variety ought to be encouraged? Agreed, the latter is not an easy notion for most Americans, with their dread of chaos and secession, and their instinct to preserve the Union, to entertain. Yet even the Anglo-Saxons, after centuries of trampling on the Scots, Welsh, and Irish, and mercilessly exploiting their labor and natural resources, have come to see that to admit the Celtic peoples who share the British Isles into equal partnership is not a sign of weakness, but of vitality, and of strength through diversity.

The people of the New Mexico pueblos not only resisted the Anglos, a century ago. What was much more difficult, they had earlier resisted the Spaniards.

Many of the Rio Grande pueblos had only been established for a scant one hundred years before the Spanish incursion; and during that century they had already had to cope with the initial depredations of the Indians who were pressing down from the north and northeast. It was to be the Spaniards who, ironically, would save them from annihilation by the Navajo, Apache, and Comanche. Yet the Spaniards, too, could on occasion behave as cruelly as their other enemies, and would drive them to revolt.

The pueblo way of life was as foreign to the Spanish or Plains Indian way of life as it is to the modern American. The Spanish soldier or priest who came to the New World was aggressive and individualistic; the Pueblo Indian, like his Mexican cousin, was passive, fatalistic, and community-minded. As for the Indian of the plains, to use the distinction employed by Ruth Benedict in her *Patterns of Culture,* he was a Dionysian, not an Apollonian like the Indian of the pueblo. True, the Pueblo Indian occasionally used mind-expanding drugs and developed an addiction to alcohol: but he lacked the frenzied, visionary proclivities of the man of the plains. He was a pragmatic and phlegmatic ploughman, not a highly strung horseman.

The architecture of the pueblos reflects the character of their inhabitants. They possess, of course, individual differences; these is no such thing as the absolutely typical pueblo. Acoma, for example, is sometimes called the "Sky City," and is a site unique in America. It is built on top of a steep-sided hill that rises, like Orvieto, out of a level plain. It stands at the end of a gravel road, fourteen miles south of Highway 66, sixty miles from Albuquerque. Bandelier wrote of it: "No other town in the earth is so nobly perched. The only foreign hints of it are the Königstein, in Saxony; and (perhaps) the Gwalior, in the Deccan." Near it is a strange, lonely outcrop of rock, the Enchanted Mesa, stationed beside it like a supernatural sentinel.

To reach the pueblo, which stands almost four hundred feet above the valley, you leave your car at the foot of the hill and ascend a tight, twisting track—the same track up which the Spaniards charged more than four centuries ago. Indeed, a line of curious peaked heads molded in adobe adorn the walls of the hilltop cemetery, and are said to be modeled on the helmeted heads of Spanish soldiers. The church, very suitably dedicated, in view of the Acomans' habit of killing their priests, to St. Stephen, is a surprise: an enormous adobe structure, 120 feet long, 30 feet wide, and 30 feet high, with walls 10 feet thick, dominated by a primitive painted altar. It represented a real offering to God on the part of the villagers. They had to carry the baskets of mud for making the bricks all the way up from the plain on that vertiginous track, as they had also had to carry the earth for their houses, their gardens, and their graveyard.

As in all the pueblo churches, there are no pews, benches, or other furniture; the worshipers kneel on their colored sarapes, on the hard-packed earth floor. You have the impression of an uncluttered faith, a directness of communication between the supplicant and God. Yet the Catholic religion of the pueblos has never been easy or orthodox. During the Pueblo Revolt, the people of Acoma murdered their priest by throwing him off the cliff, an episode that forms a chapter in Willa Cather's *Death Comes for the Archbishop*. The little sprawling presbytery from which he was dragged to his death is attached to the church. There you can see the rank remains of an herb and fruit garden, surrounded by an adobe quadrangle complete with rough cloisters. It is as if a Spaniard who had known the splendors of the Escorial was trying to recreate them out of mud, in the wilderness. It is infinitely pathetic. You receive a poignant impression of a homesick priest, striving to preserve his memories of the country of his birth, half a world away, which he would never see again. You grasp the extent of his sacrifice, the keenness of his faith, the depth of his loneliness in the middle of this huge hostile continent, among his impassive, unpredictable parishioners.

Acoma, continuously occupied for over a thousand years, is the most striking of the pueblos; but many of the others possess their own piquant character. There is the Hopi village of Oraibi, on the edge of an escarpment, disputing with Acoma the honor of being the oldest occupied township in the United States. There is Taos, not the largest of the pueblos, but impressive because in places its buildings rise to a height of five stories, and also because it has a sparkling brook running through its heart—a brook which the fathers of the community refuse to tap, since water is a sacred element that must not be forced from its chosen channel and made to flow through metal or plastic piping.

Commonly, a pueblo is a group of single-story adobe buildings built around one or more plazas. The effect is one of a flat and angular geometry carried out in soft, chocolate tones, the hard edges smoothed and rounded. Weathered beams protrude below the level of the windows, humanizing the severe black apertures of the doors and windows. The humped and conical shapes of the ovens and the fretted walls around the kivas constitute a kind of mud-brick Baroque, while the façades of the churches are often decorated with animated friezes. One of the liveliest, featuring a charming pair of prancing horses, is on the church at Santo Domingo, which also had a nasty reputation for killing its priests.

Some pueblos are richer than others, though none are rich by American standards. Many are bone poor. If the atmosphere of some pueblos is relatively prosperous, that of others is dispirited and neglected; trash and rubbish blow across the plazas and pile up against the houses. You can feel as you enter whether a pueblo is well-run and optimistic, or whether it is listless and distracted. Fortunately, in the last decade there has been a mild but noticeable

Plaza with kiva at San Ildefonso, New Mexico.

improvement in the general fortunes of the people of the pueblos. Appearances, however, are often deceptive. Among the more forward-looking and wealthier pueblos are Laguna and Zuni—yet in spite of the capable and hard-working nature of their citizens, their physical appearance is nondescript. One would not suspect the existence of the riotous altar-piece in the church at Laguna, or the elaborate jewelry in the workshops at Zuni, from the drab appearance of the pueblos themselves.

It is obviously difficult for an outsider to form an accurate estimate of the life of the pueblo people. You can make subjective judgments, but you will receive little assistance from the inhabitants themselves. Why should you? What has a white man done that he should become the confidant of the Indian? What has the white man left the Indian but his tattered dreams and the secrets of his religion? And even the latter have been damaged, though not destroyed. To speak of them to outsiders would be to rob them further of their power and mystery.

When you enter an Indian pueblo, you are entering a hermetic world. These small, brown, stocky people, with faces that bear witness to their Mongoloid ancestry, are perfectly polite to you—but also perfectly reserved. They will allow you to wander about, occasionally even talk to you in a polite if neutral manner, sometimes even invite you into their houses. But there is always a sense of wariness, of being kept at arm's length. So in Britain the Celt looked at the Saxon, and the Saxon later looked at the Norman. The worst wounds are the slowest to heal. The interior of the houses, with insignificant exceptions, are very poor. An earth floor with a mat or two; a bedstead with a mattress and a blanket; a couple of chairs and a rickety table. Usually there is no electric light or running water. Since the white man has taught the Indian to despise material poverty, he can hardly expect the Indian to enjoy displaying his beggary to a member of the master race, in his smart clothes, with his sleek car, strolling about the pueblo as if he owned it, his expensive cameras slung around his neck.

Even Carl Gustav Jung, most patient and subtle of interlocutors, was unable to pierce the defenses of the Pueblo Indian. In the book from which I have taken one of my epigraphs, Jung writes about his visit to Taos pueblo in 1924. "The Pueblo Indians," he says, "are unusually closemouthed, and in matters of their religion absolutely inaccessible. They make it a policy to keep their religious practices a secret, and this secret is so strictly guarded that I abandoned as hopeless any attempt at direct questioning. Never before had I run into such an atmosphere of secrecy; the religions of civilized nations today are all accessible; their sacraments have long ago ceased to be mysteries. Here, however, the air was filled with a secret known to all the communicants, but to which whites could gain no access. This strange situation gave me an inkling of Eleusis, whose secret was known to one nation and yet never betrayed. I understood what Pausanias or Herodotus felt when he wrote: 'I am not permitted to name the name of that god.' This was not, I felt, a mystification, but a vital mystery whose betrayal might bring about the downfall of the community as well as of the individual. Preservation of the secret gives the Pueblo Indian pride and the power to resist the dominant whites. It gives him cohesion and unity; and I feel sure that the Pueblos as an individual community will continue to exist as long as their mysteries are not desecrated." I may add that I have talked to young Pueblo Indians who were students at college, and have found them slightly more communicative about their problems and their view of the world than they would be if they were at home— though even then, not much, and never about their religion. Like all Welshmen, I am an incorrigible nosey-parker: but the Pueblo Indians defeated even me.

After the canny and monosyllabic fashion in which you are greeted during an everyday visit to a pueblo, you can be staggered when you return there on the day of a festival. Then you see these cagey people given over to the color, din, and excitement of the dance. You are driven to wonder even more compellingly what it can be that takes place in the depths of the kivas, far underground, where the celebrants are said to hear the magic music of the earth gods. All writers on Pueblo religion stress that its fundamental tenet is to achieve an identification with nature—and it would be hard to come closer to nature than in a kiva. Everything about a pueblo, even the houses themselves, are of the earth, and earthy.

What happens below the ground we can only speculate. We may know the secrets of cancer, of the outer stars, before we know the secrets of the kiva. But what occurs overhead, in the dusty, sun-saturated plaza, we can watch for ourselves—though even then we cannot fully appreciate or share in its significance. Fortunately, Elsie Clews Parsons' celebrated study, *Pueblo Indian Religion* (1939), yields us more than a hint. Every month of the year offers a different spectacle at one or other of the pueblos. Each observes its own feast day, when it performs its personal ceremonies, often coupled with games and contests. Special days are devoted to such saints as San Felipe, San Antonio, San Pedro, San Juan, and San Lorenzo, in addition to Christmas Eve and Christmas Day. Most of the pueblos have a dance or ceremony peculiar to themselves. At Taos there is the Llano Dance, at Tesuque the Eagle Dance, at Jemez the Bull Dance, and at San Ildefonso the Animal and Comanche dances, which take place in adjacent plazas simultaneously. Several pueblos celebrate Deer or Buffalo dances, while the Hopi, on their northern mesas, execute a series of dances of outstanding individuality and imagination.

During the first six months of the year, the Hopi perform their *kachina* or *kotsina* dances, and in late August the famous Snake Dances. The kotsina cult exists throughout the pueblos, but is especially notable among the Hopi. Kotsinas are supernatural rainmakers and culture-bringers, who taught mankind the arts of hunting and agriculture. Unfortunately, mankind alienated the kotsinas, who decided to withdraw from the world: but before they did so, as a concession, they allowed mankind to borrow their own appearance, by means of fantastic masks and costumes, and intercede for rain with the higher gods. The kotsina cult therefore represents a fusion of the personalities of gods and men—an illustration of the reciprocity between men and gods that is the cornerstone of Indian religion in general. The Snake Dance is another rain dance, performed in the driest season of the year, in which the participants handle live rattlesnakes (their venom prudently extruded beforehand) which at the climax of the dance are released to slither away into the Painted Desert.

Unfortunately, circumstances have never allowed me to travel to the Hopi mesas in midsummer to witness the Snake Dances; but I have seen kotsina dances and a good range of the other dances. The most fascinating, and the most important, are the Corn Dances, carried out at every pueblo without exception. The American Indian preoccupation with maize is still obsessive. Hartley Burr Alexander, in *The World's Rim,* a study of the Indian Great Mysteries, quotes an anonymous seventeenth century Spanish priest writing in the *Crónica Franciscana:* "If one looks closely at these Indians he will find that everything they do and say has something to do with maize. A little more, and they would make a god of it. There is so much conjuring and fussing about their corn fields, that for them they will forget wives and children and any other pleasure, as if the only end and aim in life was to secure a crop of corn." In fact, they did make a god of it; each pueblo has its own private Osiris, Tammuz, or Adonis. Since it was first cultivated, corn has been the central feature of existence. One recalls the gigantic networks of canals and ditches at Casa Grande and Pueblo Bonito.

Today, when you see a shopper pick up a loaf of bread in a supermarket, you realize that he seldom gives any thought to the mysterious, miraculous process that has gone to create it; he assumes that it sprang directly into existence in a cellophane wrapping. The sense of process, of the slow and holy evolution of things, is one of the casualties of the plastic way of life. The Indian, even now, never forgets the relationship between the cornstalk out in the field and the soft sweet loaf his wife lifts on a flat paddle from her earthen oven. He still makes the vital connection (*"Only connect!"* as E. M. Forster urged us) between the bread and the corn—which takes him on further, to the connection with God. Dante, Milton, and Goethe tell us that Hell is the condition of losing the sense of the connection with the divine.

The Corn Dance I thought the most impressive takes place at Santo Domingo during the first week in August. It begins after ceremonial preparations in the kivas, and is carried on in turns throughout the day by the two grand divisions or moieties of pueblo society. One moiety appears in the plaza as the other is danced out, sung out, played out, making a splendid theatrical entrance behind its own orchestra, its singers, its chorus, and its banner bearer. It is an extraordinary sight—a whole wide plaza filled with men, women, youths, maidens, and tiny children, all moving, stamping, wheeling, brandishing their pine branches in intricate absorbed patterns. Forty years ago D. H. Lawrence, who was then living at Taos, came to Santo Domingo to watch the Corn Dance—and today it is staged in precisely the same manner, not a detail altered, as vigorous and meaningful as ever.

Lawrence lived in the Southwest for only eight months, just long enough to write *Saint Mawr*. "Thou hast here no abiding city," declared Saint Augustine. Lawrence failed more than most of us to find a place where he could settle for more than the briefest time. Yet the preternatural sensitivity he possessed for divining the *genius loci* enabled him to acquire a greater insight into the Southwest in a few months than the rest of us could acquire in a lifetime. He tuned in to the essential life of the American Indian in the same uncanny fashion that he tuned in to the lives of Australian aborigines, or Mexican and Italian peasants. Perhaps the fact that he was poor, sick, a wanderer and an outcast helped him to identify with unfortunate people who were themselves rejected by "advanced" societies. It is pleasant to record that he seems to have enjoyed a short respite from his cares and harassments in New Mexico, and after his death at Vence, in France, his ashes were brought back by his wife to repose in a small white shrine, high in the pinewoods on the Kiowa Ranch above Taos.

Mornings in Mexico, published in 1927, three years before his death, consists of an essay on the American Indian attitude to life, two pieces on the New Mexico pueblos, and an epilogue in which he looked back nostalgically from Italy toward the American West. It is hard to realize that he was only forty-two when the book appeared. If Jung was the "Old Wise Man," perhaps Lawrence was the "Young Wise Man."

Why should I struggle to describe the Corn Dance when Lawrence has already done it so magisterially?

He opens quietly, to set the scene.

"Pale, dry baked earth, that blows into dust of fine sand. Low hills of baked pale earth, sinking heavily, and speckled sparsely with dark dots of cedar bushes. A river on the plain of drought, just a cleft of dark, reddish-brown water, almost a flood. And over all, the blue, uneasy, alkaline sky. . . .

"There below is the pueblo, dried mud like mud-pie houses, all squatting in a jumble, prepared to crumble into dust and be invisible, dust to dust returning, earth to earth.

"That they don't crumble is the mystery. That these little squarish mud-heaps endure for centuries after centuries, while Greek marble tumbles asunder, and cathedrals totter, is the wonder. But then, the naked human hand with a bit of new soft mud is quicker than time, and defies the centuries.

"Roughly the low, square, mud-pie houses make a wide street where all is naked earth save a doorway or a window with a pale-blue sash. At the end of the street, turn again into a parallel wide, dry street. And there, in the dry, oblong aridity, there tosses a small forest that is alive: and thud—thud—thud goes the drum, and the deep sound of men singing is like the deep soughing of the wind, in the depths of a wood.

"You realize that you had heard the drum from the distance, also the deep, distant roar and boom of the singing, but that you had not heeded, as you don't heed the wind.

"It all tosses like young, agile trees in a wind. This is the dance of the sprouting corn, and everybody holds a little, beating branch of green pine. Thud—thud—thud—thud—thud! goes the drum, heavily the men hop and hop and hop, sway, sway, sway, sway go the little branches of green pine. It tosses like a little forest, and the deep sound of men's singing is like the booming and tearing of a wind deep inside a forest. They are dancing the Spring Corn Dance.

"You realize the long line of dancers, and a solid cluster of men singing near the drum. You realize the intermittent black-and-white fantasy of the hopping Koshare, the jesters, the Delight-Makers. You become aware of the ripple of bells on the knee-garters of the dancers, a continual pulsing ripple of little bells; and of the sudden wild, whooping yells from near the drum.

Then you become aware of the seed-like shudder of the gourd-rattles, as the dance changes, and the swaying of the tufts of green pine-twigs stuck behind the arms of all the dancing men, in the broad green arm-bands.

"Gradually come through to you the black, stable solidity of the dancing women, who poise like solid shadow, one woman behind each rippling, leaping male. The long, silky black hair of the women streaming down their backs, and the equally long, streaming, gleaming hair of the males, loose over broad, naked, orange-brown shoulders.

"Then the faces, the impassive, rather fat, golden-brown faces of the women, with eyes cast down, crowned above with the green *tableta,* like a flat tiara. Something strange and noble about the impassive, barefoot women in the short black cassocks, as they subtly tread the dance, scarcely moving, and yet edging rhythmically along, swaying from each hand the green spray of pine-twig out—out—out, to the thud of the drum, immediately behind the leaping fox-skin of the men dancers. And all the emerald-green, painted *tabletas,* the flat wooden tiaras shaped like a castle gateway, rise steady and noble from the soft, slightly bowed heads of the women, held by a band under the chin. All the *tabletas* down the line, emerald green, almost steady, while the bright black heads of the men leap softly up and down, between.

"When you look at the women, you forget the men. The bare-armed, bare-legged, barefoot women with streaming hair and lofty green tiaras, impassive, downward-looking faces, twigs swaying outwards from subtle, rhythmic wrists; women clad in the black, prehistoric short gown fastened over one shoulder, leaving the other shoulder bare, and showing at the arm-place a bit of pink or white undershirt; belted also round the waist with a woven woollen sash, scarlet and green on the hand-woven black cassock. The noble, slightly submissive bending of the tiara-ed head. The subtle measure of the bare, breathing, bird-like feet, that are flat, and seem to cleave to earth softly, and softly lift away. The continuous outward swaying of the pine-sprays.

"But when you look at the men, you forget the women. The men are naked to the waist, and ruddy-golden, and in the rhythmic hopping leap of the dance their breasts shake downwards, as the strong, heavy body comes down, down, down, down, in the downward plunge of the dance. The black hair streams loose and living down their backs, the black brows are level, the black eyes look out unchanging from under the silky lashes. They are handsome, and absorbed with a deep rhythmic absorption, which still leaves them awake and aware. Down, down, down they drop, on the heavy, ceaseless leap of the dance, and the great necklaces of shell-cores spring on the naked breasts, the neck-shell flaps up and down, the short white kilt of woven stuff, with the heavy woollen embroidery, green and red and black, opens and shuts slightly to the strong lifting of the knees: the heavy whitish cords that hang from the kilt-band at the side sway and coil for ever down the side of the right leg, down to the ankle, the bells on the red-woven garters under the knees ripple without end, and the feet, in buckskin boots furred round the ankle with a beautiful band of skunk fur, black with a white tip, come down with a lovely, heavy, soft precision, first one, then the other, dropping always plumb to earth. Slightly bending forward, a black gourd rattle in the right hand, a small green bough in the left, the dancer dances the eternal drooping leap, that brings his life down, down, down, down from the mind, down from the broad, beautiful shaking breast, down to the powerful pivot of the knees, then to the ankles, and plunges deep from the ball of the foot into the earth, towards the earth's red centre, where these men belong, as is signified by the red earth with which they are smeared . . .

"And all the while, all the while the naked Koshare are threading about. Of bronze-and-dark men-dancers there are some forty-two, each with a dark, crowned woman attending him like a shadow. The old men, the bunch of singers in shirts and tied-up black hair, are about sixty in number, or sixty-four. The Koshare are about twenty-four.

"They are slim and naked, daubed with black and white earth, their hair daubed white and gathered upwards to a great knot on top of the head, whence springs a tuft of corn-husks, dry corn-leaves. Though they wear nothing but a little black square cloth, front and back, at their middle, they do not seem naked, for some are white with black spots, like a leopard, and some have broad black lines or zigzags on their smeared bodies, and all their faces are blackened with triangle or lines till they look like weird masks. Meanwhile their hair, gathered straight up and daubed white and sticking up from the top of the head with corn-husks, completes the fantasy. They are anything but natural. Like blackened ghosts of a dead corn-cob, tufted at the top.

"And all the time, running like queer spotted dogs, they weave nakedly, through the unheeding dance, comical, weird, dancing the dance-step naked and fine, prancing through the lines, up and down the lines, and making fine gestures with their flexible hands, calling something down from the sky, calling something up from the earth, and dancing forward all the time. Suddenly as they catch a word from the singers, name of a star, of a wind, a name for the sun, for a cloud, their hands soar up and gather in the air, soar down with a slow motion. And again, as they catch a word that means earth, earth deeps, water within the earth, or red-earth-quickening, the hands flutter softly down, and draw up the water, draw up the earth-quickening, earth to sky, sky to earth, influences above to influences below, to meet in the germ-quick of corn, where life is.

"And as they dance, the Koshare watch the dancing men. And if a fox-skin is coming loose at the belt, they fasten it as the man dances, or they stoop and tie another man's shoe. For the dancer must not hesitate to the end . . .

"And the mystery of germination, not procreation, but *putting forth*, resurrection, life springing within the seed, is accomplished. The sky has its fire, its waters, its stars, its wandering electricity, its winds, its fingers of cold. The earth has its reddened body, its invisible hot heart, its inner waters and many juices and unaccountable stuffs. Between them all, the little seed: and also man, like a seed that is busy and aware. And from the heights and from the depths man, the caller, calls: man, the knower, brings down the influences and brings up the influences, with his knowledge: man, so vulnerable, so subject, and yet even in his vulnerability and subjection, a master, commands the invisible influences and is obeyed. Commands in that song, in that rhythmic energy of dance, in that still-submissive mockery of the Koshare. And he accomplishes his end, as master. He partakes in the springing of the corn, in the rising and budding and earing of the corn. And when he eats his bread at last, he recovers all he once sent forth, and partakes again of the energies he called to the corn, from out of the wide universe."

What can one add to such a passage? I can only offer a few minor comments.

First, Lawrence renders the important figures of the Koshares in a somewhat more forbidding light than they actually appear. Nor is he quite right when, at the beginning, he slightly contradicts himself by referring to them as "the jesters, the Delight-Makers" (here he uses the title of Bandelier's novel, which obviously he had read and admired). The Koshares are not in

A Koshare being offered food during a break in the Corn Dance, San Ildefonso, New Mexico.

the least frightening or macabre. There is nothing of the gloom and oppressiveness of African rituals in the pueblo dances. The Koshares comport themselves in an amiable manner, like absent-minded choreographers, breaking off to attend to the costume of one or other of the dancers, where a ribbon is breaking loose, or a belt or necklace slipping. They show special tenderness toward the smaller children, who mimic the grown-ups or, if they are very tiny, form a little line of their own. The Koshares help them and encourage them to keep step. They have a multiple function, representing as they do not only the dead winter earth, from which the new crops will come, and the dead relatives and ancestors of the dancers, but also the dead past of the race, which is being taken into the ceremonies of the living.

Second, Lawrence does not mention the huge flaunting banner which is a central feature of the dance. It is an enormous pole, twenty feet high, which before the dance began can be seen sticking out of the entrance of one of the kivas. During the dance it is swirled above the heads of the dancers, as if scattering potency, and it takes a strong man to wield it. Its summit is decorated with a panache of eagle, woodpecker, and macaw feathers (the latter anciently traded up from Central America), a fox-pelt, and several medicine-pouches. It serves as the focus of the dance.

Next, I would like to underscore the profound impression produced by the ceaseless, fluid waving of the pine branches. It is like watching Birnam Wood flowing toward Dunsinane. Trees have special significance for the people of the pueblos. They are numinous objects. Above is the sky, below is the earth—and between them, touching the sky at one end and the earth at the other, stand the trees. More even than man, it is the trees which require the sun and the rain, and which call them down. Before man, there were the trees. They live on the high mountains; they line the rivers and canyons; they are the conductors of heavenly power, the ladders to heaven, just as a pine-pole is the ladder between the underworld of the kiva and the plaza above it. The soft undulation of the dark green boughs creates a hypnotic effect. Primitive peoples, no less than the ancient Persians (whose word for garden gave us our word for paradise), appreciate a fine tree. When Xerxes was passing through Turkey, on his way to invade Greece (where he hoped to acquire some interesting botanical specimens), he saw a plane tree that was so beautiful that he hung it with golden ornaments and left behind one of the Immortals, his personal bodyguard, to protect it. The American Indian would have understood such a gesture.

Next, there is the symbolism of all those colors that dazzled Lawrence. The custom is for one moiety to paint itself red and yellow, the other to paint itself blue. Every color has its meaning: vegetation is green; soil, red; sky, blue; clouds, white; the rainbow, red and yellow. Similarly, the patterns on the kilts, sashes, tunics, and the *tabletas* or *tablitas* of the women and girls, have a special meaning. The motif on the *tableta* represents the slopes of the mountain, like the fretted outline of the Step Pyramid or a Babylonian ziggurat. It is ornamented with symbolic stars, crescents, and crosses.

Lastly, it should be emphasized that perhaps the most emotive element in the dance is the incessant rhythmic stamping and pounding of the naked earth of the plaza. It is like the monotonous yet reverent treading in of the seed, a mystic summons to the gods deep in the ground to rise to the surface, to come forth. The bare feet of the women seem to stroke and smooth the soil rather than beat it; they knead it, palpate it, caress it. I found it hard, watching them, to cling to the existential view that the body of the world is nothing but a vast and senseless crud.

The earth, the corn, the sun, the rain. Four necessities. Four realities. And all invoked at the same moment, within a single dance.

Rain. The pueblos are still haunted by that devastating drought that struck the Southwest seven hundred years ago.

They do not intend to let it happen again. If the gods are asleep, they will be awakened. If they are angry, they will be placated.

Memories live long in the pueblos.

It might be expected that, besieged as the Rio Grande pueblos are by technocratic America, their religion would become flaccid and eventually crumble. To be sure, some writers believe this might happen, or is already happening. They expect that the shift from farming to a wage-earning economy, as the people of the pueblos travel to work in nearby cities, will inevitably undermine the fabric of religion. Other writers, however, report that during the 1960s the Pueblo religion not only held its own, but actually deepened and expanded. Several ceremonies that had lapsed were revived, and the young people embrace the traditional religion with enthusiasm, as a precious and irreplaceable possession. True, some of these revived dances and ceremonies are cynical, and some are totally artificial, faked-up for the benefit of the tourist. The most depressing dances of this sort are some of those held at Taos. To watch these gimcrack antics is embarrassing.

On the other hand, religion is so bound up with every aspect of Pueblo life that it is difficult to see how it could disappear without the collapse of the pueblos themselves. The social organization of the pueblos is a tightly knit compound of the religious and the secular. Seeking to live as they do, in harmony with nature, in both their religious and civil affairs the people of the pueblos follow a clear and simple duality, just as they do in their dances. This duality exists in nature: days and night, light and dark, warm and cold, dry and wet, hard and soft, sweet and sour, joy and pain. These are the eternal polarities, the essential opposites of existence. The moieties of the Pueblo Indians are therefore called in some pueblos the Summer People and the Winter People, and in others the Squash People and the Turquoise People. (Squash suggests fecundity and summer, while the turquoise suggests hardness and winter.)

In most pueblos the *cacique,* the religious head of the pueblo, shares power with the governor, who is responsible for civil affairs. Often the cacique is the predominant power and determines the election to the secular offices. Certainly it is impossible to be appointed to high office unless a man is prominent in the religious hierarchy. As for the governor, he is assisted by a lieutenant governor, an *alcalde,* a *fiscal,* and a council of village elders, the *principales.* In some pueblos the governor and his staff belong to one moiety and serve for half a year, when they give way to their successors from the other moiety; in other pueblos they serve for a whole year. At Zuni, which has realized that a period of six months or a year is too brief, the period has been extended to two years. The two-moiety system exists among the Tewan pueblos; the Keresan pueblos are ruled solely by a cacique and a permanent council; and the Hopi are directed by a Tribal Council alone. A few pueblos, like Laguna and Isleta, have attempted to make some separation between religious and civil affairs, while Isleta and Santa Clara have gone so far as to adopt a written constitution. The government of each pueblo looks after its finances and land holdings, and is responsible for law and order, except in the case of serious crimes, which are dealt with by the federal courts.

Zuni might be termed one of the more go-ahead pueblos. (I hesitate to use the word progressive, since I have heard it too often in Europe, where the self-styled progressive parties are usually anything but that.) In 1969, Zuni was the first to sanction the participation of women in pueblo elections, though from this it must not be supposed that women occupy an inferior position in pueblo society. Among the Tewa, membership of the moieties is through the father, but even with the Tewa the mother's side of the family is considered of equal importance. Elsewhere the descent is reckoned through the mother, and the home is the woman's property. It is as easy for the wife to obtain a divorce as it is for the husband; all she has to do is to tell him to go and he must leave her house. She may remarry when she pleases. Marriage itself is strictly monogamous, and the woman works by the man's side in a situation of complete equality. When you watch the dances, or the everyday life of the pueblo, you do not get the impression that women are helots, or are looked-down-upon.

It was Jung, in the passage I have quoted, who spoke of Herodotus, Pausanias, and the Eleusinian Mysteries in connection with the Pueblo religion. So I hope it will not be considered too absurd if I make a guarded comparison between the government of the pueblos and the Greek *polis.* The Pueblo Indians have produced no Homer, Ictinus, or Pericles; as I said, theirs are the short and simple annals of the poor. Yet their form of government does reflect, if humbly, that of the polis, however we are to translate that difficult word. Originally it meant a citadel, the fortress dominated by an acropolis to which the farmers who made up the community retreated in time of trouble. The pueblo, dominated by its church, bears a distinct resemblance to the polis in this sense. At bottom, however, the word meant "the people," as well as the place that sheltered them, just as the Spanish word *pueblo* means both "the people" and "the village." It was only later in Greek history that the word took on the overtones of "the city-state"—while Athens alone, be it remembered, never possessed a population at its peak of more than 20,000. Most Greek "city-states" were not much larger than the average Indian pueblo.

None of the modern southwestern pueblos numbers more than 5,000, which Plato thought ideal for the polis, though in the Anasazi period a few of them may have. But they all possess the requirement of Aristotle: that the polis must not become so large that its members cease to know one another by sight. That is the point: that the pueblo, like the polis, is a small, intimate, manageable unit, mainly agricultural in character, but with some manufacturing activities. (The pueblos, like ancient Athens and Corinth, rely heavily on the sale of fine pottery.) It has its own religious societies and traditions, but is able to share in the life and ceremonies of its neighbors. Even when he leaves his pueblo, the Indian feels the unbreakable attachment the Greek felt for his polis; sooner or later, whether he is in Los Angeles or Chicago, it draws him home. Nor, when he is living away from it, does he lose his rights or his voice in its affairs.

This is a mode of life that obviously has its satisfactions and consolations. Except in the smaller towns and a few of the smaller cities, it is not a mode of life that exists any more for most Americans or Englishmen, trapped in their cold and grimy conurbations. One of the many worrisome sensations the American or European feels today is that, unlike the Greek in his polis, or the Indian in his pueblo, he has little control over his own affairs; no one cares about him; he does not know to whom to address his appeals; he has no sense of redress. His only contact with the remote people who rule him is by mail, on printed forms—or if he is actually summoned to meet his superiors, face to face, he knows it can only be for an unpleasant purpose. And all this applies not to the poorer and more obscure members of society, but to nine-tenths of the community as a whole: alienation and *anomie* are almost universal. In America, the situation is not quite so bad as it is in Europe; American legislators are often surprisingly close to the electorate, and most Americans have not yet reached a state of despair with regard to the possibility of influencing their representatives. I shall be discussing in my last chapter the unusual sense of comradeship that exists between individual Americans, even between ordinary people and politicians. In Britain, on the other hand, the men at Westminster are sadly out of touch with the people who vote for them. With few exceptions, MPs are party wheelhorses, foisted on the constituencies by the Central Offices; their constituents seldom know anything about them and usually dislike them, even when they belong to their own party. To be fair, nobody pretends that the six hundred members of the Mother of Parliaments constitute a group of the most vigorous and intelligent men and women in the British Isles; but there is not much sense of the polis, of government by mutual discussion and consent, about modern Britain, sent staggering by dubious agencies from one crisis to another, while the faith of reasonable men in the efficacy of the system is sorely shaken.

The people of the pueblos have their troubles—terrible ones. Their material problems are more crushing than those experienced in the surrounding cities. Child mortality, tuberculosis, and other diseases are common, though medical care is improving. There is a great deal of illegitimacy, reflecting the sexual ferment in the world around them; and there are outbreaks of vandalism and juvenile delinquency. In perhaps a majority of the pueblos there are severe disagreements between one party, or one generation, and another, leading at times to social paralysis. Sometimes a crisis occurs because of the antagonism between the theocratic and technocratic interests; or the ruling faction is accused of being dictatorial; or the clash between age and youth is bitterly divisive. The struggle between the generations is partly responsible for the worst single problem in the pueblos: drunkenness. The old men get drunk because their sons work in the cities, earn more money than they do, acquire new ideas, and lose the traditional respect for their fathers. This, of course, is a phenomenon that has become acute in recent years in the Western world as a whole. As for the young men, they get drunk because the elders who run the pueblos form a closed corporation which they cannot penetrate.

Strong drink was deliberately introduced into Indian life at the period when it was official policy to break the Indian by wrecking his character and institutions. The gambit succeeded only too well. Finally the government became disgusted with its own actions, and tried to cut off the flow; but by then the damage had been done. The Plains Indian in particular swallowed the stuff with a fatal enthusiasm. Chain Lightning or Old Red Eye, he found, was very effective in producing the visions he coveted. The Indian had had no acquaintance with alcohol; strong spirits were no part of his tradition; he was a stranger to the idea of being able to take-it-or-leave-it. It was like allowing a child to play in the proverbial sweetshop. Unfortunately, too, the introduction of bad whiskey by the white man coincided with the critical period when the Indian, having suffered defeat, was desperate; it was the period of the Ghost Dances, the Earth Lodge cult, the cult of the Dreamers, the Sun Dance, the Indian Shaker movement.

It was a tense, fervid time for the Indian. Even the Pueblo Indian, Apollonian by temperament, was attracted by drink, though he did not indulge in the mad, messianic practices of the Plains Indian. However, he had long been a devotee of the peyote cult, the eating of the button of the peyote cactus (*Lophophora williamsii*), which is found in the Rio Grande valley. The practice had reached him from Mexico. The peyote contains nine alkaloids, including mescaline, and is strongly hallucinogenic, though not addictive. In the late nineteenth century, its use spread from the pueblos, where its use in religious ceremonies was strictly controlled, to the surrounding Indian tribes of Oklahoma, Nevada, Colorado, and Utah. There its employment was indiscriminate, and soon brought the whole cult into disrepute. And by that time the Pueblo Indian had also taken to drink—the white man's Delight-Maker—in his turn.

With the degeneration of Indian culture, the effects of drink took hold. Even in pueblos which had maintained their standards better than most, drink became a panacea for the general misery. It helped to make the Indian forget the disintegration of his nation, with its concomitants of disease and unemployment. Unemployment is an even grimmer problem than alcoholism in the modern pueblos. In some, the rate of unemployment among males of working age runs as high as 90 percent, and is nowhere less than 40 percent. Most pueblos average around 45 percent to 50 percent unemployment at any given time. There are simply not sufficient jobs available. The average per capita income of pueblo residents is $500 a year. Even the average family income is less than $2,000 a year—well below the official American poverty line (though well above the poverty line, be it noted, in all other countries).

The men work the fields; but the fields are too small. They work in the towns; but they lack education to obtain good jobs, and often there is prejudice against them. Sometimes, too, if the pueblo is under the control of an excessively religious caucus, there is no scheduling of dances and ceremonies to accommodate a man's outside employment. However, the men of the pueblos are acquiring an ever-increasing range of technical skills, and also making a sound start on supplementing their income by work they can do at home, either on a full- or part-time basis. There are fees from tourism, charged to enter the pueblo or to watch the dances. There is the sale of pottery, which has never died as an art, and which in the hands of such geniuses as the Hopi woman Nampeyo at Hano, or Maria, the great potter of San Ildefonso, has reached great heights. A fine piece of pueblo pottery may now command $300 to $400. Then there are baskets and rugs, sold either in the towns or at the Indian trading posts, and paintings that find their way to major art galleries. There are the exquisite kachina dolls of the Hopi. Above all, there is the jewelry. Most Indian jewelry, even at Zuni, is made on a part-time basis, and most of the profit is reaped by the white middlemen; the latter, as pawnbrokers, snap up the best specimens of antique Indian jewelry for next to nothing, making 1000 percent profit on them. Most silversmiths at Zuni make only $500 a year from their efforts. On the other hand, several communities are learning how to make a good income from their property and communal farming, and some have even attracted light industries to the pueblo. At Laguna, an electronics firm has discovered that the Indians have an unusually

Maria and Julian Martinez, potters at San Ildefonso, New Mexico. (NEW MEXICO
DEPARTMENT OF DEVELOPMENT)

deft touch with electrical equipment, like the workers of Taiwan and Hong
Kong.

If I dwell somewhat nostalgically on the government of the pueblos, it is
because it conforms to a type of government I think most people feel in their
bones might have existed in the world's happier times. It is a type of government which we pray may some day return. It meets most of the requirements
of Plato and Aristotle, of Proudhon, or of Kropotkin in that noble and neglected book, *Mutual Aid;* it fulfills one of the more sensible precepts of Rous-
seau, who held that in the ideal state the citizens should be able to observe
their rulers and criticize them on a man-to-man basis. Americans, with their
terror of things falling apart, are not yet willing to embrace such a devolu-
tionary idea; yet it is widely admitted that the best human unit is the small
one, the smallest possible. Local politics are exciting and personal; national

and international politics are remote and intimidating. As a general rule, it is more satisfying to live in a town than a city, in a village rather than a town. As my old Welsh aunts used to say—and they had not read Virgil or Horace— *Cais ddoeth yn ei dyddyn: Seek out the wise man in his cottage.* Similarly, any sailor will tell you that it is better to serve in a corvette or a destroyer than in a cruiser or an aircraft carrier. There is a greater sense of comradeship. As the units grow larger, so does the feeling of: "They-don't-give-a-damn-about-us."

Practically everybody in Western society today is being dragged along the road to collectivization. Everyone hates it: but there is no perceptible escape. People are hustled toward a state of existence which they feel will prove even more emasculating and depersonalizing than the lives they lead now. They feel they are being sacrificed to the fashion for bigness: big government, big bureaucracy, big corporations, big unions, big everything. They are helpless because the high priests of bigness—the professional politicians, the men who run huge companies and nationalized industries, and the trades union leaders— are ruthless in their pursuit of the big and bigger unit. They all have a vested interest in oiling their machines and in keeping the cities that house them in a bloated condition. If you live in an Indian pueblo, your government may be a bit slapdash: but at least you are dealing with the devil you know, and whom you know by his first name. The devils we have to deal with in our own society are so frightening because they are so faceless. You cannot call computers by their first names. One of the evil things that socialism has brought about in Britain has been to remove the visible, identifiable heads of industrial or family concerns and replace them with unknown and inaccessible bureaucrats. Once you could at least pound the boss's desk and call him a brandy-nosed old bastard; at least you got sacked by a real person, not a card index. Now that the government owns big industry, when a worker goes on strike, he is not expressing a private grudge, he is committing treason, a crime against the state. It is too complicated and bewildering for a simple man to cope with. Would it not make sense to ignore the wailing of the politicians, the trade union bosses, the more voracious kind of industrialists, and reduce things once more to human proportions? We must heed the warnings. The American President visits the Soviet Premier in Moscow; the Soviet Premier flies to Washington. The apostles of Big Capital and Big Socialism are wondering how they can resolve their differences in order to combine and crush us.

But perhaps, in the end, it will be those very economic recessions that continually plague both big systems that will finally save us. They may make people realize, eventually, that bigness is stupid, that it is in fact a principal cause of our economic dislocations, of our psychological anxieties. Perhaps we can abandon an over-collectivized life and return to a more individual one.

Anne M. Smith, interviewing young pueblans for her study *New Mexican Indians* (1966), talked to one who said: "When any Pueblo Indian is

Chimayo, New Mexico:
a typical pueblo church.

asked questions about himself as an individual, the thing that pops into my
mind is the word 'group.' Whatever I have, I want to make sure my grand-
mother who is blind has. And there are many other factors involved in helping people than handing them a few bucks occasionally." Another young man
said: "The problems of the village are a problem for everybody. It does not
only concern the individual, whether he lives in Albuquerque or if he lives in
any other part of the state, or even out of the state, but since he grew up in a
village, he has to be concerned with what will happen eventually to the people
living in the village. You can't get away from it."

    Jung found that these people, so poor in those goods which are the index
of value in the world around them, believed that they were not only brothers
to each other but, in spite of having been badly used, brothers to all other men.
When he was speaking to the chief of the Taos pueblo, the latter said: "The
Americans want to stamp out our religion. Why can they not let us alone?
What we do, we do not only for ourselves but for the Americans also. Yes,
we do it for the whole world. Everyone benefits by it." The chief felt himself
to be "the son of the sun." "I then realized," Jung continued, "on what the
'dignity,' the tranquil composure of the individual Indian was founded . . .
His life is cosmologically meaningful . . . If we set against this our own

self-justifications, the meaning of our own lives as it is formulated by our reason, we cannot help but see our poverty. Out of sheer envy we are obliged to smile at the Indians' naïveté and to plume ourselves on our cleverness; for otherwise we would discover how impoverished and down at the heels we are. Knowledge does not enrich us; it removes us more and more from the mythic world in which we were once at home by right of birth." The pueblo chief said a terrible and enlightening thing to him. " 'See how cruel the whites look. Their lips are thin, their noses sharp, their faces furrowed and distorted by folds. Their eyes have a staring expression; they are always seeking something. What are they seeking? The whites always want something; they are always uneasy and restless. We do not know what they want. We do not understand them. We think that they are mad.' I asked him why he thought the whites were all mad. 'They say that they think with their heads,' he replied. 'Why, of course. What do you think with?' I asked him in surprise. 'We think here,' he said, indicating his heart."

This is precisely the point that Aldous Huxley wished to make in *Brave New World*, a novel that is now, over forty years later, even more timely and absorbing than when it was published in 1932. The crux of the book is the contrast that Huxley draws between the way of life of the Indian pueblo, personified by the Savage, and the way of life of perfected Socio-Communistic society, personified by the World Controller. It will be remembered by those who know the novel that the Controller allows Bernard Marx, a young technocrat who has begun to have doubts about the Bravery of the New World, to satisfy his curiosity about the primitive life on the Reservation. So Bernard, with his beautiful, sanitized, and vacuous girlfriend, Lenina, takes the Blue Pacific Rocket to New Mexico. "They slept that night at Santa Fe. The hotel was excellent. Liquid air, television, vibro-vacuum massage, radio, boiling caffeine solution, hot contraceptives, and 8 different kinds of scent were laid on in every bedroom." (This is an uncannily accurate forecasting of the pleasures of the modern American motel, hot contraceptives presently excluded.) As he goes to sleep, having taken his two grams of *Soma,* Bernard's thoughts carry him "over Taos and Tesuque, over Nambe and Picuris and Pojoaque, over Sia and Cochiti, over Laguna and Acoma and the Enchanted Mesa, over Zuni and Cíbola and Ojo Caliente."

Next day they are taken into the Reservation. There is a lively account of the Hopi Snake Dance, which those who are interested might compare with Lawrence's. (Huxley and Lawrence had considered, by the way, a scheme to settle together in the United States and establish a community there.) Lenina, a girl who might have walked straight out of a TV commercial, is appalled by everything she sees. "The dirt, the piles of rubbish, the dust, the dogs, the flies. Her face wrinkled into a grimace of disgust. She held her handkerchief to her nose. 'But how can they live like this?' she broke out in a voice of indignant incredulity. (It wasn't possible.) Bernard shrugged his shoulders philosophically. 'Anyhow,' he said, 'they've been doing it for the last 5 or 6 thousand years. So I suppose they must be used to it by now.' 'But cleanliness is next to fordliness,' she insisted. 'Yes, and civilization is sterilization,' Bernard went on, concluding on a tone of irony the second hypnopaedic lesson in elementary hygiene.''

They encounter the young John Savage, a Pueblo Indian whose mother was a "civilized" woman who was lost in the Reservation many years before. She is married to an Indian called Popé, has never adjusted to Indian life, and has developed a twin addiction to mescal and peyote that has made her a swollen, sodden wreck. (Huxley must have received the germ of the idea for Lenina from Lawrence's *The Woman Who Rode Away*.) Bernard takes John and his mother back to London. The "Savage," who—because his mother is an outsider—has found life in the pueblo harsh, and has not been allowed to know the mysteries of the kiva, is as eager to escape from the Reservation as Bernard is to escape from "civilization." Nevertheless, when he reaches London, where he is treated with the kind of *réclame* that attends a Wild Man of Borneo, he is quickly disillusioned with the socialized society of A. F. (After Ford) 632. He loathes it all: *Soma;* Orgy-Porgy; Community-Sings; his visit to the Feelies, where he watches *Three Weeks in a Helicopter,* and hears a Herbal Capriccio on the scented organ; the crematoria with their apparatus for reclaiming phosphorus from the corpses; the Internal and External Secretions Corporation; the lovely, brainless, ageless girls with their Malthusian Belts; above all by the process in the Hatchery, where the embryos are budded by the Bokanovsky Process into five standard types of individual, ranging from the governing type, the Alpha, to the Epsilon type, the proletarian worker. (Huxley's budding process has now become a reality; biologists call it "cloning.")

The Savage breaks into the Park Lane Hospital, curses a "khaki mob" of workers in English and Zuni, and shouts at them: "Do you like being slaves?" He throws their ration of Soma out of the window, which causes the wretched creatures to panic. He is taken before the World Controller, who expounds the philosophy of the World State's motto: *Community, Identity, Stability.* "The world is stable now. People are happy; they get what they want, and they never want what they can't get. They're well off; they're safe; they're never ill; they're not afraid of death; they're blissfully ignorant of passion and old age; they're plagued with no mothers or fathers; they've got no wives, or children, or lovers to feel strongly about; they're so conditioned that they practically can't help behaving as they ought to behave. And if anything should go wrong, there's Soma. Which you go and chuck out of the window in the name of liberty, Mr. Savage. *Liberty!* Expecting Deltas to know what liberty is!" And when the Savage talks of God, the Controller answers: "God isn't compatible with machinery and medicine and happiness. You must make your choice. Our civilization has chosen machinery and medicine and happiness.''

'' 'But I don't want comfort,' said the Savage. 'I want God, I want poetry,

I want real danger, I want freedom, I want goodness, I want sin.' 'In fact,' said the Controller, 'you're claiming the right to be unhappy. Not to mention the right to grow old and ugly and impotent; the right to have syphilis and cancer; the right to have too little to eat; the right to be lousy; the right to live in constant apprehension of what may happen tomorrow; the right to catch typhoid; the right to be tortured by unspeakable pains of every kind.' There was a long silence. '*I claim them all,*' said the Savage at last. . . ."

In 1946, Huxley wrote a new preface to his novel. It mainly concerned what he called "the welfare-tyranny of Utopia." "All things considered," he observed, "it looks as though Utopia were far closer to us than anyone, only 15 years ago, could have imagined. Then, I projected it 600 years into the future. Today it seems quite possible that the horror may be upon us within a single century." (And that was in 1946. . . .) He had some very interesting additional reflections. "If I were now to rewrite the book," he said, "I would offer the Savage a third alternative. Between the utopian and the primitive horns of his dilemma would lie the possibility of sanity—a possibility to be actualized, to some extent, in a community of exiles and refugees from the Brave New World, living within the borders of the Reservation. In this community economics would be decentralist and Henry-Georgian, politics Kropotkinesque co-operative. Science and technology would be used as though, like the Sabbath, they had been made for man, not (as at present and still more so in the Brave New World) as though man were to be adapted and enslaved to them. Religion would be the conscious and intelligent pursuit of man's Final End, the unitive knowledge of the immanent Tao or Logos, the transcendent Godhead or Brahman."

It is worth, in conclusion, translating the French epigraph from Nicolas Berdyaev that provided Huxley with his original *donnée.* "Utopias," it runs, "appear more realizable than one would have previously imagined. And we now find ourselves actually facing an agonizing question: How are we to prevent their definitive realization? . . . Life marches towards Utopias. And perhaps a new century will begin, a century where the intellectuals and cultivated classes will dream of ways of escaping the Utopias and of returning to a society which is not utopian, less 'perfect,' and more free . . ."

FIVE

HOHOKAM, ANASAZI, Pueblo Indians—I imagine that these outlandish names may still be causing the heads of many readers to spin. Well, I am now about to explore the Spanish layer of my cultural cutting, so I hope that some of my English readers at least will start to feel on much firmer ground. The Spaniards, after all, are Europeans.

They are not, of course, to the British way of thinking, very typical Europeans. For almost eight hundred years Spain was occupied by the Moors, and to some extent it can be said that Africa begins at the Pyrenees. The appearance of the land, the tempo of life, the character of the people, all have a subtle African flavor. Flamenco, *canto hondo,* and other facets of Spanish culture have an unmistakable Arab origin. In some ways, the atmosphere of Madrid is closer to that of Cairo or Damascus than it is to Paris or Rome, while many Spanish towns, particularly in the South, might have been transferred bodily from Morocco or Tunisia.

Spain is not a country that has sent many emigrants to America. It does not bulk large in the American consciousness. As for the Spanish Empire, with which I am now about to deal, its reputation is as poor in America as in most of the rest of the world. Not only are empires unfashionable, but Americans are by nature hostile to the imperial idea and cannot be expected to consider it impartially. Americans also recall how easily they beat the Spaniards in the Spanish-American War, taking advantage of the travails of Spain during the nineteenth century to do so, and overlooking the fact that neither they nor anyone else would have knocked her out so quickly in the days of her glory.

Indifferent to history, and with a pragmatic view of human affairs, Americans regard the Spaniards as among history's losers—and a loser is someone Americans fear and shun with a superstitious horror.

It has become the custom in Britain, no less than elsewhere, to denigrate the era of empire. It also happens that the world empires tend to be judged by their later periods, their periods of decline, which are the most recent and therefore the most clearly remembered. They are seldom seen for what they may have been in their prime. This is what has happened to the British Empire; the years between 1920 and 1950 are regarded as representative, instead of the era of toothlessness and moribundity. So it is with the Empire of Spain, which is also viewed through the wrong end of the telescope. The image that has persisted is that of decay and defeat. The Spanish Empire is additionally difficult for an Englishman to understand because it was not, like the later empires, the Dutch, French, German, and Belgian, and like the British Empire itself, almost exclusively a mercantile concern. It was devoted as much if not more to the ideals of chivalry, adventure, and religion as much as to commercial purposes. Again, in a secular, skeptical age, such concepts are unlikely to earn any credit.

It would be false, of course, to call the conquistadores who brought Spanish rule to the New World the crown and flower of Christian chivalry. Many, like the scabrous Pizarro brothers and the vulpine Pedrarias Dávila, had nothing to recommend them but their crazy courage, their willingness to lay their lives on the line. Some were young men out for a lark, like Vasco Núñez de Balboa or Francisco Vázquez de Coronado. Others were straightforward opportunists, like Cortés' lieutenant Pedro de Alvarado; or serious soldiers, like Cortés' young and unlucky chief of staff Gonzalo de Sandoval, a real *preux chevalier* who was one of a generation born too late to take part in the Gran Capitán's campaigns in Italy. Cortés himself, as I have tried to show in my *Cortés and the Downfall of the Aztec Empire,* was unique among the original conquistadores in that he was not only a conquistador but a *fundador*—a man of brains as well as bravery, a prodigiously gifted diplomat and administrator. He was also unique among the conquistadores in the opacity of his character. He was an enigma, a young man of thirty-three who was compounded of equal parts of fire and ice, of steel and velvet. He was practical and far-sighted, hiding his thoughts and feelings behind a courteous and formal mask. Like all the conquistadores, he has had to pay for the excesses of the Pizarros; and it was inevitable that, with modern Mexicans building on the neo-Aztecism of the nineteenth century, and striving to rehabilitate their own past, Cortés should have been increasingly vilified as the absurd demon one can see in the crude murals of Rivera. Some of the conquistadores, within the limits of their profession, can be fairly represented as noble and inspiring. Among the latter I would place the courtly Pedro de Valdivia, the conqueror of Chile, who died in an ambush rather than desert his friend and chaplain. And New

Mexico, in a later generation, was to know a Spaniard who was among the pick of the bunch—Don Diego José de Vargas Zapata Luján Ponce de León y Contreras, whose career in the Southwest I shall be describing shortly. There was something about the conquistadores that was so precisely quixotic that I am sure Cervantes must have had one or other of them in mind when he began his novel. Like the Don, they were a mixture of the earthy and the ideal, the absurd and the practical; their violent physical energy was mingled with mental cloudiness and confusion. Like him, they rode off madly in all directions in search of extravagant adventures, only to limp home with broken limbs and bloody heads.

It is remarkable how many of the conquistadores were natives of a single Spanish province, Extremadura. Cortés, the bastard Pizarros, Núñez de Balboa, Pedrarias Dávila, Valdivia, Hernán de Soto, all were Extremeños. They were mostly poor boys, and Extremadura was a poor province. Blocked off from winning wealth and fame at home, since the whole of Spain was tightly controlled by a small clique of grandees, they were forced to work out their frustrations elsewhere. There was no place in the Church for them; they had no advantages of birth to launch them on a career at court; they disdained to follow the dusty life of the law. As would-be gentlemen, the trades were closed to them because of *el deshonor de trabajo,* which meant that all the skilled activities that kept Spain going were performed by Italians, Flemings, Frenchmen, Germans, and other foreigners. The conquistadores, ambitious young scapegraces, were determined to live by their sword, their pride, their insolence, and their wits, like the picaresque heroes of *Lazarillo de Tormés* or *Guzmán de Alfarache.* They rode or walked to the nearest port, where they took passage for distant shores. Some went to fight the French in Italy; some to fight the Turks in the eastern Mediterranean: but the most daring spirits sailed west, to the New World. There, in those lands of mystery, they stood the best chance of performing stirring deeds and acquiring titles and broad estates. They would be free agents, far from the watchful eye of authority; an occasional enthusiastic dispatch was all that would be required of them. "They were not," J. H. Parry wrote of them in his *Age of Reconnaissance,* "the stuff of which bureaucrats are made." If they failed, there was no one to come to their aid in those obscure fastnesses. Four out of five of them were to find unmarked graves in the swamps of Florida, Darien, and Tabasco, the rain forests of Chiapas, Honduras, and Brazil, or the rocky hillsides of Mexico, Bolivia, and Peru. Not many of them expected to get back to Spain alive—but if they did, they meant to go back filthy rich. They also meant to strike their blow for the greatness of their King and the glory of their God. If half of their nature was unalloyed self-seeking, the other half was dedicated to the promotion of their Fatherland and their Faith.

We should understand this when we consider the Spanish soldiers and settlers who carried the banners of Spain to the American Southwest, and to California. It is no good trying to judge such men, such individualists, by the standards of the Welfare State. We must also bear in mind that they were the product of what might be called "the generation of '92." The age-old wars against the Moors, waged over the course of almost a millennium, came to an end in 1492 with the capture by Ferdinand and Isabella of Granada, the last Arab stronghold in the peninsula. It was the most intense moment of national emotion that Spaniards have ever felt. Even in times of more spectacular triumph—even today—Spaniards look back to it with a special reverence. *Los reyes Católicos*—the title was bestowed on them by the Pope in 1494—had united Spain's two great kingdoms. They then went on to subdue half of Italy, regain Navarre from the French, chastise the Barbary pirates, reform the Church, establish the Holy Brotherhood, tame the Military Orders, and institute the royal inspectorate, or *corregidores*. They gave the martial but divided Spaniards the feeling of being knit together, the feeling that there was now nothing they could not do. In the year when Granada fell, Isabella sent Columbus on the voyage that took him to the Americas; and she and her husband were scarcely dead before the conquistadores sailed west to show that the soldiers of Spain could crush the Infidel and spread the Faith not only on the soil of Europe, but on the soil of the New World. They were carrying over into the reign of the youthful, handsome, chivalrous new Habsburg monarch the momentum they had been given at the close of the previous century.

When they reached the New World, the Spaniards were gratified to discover that the natives bore a close physical resemblance to the Arabs—which increased the sensation of continuing the Reconquest. In the Spanish Empire, there was not to be that absolute physical barrier between the rulers and the people they ruled that there was with the later empires. And to make them feel even more at home, many of the conquerors found that the landscape of much of the New World closely resembled Spain. Great stretches of Mexico and the part that was to become Southwest America looked hauntingly like Extremadura, or the harsher parts of Castile.

In other respects, they were stepping into an environment as strange as if they had landed on another planet. A few travelers had returned to Europe from Tartary, or from the kingdom of Prester John, to bring news of distant marvels; but it is impossible to exaggerate the effect that Mexico made on Cortés and his six hundred men when, on Good Friday in 1519, they landed on the island of Cozumel and made their first contact with Mexican culture. One of the sturdiest and most levelheaded of the company, bluff and honest Bernal Díaz del Castillo, found that when he tried in old age to recapture the effect produced by those wonders that words often failed him. No European had seen such sights before; he had nothing with which to compare them. It was fortunate for us that Bernal possessed a quick eye, a capacious memory, humanity, and common sense, and that he wrote his *True History of the Conquest* in the salty, direct, emphatic style which was the birthright of the Spaniards of the Golden Age.

Today, the world of the ancient Mexicans seems even more eccentric and bizarre than the world of classical Spain. Their way of life was quite different from that of the general run of humanity, stranger by far than anything encountered in Europe, Asia, or Africa. As for the Aztecs, the last of the great empires of Mexico, they were unique. Nowadays, they are being sentimentally rehabilitated, represented as noble and innocent victims of a pack of rapacious adventurers: but nothing could be further from the truth. It would be impossible to name any people more repulsive and blood-sodden than the Aztecs. I wrote in my book on Cortés that: "The contest between the Spaniards and the Aztecs was not an unequal struggle between an arrogant and aggressive culture on the one hand, and a mild and pacific one on the other. It was a clash between two cultures that could both be described as advanced and self-assertive; both had reached a point in their development where they were accustomed to carrying all before them." The difference between them, I think, was that the energy of the Spanish soldiers and priests was in general normal and healthy; they were capable of a generous ardor; they could be selfless and disinterested. The energy of the Aztec counterparts, on the other hand, was cruel and negative, totally nihilistic.

And yet, when Cortés and his legion trudged down from the mountains, and saw below them the Aztec capital of Tenochtitlán, a white and dazzling city built out into Lake Texcoco, connected to the mainland by three mighty causeways, those of them who had served in Italy exclaimed that it was more beautiful than Venice. It gave no hint of the horrors enacted within it. But already, on the coast, the Spaniards had been dismayed by some of the habits of the tribes who paid tribute to the Emperor, Moctezuma Xocoyotzin. They had found that these tribes worshipped blood-smeared images, that they practiced human sacrifice, ritual cannibalism, homosexuality, sodomy; some of them maintained cadres of boy prostitutes, dressed in women's clothes. Today homosexuality is open and widespread, though still nothing to boast about in Spain; but to Spaniards of Cortés' day it was as horrible as human sacrifice or cannibalism. It came as an additional shock to them to discover that the Aztec overlords, far from eschewing such abominations, also carried out human sacrifice and cannibalism in an extreme degree and on a staggering scale, and had actually introduced them to their subject peoples.

In fact, after Cortés had imitated Julius Caesar by burning his boats at Veracruz, and had marched inland "to take a look at Moctezuma," as he put it, he was gratified to learn, after some hard fighting, that the vassals of the Aztecs were eager to join the Spaniards in the war against their masters. Chief among them were the Tlaxcalans, who dwelt midway between the coast and Tenochtitlán, and who had endured more than most because of their proximity to their rulers. The Tlaxcalans and their old blind king, their word once given, stuck to Cortés through thick and thin, even in the darkest hours of the campaign. When Cortés, in January 1521, ordered his army forward in the last all-or-nothing assault on Tenochtitlán, he commanded more than 100,000 men, of whom 550 were Spaniards, and 10,000 were Tlaxcalans. The remainder were contingents from the many Mexican peoples who were clamoring to strike a blow at the Aztecs. It is absurd to think that Cortés could have defeated a million Aztecs and overrun the huge Aztec Empire with a handful of Spaniards supplemented by a few unreliable cannon and sixteen horses. He conquered it because the Mexicans appointed him their leader in what was less an invasion than a civil war, a war they viewed as a war of liberation. To them he was *liberador,* not *conquistador:* and indeed he relieved them for two centuries of the nightmare Mexico was not to know again until the nineteenth century, when the decencies once again collapsed after the withdrawal of the Spaniards.

What had the Aztecs done, to make themselves so universally hated? In the first place, they were unpopular even before their rise to supremacy. They were not native to the Valley of Mexico, the most populous part of the country. They were not people of any pedigree; they were interlopers and parvenus. They themselves did not know where they came from. They were a wandering band of armed scavengers from somewhere in the north of Mexico, a vague spot called Aztlán which no one has ever identified. It is probable that it was situated on the northwest coast, somewhere in the vicinity of modern Mazatlán. They were one of a complex of fierce northerly tribes who roamed impartially down into Mexico or up into the Southwest. Fortunately for the people of the pueblos, and for the United States, the people of Aztlán decided to migrate southward instead of northward. If they had chosen otherwise, the history of the Southwest would have been even more bloody than it was. Dealing with Apaches and Comanches was to be difficult enough—but dealing with Aztecs, into the bargain? . . .

In 1325, the Aztecs found a permanent home in the Valley of Mexico, in a boggy part of the lake which none of their neighbors wanted. They were regarded as miserable squatters, and their personal habits were deplorable. They ate rats, toads, newts, water beetles and rattlesnakes; they manufactured a sort of cheese out of the scum on the top of the surrounding marshes. They were robbers, murderers, and rapists, cutting off the ears and noses of their prisoners and dancing in the flayed skins of captured women. When they were asked what they were going to put into the roomy new temple they had built in honor of their sinister war god Huitzilopochtli, they answered, "Bleeding hearts and blood"; whereupon their scandalized neighbors threw rubbish into the sanctuary.

Their neighbors, however, made the capital mistake that has brought low so many cities and countries throughout the course of history: they began to hire the despised interlopers as mercenaries. Within two centuries, under the eight ferocious kings who preceded Moctezuma Xocoyotzin, who became king in 1502, the Aztecs not only devoured the city-states of the Valley of Mexico but advanced the boundaries of their empire from Veracruz to Guatemala. It was a military success story, an explosion of energy not unlike the Spanish explosion that began in 1492. Unfortunately, the manners of the Aztecs did not mend with the mushrooming of their fortunes. They refined their revolting practices and carried them out on a grander scale, establishing a regime that can only be compared with that of Nazi Germany. They were in no way worthy successors of the high cultures that had existed in Mexico since the days of the Olmecs, two thousand years before. They were perhaps the most powerful empire ancient Mexico ever saw: but in spite of the superficial attractions of Tenochtitlán, they never equalled, in any activity except warfare, the achievements of the Olmecs, Mayans, Toltecs, Totonacs, Mixtecs, Zapotecs, or any of the other peoples with whom I shall be briefly dealing in a later chapter.

It would be a libel on the Spartans, who were notoriously reluctant to start a war or venture beyond their own boundaries, to compare them with the Aztecs. But the Aztecs, like the Spartans, were wholly preoccupied with the idea of military prowess, and also lived in constant terror of slave revolts. Aztec society was severely stratified. It ascended through slaves, peasants, workers, artisans, and merchants, to the *tecuhtli,* or noblemen. Every Aztec youngster had his chance to become one of the tecuhtli. All he needed to do was to prove himself in battle. For that, he never lacked an opportunity.

The Aztec nation was deliberately kept in a permanent state of war. War not only was practical, it was a religious necessity. The Aztecs were not primary producers; they were parasitic on their neighbors, from whom they wrested fearsome annual exactions. Even the Aztec traders, who brought the parrot feathers and bronze bells to the villages along the Rio Grande, were professional soldiers. They traveled in armed convoys, and were trained as diplomats, professional spies and provocateurs, adept at staging fake border incidents to justify an Aztec invasion. Even more important, the Aztecs needed war because they needed prisoners to serve as sacrificial victims. Sacrifice was necessary to keep both the machinery of the empire and the machinery of the universe running. The Aztec gods demanded blood, fresh blood, continuous outpourings of it. This was what gave the Aztec manner of warfare its special character. The Aztec warrior, provided with sling, darts, lance, club, and wooden sword edged with razor-sharp pieces of obsidian, strove not to kill his opponent but to stun and bind him. The prisoner was then brought to Tenochtitlán, to be sacrificed. One of the odder manifestations of this conception of warfare was the institution known as the War of Flowers. This was an artificial tournament, or gladiatorial combat, in which the Aztecs and their allies forced the Tlaxcalans and their associates to engage in a formalized battle whose purpose was the taking of captives. In this way, the Aztecs secured the blood of brave men for the sticky altars of Huitzilopochtli and Tezcatlipoca, while the Tlaxcalans at least got the satisfaction of doing to death a few of their oppressors.

The choicest prisoners were dressed in a white robe, then tied by a rope around their waist to a special stone. Armed with a wooden sword, they fought as long as they could against a number of Aztec warriors wielding the fearsome flint-edged *macquauitl*. When they were fatally weakened, their breasts were slashed open and their hearts torn out in the usual way. Sometimes the Aztecs could not wait. When Moctezuma Xocoyotzin—who came to the throne because his elder brother had perished in the War of Flowers—subdued the Yopotzingo of Oaxaca, he tore the hearts out of 12,000 prisoners on the spot. The number is not exaggerated: he had them carefully counted and the number written down.

The ripping out of the heart while the victim still palpitated was the normal Aztec method of sacrifice. The tall pyramidal temples we admire today were once thickly coated with a tacky sheath of blood. The victims were driven or dragged to the top, where black-costumed priests awaited them. These men, too, had qualified for their trade on the battlefield, punishing their bodies with drugs, and thrusting cactus spines through their cheeks, tongues, forearms, thighs, and penises. The victim was held face upward on the sacrificial stone, his chest gashed open, his heart plucked out. His body was then thrown down the steps to his captor, or to the merchants or trade union members who had clubbed together to buy a slave for sacrifice. They sliced off the tenderer portions and took them home for a family feast. The corpse was decapitated, and the head placed on one of the *tzompantli,* or skull-racks, ranged at the foot of the pyramid.

There were seven gigantic tzompantli, each holding thousands of skulls, attached to the Great Temple of Tenochtitlán, which was one of the six temples at the center of the city. The Great Temple was dedicated to Huitzilopochtli by the Emperor Ahuízotl, Moctezuma Xocoyotzin's predecessor. On that occasion, a conservative estimate of 20,000 prisoners, marshalled in four lines stretching for more than four miles, had their chests opened and their hearts extracted. The ceremony, which lasted from dawn to sunset for several days, caused the city to stink horribly for years, and brought on numerous outbreaks of plague.

One of the more temperate Spanish chroniclers states that 50,000 men and women were sacrificed annually at Tenochtitlán—that is, 1,000 a week, or 150 a day. Nor was the practice of opening the breast the sole method of sacrifice. Different gods required different techniques. Sometimes batches of victims were burned in ovens, the priests snatching out the body with hooks at the last moment so that the precious hearts could be retrieved. Other gods demanded that groups of women or children be drowned, exposed on moun-

❖ 99 ❖

tainsides to freeze, or starved to death in caves. Nor did the Aztecs carry out these actions secretly, as the Nazis tried to do: they boasted of them. One of their more ingenious deities was Xipe-totec, the Flayed One. His devotees peeled off the skins of dead victims, scraped the interior, stitched themselves inside them, and went capering round the city begging alms. Sir James Frazer, in *The Scapegoat,* relates of these "filthy but sanctified ruffians" that when, after twenty days, the skin eventually stiffened and shrivelled, "they walked in solemn procession, wearing the rotten skins and stinking like dead dogs, to the temple called Topico, where they stripped themselves of the hides and plunged them into a tub or vat, after which they washed and scrubbed themselves thoroughly, while their friends smacked their bare bodies loudly with wet hands in order to squeeze out the human grease with which they were saturated."

A nightmare civilization—worshipping, as one can see in the museums of Mexico, nightmare gods and goddesses. The celebrated anthropologist A. L. Kroeber calls the Aztecs sadists—that is, people who took delight in the deliberate infliction of pain. Mlle. Laurette Séjourné, in her authoritative *Burning Water,* a study of religion and philosophy in ancient Mexico, considers that, being *parvenus,* they had no profound ideas of their own to guide them. They were forced to seize on and pervert the noble religion of the Toltecs, with the majestic figure of Quetzalcóatl in the foreground, "to prop up their bloody state." She calls their religion a "low witchcraft," filled with "lying formulae," a fraudulent structure designed to promote terror, "a political weapon in the hands of despots."

I think that this is the correct way to view the Aztecs—not as the peak of ancient Mexican civilization, but as the culture that betrayed it. In contrast to the Toltecs, the Mayas and the others, they were sick, diseased, neurotic. The Aztec empire, I wrote in my book on Cortés, "was not the culmination of centuries of civilization in Mexico. Instead, it constituted a tumor on the Mexican body, a hot and feverish growth that drained Mexico of its strength and reduced its capacity to resist. The Aztecs weakened Mexico. It was the universal loathing of the Aztecs that gave the Spaniards their chance."

Diseased or not, Cortés did not find the business of reducing Tenochtitlán a War of Flowers. It was no *Blumenkorso,* as the German generals called an easy campaign. There came a time when he and his Spaniards were cut off from their Indian allies and trapped inside the city. They broke out. They conducted a retreat that developed into a rout. Cortés was nearly captured; he was twice wounded, in the head and hand, and bore the scars to his grave. At the end of it all, when he was the master of Tenochtitlán, only a handful of his original band were left, and less than one thousand of the plumed legions of the Emperor Cuauhtémoc, who had succeeded the murdered Moctezuma. It had been a war to the death, a test of will and courage, neither of which had failed either the Spaniards or their opponents.

What had finally enabled one imperious people to prevail over the other were two factors. First, in Vaillant's telling distinction, the Aztecs were only warriors, whereas the Spaniards were soldiers. The Aztecs were limited to little more than the simple mass frontal attack, while the Spaniards knew how to adopt sophisticated formations and how to maneuver. Second, the Spaniards were the products of Western civilization, individualists, men capable of exercising the reason and logic which is at once the Westerner's glory and his curse. The Aztecs, for all their panache, lived only through the tribe, and were subject to tribal fears, superstitions, and sudden panics. They were strangers to the notion of cause and effect. The psychological advantages were therefore with the Spaniards, and we should bear this in mind as we follow the Spaniards from Tenochtitlán to the American Southwest and watch their impact on the American Indian.

It was only by chance, in fact, that the Southwest United States was not conquered by Hernán Cortés, in the prime of his youthful pride and energy. At thirty-five, he was Captain-General of more territory than his royal master ruled in Europe. He had great plans. Alas, they were not destined to be fulfilled. He was to be condemned to a frustrated maturity and an embittered old age. Shrewd and capable, he was nevertheless considered too willful to be appointed New Spain's first Viceroy, and another man was put in over his head. Yet when he was fifty, after years of humiliation, and following a disastrous expedition to Honduras, he was the first man to attempt the exploration of the north.

He was convinced that in the American Southwest was to be found the fabled land of Cíbola, richer than the realm of the Great Inca which his old rival Pizarro had discovered far to the south. In 1535, he took six ships and three hundred men to the isthmus of Baja California, whose vast enclosed waters henceforward bore the name of the Sea of Cortés. As in the case of Honduras, it was an ill-starred expedition from which he was lucky to return alive. Yet, four years later, he depleted his private fortunes further by outfitting another fleet and sending it north. It did not find Cíbola, but its captain was the first European to explore the coast of California. The following year he clashed again with the Viceroy, demanding to be placed in command of a large force that was being prepared for the first serious *entrada* of the north by the overland route. To the fury of the battered old conquistador, the leadership was given to a whippersnapper called Francisco Vázquez de Coronado, whose name instead of his is now emblazoned on numerous banks, public edifices, streets, schools, and stadiums throughout West Texas and New Mexico.

Coronado was not the first Spaniard to set foot in the territory north of the Rio Grande. That distinction belongs to Alvar Núñez Cabeza de Vaca, one of the survivors of the voyage of Pánfilo de Narváez to Florida in 1528. It was supposed that the 250 members of that expedition were lost without trace. Then, incredibly, seven years later, four starving, emaciated, sun-shrivelled men, three white and one black, shambled into one of the Rio Grande pueblos to the north of what is now El Paso. Thence, after resting, they made their way to Sonora, where they encountered an astonished band of Spanish prospectors on the Pacific Coast. These four men—Cabeza de Vaca, Alonso de Castillo de Maldonado, Andrés Dorantes de Carranza, and Dorantes' Moorish slave Estebánico—had made a westward journey, on foot, of more than fifteen hundred miles. They had survived the original shipwreck, somewhere near present-day Galveston; they had subsisted on raw fish and raw clams; they had scavenged for rats, worms, ants, and lizards; they had gnawed roots, bark, moss, and dried animal droppings; they had been servants and carriers for one Indian tribe, doctors and shamans for another. It was a fantastic story: and when Cabeza de Vaca told it personally to the Viceroy and Cortés, in Mexico City, he further fired their imaginations with tantalizing remarks about the land of Cíbola, whose southern boundaries he was convinced he had skirted on his painful trek.

Concerning the nature of Cíbola, there were many theories. One school held that it was the island of Atlantis. Cortés had certainly believed that it was an island when he tried to reach it by sea. Others asserted that it was a lost land like the kingdom of Prester John, and that it had been founded by a Portuguese bishop who fled to the New World when Iberia was overrun by the Moors. Whatever its origin, it was supposed to consist of seven cities, whose palaces and dwellings were constructed entirely of gold. Indeed, gold was so common that men and women scraped the sweat from their bodies with golden strigils, and plated their boats with it.

Cabeza de Vaca and his white companions were in no condition to take part in a fresh exploration of the north. Cabeza had returned to Spain, to recuperate and to report to the King, though later he would return to the New World to become Governor of Paraguay. Castillo and Dorantes had married and were settled in Mexico City. The Archbishop of Mexico proposed to the Viceroy that a much-traveled Franciscan friar, an Italian called Marcos de Nizza, was a proper man to undertake a reconnaissance. To guide him, Fray Marcos took Estebánico, Dorantes' flamboyant and durable black, now a freedman. Meanwhile a full-scale expedition was organized, and Vázquez de Coronado was named its leader. The Viceroy at that moment, Antonio de Mendoza, was a forceful executive who, after fifteen years as the first Viceroy of New Spain, would be sent as Viceroy to Peru, to clean up the mess left by the Pizarros. He had high hopes that Coronado would make a mighty addition to the Spanish crown, and he bestowed the name of New Mexico in advance on the yet-to-be-annexed territories.

The choice of Coronado was sound. Not yet thirty, he was vigorous, ambitious, and had an excellent record. As *adelantado,* or governor, of the then northern province of New Galicia, which had been unsettled by revolts against a ruffian who had been packed back to Spain in irons, he had shown the right mixture of conciliation and firmness. He knew the Indians, and knew something about the physical nature of the mysterious and barren north. Twenty years after the conquest, few Spaniards had yet ventured far into the wastes that stretched beyond the mining camps of Guanajuato and San Luis Potosí. Beyond New Galicia were only the hazy boundaries of New León, New Biscaya, and New Navarre. And beyond those ill-defined provinces was the parched emptiness that served as the barrier to the riches of Cíbola.

Coronado left his headquarters at Compostela in New Galicia in February 1540. He would be away for over two years, and would make one of the greatest land explorations known to history.

What did he and his men look like, as they rode or marched along? Coronado and the other horsemen carried both full armor and half armor in their baggage, donning it for battle or for making an imposing entry into a camp or pueblo. Most of the time, they would have been in shirtsleeves, or wearing the quilted cotton jacket that went under the armor. On their saddlebows were slung their burgonet-type helmet, their *schiavona,* or five-foot-long broadsword, their cup-hilt rapier, their *adarga,* or shield, painted with their personal coat of arms, the case with their pistols, and their *escopeta,* or short musket, hanging in a sash or in the *funda,* or sheath. The foot soldier also tramped along in shirtsleeves, with his chain mail skirt and his bowl-shaped cabasset-type tin hat slung on his back. Over his shoulder he hefted his huge lance, slanted at such a striking angle that to this day a common species of cactus is called Spanish Bayonet—and, indeed, a clump of them on the horizon looks uncannily like a platoon of the Gran Capitán's infantry. Those towering ash-spears, which can be seen bristling against the sky in Velázquez's *The Surrender of Breda* (which is known in Spain as *Las Lanzas*) won Spain her empire in Europe and the New World. They were the most telling weapon of the age. In the Army Museum in Madrid there are examples which are a full twenty feet in length.

Before Coronado set out, he had been heartened by a dispatch from Fray Marcos to the effect that Cíbola definitely existed, and that it needed only the resolve to reach it. He could not know that the encouragement was false. Estebánico had been killed by Indians, and Fray Marcos had done nothing more than traipse aimlessly around the Sonora desert; but the good father was understandably reluctant to be the bearer of bad news. Coronado thus led out his force of 1,500 regular troops and auxiliaries, reinforced with 1,000 horses, 500 cattle, 5,000 sheep and hundreds of camp followers, in a mood of false optimism.

He made his way up the west coast, by way of Culiacán. Then he struck

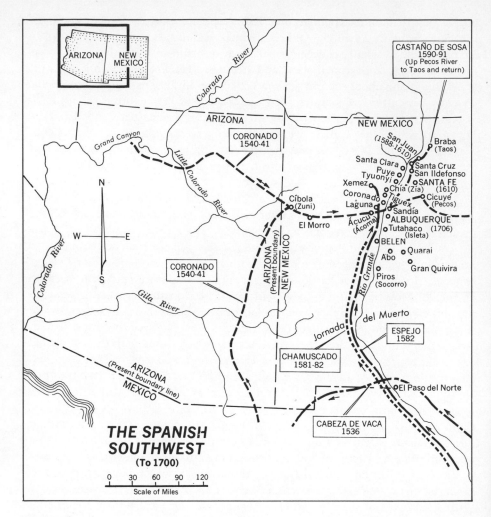

FIGURE 8

inland, crossing into what is now Arizona somewhere south of the mining
town of Bisbee. He followed the San Pedro River through the country of the
old Mogollon-Hohokam culture, crossed the Gila, and after six months struck
the Rio Grande somewhere in the neighborhood of modern Truth-or-Consequences. There he turned north. Like all explorers in North America, he followed the rivers because they were landmarks, because they provided water,
and because they passed through lush valleys; beyond them, on the empty
plains and among the endless ranges, lay the possibility of a terrible death.
After passing through the pueblo of Piros, near modern Socorro, it seems

quite probable that he settled down for his first winter in the neighborhood of the pueblo then called Kuaua, now the Coronado National Monument, which I described in the previous chapter.

He had instituted and strictly enforced a policy of goodwill toward the Indians. It was thus an unpleasant surprise when, after he broke camp in the spring and swung northwest in the direction in which Cíbola was supposed to lie, he was greeted at the pueblo of Hawikuh with fierce hostility. Hawikuh was the present pueblo of Zuni, and it put up a strong resistance. Coronado, in his golden armor, was twice knocked over by slingstones, and had to be dragged to safety by his lieutenants. The rocks, arrows, and javelins of the Indians made a telling response to the crossbows and harquebuses of the Spaniards, and Coronado was compelled to leave his horses in the rear. Finally, however, the Indians abandoned Hawikuh and the Spaniards moved in. If this was one of the cities of Cíbola, or an outpost of it, their haul was meager: no gold, no silver, no precious stones—merely the unpretentious possessions of peasant cultivators.

Discouraged, Coronado turned back toward the Rio Grande. Before abandoning this unproductive territory, he sent his three senior lieutenants further to the west, on scouting forays. Pedro de Tobar went into the territory of the Tusayan or Hopi, whom he "pacified"; Melchior Díaz seems to have got as far as the Imperial Valley in southern California, where he met with a fatal accident; and Cárdenas and his twenty-five horsemen were brought up short, as I mentioned earlier, by the Grand Canyon. None of the columns had good news to bring back to the main body, though Tobar had been told by the Hopis—who no doubt used it as a device to get rid of him—that somewhere due east lay a great river ruled over by a rich and mighty king. This king sailed about in a giant barge, of which the masts, rudder and rowlocks were solid gold.

Coronado quickly detached another of his lieutenants, Alonso de Alvarado, eastward on yet another scouting expedition. Alvarado set off eagerly. He coursed busily about, prudently bypassing the "Sky City" of Acoma, and visited numerous pueblos in what he named the Tiguex area, including Braba (Taos) and Cicuyé (Pecos). He stumbled upon nothing more hopeful than a prisoner called El Turco (probably a Pawnee Indian) who confirmed the story of the kingdom to the east, and even gave it a name: Gran Quivira.

Disappointed in Cíbola, Coronado was only too ready to be convinced about the existence of another El Dorado. Things were beginning to go badly. He was reluctant to face the possibility of having to retreat to New Spain and report to the Viceroy empty-handed. There was dissension in his army. Relations with the Indians had turned sour. He was compelled to fight punishing battles against two large pueblos, costing heavy casualties, which laid the basis for the hatred of the white man that persisted ever after. It was in a dangerously euphoric mood that he once more broke up winter quarters on the Rio

Grande, late April 1541, and took his entire force due west. El Turco, who was a strange character, poured a stream of fairy stories in his ear. Yes, the king of Quivira, who was called Tatarrax, had a golden boat, with a huge golden eagle at the prow. Yes, he took his siesta under a tree hung with hundreds of tinkling golden bells. Yes, his humblest subjects ate off dishes of the purest gold.

Coronado's army climbed the escarpment of the *Llano Estacado,* the Staked Plains. It is possible that the Plains received their name because Coronado drove in posts to guide him, although it may derive from the palisaded or stockaded appearance of the escarpment itself; certainly at a later date the buffalo hunters put up buffalo skulls on poles as markers. He was crossing what would be the Texas and Oklahoma panhandles and advancing into Kansas. Finding it impossible to move fast with the unwieldy main force, he took a band of horsemen and thrust on by himself. He advanced farther and farther into unknown territory, fording the upper waters of the Canadian, Cimarron, and Arkansas rivers. Ironically, at that exact moment the great Hernán de Soto was only three hundred miles away, on the banks of the next big river, the Mississippi. There he would perish, without either man ever learning of the existence of the other.

Coronado advanced six hundred miles from the Rio Grande before he found Gran Quivira. For find it—incredibly—he did. Unfortunately, it turned out to be nothing but a poverty-stricken Wichita Indian village. Its *"tatarrax,"* or headman—for that was what the magic name proved to mean—was a naked, skinny old man whose wealth consisted of a single copper bangle. No golden barges, no golden bells, no golden tableware. No new Moctezuma. El Turco was garroted.

It was time to leave Kansas and retire despondently to New Mexico. On the way, in December 1541, a personal disaster overtook Coronado. The gods have a nasty habit of hitting a man when he is down. He fell from his horse and was kicked in the head during the course of an impromptu race. His sorrowing troops carried him back home, paralyzed and speechless, like some defeated Don Quixote. At least he was unconscious of his failure. All the gold he brought back with him was the gold veneering on his own hacked and dusty armor. He never recovered, lingering on in a feeble-minded twilight until he died twelve years later, at the age of forty-four. He was an exceptional man; his fate was hard.

The expensive fiasco of the Coronado expedition had merely proved something that did not need proving: that Spaniards are courageous. It was a disaster on such a huge scale that it damped down the desire to find out what lay to the north of New Spain for another forty years.

Then, in 1581, three Spanish Franciscan friars, with an escort of nine soldiers in charge of the elderly Captain Francisco Sánchez Chamuscado—another quixotic figure—took the direct route for the first time up the Rio Grande to find out whether any trace remained of the three Franciscans who had said farewell to Coronado and chosen to remain among the Pueblo Indians. Chamuscado and his holy men, who visited Zuni, Acoma, and Pecos, in addition to the river pueblos, discovered that their predecessors were dead; two of them had been deliberately done to death, becoming the first Catholic martyrs on American soil. Nonetheless, all three of Chamuscado's friars decided to follow the same example and remain in the north: and the old soldier himself succumbed before reaching home.

To discover what had happened to them, and bring them relief, another Franciscan set out the following year, accompanied by an inquisitive Spanish merchant named Antonio de Espejo. The latter was in trouble with the law, and thought it prudent to make a little *tour de l'horizon*. They valiantly covered the same ground as Chamuscado's party, and learned that all three friars had been killed. They themselves managed to return safely, the Franciscan going down the Rio Grande, but Espejo electing to blaze a new trail down the Conchos River, 150 miles to the west. Clearly the Southwest in the sixteenth century was unpromising soil for Christianity. In New Spain, the Spanish missionaries had been greeted as deliverers, as bearers of a message of hope; in New Mexico, they were intruders.

It was up the Conchos, in Espejo's footsteps, that the first Spanish immigrants were to come to the Southwest, in September 1590. There were 170 of them, the entire population of a Spanish mining town in the province of New León. Their leader was their lieutenant governor, Gaspar Castaño de Sosa. He reached the upper river, crossed to the Rio Grande, and established his "capital" close to the pueblo of Santo Domingo. He then proudly sent back word of his exploit to the authorities in Mexico City. Their reply was to dispatch an officer to arrest him for undertaking an expedition within the royal domains without obtaining permission—a very serious crime. He protested that he had kept his superiors completely informed of his plans and progress—but either the mails were slow, or the bureaucrats were behaving in their usual dilatory way. He was brought back to Mexico in chains, court-martialled, and his property confiscated. He was then exiled to China. As for his 170 colonists, they vanished into limbo, the first group of whites, but by no means the last, to be exterminated or absorbed by the Indians. One must always remember how much mixed blood there is in the Southwest.

Not surprisingly, de Sosa's mistake was not made by the leader of the first successful party of colonists, whose advance guard crossed the Rio Grande in the vicinity of modern Juárez–El Paso in April 1598. Count Juan de Oñate had been invested beforehand with the resounding titles of *adelantado*, Captain-General, and Governor of the province of New Mexico, which he had been instructed to create. The Spanish frontier in northern Mexico had now reached the mines of Santa Barbara, 700 miles from the capital, and there were only another 200 miles to go to reach the Rio Grande. Moreover, the Spaniards were becoming acutely conscious of the colonizing activities of the French, the English, and Dutch on the North American mainland. They determined to extend their grip on as much of the continent as they could, and as quickly as possible.

Although Oñate was middle-aged, the authorities were putting their trust in no obscure soldier of fortune. He was a magnate, a great grandee. He had made and squandered several fortunes, but was still one of the five richest men in New Spain. His father had succeeded Coronado as Governor of New Galicia; his wife was the granddaughter of Cortés and the great-granddaughter of Moctezuma; her father was Coronado's able lieutenant, Tobar.

A man of decision, the Count marched across the Chihuahua Desert (though there was no city of Chihuahua at the time) and took the straight route up the Rio Grande. It was a daring gambit. He was moving forward from his base camp in southern New Biscaya not with a picked platoon of soldiers, but with a vast and vulnerable host. He had 138 families, 400 single men, 83 wagons and carts, 11 Franciscan friars, 7,000 cattle, and 3,000 sheep. It was the largest convoy to enter New Mexico since Coronado's *entrada,* sixty years before, and the largest that would enter it during the entire Hispanic era. The colonists came largely from Zacatecas, Puebla, and other Mexican towns, summoned to the enterprise by drum and trumpet. They were lured not only by the prospect of land, but by the bogus promise that everyone of them would be considered a *hidalgo* thenceforward. Social climbing was an even greater obsession with the Spaniards of that time than the desire for money.

Oñate's main body reached the Rio Grande at the end of April. He paused on what is now the Mexican side of the river, where everybody put on their best clothes and gave thanks to God. Dressed in one of his six suits of armor, he solemnly annexed the territory of the Rio del Norte for the King. Then, assisted by a band of friendly Indians, he crossed the river and continued upstream through the fearful stretch of desert which, as he knew from past travelers, separated him from his next oasis, the fertile uplands where clustered the Indian pueblos.

He was blazing the trail of what was to become the Camino Real—the "Royal Road" that would be the backbone of Spanish colonization of the western United States. It would stretch thirteen hundred miles, anchored at one end in the great main square or Zócalo of Mexico City, flanked by the cathedral and the palace begun by Cortés, and at the other in the little plaza of Santa Fe. Along it would clatter the wagons, gallop the horsemen, and tinkle the mule trains that would tie New Mexico to the capital. Even today it is a hard three-day drive down the length of the Camino Real, and for three-quarters of it you are crossing the sorriest kind of desert. Oñate's caravan, on that first passage, not only had to face the dry terrain and erratic flow of the

Rio Grande: it also had to traverse the fearsome Jornada del Muerto—the "Day's March of the Dead Man." This portion of the trail extended eighty shadeless, waterless, pitiless miles, across the desert of southern New Mexico. Later it was to become the focus of the Apache and Comanche raids which were to be the chief terror of travelers for almost two centuries.

Santa Fe was not Oñate's capital. He chose a place on the river, above modern Santa Fe, between the present-day pueblos of San Ildefonso and Taos. He called it San Juan de los Caballeros, and it was from here that he made his forays eastward and westward, searching for gold, silver, and precious metals. He made a fifty-nine-day journey in the direction of Kansas, searching once more for Gran Quivira. He made an even more difficult expedition to the Gulf of California, at the mouth of the Colorado River, looking for the South Sea, the route to China, and the Spice Islands. This was the mirage that had beckoned Cortés before him.

He was involved in much fighting. In December 1598, when he was absent from San Juan, his deputy and nephew, Vicente de Zaldívar, found it necessary to send out his young brother to attack and storm the pueblo of Acoma, the center of Indian disaffection. Juan de Zaldívar's performance constituted a miniature epic. At the head of 30 men—his whole force—he stormed the 400-foot-high cliffs, lined by 3,000 Indians. After three hours, a few Spaniards reached the top, where they died in hand-to-hand combat or were hurled onto the rocks below. Juan de Zaldívar, wounded three times, died with his knife in an Indian's belly, with the Indian's spear in his own. Only three survivors struggled home to San Juan.

When Oñate learned of the disaster, his rage was terrible. He dispatched Vicente de Zaldívar with 70 picked men to avenge his brother. The second battle began on January 21, 1599. It lasted three days. On the first day, Zaldívar and 11 men climbed the cliffs and effected a lodgment. Next day, they were joined by the main body. On the evening of the third day, the 600 Indians who still remained decided to surrender. They had lost 900 men charging the harquebuses, brass culverins, and bristling spears of the entrenched Spaniards, almost all of whom were wounded, though only 2 died. Another 900 Acomans committed suicide by leaping from the summit. Like the Persians at Thermopylae, they had attacked suicidally on a narrow front, and were slaughtered.

Oñate exacted a dreadful vengeance. All male Acomans over twenty-five had a foot cut off, and were sentenced to twenty years servitude; males between twelve and twenty-five, and all the women, were given the same term of slavery; and 60 children were sent to Mexico City to be distributed among the convents there for reeducation. Not surprisingly, Indian resistance grew increasingly furious. The next year, Vicente de Zaldívar had to repeat his feat in other localities, killing a further 900 Indians. It was not a reassuring start to the new century.

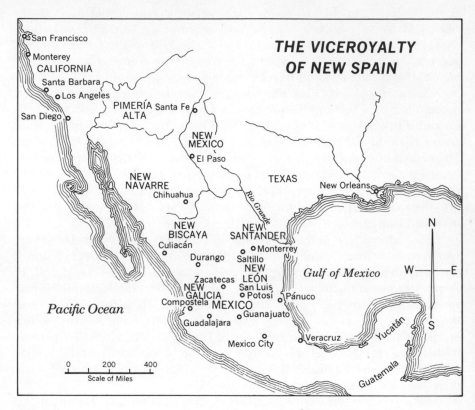

THE VICEROYALTY
OF NEW SPAIN

FIGURE 9

Frightened, the citizens of San Juan began to pack up and leave. Soon, only eight hundred people were left in Oñate's mudhut capital. He sent Vicente de Zaldívar on a voyage to Madrid, appealing over the head of the Viceroy to the King himself for funds and reinforcements for the besieged province. The request was refused, for the Governor's frantic excursions had produced no profits to justify such a major expenditure. Moreover, the motherland herself was virtually bankrupt. Philip III instructed the Viceroy to terminate all further exploration in New Mexico, and to recall Oñate to Mexico City. Oñate received the news as he was straggling in from a last brave but abortive journey to discover the South Sea. After seven years, he was compelled to accept defeat. The fates speeded him on his way with the same kind of low blow that they had dealt to the beaten Coronado. As he limped down the Rio Grande toward El Paso, he was ambushed by Indians in the Jornada del Muerto, and his only son was slain.

The old man returned to Madrid, to what he knew would be lingering last years of recrimination, litigation, imprisonment, and obscurity. The ungrateful north had beaten him as it had beaten his predecessors. Yet, as the first Governor of New Mexico, he left a mark on the dominion which was as bold as the mark Cortés left on New Spain. Thirty miles from Zuni, midway between that pueblo and Acoma, is an outcrop of soft sandstone, a huddle of cliffs as lonely as a landmark on the African veldt. Its Spanish name is El Morro, the "Bluff" or "Headland," but in Zuni it is called *Atsinna*, "The Writing on the Rock." There is a prehistoric village there, complete with kivas, and from the beginning of time the supply of water hidden at its heart had slaked the thirst of animals and men. At the twelve-foot waterhole, holding a quarter of a million gallons, Spanish soldiers, priests, caravans, and wagon trains would pause to refresh themselves; and in the nineteenth century Mexicans, English explorers, and Americans on the tremendous journey to California, followed the Spanish custom of carving their name and destination there. Twelve feet up on the sheer, smooth rock face is the testament of Juan de Oñate. His name and style have been incised on the stone in an elegant and confident hand, embellished with arrogant curlicues. Looking at those sweeping strokes, typical of the inscriptions left there by the distinguished Spaniards of the period, one feels that they must have been scored by the knife point of the Governor himself, standing on one of the carretas or carts with which he trundled around his kingdom. Accompanying the splendid

The inscription of Juan de Oñate at El Morro, New Mexico.

signature is the proud declaration: *"Governor Juan de Oñate passed here, on his way to the discovery of the Southern Sea, April 16th, 1606."*

Arizona, West Texas, Colorado, Nevada, Oklahoma, Kansas, New Mexico itself—all had been brought into the orbit of New Spain, as a result of his exertions.

Pasó por aquí.

SIX

SOMEHOW, in spite of setbacks, the Spaniards managed to maintain their northern fingerhold. Slowly, very slowly, their numbers grew, though during the next one hundred years they never numbered more than 3,000 among an Indian population which they themselves estimated at 30,000. Like the British in India, who were at an even more serious numerical disadvantage, they dominated their subjects by a mixture of threats, cajolery, and bluff. The Indians in the New World did not know, any more than the Indians in the Asian subcontinent, that the imperial homeland was diminutive in comparison with theirs; nor did they realize that its resources in manpower were similarly puny. It was when, throughout the world, the reality of the situation began to register on the subject peoples, with the spread of literacy and education, that the imperial jig was up.

Oñate's successor as Governor, Pedro de Peralta, himself to be disgraced within a few years, moved the capital in 1609 from San Juan to a site thirty miles to the southeast. It was situated not on the Rio Grande, but on the rolling uplands in a spot highly favorable to the animal husbandry which was the specialty of the colonists. Peralta named it La Villa Real de la Santa Fe de San Francisco, or more simply Santa Fe. It is the oldest state capital in the United States, and the most charming and individual. To its first church, in 1625, Fray Alonso de Benavides brought the little doll-like figure of the Virgin, dressed in the robes of a Spanish queen, which he called *La Conquistadora*.

Quickly, over thirty Spanish settlements sprang up. They stretched three hundred miles along the river, from the point in the south where the Jornada del Muerto ended as far as Taos in the north. They were little more than hamlets, Spanish enclaves constructed close beside the Indian pueblos from which they derived their labor and their supplies. The territory north of the point where the Rio Salado meets the Rio Grande, where most of the Spanish settlements existed, was known as the *Río arriba,* or Upper River; the territory south of it was the *Río abajo,* or Lower River. The chief villages of the Río Abajo were the missions, clustered about the mother-town of El Paso del Norte, which quickly came to rival Santa Fe in importance. The El Paso mission was not established until 1659; but when, in 1668, the great Franciscan, Fray García de San Francisco y Zúñiga, dedicated his church to the Virgin of Guadalupe, its population already numbered over 1,000, with 9,000 cattle, and 13,000 sheep and goats.

Domestic animals, which included the pig, the chicken, and the cat, were a specifically Hispanic contribution to the economy of the Southwest. The first shipload of cattle is said to have reached New Spain from Santo Domingo as early as 1521, almost as soon as the Conquest had been completed. They were brought over by Gregorio de Villalobos, and were descended from the stock Columbus had carried on his second voyage to the New World in 1493. The small, hardy Spanish cattle were already well adapted by the semiarid conditions of their homeland to the similar conditions of New Mexico. The Spaniards were also the leading sheepmen of Europe; the shepherds of the great corporation known as the Mesta annually drove vast flocks from the uplands of northern Spain to winter in the south, returning north in the spring. Spanish shepherds, particularly the Basques, with their huge cloaks and flapping berets, have been for over three centuries a feature of the southwestern scene. A second contingent arrived in the 1840s, and another in the 1940s, as a result of civil wars that drove them from their native ranges.

More exotic than cattle or sheep, and producing a momentous impact on the history of North America, was the introduction of the horse. For this too Juan de Oñate was responsible. There is no truth in the often-repeated story that the wild herds of America, which once covered the land so plentifully that the plains shimmered like the sea, were the outcome of chance matings between animals escaped from the remudas of Coronado and de Soto. Coronado had only 2 mares among his 600 horses, and de Soto's horses were all killed and eaten by the Indians who murdered him. It took the Plains Indians thirty years to decide to ride horses instead of treating them as an interesting change of diet. As late as the 1660s, tribes who would soon become expert horsemen still hunted game on foot. The real source of the horses of the United States were the 100 mares and 700 stallions Oñate brought with him to New Mexico. In 1900, there were as many as a million mustangs running on the plains. Their number has now been reduced to about 17,000. Farmers and licensed scavengers shoot them out, selling their flesh for dog food.

The Spaniards also introduced to America every variety of crop and fruit. They brought the plow, the wheeled vehicle, and scores of farming and household utensils. They naturalized not only the grape and the olive, which were the staples of their Mediterranean homeland, but the apple, orange, fig, pomegranate, pear, plum, lime, lemon, raspberry, strawberry, cherry, peach, apricot, almond, and walnut. They planted flax, alfalfa, cotton, and the first strain of wheat to appear in the United States. They introduced those two boons of civilized living, wine and cheese. In short, they were proficient husbandmen, concerned with nurturing the arts of peace as well as the arts of war.

The Spanish missionaries do not enjoy a high reputation in the eyes of non-Spanish and non-Catholic posterity. The reasons for this are the Holy Office and the *leyenda negra,* or the Black Legend. The Inquisition was introduced into Mexico soon after the Conquest; but at least until the end of the eighteenth century, when it became as much a political as a religious instrument, its behavior was fairly mild. It reached New Mexico and the other northern provinces correspondingly later, and in any case was administered throughout the New World not by the Dominicans, who had charge of it in Spain, but by the Franciscans, who lacked the Dominicans' fanaticism and disliked the institution. As for the leyenda negra, it stemmed from two massive and eloquent works by the Dominican "Apostle of the Indies," Bartolomé de las Casas. These were the *Historia General de las Indias,* and its equally intemperate sequel, the *Destrucción de las Indias.* Las Casas, who eventually became a Bishop, spent his life laboring in the cause of the Indians, and was appointed their official protector by the Emperor Charles. His main target was the system of the *encomienda,* by means of which Indian families and villages were allotted to Spanish settlers. He regarded it, rightly, as a form of slavery; but it seems fair to say that later writers have concluded that, in the chaotic situation for which the Aztecs and not the Spaniards were responsible, the system produced a stabilizing and unifying effect. Nor was it a system that ever worked efficiently in New Spain, or elsewhere, while in New Mexico it was scarcely applied at all. Nevertheless, Las Casas provided the critics of Spain with much damaging material, material that few of them bothered to verify, even if they had had the means or inclination to do so.

The Franciscans in New Mexico were faced with a problem that had not existed eighty years earlier, in New Spain. In New Spain, it was an easy task for Christianity to establish itself under conditions of a complete social and spiritual breakdown. It was simply filling a vacuum. The Mexicans embraced Christianity as unhesitatingly as the Germans and Japanese embraced new political forms in 1945. In the Rio Grande pueblos, however, it was another story, for no such breakdown had occurred. Pueblo religion was altogether tougher and healthier than Mexican religion had been. The most the Franciscan fathers could do was to effect an amalgam, a mingling of the two creeds in which Christianity was queerly changed by the Indian religion, while the latter was queerly changed by Christianity.

The fathers tried hard. They never shirked hardship and loneliness, the threat of martyrdom, or martyrdom itself. They tried to educate, to introduce enlightenment as they understood it. But often they grew irritated with the stubbornness of their charges, and as the seventeenth century progressed their attitude grew harsher and more impatient. The Pueblo Indians did not respond with the childlike trust and affection of the peoples of Mexico; they constantly caused trouble, they resisted. The Indians of New Spain had kneeled in tens of thousands before their bishops, begging to be converted; the Indians of New Mexico sometimes had to be locked at night in the mission compounds for fear that they would escape and slide back into their pagan ways. Many fathers became more inflexible than the Spanish military or the Spanish settlers. It became a test of wills, a competition of faiths.

The Apache-Navajo incursions only increased this tendency. The outlying pueblos were abandoned; the population retreated even closer to the river. The pueblos were fortified, and inside the fortress the priest often became more powerful than the Spanish alcalde. Where missions existed separately, they were protected by new *presidios,* or military encampments, which added to the rigid, siege-mentality of the religious as well as the civil arm. When the behavior of the priests caused incidents, they were forced to summon the military to punish their parishioners, whereupon they were regarded as oppressors, not benefactors.

The first raids by Plains Indians began in the 1660s. For two hundred years thereafter the Rio Grande settlements were, in the words of D. W. Meinig, in his excellent short account of the Southwest, reduced to the status of "islands of civilization in the midst of vast tides of savagery which pounded upon every shore." The threat by hostile Indians had been gathering for half a century. By the 1630s, the Apaches de Navajo, as the Navajos were originally called, had been trickling into the abandoned villages of the Anasazi and noting the enviable quality of life of the Anasazi-Pueblo people. Splitting away from the Apache, they took to horses, then became gifted sheepmen, weavers, and eventually jewelers and artisans. However, it should be noted that accommodation was normally possible between them and their neighbors, even though they mounted dangerous raids on the pueblos from time to time.

There were other, non-pueblo Indians who were eventually absorbed quite peacefully into the Spanish orbit. The mild policies of the Franciscans at El Paso attracted the Manso and Suma Indians to the valley, while the Jesuits in Arizona became the instructors and protectors of the Pima and Papago. To the east of the Camino Real, between thirty and fifty miles away from the highway, at a point equidistant between El Paso and Santa Fe, the Franciscans had also achieved remarkable work among the Las Humanas, or Jumano Indians. These were outlying relatives of the Pueblo Indians, remote descendants of the Mogollon people who had occupied this lonely area for seven centuries. There, in three populous villages called Abo, Quarai, and Gran Quivira, flourishing communities sprang up which bore a fine promise for the future. The handiwork of the devoted Franciscans can still be visited, in the remote and beautiful Manzano Mountains: yet over these impressive cities of stone there hangs an aura of tragedy. They were among the first places to suffer from the depredations of the Apaches, operating from a seasonal haunt in the Sierra Blanca, fifty miles further east. In a culminating incident, the Franciscan priest of Abo was stripped by Apache raiders, bound, flogged, and killed with an axe. In the 1670s the Jumanos abandoned their villages and fled westward to the Rio Grande, eventually seeking the safety of El Paso. The Apaches, with the Utes and, toward the end of the century, the Comanches, were never to be appeased or satiated. To the end, as we shall see, they would remain marauders, their names synonymous with murder, torture, rape, and terror.

It was unfortunate that the menace of the external Indians, attracted to the valley by the prospect of horses, cattle, captives, women, strong drink, and novel foodstuffs, should have coincided with the growth of dissident feeling in the pueblos. A number of Catholic padres had become overzealous in their efforts to stamp out all manifestations of the native religion. As we have seen, pueblo religion was a sturdy growth, and chopping at it only made it stronger. Some of the padres had recourse to imprisonment, flogging, and the halter for what they termed the crimes of sorcery and trafficking with the devil, which were actually nothing more than the persistence of the Indians in celebrating their own rites.

Matters came to a head in 1675, when Governor Treviño arrested forty-seven Indian shamans, hanged three of them, and jailed most of the rest. Among the latter was the shaman Popé, of San Juan pueblo. The Governor would have done better to have hanged him. "Stone dead," as Strafford used to say, "hath no fellow." (His enemies showed they agreed with him, by cutting his head off.) Popé had been attempting to organize a revolt for ten years: and now the Spanish friars had provided him with a favorable climate.

He traveled secretly from pueblo to pueblo, laying the groundwork of a soundly conceived and cleverly organized rebellion. The date for the uprising was to be August 13, 1680. Runners went around the countryside, carrying cords in which knots had been tied to give the day. The cords were like the lotus and other signals used as signs in the Indian Mutiny against the British. Indeed, the Pueblo Revolt and the Indian Mutiny have points of resemblance, not least in the manner in which the Spaniards and the British ignored the warning signs and were taken completely unaware. Popé's security was so thorough that he executed his own son-in-law, whom he thought was a security risk. Nonetheless a hint reached Santa Fe that something was amiss, and Governor Antonio de Otermín hastily ordered all Spaniards to retire on the capital. Popé promptly advanced the date of the revolt by three days, and although most of the Spaniards escaped his net he made a good enough haul. His men killed an estimated 500 of the 2,500 Spanish settlers, including 21 priests, whose bodies were stacked on the altars; 2 priests were killed at Jemez, 3 at Acoma, 3 at Zuni. The manner of their deaths was not edifying.

The Spanish settlers in the Río Arriba fled to Santa Fe, those in the Río Abajo to Laguna. Both towns were besieged and put up heroic defenses. With Santa Fe burning around him, Otermín marched out his people on March 21st and, like Cortés at Mexico City during the *noche triste,* got them away to safety. He fought his way downriver to Laguna, rescued its garrison, and took them on down to El Paso. They reached it, "looking as if they were dead," as a Spanish chronicler wrote, on September 18th.

New Mexico had ceased to exist. "The whole province," writes C. L. Sonnichsen, in his *Pass of the North,* a classic of local historiography, "had gone in a welter of blood and smoke. Everything—the fruits of nearly a hundred years of occupation—was lost."

The loss was more of a blow to Spanish pride than Spanish power; New Mexico was not of overwhelming military or economic importance to New Spain. Nonetheless, the reverberations were felt as far south as Mexico City, where the cathedral bells tolled in mourning, and the northern provinces stood to arms.

Otermín, after waiting a year, returned to New Mexico with a small force. He reconnoitered almost as far as Santa Fe, but found the Indians intractable and the pueblos in turmoil. In a singularly honest report, he told the Viceroy that the rebellion had occurred "because of the many oppressions the Indians received from the Spaniards." Foremost of these, he wrote, was "the yoke they are forced to wear by the church." When his term of office expired, in 1683, he was replaced by a general with European experience, who was instructed merely to hold the line: and during the whole course of the 1680s, except for an occasional sortie, New Mexico was ignored and the direction of the Spanish effort north of the Rio Grande shifted toward the east. There, it had become necessary to curb the incursions of the French, whose flag had been raised at the mouth of the Mississippi by La Salle in 1682. After claiming the whole of Louisiana for Louis XIV, La Salle came west to build Fort St. Louis, on the Gulf Coast, four hundred miles west of the point where New Orleans would be founded in 1718. Although the noble and luckless La Salle was assassinated there, in 1687, and the French effort foundered, it was to counter French influence that, in the late 1680s, the Spaniards began to erect a string of forts between the Rio Grande and the Red River. They called this territory *Tejas*—or, in the old orthography, *Texas* (cf. Don Quijote/Don Quixote).

Throughout the 1680s, the Governor of New Mexico held his council meetings in an adobe house in El Paso, now swollen greatly because of the flood of refugees. In the north, the victorious Popé held sway for a full ten years, until his death in 1690. He eliminated all traces of the "Metal People," washed clean those who had been converted to Christianity with yucca suds, and abolished the use of the Spanish language. His authority was unquestioned: but unfortunately his successes went to his head, and he became a despot. He reigned as a crazy witch doctor, or miniature Shaka Zulu, and it was not long before his subjects became thoroughly weary of him. Worse, savage civil strife broke out among the pueblos, between the pro-Popé and anti-Popé factions. At the turn of the century, in 1600, the population of the pueblos had been about 50,000; it had been drastically reduced by two smallpox epidemics, in 1641 and 1671; and now it declined further because of the civil war and the wars against the Spaniards. When the Spaniards withdrew, the Apache raids became so bad that half the pueblos fell into ruins, and it was from this time that pueblo society assumed the defensive, impoverished configuration with which we are familiar today. By 1700 the population had dropped as low as 8,000—a sixth of what it was a century earlier. If the late 1600s were a miserable time for the Spaniards, they were therefore even worse for the Indians.

The Viceroy did not feel the time had come to attempt a reconquest until 1688. In that year, in an inspired hour, he appointed Don Diego José de Vargas to be Governor and Captain-General of New Mexico. Vargas was born in Madrid in 1643, fought as a young man in Italy, and married a rich wife, Doña Beatriz Pimentel de Prado de Torrelaguna. In 1673, he sailed to the New World on a royal assignment. He was then thirty, and would not see Spain again. He retained the King's trust, served in important appointments in the mining towns in the north, and was regarded in Mexico City as a man of unassailable integrity. C. L. Sonnichsen in *Pass of the North* and Paul Horgan in *Great River* paint vivid pictures of him, based on the single portrait of him that survives and on the account of Espinosa, his biographer. "He was a tall man," writes Horgan. "His long hair and large eyes were dark, his face was a long oval with a straight nose and his mustaches and beard were slender. He wore a morion and body armor. His horse-stained boots were wrinkled up about his thighs when mounted, and folded down below his knees when dismounted. In his luggage he carried court dress of much splendor, including Dutch linen shirts with shoulder-wide collars and long ballooned sleeves; knee-length vests embroidered and edged with gold lace; slashed doublets outlined with fur and tied with ribbons; knee breeches with bullion garters and bows; white silk hose; low shoes tied with double bows of silk ribbons; dark velvet hats crowned with plumes and faced under the brims with ermine; and stiff taffeta baldrics to carry his light dress rapier. These proclaimed estate. Within he carried the essence of it. His mind was orderly, clear and grave. He was without fear of all things short of God."

This characteristic image of the *hidalgo* and the *caballero* has been graven into the culture of the Southwest. There is more than a touch of the Spaniard in the hero of the Western movie. In the latter, with his fine horse, elegant weapons, dandified dress, his pride, reserve, melancholy, and *cortesía,* something of Francisco Vázquez de Coronado, Juan de Oñate, and Diego de Vargas rides again.

It took Vargas three years to secure his base at El Paso and pacify the Río Abajo. Such had been the extent of the disaster. Then, in the late summer of 1692, he marched rapidly and decisively to the north, and at dawn on September 21st marshalled his 200 veterans beneath the walls of Santa Fe. A shout, five times repeated, of "Glory be to the Blessed Sacraments of the Altar!," brought the inhabitants from their beds. As the light broadened, they saw that they were confronted by no Apache band, but by Vargas at the head of his troops, in full armor, his plumed hat on his head, bearing in his hand the banner that had belonged to Oñate and to Otermín.

After some intricate negotiations, Santa Fe surrendered to him peacefully. The other pueblos followed suit. He visited each village in turn, scolding them, then granting pardon. The Hopi, inclined to hold out, submitted quietly, and within four months Vargas was back in El Paso after a bloodless campaign. The news was greeted in Mexico City by more ringing of church bells.

Unfortunately, pacific relations were not to endure. While he was away, during the next twelve months, recruiting a new nucleus of eight hundred settlers and shepherding them north, the mood of the Indians changed. When he presented himself once more outside Santa Fe, on December 15, 1683, he was abused, jeered at, and refused admittance. For two weeks he camped outside the walls, his people exposed to the bitter weather, their children dying. Once more he sought to settle the matter by negotiation; but then, on December 28th, after once more "exhorting them with great kindness and love, and expressing regret at their rebelling and at their hard and vindictive hearts," he and his men flung themselves at the fortifications. After a day of battle, in which the Spaniards were repulsed when they attempted to scale the walls, the main gate was eventually set on fire. But at that moment the Indians of Santa Fe were reinforced by their cousins from Santa Clara, San Ildefonso, Tesuque, and Nambe. Vargas had to draw back to subdue the newcomers. Having done so, he stormed Santa Fe and captured it at four o'clock in the morning. The standard of Spain was broken out over Otermín's palace, and a cross erected over the entrance to the plaza. The Indian cacique hanged himself, and the war captain and sixty-eight of his soldiers were shot, after being subjected to a lengthy sermon from one of Vargas' seventeen friars.

The fate of Santa Fe so stiffened Indian resistance that the next nine months were occupied by ceaseless and bloody fighting. The Indians would abandon their pueblos on the approach of Vargas, taking to some nearby mesa where they could defend themselves more purposefully. Vargas overran the Portrero Viejo, where the people of Cochiti chose to fight him, but three times was beaten back by the San Ildefonsans from the slopes of the Black Butte; and although the people of Acoma were eventually forced by hunger to submit, he did not succeed, as Vicente de Zaldívar had, in reaching the summit of their "Sky City." As for the Hopi, they stood to arms on their distant mesas to such effect that they were never more than technically subdued. When one writes of the Southwest Indians, one must remember that one is writing of people who stood up to and defeated Spanish soldiers at the time when the prowess of Spanish arms was at its height.

Vargas' firing squads went to work, executing a dozen here, a score there, fifty somewhere else. It was not surprising that, in 1696, as he neared the end of his term as governor, he was compelled to deal with another revolt which, had he not acted promptly, might have resulted in a second disaster to the colony. He managed to bring it under control with a loss of twenty-one settlers and five priests. One feels, again, that the men of God, in the American mission fields of the seventeenth century, did not constitute good insurance risks.

Vargas had become unpopular with his own people. He petitioned to have his governorship renewed, and was rebuffed. Then he underwent one of those petrifying reverses of fortune which habitually struck Spaniards of the epoch—reverses which would have sunk men with less of what Churchill called intestinal fortitude. His successor, Pedro Rodríguez Cubero, bought the governorship for 2,000 pesos while Vargas' application was snarled in the toils of the Madrid bureaucracy. He had Vargas arrested and put in chains, tried on trumped-up charges of extortion and embezzlement, and thrown into solitary confinement. His property was confiscated, and his remaining wealth seized for "court costs." The cell in which he lay was situated in the long, low, whitewashed adobe building, with a handsome cool colonnade where Pueblo women now sit with their wares, which forms one side of the plaza at Santa Fe. I never enter that building, now a museum, but which formerly housed the oldest state government in the United States, without thinking of the *grandeurs et servitudes* of Pedro de Vargas. He was kept in a small, dark cell at one end of the building, while Cubero wenched, drank, and gambled at the other. He would have stayed there till he died, had not Fray Francisco de Vargas, the *custodio,* or Father President of the province, courageously made the six-months-long journey to Mexico City to bring his plight to the attention of the Viceroy.

Such were the lapses of communication in those days that neither the Viceroy nor the King in Madrid were aware of the slights that had been put upon this most faithful and efficient of their servants. Reparation was instantly made. The Viceroy ordered his immediate release; the King bestowed on him the title of Marquis. Vargas hastened to Mexico City, was exonerated, vindicated, apologized to—a very rare event in Spanish annals—and reinvested with the titles of Governor and Captain-General of New Mexico. He returned to Santa Fe to make his enemies disgorge his monies and estates. He was eager to settle accounts with his chief persecutor; but Cubero, anxious to avoid having a yard of cold steel rammed down his throat, had fled. Vargas had to savor his reinstatement without the musk and amber of personal vengeance.

The new Marqués de la Nava Brazinas survived to enjoy his title only seven months. His health had been undermined by the rigors of reconquest and imprisonment. He now overtaxed his remaining energies by embarking on a thoroughgoing campaign of reorganization and reform. Under Cubero the province had been rapidly running down. The defenses of Santa Fe were dilapidated; the countryside was impoverished and its agriculture neglected; the troops had become lax and undisciplined. During the winter of 1703, Vargas began to take steps to remedy matters. He made such progress that in the spring of 1704 he was able to lead out a force in which Spaniards and Indians marched side by side to combat the ever-pressing threat of the Apaches. He moved downriver, then headed east for the Manzano Mountains to attack that same Apache warband that twenty years earlier had destroyed Abo, Quarai, and Gran Quivira. He was hot on their trail when he was taken ill, and his troops had to carry him back to the Rio Grande, to the Spanish settlement of Bernalillo.

He knew he was dying. He made his peace with his Maker, then drew up his will, which was witnessed by five of his officers. He divided his armor, fine clothes, and horse furniture between his two natural sons, who shared his fortune equally with a natural daughter in New Spain. He freed the two slaves who were his personal servants, paid his debts, and ordered his silver plate and jewelry to be sold to pay for Masses for his own soul and for the souls of the Spaniards who had died under his command in the reconquest of New Mexico. He had strength enough to sign the will with the same extravagant flourish with which Oñate had signed the rock at El Morro.

His body was taken back to Santa Fe to be buried in the parish church, beneath the high altar. Again, I can never enter the church, with its little figure of *La Conquistadora,* without remembering Vargas. Horgan writes that "the earth for which he fought and which he defended was over him in peace, and, in the peace which he had brought to it, the upper river kingdom lived." Paul Wellman, in *Glory, God and Gold,* notes that he was "the savior of New Mexico, as Oñate was its father." And Sonnichsen observes, "The great September Fiesta in Santa Fe still celebrates his recovery of New Mexico for the Crown and the Cross, and his name is still honored in his old haunts. These were the rewards Vargas worked and suffered and died for, and from what we know of the man, he probably would not have considered the price he paid too high."

It is doubtful whether the Pueblo Indians, whose land the Spaniards usurped, would endorse such encomiums to a foreign interloper. However, it was the leadership and military experience of the Spaniards that enabled them to survive. Otherwise they could not have withstood the Navajo-Ute-Apache-Comanche onslaught.

In New Mexico, the Anasazi-descended peoples, under the tutelage of the Spaniards, and as a result of fighting them, learned the skills which were necessary to beat off their savage brethren. In Arizona, the more pacific peoples descended from the Hohokam had a far worse time of it. There, the Spaniards never managed to effect more than a temporary lodgment in the face of the nomadic and aggressive Indians. It was only in the 1680s, when Popé's revolt had extinguished the Spanish presence in New Mexico, that Spain turned her attention briefly to the western portion of the Southwest, in the way she was also shoring up the line in the east, in Texas. The strategy was to strengthen and hold the periphery of New Spain until the center could once more be brought under control.

Arizona was explored and mapped, in a series of journeys beginning in 1683, by one of the most impressive and remarkable men in the history of the United States, Father Eusebio Francisco Kino. Eusebius Kino was born in Segno, a little town in the Italian Tyrol, in 1645. He became a Jesuit at twenty-one, distinguishing himself in his studies at Innsbruck, Munich, and Ingolstadt, where the Duke of Bavaria invited him to teach science and mathematics. During a severe illness, St. Francis Xavier appeared to him in a vision, and instructed him to leave Europe and enter the mission field. He took his middle name, Francisco, in gratitude for his recovery. He was already in his middle thirties when he sailed from Cádiz to Veracruz, a passage of ninety days, never to see his home, family, or native land again.

A man of preternatural vitality, he was sent first to the Baja California of Mexico, where he labored for six years among the singularly savage and primitive tribes of that barren peninsula. His years there inculcated in him a desire to reach northern California—which, like everyone else, he assumed was an island—that obsessed him for the remainder of his life. Then, in 1687, he was transferred to Sonora and the *Pimería alta,* where he was to enter into immortality.

Within ten years, he had laid the foundations of a string of seven major missions, fourteen minor ones, and countless wayside chapels across Sonora, in the remotest part of northwestern Mexico, then in the province of New Navarre. His headquarters was at Nuestra Señora de las Dolores, from which his activities spread out along the rivers to the north and south. His first churches were small, but later they became ambitious adobe structures. The churches at Caborca, Cabórica, Tubutama, Remedios, Cocóspora, and Santa Maria were particularly lofty and impressive. From Dolores he rode northward, eventually exploring the whole of southern Arizona as far north as Casa Grande.

It was at Tumacácori, just north of the twin Mexican-American towns of Nogales, on the road to what was to become Tucson, that he established his first mission on American soil. It was founded as a result of direct representations from the local Pima Indians. They had heard of the wheat, livestock, and fruit trees that he had introduced further south, and wanted him to confer the same benefits on them. Today Tumacácori is a splendid shell: a complex of buildings dominated by a half-finished basilica where, above the wrecked altar, the Crucifix was ripped from the wall and its outline can still be seen. The mission perished in the troubles that overwhelmed the Pimería Alta and the *Papaguería* after the collapse of Spanish power. In the wall of the enclosed garden where the fathers tended their orchard are the marks of bullets where men were shot in the Mexican and early American periods.

For Father Kino, Tumacácori was the jumping-off point for his third tier of missions. In 1692 he founded a mission at Guevavi, now a ruin, and came to the place called Bac, or The Spring. It was inhabited by the Papago Indians, whom he found "very affable and friendly." Father Charles Polzer, in his comprehensive monograph on Kino (1972), tells us that he "spoke to them of the word of God, and on a map of the world showed them the lands, the rivers and the seas over which Fathers had come from afar to bring them the saving knowledge of our holy faith. And I showed them on the map of the world how the Spaniards and the Faith had come by sea to Vera Cruz and had gone to Puebla and to Mexico, Guadalajara and Sinaloa. They listened with pleasure to these and other talks concerning God, Heaven and Hell, and told me that they wished to be Christians, and gave me infants to baptize." On a second visit, in 1697, he brought them cattle, sheep, goats and horses, and found that the wheat which he had previously planted was growing satisfactorily; and on his third visit, in 1700, he founded what he named "the very large and capacious church of San Xavier del Bac, all the people working with much pleasure and zeal, some in digging the foundations, others in hauling many and very great stones of *tezontle* (volcanic rock) from a little hill which is almost a quarter of a league away. And that place, with its large court and garden nearby, will be able to have all the water it may need throughout the year, running to any field or workplace that requires it."

At Tumacácori, there is an equestrian statue of Father Kino, and others stand in the halls of Congress at Washington, at Tucson, and in the principal concourse of Hermosillo, the spacious, handsome capital of Sonora. All are imaginary. We do not know what the redoubtable Father looked like, though Wellman has culled from various sources a catalogue of his personal habits. "He was an ascetic in the absolute sense, taking his food without salt, and with mixtures of herbs 'which made it more distasteful.' He neither smoked nor took snuff, as did many religious of his day. The only wine he ever tasted was

Father Kino's first mission on American soil, Tumacácori, Arizona. (PHOTO BY AUTHOR)

when he celebrated mass, and he slept always on the floor, on mats or horse blankets, refusing to take to a bed. At times he appears to have submitted to flagellations, to further curb his flesh, and when he fell sick with fever he tried no remedy for six days, except to celebrate mass and then retire to his horse blankets again. When it was necessary to reprimand a sinner he could grow 'choleric,' but otherwise he was mild and meek, never appearing to resent abuse, which was sometimes directed at him. In saying the mass he invariably wept. As his companion Fray Luis Velarde wrote of him, 'he was merciful to others, but cruel to himself.' "

It was in 1711, while he was celebrating a mass at Magdalena to dedicate a new chapel to St. Francis Xavier, that his strong body finally failed him. He was sixty-seven. The grand old man whom even in his lifetime his superiors in Rome had not hesitated to compare to St. Francis Xavier, collapsed and was taken to his deathbed. We are told it consisted of "two calf-skins for a mattress, two blankets such as the Indians use for covering, and a pack-saddle for a pillow." As Father Velarde said, "He died as he had lived, in genuine humility and real poverty." It was only fitting that he should have died with his head on his saddle, for he was one of the great horsemen of the Americas. He had ridden as many miles in his life as those friends of my youth, Roy Campbell and Tschiffely. In twenty-four years on the frontier, "the padre on horseback" made more than forty epic journeys of up to six hundred miles apiece

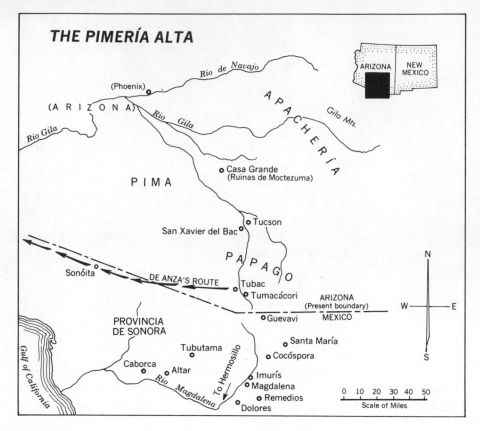

THE PIMERÍA ALTA

FIGURE 10

to explore and to save souls. He charted the Colorado River from the Gila to the Sea of Cortés, and his maps remained the standard source of information for over a century. Herbert E. Bolton relates that at fifty-one he rode 1,500 miles from the Pimería Alta to Mexico City in fifty-three days. Once he rode seventy miles in twenty-four hours, from Tumacácori to San Ignacio near Magdalena, to save the life of an Indian who had been unjustly sentenced to death.

Magdalena, a town fifty miles south of the border, at the Nogales crossing, is now officially named Magdalena de Kino. There the state of Sonora has erected a magnificent mausoleum to Father Kino. When I first visited it, it was not completed, but was a splendidly imaginative construction of flying white archways and arcades, surrounding a spacious modern plaza. On my last visit, three years later, it was not only finished but had already collected the graffiti, scrawled obscenities, and general scruffiness endemic to most Mexican towns, a habit that Mexico certainly did not acquire from Spain, that house-proud country. The skeleton of the Father is displayed in situ, at the bottom of an opened grave—another characteristically Mexican touch. There is some slight remaining dispute as to whether the bones really are Kino's, though the strong square skull and legs bowed from 80,000 miles in the saddle suggest that it is. It does not greatly matter. Kino himself would not have cared, and what counts is this generous tribute to his place in Mexican history.

On the American side of the border, this frugal servant of God is com-memorated by a monument which is even more striking. There is nothing left of his original church at San Xavier del Bac, close to Tucson: but the church that stands there today may be justly considered his memorial. Ironically, the church as we know it was not even built by the Father's own Order, whose five thousand missionaries were expelled by King Charles III from the Pime-ría Alta in 1767, and suppressed throughout the whole world in 1773. It was Father Francisco Hermenigildo Garcés, the first Franciscan to take charge after the Jesuit expulsion, who began the second church in 1783. A man in every way worthy to continue Kino's work, he was formed in his predecessor's mold: priest, explorer, trailblazer. He pioneered the road that would lead from Durango to San Francisco; he was the benefactor of the Hopi, and of the savage Yumas, by whom he was eventually murdered.

I would say unhesitatingly that, for me, San Xavier del Bac is the most attractive single building I have encountered in North America—and I am not forgetting some of those I have seen in New Orleans, Natchez, Annapolis, Georgetown, and elsewhere. San Xavier deserves its name of "The Dove of the Desert." It rests, light and dazzling, like the Holy Ghost, on a bare land-scape, with the glistening slopes of the Catalinas beyond. The architecture is a cool blend of Moorish and Byzantine, Baroque, and Spanish Colonial. It rises from the flat desert in a dreamlike assemblage of domes and vaults, tow-ers and pendentives, pillars and buttresses, finials and arabesques. Its churri-guresque portal, stuccoed walls, tiny walks and gardens planted with agave, ocotillo, tamarisk, and saguaro, are all immaculate. Franciscan Fathers and Pa-pago Indians tend it with pride and devotion. Its atmosphere belongs to a sim-pler and earlier world, a simpler and earlier church. Whenever I drive through Tucson, I make a point of spending an hour there. At San Xavier, and some of the other mission churches of the Southwest, I sometimes experience the sensations I feel in buildings at the other end of the religious scale—the cathe-drals of Lincoln, Compostela, Reims, or Strasbourg. There is even an echo of Chartres, where I would pause on my journeys from Spain to stand where the wine-purples of the rose window spill across the flagstones. San Xavier del Bac could be inserted in a disregarded corner of Chartres: yet it is replete with God, like the cells of the Celtic hermits tucked away in the lost valleys of Car-digan and Carmarthen. God overwhelms us with his greatness—but also knows the trick of making himself small. It is fortifying to sit in the little church,

Uncovering the bones of Father Kino at Magdalena, Sonora, Mexico.

gleaming with gilded plasterwork and with *trompe l'oeil* pictures which must have seemed magical to Indian eyes. In its side chapels preside the Virgin and St. Francis Xavier. A plasterwork imitation of the Franciscan cord runs the whole way round the ceiling—a cord whose knot, tied above the high altar, represents the knot that binds man to God.

The church and its buildings have not always existed in such a state of miniature perfection. Soon after the Spaniards withdrew, and the frontier was left to its fate, the site was abandoned. In 1851, when Arizona had just become American territory, a traveler noted, in a passage that would have pleased St. Francis of Assisi, that "its only occupants are the birds, and they sing praises from morning until night. They build their nests on the heads of saints and warble their notes of joy while perched on their fingers. The door of the church is open, but the property of the church is undisturbed. The natives look upon the structure with awe and could not be persuaded to deface or injure it." The church was later damaged by a cyclone, and its roof could not be restored until 1908, thanks to the labors of Bishop Granjon of Tucson. In this century there have been two more cyclones, the second as recently as 1964; but the work of renovation has gone steadily forward, supervised in the 1960s and 1970s by Brother Lawrence Hogan and Father Kieran McCarty, with the assistance of a group of lay benefactors.

Whatever the condition of the mission church, the Papago Indians, on whose 71,000 acre reservation it stands, have not lacked a priest since 1670. But the history of Spanish settlers and sedentary Indians in Arizona was even more disaster-racked than that of New Mexico. The Rio Grande valley was fertile and possessed good grazing; after the decline of the Hohokam and the decay of their canal system, Arizona became almost entirely barren and devoid of adequate water. During Father Kino's heyday, there had been a very brief period of prosperity, occasioned by the discovery of a vein of silver at a place called Arizonac, on the Alta River, just south of the present Mexican border. The find was a nine-day-wonder, and fanned that chronic Spanish expectation of a bonanza in the far north that would rival the earlier bonanzas in New León and New Galicia. But the Apaches made mining in Arizona dangerous and impossible; the officials and entrepreneurs in Mexico City quickly withdrew their support; the miners concealed their tools and equipment in their

Mission of San Xavier del Bac, near Tucson, Arizona.

mines, boarded them up, and departed. Father Kino's last years were overshadowed by financial troubles as he strove to keep his missions alive. Nor were the troubles only financial. Already in 1695 the normally peaceful Papago, whom he was trying to protect, rose in revolt and murdered one of his priests. They would have murdered him, too, had he shown fear: but he stood up to them and dared them to kill him, and they backed away. In 1771, there was a second rebellion that almost swept the handful of Spaniards from the province: and the struggle for survival was not improved by the hiatus caused by the expulsion of the Jesuits. Michael Foss, in his *The Founding of the Jesuits,* observes that "In time the Society began to show some of the less fortunate attributes of the military mind—narrow, rigid and doctrinaire. The Jesuits became proud, the great temptation of soldiers, and they tended to equate the interests of the universal Church with their own interests. The Church had enough of them and for various reasons, both honorable and dishonorable, temporarily suppressed the Society from 1773 to 1814." Certainly Father Kino and his colleagues possessed some military virtues: but one feels that they were scarcely of the stamp of those Jesuit generals in Paraguay who, beginning in 1607, organized 100,000 Indians into a wealthy and wide-ranging state. The followers of the great "Apostle of the Pimas," on the "rim of Christendom," were temperate men. They included Father Bernard Middendorf, who founded San Cosme de Tucson in 1757, and another great traveler, Father Jacobo Sedelmayr, and his colleague Father Ignatius Keller. Their fate was therefore all the more terrible. All fifty-one of them were rounded up, without warning, by officers acting under sealed orders. They were dragged from their missions, put in carts, and taken down to the Pacific Coast at Mazatlán. There they were kept for weeks in an old warehouse, until a ship came tardily to fetch them. They were then marched across the isthmus to Veracruz and transhipped to Spain. Over twenty died from the rigors of the march, or from previous exposure on the beach; some went mad. It is impossible to estimate the depth of their bewilderment, or envision their attempts to resist falling into the sin of despair. Tough old Father Sedelmayr was one of those who survived, and he wrote a Latin elegy on the deaths of his comrades. Their departure was not attended by the immediate collapse that occurred in Paraguay, where thirty mission-cities went back to the jungle; but an already shaky province was further weakened.

The government in Mexico City could seldom be prevailed on to help the Pimería Alta. Funds, military reinforcements, or drafts of fresh settlers, were always minimal. New Mexico had too much on its own hands to be able to assist its neighbor. In any case, the whole intervening area between New Mexico and Arizona was seething with hostile Indians. The Apaches had become immovably entrenched in the Gila country, forming an impassable wedge between the two territories. Many of the pioneer Arizonans, tired of living in cramped presidios, finally took the opportunity of joining the colony which Juan Bautista de Anza led to California in 1776.

De Anza had made his first march the previous year, forming up his column at the presidio of Tubac, which guarded the route between Tumacácori and San Xavier del Bac. He was following the lead given him, almost seventy-five years earlier, by Father Kino, who in 1702 had finally succeeded in reaching the Colorado River and had actually crossed it. Kino was the first white man, apart from casual mariners, to set foot in California, and to prove it was not an island. Tubac, today, is only an agreeable but insignificant stopping-point on the road to Mexico. It is hard to associate that sleepy hamlet with what has been called the *Anabasis* of California history, an extraordinary feat of courage and endurance.

The first settlers in California were relieved to find that the Indians of the West Coast, though much more numerous, lacked the ferocity of the Indians of New Mexico and the Pimería Alta. De Anza was only able to feel out, not establish a regular overland route; two Mexican officers and a Dominican father went over the same ground in 1823, but it was not until 1846 that a true Arizona-California wagon road was opened. But though the immigrants continued to come by sea, within five years they had founded the presidial towns of San Diego, Santa Barbara, Monterey, and San Francisco, also the pueblos of San Jose and Los Angeles. The colonization of California was a more relaxed proceeding than the colonization of the Southwest—except for the Indians, whose ruthless extermination, after the Spaniard and Mexican had been replaced by the Anglo, was the more depressing in that it was totally unprovoked. In 1849, a year after the United States had annexed California, and at the start of the Gold Rush, the Indian population of California was estimated as between 110,000 and 130,000. In 1880, thirty years later, it was 20,000. The systematic destruction of the California Indian is one of the saddest episodes of American history, just as Theodora Kroeber's *Ishi in Two Worlds: A Biography of the Last Wild Indian in North America,* which chronicles it, is one of America's saddest books.

Carey McWilliams, in *North from Mexico, the Spanish-Speaking People of the United States,* describes the effects of poverty, isolation, and incessant nomadic Indian attacks on the main areas of Spanish settlement. "The Spanish scheme for colonizing the borderlands," he says, "called for a strong central colony in New Mexico, the establishment of widely separated outposts in California, Arizona and Texas, and, eventually, the linking of those settlements into a broad band across the northern part of New Spain. The central colony of New Mexico was finally anchored, after great effort, but more than a hundred years passed before the colonization of the three outlying provinces could be undertaken. While these salients were ultimately established, the colonies were never consolidated. During their existence as Spanish outposts, they went their separate and different ways, with little intercommunication or exchange; each with its own pattern, its own special problems.

"The failure of Spain to consolidate the borderland outposts has had important latter-day consequences. For the Spanish-speaking of the borderlands remain, to some extent, separate and disparate groups, sharing a common heritage but never having known the experience of functioning together. Spanish-speaking people in California know little of the experience of their compatriots in New Mexico; and those in New Mexico are unacquainted with conditions in Arizona and Texas. No effective liaison has ever existed between these groups; their experiences have run parallel but have never merged. For the border was broken, the links were never forged."

Again, as a European, one is reminded that, for Americans, the beauties and freedoms of North American geography are outweighed by its lonely terrors.

The component areas of Spanish North America, then, were never welded together. Equally significant was the fact that, from the beginning, the links with the motherland through New Spain had never been strong; they were constantly thinning and fraying. Furthermore, when Oñate went north to plant the colony, imperial Spain was already moribund—although, as is the way with empires, neither Spain nor her rivals realized it at the time. At sea, the decline of Spain had begun with the defeat of the Spanish Armada in 1588, and was augmented by the destruction by storms of a second fleet the fatally stubborn Philip II amassed for another "enterprise of England." On land, after the young French general Condé had routed the Spanish in Flanders at Rocroi, in 1643, there could be no doubt that the *siglo español* had ended, and that the *siècle français* had begun. In 1700, Spain accepted a Bourbon king, the nephew of Louis XIV, and was reduced to the status of a French client.

From the outset, New Mexico had been living on borrowed time. The only reason that the French and English did not attack and dismember the Spanish empire was because they were fighting one another and were busy with absorbing the large slices of the world which they had already acquired. The Spanish colonies in the New World were like outer limbs still functioning when the central organs have been stricken with a fatal disease. Or, to change the metaphor, they were like the crew of an ocean liner who have not noticed that the engines have stopped turning, that the ship is moving forward only because of its previous momentum. Englishmen can now recognize that, in their case, the engine room began to fill with water in 1919, though it only fell silent in 1945. Historical processes take a long time to work out, and their implications only very slowly become apparent.

All the same, it would be wrong to expect a powerful organism like the Spanish empire to succumb without some vigorous terminal twitchings. New

Spain had, in general, prospered in the sixteenth century, then stagnated in the seventeenth; then in the eighteenth century—paradoxically—it boomed once more, even though the night was already descending. Sometimes, close to the end, a patient suffering from cancer or tuberculosis will have a deceptive remission. This imperial Saint Martin's Summer was the result of wise reforms which produced excellent results both in Spain and her overseas possessions. They were the work of Ferdinand VI (1746–1759), Charles III (1759–1788), and their able ministers. New Spain was ruled by two exceptionally capable viceroys, Bucareli and Revilla Gigedo, both of whom have streets named after them in Mexico City, and by such gifted men as José Campillo and José de Gálvez, the founder of Galveston. It ought to be remembered that, in spite of corruption and top-heavy bureaucracy, lively experiments in colonial government were being made within twenty years of the final collapse.

The New Mexican settlers hung on through nomadic Indian oppression, outbreaks of pestilence, and a host of other troubles. They founded important towns: Bernalillo, Belén, Tomé, Sandía, Albuquerque. Chihuahua came into existence as an intermediate station on the Camino Real between El Paso and Mexico City. In Texas and Arizona, and later California, the presidio system was in operation; in the Rio Grande valley the settlers and Pueblo Indians had become fused into some sort of amity, drawn together by their mutual need to resist the Navajo and Apache, then the Comanche. As in India, after the Mutiny, the occupying power had learned to rule with a lighter touch, to comport itself more tactfully. The process of rapprochement was also aided by the fact that the settlers, like Cortés at Veracruz, had burned their boats. Spain, for the few of them who may have known it, was merely a memory. They were separated from New Spain and Mexico City by the perilous march downriver, across the Jornada del Muerto. No doubt most of them had only the haziest notion of events in Mexico, let alone Spain. When De Anza was setting out from Tubac, he was ignorant of the existence of the men who were at that moment signing the Declaration of Independence, and they were ignorant of him. The blood and language of Spain were not grafted on to the Indian stock as the result of a casual, makeshift relationship, but as the result of one that was destined to be permanent. The Spanish settlers were there to stay. They could not keep themselves to themselves, and then, when the flag was hauled down, step aboard a P. and O. liner or a BOAC plane, like the English settlers returning from Kenya, Nigeria, or India.

We have noted that, by 1800, because of the wars with the Spaniards, the civil wars fought between 1680–1690, and particularly the epidemics, the number of Pueblo Indians had dwindled from 50,000 to about 8,000. The numbers of people with Spanish blood, however, had increased from Oñate's 500 to 20,000, largely because the Spaniards possessed a natural immunity to the diseases they brought with them. Few of that 20,000 were *peninsulares*—men and women born in the Iberian peninsula. Only a few senior officers and officials could claim that privilege, and were wealthy enough, if they survived the hazards of their tour of duty, to make the voyage home to Spain. The bulk of the population were either *criollos,* persons of pure Spanish parentage born and domiciled in the New World, or *mestizos,* persons of mixed Spanish and Indian blood. The word *mestizo* comes from *mezclar,* to mix, and in due time the *mestizo*—sometimes also called the *ladino*—became the dominant breed, and ultimately the so-called Hispano or Hispano-American.

Nonetheless, in spite of cross-breeding and acculturation, the Spaniard preserved many of the elements of his original life style. He lived in an Indian-type adobe house, but he provided it with the big carved doors and plain, ponderous furniture in the taste of his father and great-grandfather. Its thick clay walls were provided with *pergaminos,* or thin oiled rawhide windows to admit the light, and barred by the traditional ornamental *rejas.* He ate chile, tamales, tortillas, and *atole* (a mixture of cornmeal and brown sugar), ground in a metate of tezontle, and served on an earthenware platter called a *comale* or *comalli.* But on formal occasions he would bring out the heavy silver or pewter tableware that had been carried by mule-train up the Camino Real, and earlier across the Atlantic.

Like his kinsman in New Spain, the Spaniard in New Mexico gradually evolved a distinct appearance. His garb was an elegant variation on the costume of the caballero, the conquistador, the romantic lover and horseman of Andalucía, of whom he was or fancied himself to be the heir. He wore a heavy stiff woolen sombrero with an enormous brim and high *copa* or crown; a woolen *poncho, manta, tilma,* or *serape de boca manga;* a long soft leather *cuero,* or soft garment of leather, necessary in the harsh brushcountry; and the *botas de ala,* the wing leggings, that were to become the *chaparreras* or chaps. He carried a muzzle-loading flintlock, or *escopeta,* a flintlock pistol, or *Miguelete,* an *espada ancha* or *machete,* and a *hoz* or hook for cutting grass for forage. On his saber was invariably engraved the legend *Por mi ley y por mi rey*—"For my law and for my king"—because even though no Spanish king ever visited his overseas dominions, he was the fountain of all wisdom and authority, and an object of the profoundest veneration. Our caballero had also adopted the New World habit of smoking cigarras or cigarillos made of tobacco wrapped in cornhusks, which he lit with a *mecha* or strike-a-light. His person and possessions were lavishly inlaid and festooned with silver, the precious metal which Spain had found in vast quantities in the New World, and which was both a boon and a curse to her: silver braid, silver buttons, silver spurs, silver saddles—something to flash and twinkle in the brown and dusty landscape.

He has also left his mark on the Southwest in such things as the design of his towns, his political organization, his dreamy and quixotic attitudes, and, above all, his language. The Indians had their own tongues; but the Hispano, later reinforced by the Mexican, introduced into the Southwest the language that until the arrival of the Anglo was the medium of government, commerce, and daily interchange. Even today it is in most areas the preferred or mother tongue. It is Spanish that gives the English of the Southwest its spicy character.

Many of these Spanish loanwords in southwestern English are, appropriately, derived from horses and horsemanship. There are over four hundred of them, and they include bronco (sturdy horse); buckaroo (*vaquero*); hack (*jaca,* pony); burro (ass); mustang (*mesteño*); remuda (herd of horses); rodeo (cattle-market); stampede (*estampida,* runaway debt); lasso (*lazo,* slip-knot); and corral. Then there are scores of words associated with nature or agriculture, and place-names derived from them: *cañón* (canyon); *barranca* (ravine); mesa (flat-topped hill); *malpaís* (badlands); sierra (mountain-range); arroyo (watercourse); laguna (lake); *llano* (plain); *cañada* (glen, glade, sheepwalk); *bosque* (forest, grove); *loma* (rising ground); *vega* (meadow); *hondo* (deep); tornado and hurricane (*huracán*); mesquite, paloverde, ocotillo, maguey, agave, sotol, lechuga, lechuguilla, saguaro, cholla, chamiso; álamo (poplar) and nogal (walnut); grama (grass); alfalfa; *algodón* (cotton), *henequén* (hemp). A whole series of words describe buildings or architectural features: hacienda; ranch (*ranchería*); *cabaña* (cabin); stockade (*estocada*); calaboose (*calabozo,* dungeon); hoosegow (*juzgado,* court); presidio; adobe, corbel, portal, patio, plaza; *azotea* (flat roof); *viga* (beam); *ramada* (lean-to); hammock (*hamaca*). Types of people include the impresario, *comisario,* vigilante, *filibustero* (robber, pirate), imposter (*embustero*), desperado, and bandido. Among animals are numbered the coyote; jackal (*chacal*), javelina hog; cougar; *lobo* (wolf); jaguar; armadillo; and chinchilla with a sideways glance at the mosquito and cockroach (*cucaracha*). A few of the New World words connected with food or cooking are chile, cocoa, potato, tomato, avocado, banana, vanilla, charqui or *jarquí* (jerky or jerked meat), and barbecue (*barbacoa,* to roast an animal whole).

And finally, to wind up this verbal fandango, I will vamoose (*vámonos*) with a final *hasta el próximo, hasta la vista, hasta lluego,* not to mention a *vaya con dios.*

SEVEN

WE HAVE DEVOTED a chapter to the Pueblo Indians of the old Río Arriba and Río Abajo, and described their life today.

Two tribes in the Rio Grande area, related to the Pueblo Indians, but who did not survive into modern times, have also been noted in passing. These were the Manso and the Jumano. The former, who never seem to have been more than 1,000 strong, were drawn down into the El Paso region soon after the city was founded, and were there absorbed into urban life.

The Jumano, on the other hand, were one of the biggest tribes in North America. Cabeza de Vaca described them as handsome, kindly, intelligent, and prosperous, after he and his companions had passed through their territory toward the end of their long march. It was the Jumanos who had inhabited the thickly populated and ill-fated towns of Abo, Quarai, and Gran Quivira, in the Manzano Mountains. Known also as Las Humanas, Piros, or Salinas people, they were an offshoot of the Pueblo Indians to the northwest of them. Like the Manso, they were driven south to the shelter of El Paso and Chihuahua by a combination of disasters: the drought of 1666–1670, the epidemic of 1671, the intensified Apache raids of the 1670s, and the upsets attendant on the Pueblo Revolt of 1680. Of these, the most devastating were the Apache raids: and it is an indicator of their scale and frequency that a tribe which was still, at the end of the seventeenth century, several thousands strong, could be so hustled and harried that it gave up its ancestral lands and sought shelter with strangers. Like the Manso, after settling in their southern

◆ 136 ◆

NAME AND POPULATION 1970	LANGUAGE	NATIVE NAME	MEANING

APACHE
  San Carlos (4,000)
  White Mountain (4,000)
  Jicarilla (2,000)
  Mescalero (2,000)
	Athabascan	*Indeh, Tindeh*	The People

CHEMEHUEVI (700)	Shoshonean	*Nü Wü*	The People
COCOPA (600)	Yuman	*Kwi-ka-pa*	(Unknown)
HAVASUPAI (350)	Yuman	*Havasuwaipaa*	Blue-Green Water People
HUALAPAI (750)	Yuman	*Hah-wah-lah-pai-yah*	Pine Tree Folk
MARICOPA (250)	Yuman	*Pipa, Pipatse*	Men or People
MOHAVE (2,000)	Yuman	*Aha-makave*	Beside the Water
NAVAJO (90,000)	Athabascan	*Dineh, Diné*	The People
PAIUTE (150)	Shoshonean	*Paiute*	True Ute (?)
PAPAGO (12,000)	Piman	*Toho'no-o-otam*	Bean People
PIMA (8,000)	Piman	*Ah-kee-mult-o-otam*	River People
UTE (3,000)	Shoshonean	*Nunt'z*	The People
YAQUI (3,000)	Piman	*Yaqui*	(Unknown)
YAVAPAI (350)	Yuman	*En-ya-va-pai-yah* *Yawape*	People of the Sun Crooked-Mouth People
YUMA (2,500)	Yuman	*Quechan*	Following-the-Sacred-Trail

FIGURE 12. Modern tribes of the Southwest.

refuges, behind the stockades of the Spaniards, they gradually lost their identity through intermarriage and urbanization, and dropped out of history.

While the Apache band entrenched in the Sierra Blanca terrorized the pueblos and settlements east of the Rio Grande, the Apache in the Gila Wilderness did the same west of the river. The chief recipients of Apache attentions in the west were the Pima and Papago, descendants of the great Hohokam, who together made up the Piman branch of what are now called the *Desert rancheria* (i.e. desert farming) tribes. The Pima and Papago were peaceable folk, the folk of the Casa Grande, of San Xavier del Bac, and of the old Pimería Alta. Not surprisingly, they conceived a profound hatred for the Apache, and were to be instrumental in helping the white man in tracking him down.

Today the Pima, whose own name for themselves means "river people," occupy the Salt River and the Gila River reservations, both close to Phoenix. Eight thousand strong, they live side by side with some few hundred members of the Maricopa tribe, who two hundred years ago split away from the Yuma in order to join the Pima. Together, Pima and Maricopa irrigate and plow desert lands which, though unpromising, have been made to yield a fine cotton which bears the Piman name. They are industrious, inventive people, and although they are not rich their largely infertile reservations contain valuable sands and gravels. Their nearness to ever-growing Phoenix also suggests that, if they can avoid being cheated—a big *if*—there is an excellent opportunity for leasing land to the white man.

The Papago, to the south, have not been so fortunate. There are 12,000 of them, distributed among five reservations, the majority on the vast 2,750,000 acre Papago reservation, second largest in the United States. Most of the acreage on this and the other Papago reservations is dry and dusty, good for little except growing saguaros and Judas trees. The Papago, whose name in Piman means "bean people," have actually given up cultivating beans and the other vegetable items in the old Hohokam repertoire and are attempting to convert to cattle raising. Most of them, however, are forced to leave the reservation to find work in nearby towns. They have succeeded, however, in retaining many of the skills of their forefathers. The basket-wares of the Papago, and only to a slightly lesser extent the Pima, are in the forefront of American Indian manufactures, and are sought after wherever superb craftsmanship is appreciated. They are not only aesthetically satisfying, but functional, and two of them, made of yucca and devil's claw sewn over a clump of bear grass, have done duty in my household for five years and will continue to do so for fifty more.

Pima and Papago, I have found, are very warm, relaxed, easygoing people—although when need arises they make first-class fighters. It was a Papago who helped to raise the flag on Iwo Jima (and subsequently became an alcoholic because of all the free drinks that were pressed on him). At Pima and Papago festivities, you will always see a number of trim, broad-shouldered youngsters in Marine uniform. In the Rio Grande pueblos, the outsider has to tread carefully. You are subjected to wary, suspicious, even hostile glances; you leave your car at a tactful distance; you enter with an expression of consideration and decent respect; you do not go trampling and trumpeting around. Even so, with my incurable itch for poking about, I have encountered an occasional reproof or rebuff. In Pima-Papago country, on the other hand, the atmosphere is serene and good-natured, and the people are possessed of unusual gentleness and charm.

The other branch of the Desert Rancheria are the Yuma. These are in the farthest fringe of the Southwest, on the Colorado River and its delta. Except for one tribe, the Chemehuevi, who have Uto-Aztecan affinities, they all belong to the Hokan group. The Chemehuevi are a tiny but remarkable people. They have given up the tribal and religious ceremonies they practiced when they roamed the barren eastern half of the Mohave desert, and for the

Miss Papago, 1973. She later became Miss Indian Arizona and Miss Indian America.

last century have thrown in their lot with the neighboring Mohave tribe, with whom they live and work in amity. The Mohave are now the most numerous of the Colorado River tribes, though they are split into two reservations, spaced widely apart. Fifteen hundred of them share the Colorado River reservation with the Chemehuevi, and a further three hundred share the Fort McDowell reservation with, of all unlikely people, a band of Apache. The Mohave were in early times a virile, independent, athletic people, inhabiting a spectacular stretch of the Colorado from the Black Canyon, where the Hoover Dam now stands, to a breathtaking outcrop known as "Needles," from which they took their name of *Hamakhava* or "Three Mountains." Indifferent farmers, they were clever traders, middlemen in exchanging the goods of the peoples of the Rio Grande, the Salt and the Gila with the peoples of the Pacific Coast and the Gulf of California. They were also first-class warriors, and between 1840 and 1870 fought hard to keep the white man out of the bottom lands of the Colorado. Today, reduced to about 1,800, they remain a capable and constructive people, making money from tourism, hunting, and fishing. They have taken to agriculture, and have proved exceptionally skillful with machinery. But they cling jealously to their old traditions. The status of the medicine-man is high among them, and they are said to practice interesting secret ceremonies devoted to the acquisition of power by dreams.

The Yuma themselves, who give their name to the second branch of the Desert Ranchería, live almost exclusively on the west or California side of the Colorado. They acted as buffers between the Mohave and the Cocopa, who were traditional enemies. Like the Mohave, they struggled valiantly against the white invasion of their homelands, and after their defeat were confined on a reservation consisting almost entirely of naked desert. They were traders like the Mohave, but better farmers—yet all their bravery and vigor could not preserve them from the Anglo, and their numbers have shrunk to a mere 2,500.

In former times, a small Yuman tribe called the Kamia inhabited the Imperial Valley of California and the shores of the Salton Sea. They were notorious because, in the words of one authority, "they were undoubtedly the dirtiest and most degraded tribe in the Southwest. The people of the main river tribes bathed and soaped themselves regularly throughout the year, but to overcome vermin the Kamia coated their hair with mud. On hot days they weltered in mudholes like pigs. They sold their children. As there were few animals in their tortured land, they subsisted on fish, seeds, and roots. Many were dreadfully scorbutic." These poor wretches were fortunate to have become extinct a century ago.

The Cocopa were 10,000 strong in Spanish times, when they seem to have joined forces with two larger tribes called the Halyikwamai (or Quigyuma) and the Halchidhoma. There are only 1,200 of them today, and they are the most southerly of the Yuman peoples, occupying the delta of the Colorado. Half the tribe lives in the United States, half in Mexico. They too were traders, and were slightly less aggressive than their neighbors to the north. Today they farm and grow cotton. They should not be confused with the Maricopa, who, though of the same stock, live as we have seen with the Pima of Arizona on the Gila and Salt rivers far to the west. Once a Colorado River tribe, the Maricopa fought continuous bloody wars with the Yuma. In 1857, assisted by their allies the Pima, they killed 90 out of 93 Yuma who attacked them, then prudently decided to retire with the Pima to more sheltered surroundings.

The militaristic proficiency and outlook of the Yuman branch of the Desert Ranchería was not at all characteristic of the four remaining sedentary tribes of the Southwest. The Havasupai, Hualapai, Yavapai, and Paiute live to the north of the Colorado River tribes, in the mountainous uplands of northwestern Arizona. Inaccessibility has provided them with a refuge. They have been given the collective name of the *Plateau ranchería*. All are tiny, the largest tribe, the Hualapai, having 750 members, and the smallest, the Paiute, numbering a mere 150. They belong, like the Colorado River tribes, to the Yuman stock.

The Hualapai, or Walapai, the "pine tree folk," were the northern neighbors of the Mohave. They lived by hunting and food gathering, and their fate when the Anglo arrived is typical of many small agglomerations of Indians. At first, relations with the white man were friendly, until the time came when the latter felt strong enough to seize their springs and waterholes. When they tried to resist, they were rounded up and taken to one of the hottest parts of the Mohave desert. Eventually the few survivors were permitted to crawl back home, where they were given government rations. "In 1883," writes Tom Bahti in his *Southwestern Indian Tribes,* "a reservation was set aside for them in their native country, made up of those areas which the Anglos found unsuited to their own needs." He continues: "Because the Hualapai were not warlike and therefore not dangerous, the Anglos regarded them merely as an intolerable nuisance; one newspaper, the *Mohave County Miner,* in 1887 suggested editorially that rations for the Indians be mixed with 'a plentiful supply of arsenic' to solve the problem."

Stemming from the Hualapai, the Yavapai, or "people of the sun," have dwindled from about 1,500 to a present 750. Once they hunted the area between the Colorado and the Gila. Quarrelling with the Hualapai, they formed close relations with the Tonto band of the Western Apache; and when General Crook subdued the Apache, in 1872, he rounded up the Yavapai and herded them on to the new Apache reservation at San Carlos, far from their homeland. After twenty-five years they were permitted to return, to find that their land had been appropriated by the Anglo cattlemen and farmers. Today, they scratch a poor living as dirt farmers or as hired hands on white ranches.

The other branch of the Hualapai, the Havasupai, the "blue-green water people," hit on a unique way of avoiding conflict. Nine hundred years ago they separated from the main body of the Hualapai and retreated to the bottom of the Grand Canyon. There, 3,000 feet below the canyon rim, they lived during the summer on a quarter-mile strip of soil irrigated by the water of Cataract Creek, with the lovely cascade that gave them their name. During spring, they cultivated their diminutive gardens, cautiously emerging in the summer months to hunt game on the plateau. If threatened, they could speedily retire to their private labyrinth: and the proof of their success is that their numbers appear to have remained constant at a modest 250 to 300 for almost 1,000 years. They were not completely isolated, for they maintained friendly contact with the Hopi, another peaceful people. The Hopi became their intermediaries for bartering such commodities as salt and skins, and also a fine red ochre of which there was a hidden supply in the recesses of the Canyon, and which was eagerly sought for body-painting all over the Southwest. Padre Francisco Garcés visited the tribe in 1776, but it was too remote for missionizing. Even the Bureau of Indian Affairs, in its early, hectoring phase, was unable to do more than interfere with a number of Havasupai ceremonials of which it disapproved. Moreover, the eight-mile trek to the canyon bottom effectively discouraged the Anglo settlers—although the Havasupai were very careful, nonetheless, when their reservation was established in 1882, not to claim any land which they thought might turn the eyes of the Anglos in their direction. Today, with the advent of tourism, they cannot enjoy their former privacy, but they make a nice profit acting as guides to the Canyon. They run a store at the bottom, which properly charges Anglo visitors outrageous prices.

Unfortunately, it seems impossible to escape progress, even at the bottom of the Grand Canyon. The United States Air Force likes to fly helicopters down there on philanthropic missions; and no doubt in a few years the Tarahumare Indians of northwest Mexico, who inhabit the paradisal depths of the Barranca del Cobre, which is almost as vast as the Grand Canyon itself, will be subjected to similar invasions. There seems to be nowhere, now, that a primitive people can remain undisturbed—neither in Brazil, nor Botswana, nor New Guinea. If the lamasaries of Tibet, where the priests did nothing more harmful than turn prayer wheels, eat yak butter, and drink brickdust tea, could be defiled and comminuted, what hope is there for lesser peoples?

The smallest of the small tribes of the Plateau Ranchería, the Paiute, are really the Kaibab band of the Southern Paiute of Nevada. The Paiutes are the "Digger Indians" or "Digueños," whose name crops up in the annals of the Southwest as a people almost as deprived as the mud-smeared Kamia. They were too busy scavenging for the roots, insects, and reptiles that kept them alive to devise any ceremonies or rituals.

Of unusual interest, in concluding this brief survey of the sedentary tribes, is the last we shall mention, and the last to arrive in the Southwest. These are the Yaqui, who live in seven small villages on the outskirts of Phoenix and Tucson. They number 3,000, which puts them among the larger Indian groups of the area; but the circumstances of their arrival in the United States technically disqualifies them for recognition and assistance from the Bureau of Indian Affairs. The official Bureau guide to the Indians of Arizona does not mention them, and most of them are not American citizens. They are a very individual people, with a striking history. When the Spaniards originally encountered them, on the Yaqui River in Sonora, they numbered 30,000, and fiercely resisted all attempts at conquest. In 1610, they signed a peace treaty with the Spaniards, and asked that Jesuit missionaries be sent to them. They flourished under Jesuit tutelage, observed the Catholic calendar, and elaborated a repertoire of curious rituals presided over by their own priests, called *maestros*. The rituals were conducted in a mixture of Spanish, Latin, and Yaqui, which was a derivation of Piman. After the departure of the Spaniards, they continued these rituals independently of the Church, with which they maintain only tenuous relations. When Mexico became independent, in 1820, they were taxed for the first time, and were not impressed by this introduction to the blessings of civilization. They embarked on a series of bloody and unrelenting revolts. However, they found that the new masters of Mexico were even worse men to cross than the departed Spaniards. Their numbers dwindled; they fought on. Eventually, after a culminating battle, they were driven into camps, and the President of Mexico, Corral, sold them as slaves to the hemp planters of Yucatán, fifteen hundred miles away, for seventy-five cents a head. Some of them managed to flee to the United States, but the Yaqui nation was effectually shattered. And yet, against all the odds, something of their essential identity has been preserved. Their colorful and peculiar ceremonials are still being carried out. The Yaqui are outstanding dancers, and the male performers of the Matachín society, dedicated to the Virgin Mary, and calling themselves her "soldiers," possess an extensive repertoire. (The Pueblo Indians too have dances which they call *Matachines,* danced with knives or swords. The name is intriguing, as it is that of a sixteenth century dance which Peter Warlock used as the finale to his *Capriol Suite.* Danced originally in Europe by men dressed in suits of gilded cardboard, it was one of the dances the Spaniards brought to the New World, where it became embedded in Indian religion. Today, by another friendly syncretism, one can often see the figure of Cortés treading a merry measure during the pueblo festivals with Jesus and the Virgin Mary.)

One of the most striking Yaqui dances is the Deer Dance, recently made famous by the Ballet Folklórico of Mexico. In this, a solo male dancer, with a set of antlers bound to his forehead, enacts the tracking down and killing of a stag. The only music is the rustle of the gourds shaken by the bare-chested dancer, who manifests an uncanny identity with the stricken beast. The horns swing this way and that; the flanks quiver as the thrusts go home; we can see the pain and incomprehension as death takes hold, the clouding of the eyes, the last protesting twitch of the limbs, the final resignation. It is not only a threnody for a splendid animal: it is the death agony of the American Indian.

In *Crotchet Castle,* by T. L. Peacock, one of my favorite novelists, the mournful political economist, Mr. MacQuedy, declares that "Laughter is an involuntary action of certain muscles, developed in the human species by the progress of civilization. The savage never laughs." To which the robustly humorous Dr. Folliott responds: "No, sir, he has nothing to laugh at"; adding that if the savage were only exposed to the spectacle of progressive politics, it would certainly "develop his muscles."

The North American Indian, indeed, both before and after the advent of the European, has seldom had much to laugh at. Portraits of Indian leaders by George Catlin, Charles Bodmer, John Mix Stanley, and other painters, or by early photographers, seldom show them smiling. Sometimes the gravity of those sad, square, mahogany faces is due to the weight of the office, or to *machismo;* but more often it is the result of hardship and suffering. They stare at the lens with a devastatingly open and direct gaze, dignified and hauntingly tragic, men who have looked on much pain, violence, deprivation, and death.

In most synoptic accounts of the Southwest, the nomadic Indian, whom this chapter chiefly concerns, tends to be treated in a somewhat peripheral way. He left no imposing monuments behind; his settlements and burial-grounds were inconspicuous; his patches of cultivation almost nonexistent. His remains do not form tourist attractions, and today he lives mainly in the kinship-tables of anthropologists, or in occasional intertribal junketings. There he wears his paint-and-feathers self-consciously, executing dances whose original fervor and meaning have largely been lost. He is in the grip of a cultural crisis far more acute than that of the sedentary Indian whom he once despised, terrorized, and treated as a beast of burden. Yet once, between the end of the regime of the Hispano and the beginning of that of the Anglo, the nomadic Indian was supreme in the Southwest. It would hardly be too much to claim that the Spaniards, Pueblo Indians, and the Indians of the Pimería Alta existed by sufferance of the surrounding nomads, who required the fruits of their labors.

On the other hand, if the predatory Indian bequeathed posterity nothing more substantial than beads, bows and arrows, and flamboyant headdresses, if he lacked an architectural instinct, this should not be taken as a sign of an impoverished imagination. The notion of architecture, for example, was totally foreign to the nomadic Indian. He had no intention of scarring and marring the landscape with ephemeral and presumptuous rubbish: his respect for it was too strong. He went whispering through the countryside, hardly raising the dust or disturbing a leaf. He obliterated his campfires and eliminated the signs of his passing. He existed inside the scheme of things like a fine animal, enjoying the seasons or enduring them, but never divorced from them.

Until a century ago he was still the chief owner and occupant, if no longer the absolute master, of the United States. Of the names of the fifty states, twenty-five are derived from American Indian words, while the names of Alaska and Hawaii are also taken from the languages of their original inhabitants. As a matter of interest, the English gave names to thirteen states, the Spaniards to four, and the French to three; Vermont, Nevada, and Montana, though French or Spanish-sounding, were nineteenth century coinages; and the only state named after a white American is Washington. In the Southwest, New Mexico and Colorado (the Spanish word for "red") owe their names to the Spaniards; Arizona is said to be a Spanish version of a Pima word meaning "little spring place"; Oklahoma is a Choctaw word for "red man"; Utah is a Navajo word meaning "higher up," referring to the Utes who occupied the lands to the north; and Texas is supposed to be a word used by the Caddo Indians to designate friends or allies.

At the time when Columbus landed, the Indians were spread out across the continent in more than fifty families. There are several alternative methods of arranging these families into major groups, and of these the method proposed by the great linguist Edward Sapir in 1929 is still one of the more acceptable. He divided the Indian population into six main divisions: the Eskimo-Aleut; the Algonkin-Wakushan; the Hokan-Siouan; the Penutian; the Aztec-Tanoan; and the Nadene. Two of the six, the Aztec-Tanoan and the Nadene, figure in the history of the Southwest.

The Aztec-Tanoan comprises five subfamilies. Of these, the Tanoan fam-

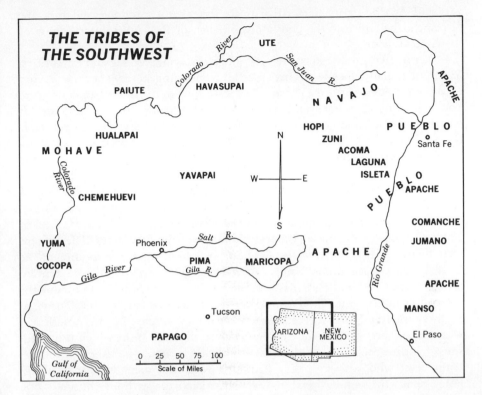

THE TRIBES OF
THE SOUTHWEST

UTE

Colorado River

San Juan R.

PAIUTE

HAVASUPAI

NAVAJO

APACHE

HUALAPAI

MOHAVE

Colorado River

CHEMEHUEVI

YAVAPAI

HOPI
ZUNI
ACOMA
LAGUNA
ISLETA

PUEBLO
o
Santa Fe

PUEBLO
APACHE

N

W——E

S

COMANCHE

YUMA

Phoenix
o

Salt R.

APACHE

JUMANO

COCOPA

Gila River

PIMA
Gila R.

MARICOPA

Rio Grande

APACHE

o Tucson

PAPAGO

ARIZONA

NEW
MEXICO

MANSO

El Paso
o

Gulf of
California

0   25   50   75   100

Scale of Miles

FIGURE II

ily includes all the Pueblo Indians of New Mexico, with the exception of the
outlying pueblos of the Zuni and of the Hopi. The status of Zuni and Hopi is
debated, the former having Penutian and the latter Shoshonean affinities. It
seems clear, however, that the Hopi belong with the Uto-Aztecan branch of
the Aztec-Tanoans, along with the Pima, Papago, and the related tribes of the
Colorado River and Colorado basin. The Aztec-Tanoans are distributed over
an area no less than two thousand miles deep, ranging from the territory of
the Kiowa in the north, in the Rocky Mountains, to two substantial groups in
Mexico in the south. The Mexican groups are the Aztecan, comprising the
Aztecs themselves, with the Yaqui and Opata, and the far-distant Mayas in
Yucatán and Guatemala. The Aztec-Tanoans are thus an immense related
community—and yet the other stock, the Nadene, is, if anything, larger still,
for it encompasses tribes from Arizona, New Mexico, and Oklahoma to as far
north as Alaska. In particular, it embraces the gigantic family of the Athabas-
cans, more than fifty tribes, scattered from Canada to the Southwest. The Na-

vajo and Apache nations are Athabascan, though their fellow predators, the Comanche, belonged to the Shoshonean branch of the Uto-Aztecan family of the Aztec-Tanoans.

Terms like group, stock, family, and nation suggest substantial entities. Yet most Indian tribes were in fact small, containing perhaps as few as 300 or at most 3,000 members. These tribes were split in turn into bands of 50 to 100, consisting of women and children looked after by 10 or 12 hunters. It was the dispersed and fragmented manner in which they lived that later made them so vulnerable to the Anglo; there were more than 500 tribes, speaking more than 300 different languages or dialects. Nor was the aggregate number of Indians as large as might be supposed. It has been estimated that the Indian population of the North American continent at the time of the landing of Columbus was not higher than two million and perhaps as low as one million. That is no more than the population of modern Arizona, or New Mexico, or Colorado, which rank among the least populous of the fifty states. The Indians were therefore distributed in the thinnest possible manner, the interior of the United States being almost empty. At least two-thirds of them were concentrated on the West and East coasts, leaving only a token number to occupy the vast spaces in between. The Pacific seaboard, as we saw, had been the original highway used by Stone Age huntsmen when they entered North America; it was thus the first area of Indian colonization, the area from which the diffusion of Indian peoples took place. Eventually there would be tribes on the Atlantic coast who, although they had long forgotten their western starting-point, spoke the same Algonkin-Wakushan language as their cousins 5,000 miles away. These coastal Indians differed from the popular stereotype of the Indian, in that they subsisted as fishermen as well as huntsmen; indeed, many were accomplished seamen, exploring the creeks, inlets and fishing grounds of the two great oceans in a variety of craft. Away from the saltwater and Canadian lakes, there was only one single large accumulation of Indians within the interior of the United States: and that was in the Southwest—so we can see, once more, how this part of America has been continuously and variously occupied for many thousands of years, since the far-off days of the Sandia, Folsom, and Clovis hunters. This is not long, of course, in terms of Grand Canyon time—but it is surely long enough on our puny human scale.

The culture of the Indian, in which every tribe was split into individual moieties, phratries, and clans, was highly diversified. It remains so today. Over one hundred distinct Indian languages still exist, and tribal fragmentation is a continuing source of weakness in the battle against the Anglo. However, to Europeans, and to many Americans, the "classic" Indian, the only real Indian, was not the sedentary Indian who comprised the vast majority of the Indian population: he was the Indian of the Plains, the Horse Indian. The

Horse Indian is the Indian of romance, of the movies, the Indian of "Cowboys and Indians."

Such has been its grip on the imagination of the world, through the medium of books, the cinema, television, and the pulp magazines, that the cult of the cowboy and the Indian has flourished for almost two centuries. In actual fact, their apogee in real life lasted barely a quarter of that time. What is the secret of their extraordinary appeal? Of course, they persist because they are folklore, representatives of the American heroic period; but that does not explain their fascination for millions of non-Americans, all over the world. Could it be that, in some deeper sense, they stand in some way for the promptings of the Id? Do they represent early, basic, unregenerate man, unreconciled to the slavery and indignity of society?

As we know, Freud considered that, in order to become "civilized," men had to be compelled to give up most of their primitive pleasures and simple aggressions. He went so far as to say that civilization emasculated men. Men recognized this; they resented the loss and the humiliation; at intervals they resorted to warfare in order to reassert themselves. Cowboys and Indians, then, may stand for *das Elementare*—men as they feel they once were, and as they ought to be again: vigorous, proud, unfettered, unencumbered by petty responsibilities, unburdened by possessions, beholden to no one, free to hunt, to fight, to ride across the limitless plains, to sleep beneath the stars.

In the dream world of the cinema, the cowboy and the red man often engage in conflict; but their struggle is often more in the nature of a joyous, childish scrimmage than a deadly antagonism. They are really on the same side. At the end of the story, there is usually a reconciliation, a recognition of their kinship. Neither of them like the soldiers, the settlers, the ranchers, the bankers, the railwaymen, or the other agents of civilization and centralization; usually they collaborate against them. The cowboy, like the scout and the mountainman, is always uneasy when he is required to assist the government or the Army against the Indian. Both are rebels and pariahs. Both are tragic figures. Like the Indian, the cowboy too will be defeated in the end by the forces of money and social compulsion, the victim of his own ingenuous and uncomplicated code of trust, loyalty, and good faith.

Is it possible that the spectator of the Western movie may sense a similarity between the fate of the cowboy and the Indian and what Freud suggested might be the fate of the Id itself? Freud thought that, if humanity managed to avoid destroying itself (he was not optimistic), then during the course of evolution it might be the destiny of the Ego to learn how to bring the Id under control. He employed the arresting simile of the Zuider Zee. "God made the world," say the Dutch, "but the Dutch made Holland." During the course of three centuries, the Dutch have pumped out the dark, salt waters of the North Sea, replacing them with clear, fresh water. Freud considered that in some such way the Ego might eventually push back the frontiers of the Id; eventually all will become consciousness and clarity. I am sure that, pessimist as he was, he recognized the danger that, if that stage is reached, the waters of consciousness might run clear enough, but might also be overchlorinated—sanitized, denatured, and unpalatable. And if that should come to pass, men may very well look back to the sweaty, disorderly, high-spirited world of the cowboy and the Indian with even more nostalgia than they do today.

After the climate-crash, the pestilence, or whatever it was that had brought them from their cliff cities to the banks of the Rio Grande, the newly established Pueblo Indians appear to have enjoyed three centuries of peace. This tranquil interlude ended when the Navajo started trickling down from their Athabascan homeland, somewhere in the distant Pacific northwest. Known at that time, as we saw, as the Apaches de Navajo, they spent some decades observing and attempting to copy the more sophisticated life of the Pueblos. They did not take over the abandoned cliff cities in the area they now occupied, because though the Navajo fear few things living, they have an in-tense terror of the dead. They continued to dwell in their traditional earth hogan, with its buttresses of three forked logs. They took to cultivating the land, they traded for sheep, and eventually, after Spanish rule had been es-tablished on the Rio Grande for half a century, they could no longer resist the temptation to steal from their southern neighbors. The cattle and sheep, and the novelties the Spaniards had brought with them from the New World, drew them like magnets. More than domestic animals, they became covetous of the remudas of horses, as did the Apache. The latter, slightly later arrivals than the Navajo, also moved into the Southwest from the region of the Rocky Mountains, motivated in their turn by pressures from the Pawnee, Ute, and Comanche. The Utes would always remain in the rear of the Navajo, harassing them as they in turn harassed the Pueblos; and the Comanche were to exert similar pressure on the Apache. However, it ought to be noted that the Navajo were not, like the Apache and Comanche, strictly speaking warriors, but rather raiders. They did not indulge in warfare for its own sweet sake, as a way of life, but sporadically, to obtain goods and animals.

Once it dawned on them that it was more sensible to ride horses than eat them, the Navajo, Apache, and Comanche took to them with the fanatical en-thusiasm of all the other Indians of the Great Plains. The sedentary Indians too, of course, also came to prize horses, but without making them, as the Plains Indians did, the peak and pivot of their existence. The latter, until then, had been scratching along in a rather undistinguished way, and the horse came to them not only as an inspiration and revelation, but as a miraculous release. Clark Wissler, in his *Indians of the United States,* writes that "the changes in Indian life brought about by this new mode of travel were even greater than those produced by the automobile in our time," and he points out that its importance lay not so much in the sphere of fighting as in that of mobility. It enabled the Plains Indian to transport his family, tents and belongings wherever he wished, and gave him "a broader outlook, new experiences, more leisure, and inhibited sedentary occupations. Many Indians of the grassland quit raising small patches of maize, squashes and beans, and increased their ranges to 500 miles and more a season." The horse-frenzy came naturally to the Indians of the prairies and the grasslands; while it became only a minor adjunct to the lives of the farmers, fishermen or forest dwellers of the east and west coasts, where the terrain was not so ideal for raising and running stock.

A frenzy it was. In the 1640s and 1650s, the Plains Indians possessed few mounts; by the 1660s and 1670s, they were acquiring them in ominous numbers; and in 1680 they enjoyed a bonus—they acquired the herds of horses that the Spanish settlers had left behind when the Pueblo Revolt drove them south to El Paso. Dipping steadily into the reservoir of Spanish mounts in New Mexico, Texas, and Louisiana, trading or stealing among themselves, by 1800 the Plains Indians of the Southwest were entirely horsed. In the inner ring were the Navajo, the Apache, the Comanche, the Ute; in the second, the Osage, the Kiowa, the Cheyenne, and the Arapaho. Beyond them lay the Pawnee, the Crow, the Shoshone, and the tribes of the great Sioux nation, including the Dakota, Mandan, Hidatsa, and Crow. And farther still, in the distant north, were the tribes of Canada and the Canadian border, the Cree, Blackfoot, Ojibway, and those splendid horsemen, the Nez Percé, with their Apaloosas. To the westward lay the tribes of Alabama, Mississippi, and Georgia—Cherokee, Creek, Choctaw, and Chickasaw—who possessed stock of French ancestry; and of course, the English settlers had contributed their share. But it seems fair to say that it was the Spaniards of New Mexico who had provided the bulk of the seed.

Within a few decades, each tribe possessed thousands of horses. There were no problems in grazing them during the long months of summer, and in winter they were allowed to forage, nibbling the bark of certain trees, especially the birch. Most warriors possessed not one but many horses, sometimes as many as twenty or thirty—nor was riding confined to men. Everyone rode, the women and children with as much dash as their husbands, brothers, or fathers. The cream of the remudas, of course, were the war-horses, treated as members of the family, sometimes even as gods, and spared workaday service. Favorite horses were painted, festooned with bells, their manes and tails plaited with ribbons, their skin rubbed with aromatic herbs. In rough country their legs were carefully bandaged, their hoofs protected by soft leather moccasins. They were trained to perform incredible evolutions, to stop, turn, and wheel like lightning. Various techniques were used to make them run faster, such as slitting their nostrils to admit more air to the lungs. The standard of horsemanship has never been surpassed. Warriors would hang with one leg

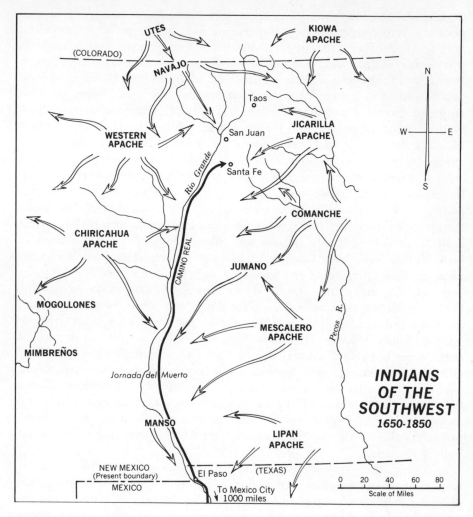

FIGURE 13

hooked over the horse's back, shooting arrows or firing beneath the horse's neck; they would dangle on the horse's blind side, to protect themselves when retreating; they could twist round and use their weapons on an enemy or a buffalo from a side-saddle position, or turn completely about; they could load muskets and muzzle-loaders—powder, ball, and wadding—while charging flat out, and pick up a wounded man at a dead run. W. H. Hudson, discussing the differences between the gaucho and Plains Indian in *The Naturalist in La Plata*, wrote that the American Indian "can die on his horse. During frontier warfare one hears at times of a dead warrior being found and removed with difficulty from the horse that carried him out of the fight, and about whose neck his rigid fingers were clasped in death." Sublime and enviable end.

It was little wonder that the Spaniards and their successors in the Southwest were so badly tormented. The Comanche, for example, were rated even in the opinion of their fellow Indians as the most skillful horsemen in the Americas. From the time of the Pueblo Revolt, it became a ceaseless, grinding struggle for the Spaniards to try and keep the Plains Indians in check. The Pueblo Indians were forced off their outlying fields and upland pastures; the number of pueblos shrank from sixty-six to nineteen. The Spanish settlements were similarly punished, and the Spanish garrisons in the presidios were forced back into a narrow perimeter which they could scarcely hold, and which provided meager grazing for the horses on which they relied to chase their tormentors away. The Indians grew increasingly insolent. They would ride up to the pueblos or Spanish settlements in war bands several hundreds or thousands strong. They would call for the cacique or alcalde, and demand a *regalo,* a present. Needless to say, in the feeble state of the province, struggling to recuperate from rebellion and civil war, they got it, in the hope that they would stay away for another six months or a year. If they were snubbed, they would not be content with routine thieving, but would overrun whole villages, killing and carrying off the women and children. Once they seized fifty women and children from Taos, none of whom were ever seen again. The "gifts" they preferred included guns, axes, knives, scissors, mirrors, combs, copper kettles, ornamental bells, beads, and copper wire. Sometimes they would deign to trade for these objects, coming into the main fairs and markets; there they would bring the loot they had stolen or exacted from villages elsewhere, and also supplies of a commodity which the settlers and sedentary Indians prized highly, jerked buffalo meat.

It may seem strange that the Indians were given guns by the Europeans, but in fact it became official policy to do so. The Indians got guns, in any case, either by threats or by taking them off the dead bodies of their victims. The authorities therefore reasoned in exactly the same way that the American and European governments now reason with regard to selling arms to Middle Easterners or South Americans: the latter are bound to get them from somewhere, so you may as well sell them yourself, take your profit in cash and goodwill, and bind them to you by controlling the rate of supply and the sale of spares. This is what happened when the Spaniards, French, and English sold weapons to the warrior tribes. Where they could, they made sure that the guns were of poor quality, or even useless, since in many cases the Indians wanted guns not to shoot but simply as status symbols. Moreover, the Indians were incapable of manufacturing gunpowder, and were thus entirely dependent on the colonists for their supply. Nor were they able to repair their guns themselves, lacking tools and mechanical training, and had to bring them into the settlements in case of failure. Tales are told of baffled Indians thwacking their guns against trees and boulders, like angry golfers smashing their clubs. Finally, few Indians, unlike the white pioneers, who handled guns from the cradle, became expert shots. They had no tradition or training, and even if they had good weapons they could seldom spare enough of their precious powder and shot to practice. In the east, where the Indians of the woodlands were in contact with the English and French, from whom they obtained superior weapons, the picture was different. By 1800 the Iroquois and the Algonkin had become good marksmen, and in the War of 1812 were using better weapons than the soldiers on both sides. But Spanish guns, with few exceptions, were poorly made, and until the Civil War brought sound weapons into their hands, it was not as musketeers and riflemen that the Indians of the Southwest posed their most serious menace.

But even with indifferent firearms, armed only with the lance and the bow and arrow, they could wreak fearful havoc. In 1748 the Spaniards were compelled, shorthanded and starved for supplies as they were, to discontinue the policy of bribes and hollow "peace treaties," and to launch as large an offensive as their resources allowed. The Indian attacks were undermining the hold of Spain on the whole of the territory north of the Rio Grande, territory which might yet prove a priceless part of those overseas assets that Spain, even in decline, was determined to keep intact. Her pride had been hurt enough in her defeats at the hands of her civilized enemies, England and France; she was not, even in her travail and weakness, going to knuckle under to a mob of savages. Yet the campaign did not go well. In its first twenty years, it was the Indians who had the upper hand, killing an estimated 6,000 persons, kidnapping more, and doing twelve million pesos worth of damage.

Yet Spain persisted. The Marqués de Rubí was sent to New Mexico to inspect and strengthen the garrisons and presidios, build new ones, and make sure that the main towns of Santa Fe and El Paso, which now had 5,000 inhabitants, were secure. In 1772, when Don Hugo O'Conor became Inspector Commandant at Chihuahua, he set about punishing the Apache, who were now unrestrainedly terrorizing all the frontier provinces. Chasing mounted Indians was an exhausting business, as O'Conor found out; but he persevered, and had some success. He killed 150 Apache, cornered and captured 150 more, and recovered 2,000 sheep and cattle. Near El Paso, assisted by the Comanche, the captain in charge of the El Paso garrison trapped an Apache force in the nearby Guadalupe Mountains and slaughtered several hundred of them. Nevertheless, the Apache counterattacks were devastating. Between 1771 and 1776, in the province of Nueva Bizcaya alone, they killed nearly 8,000 people, stole over 68,000 cattle, and caused over 100 ranches and settlements to be abandoned.

O'Conor retired to New Spain, worn out. He was succeeded as Commandant at Chihuahua by the Chevalier or Caballero de Croix, who immediately called the governors of New Mexico, Nueva Bizcaya, and Coahuila into conference. Impressive results flowed from the concerted operations that followed. De Croix cajoled the Viceroy in Mexico City, at that time enjoying a relatively untroubled existence, into sending him reinforcements, and seven years of continuous warfare took place. Thanks in most part to the efforts of the Governor of New Mexico, that same de Anza who had just returned from his heroic journeys to California, the Lipan, Mescalero, and Jicarilla Apache of the east bank of the Rio Grande (see Figure 13) were almost entirely subdued, and on the west bank the Chiricahua Apache and the other Apache of the Gila Wilderness were taught a sharp lesson. If larger political events in the world beyond had not interposed, forcing him to go on the defensive, de Croix might have achieved a striking victory. As it was, his work brought about a period of uneasy peace, broken only by the inevitable raids, that lasted the remaining thirty years of the Spanish epoch. In the late 1780s, the general truce established by de Croix was bolstered by the policies of one of New Spain's last and cleverest administrators, Bernardo de Gálvez. Gálvez, without relaxing military alertness, initiated another activity which, while it was neither elevated nor glorious, was equally effective—supplying the hostile Indians with practically unlimited drink. The wines and *aguardiente* of El Paso were already famous, and the tequilas and pulques of New Spain were even more corrosive. The horse Indians, with their fierce, Faustian view of the world, took to liquor with a hectic enthusiasm: and for the time being, it kept them happy. The Hispanic era in the Southwest drew to a close in an atmosphere of tranquillity and prosperity. With the collapse of law and order, after Spain's departure, this comfortable state of affairs would, of course, vanish.

EIGHT

"WHEN THERE WERE NO HORSES, THERE WERE NO NAVAJO." Like other peoples, including most of those who regard themselves as advanced, the Navajo had no idea where they originally came from; they only knew that life without horses was inconceivable.

> My horse has a hoof like striped agate;
> His fetlock is like a fine eagle-plume;
> His legs are like quick lightning.
> My horse's body is like an eagle-plumed arrow;
> My horse has a tail like a trailing black cloud.

Nevertheless, their early journey from their Athabascan homeland in the Northwest had been done on foot, and must have taken many centuries. Certain of their techniques of weaving, a skill they do not appear to have learned in toto from their Pueblo mentors, have been compared to techniques practiced by the tribes of the Puget Sound. Also of Athabascan origin may be such customs as shunning the dead, and the quaint taboo against looking directly at one's mother-in-law.

Excavation of several sites suggests that ancestors of the Navajo and Apache were already encamped in western and central Colorado by A.D. 1000, and were thus in touch with the Anasazi as the latter were entering their Great Pueblo Period. By the time that Coronado reached New Spain, the Navajo had already shifted their ground slightly—slightly, that is, as distance in America goes—from the Colorado highlands to those areas of northern New Mexico and northern Arizona that they occupy today; thus they have lived on the territories now allotted to them as reservations for five hundred years. Incidentally, the first Europeans who encountered the Navajo were convinced that they were Welsh, and that any Welshman could understand the Navajo language perfectly. The early Americans, of course, were always looking for the descendants of the Welsh Prince Madoc, who was reputed to have discovered America before Columbus. (Southey wrote a verse epic about him.) At other times, cranks have sought to prove that the Welsh were one of the lost tribes of Israel. In actual fact, there is a very startling similarity between Welsh and Navajo, both in their light pitch and in the frequency of the characteristic *ll* sound, which gives both of them a liquid lilt. The Navajo language, by the way, proved of immense value to the American authorities during World War Two, when the Army recruited over one hundred Navajo to broadcast messages *en clair* instead of going through the cumbersome business of putting them in code. The Japanese never succeeded in identifying and breaking down the language employed.

As in the case of all the other tribes described in the previous chapter, the word *Navajo* was not the name which the Navajo called themselves. Tribal names are names bestowed on tribes by their neighbors, or Indian or English corruptions of these, or names given to them by the French or Spaniards (see Figure 12). Like many native peoples, in America and elsewhere, the Navajo called themselves by the plain and lofty name of "The People," the *Dineh,* just as their cousins the Apache also called themselves "The People," the *Indeh* or *Tindeh,* a linguistically related word. *Nava* or *Navajo* is the Spanish word for a piece of level ground, and a *navaja* is a knife or razor, either of which would be appropriate to the Navajo; but some writers hold that the word comes from an early Navajo place-name, or from a Tewa word meaning "to take from the fields," perhaps given them by the people of Taos, who had more cause than most to regret this Navajo propensity.

Whatever their origin, the *Dineh,* as they still call themselves, were one of America's most numerous and coherent tribes, though it is only in recent times that they have come to see themselves as one tribe instead of a loosely knit confederation of matrilineal clans and extended families. They had no chief and no central organization, such as they have today in the persons of their elected Tribal Chairman and his seventy-four-man Tribal Council. Even at the abysmal low-point of their fortunes, when they were both captive and in exile, their numbers never sank below 9,500, and a century later the census of 1970 showed them to have increased to no less than 90,000. They are the largest Indian tribe in the United States, occupying the largest reservations. It ought to be added here that three-quarters of all the tribalized Indians of the U.S. are to be found concentrated within the boundaries of the Southwest, the majority of them in New Mexico and Arizona.

The Navajo are among the most colorful in appearance of the surviving

Indian tribes. It is as if they sought, by means of their bright costumes, to emulate or take into themselves the colors of Navajoland, its flaring reds, its implacable buffs, its high purples. When one sees them in their gala or ceremonial dress, they are magnificent, the men in silk or satin shirts with crimson headbands, the women in velour blouses and full skirts, both sexes laden with silver belts, silver bracelets, silver rings, and silver earrings. In fact, however, this so-called traditional costume dates only from the 1850s, during their first contact with the Americans. Both the Navajo men and women were enchanted by the silks, satins, and velvets from which the wives of the officers on the army posts made their gowns, and the women copied the ample mid-Victorian fashions. As for the famous Navajo silverwork, this too dates only from the 1850s. The first Navajo silversmith—for it is traditionally a man's craft—was Atsidi Sani, the Old Smith. He learned his skills from itinerant Mexican smiths, and began to practice in 1853. Nonetheless, if the costumes and jewelry we see now are not those of the ancient Navajo, one may still guess that, when the Pueblo Indians and Spaniards first grew aware of their presence, they already sported the bold colors that they display now, even in their everyday work clothes.

They were always an adaptable, eclectic people. From the Pueblos, they learned how to grow corn, beans, squash, sunflowers, cotton, and tobacco; how to improve their weaving; how to make pottery—although they never reached the highest standards in this art. From the Hispanos and the Mexicans, in addition to making jewelry, they took—literally—horses, guns, and captives. Indeed, it was during the period when they came into contact with Europeans and Americans that the Navajo, like all the Plains Indians, reached the highest peak of their culture. Those proud braves who flaunt themselves in the movies owe much of their peacock appearance to the cultural enrichment that they derived from alien sources—and the very people who lent it to them were the ones who took it away.

Their heyday occupied the brief period between the departure of the Spaniards in 1819 and the beginning of American rule in 1846—less than thirty years. Mexico itself, as we shall see in the following chapter, fell into such disarray when the Spaniards left that its northern provinces became almost totally neglected. Arizona was evacuated; New Mexico was preyed upon by a succession of brutal and half-witted governors, all of them incapable of administration. The predatory Indians of the Southwest assumed that such a happy state of affairs would last forever: and the Americans, so long as they were fighting Mexicans, egged them on. Thus, the Indians at this time regarded the Americans as their friends and allies, and were normally tolerant of the American wagon trains that trundled through their territory. Contacts only deteriorated when the railroad, mining, and military surveyors arrived in force in the 1850s, and the Indians began to sense dimly what was in store for them.

The worst outrages of the Mexican period were not the work of the Navajo, though they were not averse to taking advantage of the chaotic situation. The real villains were the Apache and the Comanche, peoples given over wholly to warfare and *Schrecklichkeit*. Indeed, the Hopi and other Indians customarily helped out the Navajo in hard times, and received help themselves. After the American acquisition of the Southwest, conditions quickly changed, and when the Americans decided that the time had come to crack down on the Indian, the Navajo had to suffer with the rest. America was in its first expansionist phase. United States troops had marched as a conquering army into Mexico City; Mexico had been forced to recognize the new Republic of Texas, and had ceded to the United States an area almost as large as Mexico itself (and Mexico is no small country). The government in Washington was in a buoyant and aggressive mood. It might have been possible to overlook the damage to property, though whites have always been religiously attached to property—but what struck a deeper chord, and provided the *casus belli,* were the stories of the wholesale abduction of Anglo and Mexican women and children. The Indians had certainly become accustomed, during the feverish Mexican years, to seizing this valuable human commodity. The women and children either settled down with their captors, or were traded as slaves to other tribes. On the other hand, at this period there may have been no less than 6,000 Navajo slaves in the possession of Anglos and Mexicans, who valued them, a nineteenth-century writer tells us, "on account of their tractable nature, intelligence, light skins, and the voluptuousness of the females." Interracial kidnapping had long been a feature of life in the Southwest.

Nor were all these white captives or children who were brought up by the Indians unhappy with their lot; fewer still were treated badly. An early account of an occasion when the Indians were forced to yield up their white prisoners tells us that "they delivered up their beloved captives with the utmost reluctance, and shed torrents of tears over them, recommending them to the care and protection of the commanding officer. Their regard to them continued all the time they were in camp. They visited them from day to day, and brought them what corn, skins, horses and other matters they had bestowed on them while in their families, accompanied with other matters and all the marks of a sincere affection. Nor did they stop there, but when the army marched some of the Indians solicited and obtained leave to accompany their former captives and employed themselves in hunting and bringing provisions for them on the road. Among the children who had been carried off young, and had long lived with the Indians, it is not to be expected that any marks of joy would appear on being restored to their parents or relatives. But it must not be denied that there were even some grown persons who showed an unwillingness to return. The Indians were obliged to bind several of their prisoners and force them along to the camp; and some women afterwards found means to escape and run back to the Indian towns. Some, who could not make their escape, clung to their savage acquaintance at parting, and continued many days in bitter lamentation." The writer of the above lines was made uneasy by such manifestations, indicating a definite preference for Indian to "civilized" life. He concludes: "For the honour of humanity, we would suppose those persons to have been of the lowest rank. Easy and unconstrained as the savage life is, certainly it could never be put in competition with the blessings of improved life and the light of religion." Evidently, there were those that did not agree.

It made no difference. Word had gone out from Washington. The Anglos had no intention of sharing the North American continent with its native owners. The Pueblo Indians could survive in their ancestral places, on sufferance, because they represented a useful peasantry—the kind of people who always survive wars and invasions. But the nomadic Indians had no such role to play; they were the equivalent of squatters; they had to be swept aside. Yet there was clearly more than a material question involved. There was something else, something deeper, some irreversible dislike and antagonism that sprang up between the two races. D. H. Lawrence discusses this, in another interesting passage in *Mornings in Mexico*. He opens with a warning about being too sentimental about the Indian: "White people always, or nearly always, write sentimentally about the Indians. . . . It is almost impossible for the white people to approach the Indian without sentimentality or dislike. The common healthy vulgar white usually feels a certain native dislike of these drumming aboriginals. The highbrow invariably lapses into sentimentalism like the smell of bad eggs. Why? Both the reactions are due to the same feeling in the white man. The Indian is not in line with us. He's not coming our way. His whole being is going a different way from ours. And the minute you set eyes on him you know it." And he concludes: "The consciousness of one branch of humanity is the annihilation of the consciousness of another branch. That is, the life of the Indian, his stream of conscious being, is just death to the white man. And we can understand the consciousness of the Indian only in terms of the death of our consciousness. . . . A man cannot belong to *both* ways, or to many ways. One man can belong to one great way of consciousness only. He may even change from one way to another. But he cannot go both ways at once. Can't be done."

During the 1850s, the incoming Americans constructed a dozen "Forts" in the Southwest, most of them little more than makeshift encampments in the vicinity of the more heavily populated towns and settlements (see Figure 16). Troops were thin on the ground, and few of them had any experience in waging war in the desert. They spent their time tramping or galloping around fruitlessly, encountering little success, losing as often as winning. Nevertheless, a few competent commanders began to emerge: and when the message came from Washington that the Navajo were to be crushed, it was unfortunate that the order was sent to one of the most remarkable men in Southwestern history.

Colonel Kit Carson was an effective Indian fighter because he was himself a "mountain man," part soldier, part trapper, part scout. Born in Kentucky in 1809, he was apprenticed to a saddlemaker in Independence, Missouri, and ran away at the age of sixteen to become a *coureur de bois.* Hardly more than a boy, he was already fighting Indians on the Santa Fe Trail. After a period of trapping in California, he settled at Taos in 1830, joining forces with traders like William Bent and Céran St. Vrain to supply pelts to John Jacob Astor, whose fortune was founded on the Western fur trade. Latterly, Carson had taken part in Frémont's three expeditions, including the one in which California had been annexed to the Union, and he had acted as guide and dispatch-rider for General Kearny. Married to a Mexican wife, he spoke Spanish, and had a command of several Indian tongues. All his life, and especially at Taos, he had lived close to the Indians, respecting them, knowing their ways, and being respected by them in return. Since he was intimately acquainted with the geography of the area, he was the logical man for Washington to choose: but the assignment was hateful to him. The photographs in his tiny house near the plaza at Taos show a man whose temperament, like all those who had passed their lives in the wilderness, was lonely, reserved, and ascetic. There is something profoundly Indian in the expression. He took what comfort he could from the thought that he might be able to carry out his ugly task with more humanity than a doctrinaire officer. He had been plunged into that most pitiful of all tragic situations, that in which the antagonists genuinely like and respect one another, brother against brother. But his instructions were uncompromising. It was 1863; the Civil War was at its height; the Indians had taken advantage of the white man's troubles to go on the rampage. The Rio Grande must be prevented at all costs from sliding into a disaster as terrible as that of 1680.

Carson took nine months, with a scratch force of less than four hundred men, to bring the Navajo nation to its knees. He managed to do it without undue bloodshed, and less than forty Navajo were killed. There were a number of skirmishes and pursuits, but the business was rendered easier by the help he received from the Utes, the traditional enemies of the Navajo. Moreover the Navajo had long ceased to be nomads, who could melt away into the landscape, like the Apache, but were people who sowed crops and kept immense herds of animals. By destroying these, Carson was cutting off their means of subsistence, and at the end of the winter the starving Indians began to struggle into his headquarters at Fort Defiance to give themselves up. Carson's biggest capture was made at the Canyon de Chelly, in the middle of Navajoland, where the Navajo had retreated, and where they thought they were inaccessible. On March 6, 1864, 2,400 persons, with 30 wagons, 400 horses, and 3,000 sheep and goats, were led out from Arizona by Carson on the "Long March," an ordeal comparable to the "Trail of Tears" trodden by many other Indian tribes during the process of forcible removal. The Cherokee nation, for example, lost 4,000 people on the gruesome six-month "March Where They Cried." Carson had been instructed to transfer the entire Navajo nation to Fort Sumner, in New Mexico. It was 300 miles away, on the Pecos, 180 miles east of Santa Fe. The women walked with the men; only the sick and the children rode in the wagons. When they eventually reached Fort Sumner, their numbers were swollen by the arrival of three more columns of captives, until an estimated 8,000 to 9,000 people were herded into a cramped and squalid area known as the Basque Redondo, the Round Wood. Kluckhohn writes: "Probably no folk has ever had a greater shock. Proud, they saw their properties destroyed and knew what it was to be dependent upon the largesse of strangers. Not understanding group captivity and accustomed to move freely over great spaces, they knew the misery of confinement within a limited area. Taken far from the rugged and vivid landscape which they prized so highly, they lived in a flat and colorless region, eating alien foods and drinking bitter water that made them ill." He adds: "Fort Sumner was a major calamity to The People; its full effects upon their imagination can hardly be conveyed to white readers. Even today it seems impossible for any Navajo of the older generation to talk for more than a few minutes on any subject without speaking of Fort Sumner. Those who were not there themselves heard so many poignant tales from their parents that they speak as if they themselves had experienced all the horror of the 'Long Walk,' the illness, the hunger, the homesickness, the final return to their desolated land. One can no more understand Navajo attitudes—particularly toward white people—without knowing of Fort Sumner than he can comprehend Southern attitudes without knowing of the Civil War."

Kit Carson, by the way, who had tried to mitigate the Indians' lot while carrying out his orders, did not long survive. He died suddenly of an aneurysm in 1868. He was fifty-eight.

Kluckhohn was writing in the 1940s. Even today, it is a shock to visit Navajoland and realize how intense is the Indian's hatred of the white man. When one stays in Navajo owned and operated hotels, such as the one at Kayenta, it takes an effort for the Indian staff, who are not enamored of the idea of waiting on people in any case, to bring themselves to serve you. When they do, there is a steely element in the way they look at you, a direct quality, resembling the openly distrustful way in which animals stare at you. It is at such times that I take refuge in my foreign accent, which helps to thaw the barrier, and has led to interesting discussions with the younger Navajos.

The hatred of the American Negro for the American white is fitful. The black—who does not figure in these pages, since he is not significantly represented in the Southwest—has no solid physical or psychological base from which to launch his hatred, should he possess it. Within the cramped confines of the ghetto, he is not so much strengthened by his hatred, as the free-ranging Indian is, but enfeebled and distracted by it. He is racked by a cruel identity problem. He is an orphan, an adopted child, wondering all his life where he came from. He learns Swahili; he tries to identify with the Ghanaians, the Nigerians, the Sudanese. It is all make-believe. In the final analysis, he knows that he is committed to assimilation, to being an American, nothing else.

Not so the American Indian, such as the Navajo. The Navajo, even in misfortune, draws an ancestral strength from the natural surroundings among which he has lived for so long. Although some 2,000 Navajo live in Los Angeles, and a small number elsewhere, few Navajo leave the reservation to live and work outside it, where they would not be buttressed by the folkways of the tribe. This was their fathers' place, and the place of their fathers' fathers. They certainly endure a continuing cultural crisis, for their folkways conflict continuously with the white civilization that hems them in: but they have no identity crisis. They know *who* they are: the problem is how to regain their old confidence and sense of direction. And in this respect, they possess an important advantage: they are predominantly a young nation: 60 percent of them are under the age of nineteen, another 25 percent under forty. It is as if the population explosion that has swelled their ranks tenfold since the days of the Bosque Redondo is an unconscious act of revenge.

In 1868, when the broken, depleted "People" were permitted to crawl home from Fort Sumner, they were lodged on a reservation 3½ million acres in extent. This sounds generous, until you realize that originally they had roamed over an area of some 23 million acres. Also, this allotted acreage was largely brushland, the choicer parts of their homeland having been given to the Anglos. So poor was the soil that already, by 1900, the government was compelled to double the size of the reservation, to try to keep the growing population from starving. You can get some idea of the aridity of the Indian reservations in the Southwest from the fact that the Anglos did not even bother to snap them up under the policy of severalty. Between 1887 and 1934, the Dawes Severalty Act of 1887 robbed the Indians of 86 million of their 138 million acres. "Most of that remaining," says William T. Hagan, in his authoritative *American Indians,* "was desert or semi-desert: worthless to the white population." He adds: "Worldly interests had demonstrated what can happen in a democratic society to property of minority groups incapable of political action."

Until comparatively recently, the American Indian has not possessed the vote. The professional politician has therefore regarded his plight with indifference. After his defeat, he was a "ward" of the government, his property held in "trust." It was not until 1924 that he was admitted by Congress to citizenship, and since the franchise his voting patterns have been uncertain. Many

Navajo man on his pony (1907), taken near Leupp, Arizona.

states have not played fair. Arizona, for instance, has a literacy test which effectively keeps half of its numerous Indian population from the polls. In New
Mexico, however, the Navajo in recent years have sent two of their members
as far as the State Legislature.

The Navajo, like most other Indians, is trapped by his lack of education.
The American Indian completes only about five years of schooling, while other
Americans average over eleven. Moreover, most of the teachers are white, and
in many schools the use of the native Indian languages is strictly forbidden, as
the use of Welsh and Gaelic used to be in British schools not so very long ago.
A quarter of the Navajo people receive no formal education at all. Few go to
high school, and most of those who do fail to finish. The Navajo is also
trapped by poverty. Fifty percent of families earn less than $1,000 a year, and
75 percent less than $2,000 a year. Only 10 percent earn more than $4,000.
(However, it ought to be borne in mind that the Indian is not alone in this;
the per capita income of the non-Indians of the Southwest is only about $2,000

a year.) On both the economic and educational fronts, the Navajo are making courageous efforts to better the situation, through their Tribal Council and the one hundred local chapters of which it is composed. They have their own newspaper and radio programs to spread the message. But life on their beautiful reservation is hard, inducing not only poverty but ill health. After their return from Fort Sumner, where their spirit was almost broken, they were ravaged by the diseases of despair: malnutrition, syphilis, tuberculosis. In the 1960s, the incidence of syphilis was 50 percent higher, of tuberculosis 100 percent higher, than among other Americans. The life expectancy of an American Indian is forty-three, of a white man, sixty-eight.

It is the same with that other symptom of despair: drunkenness. In Gallup, where the Navajo go to do their off-reservation drinking, and where there are fifty-four bars in an area of 50,000 people, there are up to 10,000 arrests a year for drunkenness. There are more bars per head of the population in Gallup than in any other town in America. Not surprisingly, the toll taken by drunken driving is horrible. The Tribal Council has a Committee on Alcoholism, and several chapters of Alcoholics Anonymous exist. Liquor has always had a fatal attraction for the Indian, and the whites have never hesitated to use it to sap his strength and self-respect, bolstering their own sense of superiority in the process and providing themselves with a rationale for thievery.

In Gallup, a featureless town, run up on the cheap out of plywood and plasterboard, much of the better stock in the stores is jewelry that has been sold or pawned to buy drink. These are the pieces made by the Navajo for themselves, often family heirlooms. "Pawn" is a recognized category of Navajo jewelry. When the Navajo don their personal ornaments for special occasions, men, women and children aglitter with a mass of silver, it is difficult to remember that they are financially poor. To the Navajo, their silver not only enables them to make a proud, brave show: it has come to assume psychological and religious significance. They treasure it, make agonizing sacrifices for it, only relinquishing a precious piece in the event of a material extremity—or an ungovernable thirst. Oliver La Farge, at the end of his novel *Laughing Boy,* conveys what their silver means to the Navajo. Laughing Boy, the young hero, who is a gifted jeweler, is riding with Slim Girl toward Moonlight Water, a place on the northernmost boundary of Navajoland where they hope to live out of reach of the white Americans. "They prepared to move," writes La Farge, "in beautiful, clear, cold, sunny weather following a first light snow, the slight thawing of which assured them of water. Their goods made little bulk—well over a thousand dollars in silver, turquoise, and coral, several hundred dollars in coin, his jeweller's kit, her spindle, batten, cards, and fork, half a dozen choice blankets, some pots and pans and provisions. They carried a good deal on their saddles, and packed the rest, Navajo-fashion, which is to say badly, on the spare pony. They set out with fine blankets over their shoulders, their mounts prancing in the cold, their saddles and bridles heavy with silver and brass, leading the pack-horse by a multi-colored horsehair rope, a splendid couple." They have scarcely begun their journey when they are ambushed by the jealous Red Man, who shoots and kills Slim Girl. Laughing Boy carries her body to a crack in the cliffs, covers her with her blankets, and places food, cooking implements and weaving tools around her. Then, as the snow begins to fall, he starts on his four-day vigil beside her. He puts upon her his silver bridle, and packs around her "his heavy silver belt, his turquoise and coral necklace, his two bracelets, his garnet ring and his turquoise ring, his earrings of turquoise matrix, laying each one gently upon the heap." In the Beyond, she will possess the status and protection afforded her by these sacred objects.

A thousand dollars in silver, together with several hundred dollars in coin, sounds a great deal; but it represents Laughing Boy's entire capital and stock-in-trade. In fact, the manufacture of jewelry does not represent such a high proportion of the tribal income as might be supposed. The good pieces involve much time and heavy investment, and are slow to find a customer. During the late 1960s and early 1970s, the price of a piece of fine silver and turquoise quadrupled, as Indian jewelry became a fad among wealthy Easterners and Californians. The Indian himself derived little increased benefit from his products, for most of the profit went to the middlemen who always turn up like sharks when they scent that there is money to be made. The Indian craftsman seldom receives more than a modest percentage for his labor. However, he is now learning how to sidestep the entrepreneur by selling direct to the public.

As we saw, the first Navajo silversmiths began work in the 1850s, borrowing from outside. During the Hispanic and Mexican periods, itinerant painters and carvers, as well as silversmiths, had been working in the Rio Grande valley. One entire school of traveling artists, the *Santeros,* specialized in the making of holy images and pictures, *santos, retablos,* and the figures in the round called *bultos.* Their work, whether on a large or small scale, is accomplished, often masterly; and although the names of many became celebrated, most of them worked in obscurity, for God alone. All these wandering artists brought their designs with them, and the traditional designs of Navajo jewelry are derived from Spanish and Mexican prototypes. Thus the heavy ornament at the end of the typical necklace, which looks like an inverted horseshoe, is patterned on the crescent-shaped ornament, or peytrel, which Spanish horsemen hung from the center of the bridle, and which they themselves copied from the Moors. Similarly, the squash-blossoms on the necklace itself stem from the little silver pomegranates the Spaniards used as cape and trouser ornaments. The famous *concho* (shell) belt is not Spanish, however, but a copy in silver of the belts of shells worn by the Plains Indians.

The Navajo transmitted the art of silversmithing first to the Zuni, then to the Hopi. The Zuni concentrate on bright, delicate arrangements of turquoise, shell, coral, and jet. They are decorators, specializing in brilliant inlay, while Hopi work is sober, with incised running patterns and representations of men and animals. The Zuni also make a delightful range of small carved animal fetishes, which Tom Bahti in his book on Southwest Indian arts and crafts says are "treated with reverence, and when not in actual use are carefully stored in fetish jars and ceremonially 'fed' with cornmeal or pollen." The Hopi have branched out into manufacturing their celebrated kachina dolls, of which more than 250 different examples exist. Navajo jewelry, on the other hand, whether sand-cast or overlaid, tends to retain a massive simplicity, though often there is an exaggerated employment of turquoise, which in large chunks can be a vulgar and glaring stone. Not much used until the turn of the century, it could then be found in plentiful supply throughout the Southwest (and nowhere else in America). Now that the supply has dwindled, the Indians purchase most of their turquoise, as they purchase their bar-silver, from white agencies. Buyers should note that there is a great deal of fake turquoise in circulation, concocted of baked and painted pastes. Similarly, they should also remember that the number of really first-class silversmiths is dwindling, as mass-production methods come into vogue.

The artistic genius of this thoughtful people is not confined to jewelry. In common with the other Indians of the Southwest, they have produced many striking painters, who model their style on the ancient Indian modes. Modern Navajo artists draw inspiration from the sand paintings which were done by the medicine man during the three-day or nine-day "sings" or "chants," to cure a sick patient. The sufferer watched all day as the painting was slowly executed around him as he sat on the ground. His ill humors were simultaneously absorbed into it; the gods whose figures were incorporated into it exerted their influence. Then, at the moment of sunset, the magnificent design was effaced, the sickness departing with it. Many striking examples of sand painting can be seen in the small but artfully arranged Museum of Navajo Ceremonial Art in Santa Fe. The name "sand painting" is really a slight misnomer, as sand is actually the background to the painting, whose primary ingredients are pollen, cornmeal, charcoal, and materials derived from powdered rocks and plants. These are trickled on to the sand between the thumb and forefinger, in designs entirely drawn from memory. It should be noted that sand paintings are not exclusively Navajo; the Papago, Apache, and Pueblo Indians execute them also.

The inexhaustible ability of the Navajo to invent two-dimensional decoration is also shown in their rugs, made from the wool of their own flocks. The different designs possess exotic names, after the part of the reservation where they were devised: Yei, Klagetoh, Teec Nos Pos, Nazlini, Ganado, Chinle, Crystal, Two Gray Hills. The brio of the design often leads a would-be buyer, who may be dismayed by their high price, to forget the amount of time and effort that went into their making. Anyone who has watched a Navajo woman, seated on the red earth outside her hogan, working with her children around her at her large loom, or working indoors at her small one, will appreciate the devotion which is expended on the Navajo rug. And the weaving is only the last and least laborious of many processes—teasing, carding, spinning, dyeing —that have gone into its creation. Like any truly satisfying object, a Navajo rug or blanket is not something clacked out by a machine; it is a portion of somebody's life, a sliver of an individual soul. One should not expect to get it for nothing.

Apart from sand painting, the decorative designs of most Navajo artifacts do not in themselves possess any elaborate religious significance. The Navajo do not appear to be among the most spiritually complex of Indian peoples. They are pragmatic, and although they believe in an afterlife, which is to be lived underground in some vague place in the north, they are chiefly concerned with enjoying the present existence as much as possible. They have their festivals, some of them lasting several days—the Fire Dance, the Enemy Dance, the Night Dance—but they have not evolved the subtle and profound rituals of the Pueblo Indians. Their myths and deities are pretty but uncomplicated. The People today are held to be descended from several races of First People who lived underground, and who eventually emerged from a badger hole in southern Colorado. The upper world was created by First Man and First Woman, the incarnation of Nature in all her moods; she was sometimes called Turquoise Woman, and was sister to the moon. The moon, White Shell Woman, was visited nightly by the sun in her home in the western ocean. The principal feature of Navajo religion is its poetic personification of Nature; no feature of the landscape, whether mountain, mesa or river, lacks its tutelary god or goddess, if it is not indeed a god or goddess itself. On the other hand, it is characteristic of the Navajo that they rejected all the ardently religious or revivalist movements in their area, including such fanatical manifestations as the Comanche Sun Dance of the 1870s, and the two outbursts of the Ghost Dance in the 1870s and 1890s. The successor of the last Ghost Dance was the peyote cult; but, again, the Navajos only took to using peyote in the 1920s, and then on a restricted scale. What peyote signifies in the life and religion of the Indians of the Southwest is demonstrated in N. Scott Momaday's *House Made of Dawn,* where much of the second portion of the book is devoted to describing its effects. Some writers have ascribed the Navajo rejection of the Ghost Dance, almost alone of the Horse Indians, to their dread of the *chindi,* the walking spirits of the dead. In his *Religions of the Oppressed,* in which there is a fascinating discussion of this and other prophetic movements among the American Indian, Vittorio Lanternari writes: "Some students ascribe the strenuous opposition to the cult by the Navajo to the fact that they had not experienced spiritual and social deprivation. Others believe the Navajo were skeptical by nature and privileged among the Indian population because of

Navajo weaver.

their prosperous sheep-, horse-, and cattle-raising economy." A flexible people, the Navajo will one day effect the necessary change and adjustment to the
white culture that lashes like a tide around their reservation: but they will do
it calmly and sensibly, in their own way.

Material deprivation, yes—that happened at the Bosque Redondo. But as
Lanternari says, spiritually and socially, perhaps for the very reason that their
religious beliefs were broad-based, unspecialized, and anchored in their native
scene, the Navajo have kept themselves together. As I have been trying to indicate to my English friends, the Southwest is a numinous place. The soil of
Navajoland may be poor, but the gods everywhere ride their high horses across
that mighty landscape. It is a cosmic cathedral, where the sun, the sky, the
rocks, and the earth are the colors of stained glass.

When you drive north from Gallup, toward the Four Corners area, the
place where Arizona, New Mexico, Utah, and Colorado all meet, you are in
Navajoland, within easy distance of Chaco Canyon, the Canyon de Chelly, the
Aztec and Mesa Verde National monuments, and the Hopi villages. (At Four
Corners, you get a friend to photograph you on all fours, straddling the bronze

marker, with a limb in each of the four states.) As you near the end of Route 666—where many of the drunk-driving crashes occur—you will pass a free-standing mesa of immense grandeur. It is called Shiprock, because it seems to breast from the flat plain like a great thrusting galleon. To the land-bound Navajo, however, it is not a ship but the body of a sleeping god, in the form of an eagle. I always stop at Shiprock, to eat my sandwiches, drink my coffee, and walk about a little on that gigantic outcrop. Always there are dust devils, cavorting puffs of loose brown soil, twisting and twirling around its base. They are like little acolytes. There are always five or six of them—more than you are likely to see at other times in the course of an entire day. They are at home at Shiprock; they are the grace notes of a living, singing landscape. The eagle is not dead. It rests; sleeps; recuperates. It embodies the soul of the Navajo nation, which one day will soar again.

Toward the close of *Death Comes for the Archbishop,* Father Latour, then a bishop, is riding back to Santa Fe in the company of Eusebio, a Navajo. Willa Cather, in a long passage, captures the essence of the Navajo—and by extension, the American Indian's—attitude to Nature.

"The ride back to Santa Fe," she writes, "was something under four hundred miles. The weather alternated between blinding sand-storms and brilliant sunlight. The sky was as full of motion and change as the desert beneath it was monotonous and still—and there was so much sky, more than at sea, more than anywhere else in the world. The plain was there, under one's feet, but what one saw when one looked about was that brilliant blue world of stinging air and moving cloud. Even the mountains were mere ant-hills under it. Elsewhere the sky is the roof of the world; but here the earth was the floor of the sky. The landscape one longed for when one was far away, the thing all about one, the world one actually lived in, was the sky, the sky!

"Travelling with Eusebio was like travelling with the landscape made human. He accepted chance and weather as the country did, with a sort of grave enjoyment. He talked little, ate little, slept anywhere, preserved a countenance open and warm, and he had unfailing good manners. Father Latour was rather surprised that he stopped so often by the way to gather flowers. One morning he came back with the mules, holding a bunch of crimson flowers—long, tube-shaped bells, that hung lightly from one side of a naked stem and trembled in the wind.

" 'The Indians call rainbow flower,' he said, holding them up and making the red tubes quiver. 'It is early for these.'

"When they left the rock or tree or sand dune that had sheltered them for the night, the Navajo was careful to obliterate every trace of their temporary occupation. He buried the embers of the fire and the remnants of food, unpiled any stones he had piled together, filled up the holes he had scooped in the sand. Father Latour judged that, just as it was the white man's way to assert himself in any landscape, to change it, make it over a little (at least to leave some mark of memorial of his sojourn), it was the Indian's way to pass through a country without disturbing anything; to pass and leave no trace, like fish through the water, or birds through the air.

"It was the Indian manner to vanish into the landscape, not to stand out against it. The Hopi villages that were set upon rock mesas were made to look like the rock on which they sat, were imperceptible at a distance. The Navajo hogans, among the sand and willows, were made of sand and willows. None of the pueblos would at that time admit glass windows into their dwellings. The reflection of the sun on the glazing was to them ugly and unnatural—even dangerous. Moreover, these Indians disliked novelty and change. They came and went by the old paths worn into the rock by the feet of their fathers, used the old natural stairway of stone to climb to their mesa towns, carried water from the old springs, even after white men had dug wells.

"In the working of silver or drilling of turquoise the Indians had exhaustless patience; upon their blankets and belts and ceremonial robes they lavished their skill and pains. But their conception of decoration did not extend to the landscape. They seemed to have none of the European's desire to 'master' nature, to arrange and re-create. They spent their ingenuity in the other direction; in accommodating themselves to the scene in which they found themselves. This was not so much from indolence, Father Latour thought, as from an inherited caution and respect. It was as if the great country were asleep, and they wished to carry on their lives without awakening it; or as if the spirits of earth and air and water were things not to antagonize and arouse. When they hunted, it was with the same discretion; an Indian hunt was never a slaughter. They ravaged neither the rivers nor the forest, and if they irrigated, they took as little water as would serve their needs. The land and all that it bore they treated with consideration; not attempting to improve it, they never desecrated it.

"As Father Latour and Eusebio approached Albuquerque, they occasionally fell in with company; Indians going to and fro on the long winding trails across the plain, or up into the Sandia mountains. They had all of them the same quiet way of moving, whether their pace was swift or slow, and the same unobtrusive demeanor: an Indian wrapped in his bright blanket, seated upon his mule or walking beside it, moving through the pale new-budding sagebrush, winding among the sand waves, as if it were his business to pass unseen and unheard through a country awakening with spring.

"North of Laguna two Zuni runners sped by them, going somewhere east on 'Indian business.' They saluted Eusebio by gestures with the open palm, but did not stop. They coursed over the sand with the fleetness of young antelope, their bodies disappearing and reappearing among the sand dunes, like the shadows that eagles cast in their strong, unhurried flight."

As a result of Kit Carson's roundup at the Canyon de Chelly, the Navajo were effectively suppressed. They gave the Anglo little trouble thereafter. Contrary to the accepted stereotype, although feuds and rivalries were endemic to the Indian way of life, most Indian tribes were relatively peaceful and tolerant, practicing a general policy of live and let live. For the most part, the Indian lacked the consistent aggressiveness of the Anglo, and was unable to compete with him in that department.

Not so the Apache. The Apache, above all else, have given rise to the notion of the bloodthirsty Indian, the Indian on the warpath. The Apache are the Indians of the more violent Westerns, the Indians who gave their names to urban street gangs. In effect they were not physically impressive or gorgeously attired. They were squat, scruffy, and unfeathered. Their only sartorial extravagances were their painted shields, their elaborate war necklaces, and the bright piece of flannel or cloth they wore around their forehead and which they took off and hung on a bush to draw the enemy's fire during a battle. They were not even good horsemen, unlike the Navajo and the phenomenal Comanche. They long clung to the habit which most other Indians had outgrown, preferring to eat horses rather than ride them. They liked horsemeat above other kinds, and were wretched horse-wranglers, callous and ignorant in their treatment of their mounts. They rode mules and donkeys as readily as horses, and when they fought they sent the horses to the rear and fought on foot. They were indifferent potters and weavers, and apathetic agriculturists. Their houses were not the solid, earth-hugging, wood-and-soil hogans of the Navajo, but were flimsy, rickety wickiups of brushwood and beargrass, lashed together with yucca fiber. Their beadwork was passable, and their only marked domestic ability lay in the making of baskets. They were not even particularly numerous, since it is doubtful whether at their peak all the Apache bands together numbered more than 15,000 to 20,000 people. This is scarcely as many people as would fit into a modern suburb; yet few small peoples in history have made such an impression on posterity.

For the Apache had one notable skill. In spite of their unprepossessing appearance, they were tremendous fighters. They were so greatly gifted in this respect that it more than made up for their lack of numbers, making them seem a hundred times more numerous than they were. Their battles with the Spaniards, the Mexicans, the Americans, and their fellow Indians lasted for two hundred years, and they performed such feats of enterprise and hardihood that the final phase, when thirty-five starved braves were standing off 5,300 men of the American army, has been given the ringing title of the Apache War.

The Apache have bestowed on the American Indian an unfading glamour, while giving him an ugly and misleading reputation. They have their apologists. Gordon C. Baldwin, in his *Warrior Apaches,* a study of the Western and Chiricahua Apache, declares that: "The Apache were no more cruel than other people. They learned a lot of their tricks from their Spanish, Mexican and American neighbors. As one officer who should know expressed it, the Apache were mere amateurs compared with the Americans and Mexicans when it came to treachery, thievery, and the murder of women and children. However, such acts of the Americans and Mexicans did not make the headlines. Rarely was a white man ever punished for killing an Indian. Yet the slightest mistake by an Apache was immediately seized upon and heralded far and wide as another frightful Apache atrocity." He concludes, agreeing with the opinion of D. H. Lawrence which I have quoted above, that "the truth was that the white man could not understand the Apache's point of view or ways any more than the Apache could understand the white man's. The two were complete opposites."

All the same, many of the "mistakes" of the Apache to which Baldwin refers were gross. It was the Apache who, alone of the tribes of the Southwest, specialized in such practices as castrating both the living and the dead, pegging prisoners out on antheaps, skinning them alive, crucifying them with cactus spikes, or tying them upside down and lighting a fire beneath their heads. In 1872, a party of young Englishmen who were traveling through Arizona had the misfortune to fall in with an Apache war party. Most of them were butchered at once. They were lucky. An American officer later described how the two survivors had been tied to saguaros by their captors, who then "proceeded deliberately to fill them with arrows. One of the poor wretches rolled and writhed in agony, breaking off the feathered ends of the arrows, but each time he turned his body, exposing a space not yet wounded, the Apaches shot in another barb." It is not surprising that, with their relish for bloodshed, the Apache had almost no friends, even among their fellow Indians. The only people who would have anything to do with them were the Yavapai, who had enlisted their aid during their struggle against the Hualapai. Other Indians feared and hated them, and hundreds of Indians from many tribes eventually became Army scouts in the campaigns against them, just as the Mexicans had joined forces with Cortés to exterminate the Aztecs. The very word "Apache," which the Apache adopted with disdainful pride, was taken from the Zuni word *Apachu,* which meant The Enemy.

It was inevitable that the Apache should be blamed whenever any act of violence occurred. Their name was synonymous with terror. From the beginning they were outlaws, self-confessed bandits, living by the premise that every man's hand was against them. They gave no quarter and sought none. Nevertheless, it was unfortunate that their status as a tribe was so confused that it was easy to blame one Apache band or another for any indiscriminate outrage. If one segment of the Apache nation was temporarily at peace, digesting the proceeds of its latest raid, others were bound to be on the warpath. From the outset, there had been a bewildering multiplicity of such bands. Small in aggregate, they divided their numbers still further, roaming the

Southwest in groups that were no more than extended families. The situation was further confused by the fact that, like the Navajo, the Apache had no chiefs. There was no one to unite the various groups in an emergency. Most of the bands were strangers to each other, scarcely knowing of the others' existence.

It is fairly generally accepted that the Apache nation was divided into six tribes (see Figure 13). Four of them occupied territories east of the Rio Grande, and two on the west. In the far northeast were the so-called Kiowa Apache, an Apache outlier which had become attached to the Kiowa. They lived in the region of the Oklahoma Panhandle, and made forays in the direction of Taos and Santa Fe; Coronado seems to have made contact with them during his futile search for the Gran Quivira. Closer to Taos and Santa Fe, in the wooded fastnesses of southern Colorado and northeast New Mexico, were the Jicarilla Apache; and south of the Jicarilla, in the pine-covered retreat of the Tularosa Basin and the Sacramento Mountains, were the Mescalero Apache, who had made life so miserable for the Jumanos. Last of the eastern group, in western Texas and northern New Mexico, utilizing as their heartland the superb portion of the Southwest known as the Big Bend, were the Lipan Apache, who for two hundred years had threatened the very existence of El Paso. These four tribes were populous, which is to say they probably numbered between 1,500 and 2,000 apiece. Although they were never fully pacified, these four eastern bank tribes had lost much of their cutting edge during the latter part of Hispanic rule. The Spaniards were constantly exasperated by the uncentralized nature of Apache social organization, which made it impossible for them to reach a satisfactory general peace agreement; nevertheless they had brought many Apache into the vicinity of the settlements, where they could be made dependent on regular rations, liquor and supplies, and where they could be watched.

With the west bank Apache, who had successfully wrecked all attempts to colonize Arizona, it was a different tale. In the southwest, the Chiricahua Apache were entrenched in the terrific canyons and mountains of the Gila Wilderness and the Mexican-American borderlands—the Chiricahuas, Dragoons, Winchesters, Mules, Mazatzals, and Mogollons. They were the savage lords of the territory where the Hohokam, Mogollon, and Mimbreños had once lived, and the even more ancient Cochise people. Indeed, they often sorted through the debris of these dead peoples and retrieved a useful utensil or an ornament that was of more refined craftsmanship than anything they could make themselves. The Chiricahuas were split into three main bands, East, Central, and Southern, and although they probably never numbered more than 1,000 in all, they plundered and murdered over a tremendous area, ranging far across Arizona and deep down into Sonora as far south as Hermosillo. In the 1770s, they attacked and totally destroyed Father Kino's last resting-place, Magdalena. It was the Chiricahua who, a century later, and forty years after Mexico had ceded the Southwest to the United States, were still keeping the flame of Indian resistance very much alive.

Finally, to the north of the Chiricahuas, around and beyond the Salt and the Gila, were more than a dozen Apache bands to whom the collective name of Western Apache has been given. The Western Apache occupied the inaccessible places of northern Arizona, but often thrust westward to the middle and upper reaches of the Rio Grande. Customarily, they were divided into five groups: White Mountain (Eastern and Western bands); Cibicue (Cibicue, Canyon Creek, and Carrizo bands); San Carlos (San Carlos, Apache Peaks, Araiva, and Piñal bands); Northern Tonto (Oak Creek, Fossil Creek, Bald Mountain, and Mormon Lake bands); and Southern Tonto (Mazatzal band). All together, the Western Apache congeries may have numbered as many as 5,000 to 6,000 people on the eve of the great confrontation with the whites.

Ironically, the Apache nation was delighted when the Americans took over after the Treaty of Guadalupe Hidalgo. Were not the Americans, also, the enemies of Mexico? Would they not together, side by side, continue with the laudable business of slaughtering Mexicans? The Apache had had a glorious time, in the quarter of a century between the withdrawal of Spain and the onset of the Americans, assailing the enfeebled provinces of northern Mexico. Even after the Americans arrived, and were themselves at first too uncertain of the area to take decisive action, the great Apache splurge continued. The white man was thin on the ground, outnumbered by the Indian; the wagon trains had hardly begun to lumber westward. There was plenty of room for all. The removal of the Navajo to Fort Sumner, of course, was a portent, had the Apache been able to recognize it; and there had been heavy fighting between the whites and the Sioux and Cheyenne, and other Indian nations, somewhere on the plains of the north. But the country was large, the small nomadic Apache bands were left undisturbed in their remote corner, and they had reason to feel confident in their capacity to survive and to handle any opponent. For the Western and Chiricahua Apache, the thirty years from 1820 to 1850, covering the Mexican and early American period, was their Golden Age.

Nevertheless, there had been storm signals, even in the Southwest, as early as the 1830s, when the Mexican governor of Sonora was paying Texan scalp hunters as much as $200 a head for dead Apache. However, the Apache even more readily killed the scalp hunters, gratis. Similarly, when in 1836 the American miners at Santa Rita had massacred Juan José, head of the Eastern band of the Chiricahuas, with his entire family, the Apache were able to revenge themselves to the tune of twenty-two American dead. The real trouble started in the 1850s and 1860s, when American trappers, traders, copperminers, and goldminers, as tough and predatory as the Apache themselves, increasingly antagonized two exceptionally spirited Apache leaders, Mangas

Coloradas of the Eastern Chiricahuas, and Cochise of the Central Chiricahuas.

Mangas or Mangus Coloradas was unusual for an Apache, in that he stood 6 feet 6. His name meant "Red Sleeves," or "Red Shirt," because of a flannel undershirt he had taken from a dead American and which he wore constantly. He was ruthless, intelligent, had several wives, and was an excellent general. When he decided to punish Santa Rita for murdering Juan José, he patiently besieged it, cut off its water and supplies, and when the inhabitants fled south, killed them on the march. Only a handful out of 300 to 400 people reached safety. A few years later, the miners of another mining camp, at nearby Piños Altos, north of Silver City, laid hands on Mangas when he had ridden in under a flag of truce. He wished to tell them of a vein of gold, to which he promised to lead them. The offer may have been sincere; it may have been a ruse to get them out of his part of the country, or to trick them into an ambush. In any event, they took no chances. Instead of letting him ride away, they tied him to a tree and gave him a fearful lashing with a blacksnake whip. It was the same mistake the Spaniards had made when they whipped Popé. They should have finished him off.

In 1861, an inexperienced and probably scared young lieutenant, fresh from West Point, made a blunder that needlessly antagonized Cochise. The origin of the word *Cochise* is obscure, but it may signify "Hard Wood." Like Mangas Coloradas, he was already in his sixties at this time. Western historians dispute as to which was the greater of the two, but there is no doubt that they stand head and shoulders above other recorded leaders of the Apache nation. Coloradas was perhaps the more bloody, bold and resolute, while Cochise was the more thoughtful and sagacious. The latter was thrown uncharacteristically out of stride by the young West Pointer, Lieutenant Bascomb, in a dispute at the Bowie stagecoach station. Bascomb had accused Cochise, wrongly, of carrying out a raid which was actually the responsibility of a band of Western Apaches. At that time, Cochise was actually trying to live a virtuous existence, supplying the Bowie station with wood as one of his enterprises. Both sides lost their heads. Cochise took six people off a stagecoach and killed them; Bascomb retaliated by hanging six Apache captives. Cochise, seized and held prisoner in a tent, cut his way out and escaped. He rode away with three bullets in him, convinced that there could be no further compromise with the white man. He sought out Mangas Coloradas, and the two men made common cause together.

The two Apache captains honestly believed that they could expel the Americans from Apacheland. They believed that they could secure it permanently for their own people. Of course, they were totally ignorant of the geography of the world beyond their own homeland: but they must have had some idea of the odds against them. It is impossible not to admire them. And amazingly enough, at first they swept everything before them. They were helped, of course, by the outbreak of the Civil War, and by the fact that the Mescalero

Apache had wiped out an American cavalry column, inducing the Americans to concentrate their efforts on the opposite bank of the Rio Grande. Mangas and Cochise struck mercilessly. In August 1861, the *Arizonian* reported: "We are hemmed in on all sides by the unrelenting Apache. Within but 6 months, nine-tenths of the whole male population have been killed off, and every ranch, farm and mine in the country has been abandoned in consequence." The situation was so bad that Colonel Baylor, who was governing Arizona and New Mexico for the Confederates, recommended to Jefferson Davis the systematic extermination of all Indians, men, women and children. Davis, to his credit, promptly recalled him. The white Arizonans abandoned their outlying towns and settlements and retired on Tucson: but Mangas trapped the population of Piños Altos, where he had been flogged, penned them up, and prepared to do with them what he had previously done with Santa Rita. Piños Altos has long been a ghost town, struggling to be reborn as an artist colony; Santa Rita, acquired by the Anaconda Corporation, ultimately became one of the biggest copper mines in the world, an immense amphitheater, the color and texture of Stilton cheese, itself ghostly and deserted now. But when I pass through one or the other, on the way to fish in the lakes beyond Silver City, I always remember the brutal beating of the giant Apache, and its even more brutal aftermath.

For a year the Apache were triumphant. They believed they had prevented the whites from settling in Apacheland. Then, in the summer of 1862, after the Confederates had been forced out, General James Carleton marched into the Southwest with an army of 3,000 California volunteers. California had had some trouble making up its mind which side it was on, but once the decision was made it acted decisively. Carleton's instructions were to break the back of the Navajo and Apache, who had dared to throw up a barrier and block communications between East and West. Mangas Coloradas and Cochise shadowed him, let him move east from Tucson into the Chiricahua Mountains, on the way to relieve Piños Altos, and struck at him when he reached Apache Pass, the apex of the great escarpment which would bring him down into New Mexico.

It was a remarkable strategic conception, and the Apache leaders were operating on their home ground. To prevent the Americans coming through the pass, the Indian leaders had built stone breastworks and dug themselves in. It must be remembered that at this point the Indians had passed beyond the bow-and-arrow stage, and were using repeating rifles, particularly Winchesters, as well as such refinements as field glasses. The three hundred men of Carleton's advance guard entered the pass—and suddenly heard the petrifying Apache yell and came under heavy fire. They were taken completely by surprise; but their senior officer, Captain Roberts, behaved coolly, called forward two howitzers to shell the heights, sent back word to Carleton and the main body, and got ready for what he expected to be a major battle next day. He spent an anxious night—but then, at dawn, he found that the Apache had mysteriously departed.

What had happened? It was afterward learned that, late in the previous day's engagement, an American cavalryman, Private John Teal, had lost his mount in the open and saw a party of Apache about to ride down on him. Among them was an exceptionally tall man. Teal took aim and knocked the big Apache off his horse. He believed it was the last shot he would ever make: but, to his astonishment, the Indians swerved aside, picked up their fallen comrade, and galloped off. He had hit Mangas Coloradas. Such was their concern, the Indians broke off the engagement. They bore Mangas south to a Mexican town, where they forced an American doctor to operate on him. He did so successfully, and his life was spared.

After the battle of Apache Pass, in July 1862, the fortunes of the Apache began to wane. Piños Altos, its last thirty defenders reduced to eating grass, was relieved. Five months later, in January 1863, Mangas Coloradas, still suffering from the effects of his wound, was enticed into Piños Altos by its deliverer, Captain Shirland, under safe conduct, with a view to talking peace. Colonel West, commanding at Fort McLane, rode over, saw Mangas Coloradas, and told two of his soldiers to dispose of him. First they tortured him with red-hot bayonets, then shot him down "attempting to escape." His death ended the grand alliance between the branches of the Chiricahua; and at the same time the Mescalero, who had been keeping the cauldron bubbling on the other side of the Rio Grande, were defeated by Carleton's men at a sharp encounter in the Canyon del Perro. Knowing that Carleton had given orders that all male Apache prisoners were to be shot, the surviving Mescalero rode north and surrendered instead to Kit Carson, who was on his way at that moment to deal with the Navajo. "You are stronger than we are," Chief Cadete told him. "We fought you as long as we had rifles and powder, but your weapons are better than ours. Give us good weapons and turn us loose and we will fight you again. But we are now worn out, have no more heart, no provisions, nothing left. Your troops are everywhere, and have driven us from our best and final stronghold. Do what you want with us: but remember that we are men and warriors." Carson gave them food, ignored Carleton's barbarous injunctions, and sent the Mescalero to the newly established encampment at Fort Sumner that was being readied for the Navajo.

Cochise stayed out. During the next seven years, he and his band took refuge in the Gila Wilderness, striking more or less at will. It is a remarkable thing that no Apache band was ever captured by Spaniards or Americans during active warfare. They rank among the most talented guerrilla fighters of all time. But their luck was running out. During the late 1860s, they had to face a new and plentiful supply of regular troops, seasoned in the Civil War. These kept them exhaustingly on the run, and efficiently protected the growing white settlements. The frontier had finally reached the Southwest and was advancing beyond it. The railroads began to thrust east and west to girdle the continent, and soon the Golden Spike would be driven into the track at Promontory Point in Utah.

Power had swung to the settlers. The days of giving the Indians their regalos were over. In 1864, thirty-five members of an Apache band, who had come in to ratify the so-called "Pinal Treaty," were gunned down; in 1870, at Tucson, eight Apache warriors and seventy-seven women and children were massacred after they had walked into Camp Grant and had voluntarily surrendered. Cochise had a last glorious military moment when, in May 1871, he ambushed twenty-three soldiers who had foolishly entered his mountain redoubt and killed them, including an officer who had been tracking him for years. But it was in that same summer that General George Crook was placed in command of the Department of Arizona, with orders from President Grant to pacify the territory. Fortunately for the reputation of the white race, Crook was no brute, like Carleton. He was not only an experienced "Indian fighter," but was a sensible, honorable and compassionate man, with a sense of humor. Not in the least blimpish, he seldom wore his general's uniform, and conducted operations in a white duck suit and a straw hat. The Apache trusted "Gray Wolf," as they came to call him, and within a few months he had got the Western and Chiricahua Apache settled on reservations. Cochise made peace with him in September 1871; but when the general had to tell him, with reluctance, that he and his people must leave their homeland, and move to the Tularosa reservation, across the Rio Grande, the old Indian promptly declared war again and vanished into the hills. Another fifty settlers fell to Apache bullets before the government came round to Crook's and Cochise's point of view; and until his death two years later, in June 1874, he dwelt tranquilly with his band on their newly established reservation on ancestral soil.

The rest of the Apache story is essentially an anticlimax. Crook cleared up the remaining pockets of resistance, striving hard to treat his enemies generously. He also sought to teach them the domestic skills that he knew they would now need if they were to live productively on their reservation. Unfortunately, he was replaced in 1875, by which time the government and the white settlers between them had already ensured another ten years of pointless bloodshed and bitterness. The government, particularly when the reservations showed signs of yielding valuable minerals, kept shifting the Indians about in an abrupt and arbitrary way, which inevitably brought about a long succession of breakouts and rebellions.

Victorio, successor to Mangas Coloradas, escaped from Ojo Caliente in 1879 with 100 warriors. He reached the Big Bend country, crossed into Mexico, and before he was run down by the Mexican army north of Chihuahua had killed 100 soldiers and 500 settlers. In 1881, a mixed band of Mescalero and Chiricahua Apaches, under a rheumatic, half-blind septuagenarian called Nana, got loose. In two months, they traversed 1,000 miles of territory, fought eight successful battles against 1,000 soldiers and 400 vigilantes, killed 40 of them, and captured 200 horses and mules. Nana's band never numbered more than 40 warriors, and they vanished clean away into the mountains of Mexico. In March 1883, Chato, who had given warning of his mettle before, bolted with 26 Chiricahua warriors and led them through the Southwest and Mexico, dodging 500 American and 4,000 Mexican troops, traveling seventy-five to one hundred miles a day, killing twice their own number, and losing only 2 men. Most spectacular of all, Ulzana, with 10 Chiricahuas, cut a terrible swath through the same area in the early winter of 1884. In five weeks, he rode 1,200 miles, evaded 3,000 soldiers and scouts, killed 35 civilians and 5 soldiers, lost 1 man, and stole back again to Arizona. Not all such episodes ended so happily for the Apache. In 1882, Loco and 78 Chiricahuas, mostly women and children, were killed in a battle with the Mexican army, after accounting for 20 soldiers; and in the same year 50 Western Apache were surrounded by 500 troops in the Mogollons, only half of them slipping alive through the enemy lines.

A special word must be said about Geronimo, today the most famous, though not historically the most important, of the Chiricahua chieftains. He has come to possess a special romantic appeal, because of his name, his cunning, his ferocity, and the fact that he was the last hostile American Indian to remain at large. He has become a symbol of that truly free, independent man that the American once felt himself to be; his exploits are the last threshing of the American Id before it had to submit to the dictates of modern society. Compared with Cochise, Mangas Coloradas, and other Apache leaders, Geronimo was a squalid character—yet, cutthroat and renegade though he was, it is impossible to take away from him the glory of that last defiant year. "Many a mad magenta moment," sang the poet, "stains the lavender of life." Geronimo certainly provided the world with one of its gaudier interludes.

He was born a Southern Chiricahua, and was never actually a leader of his people. His name in the Indian tongue was Goyaklah, "He Who Yawns," from a sinister habit he showed in times of excitement. Lieutenant Britton Davis, who took part in the Chiricahua campaigns of the 1880s, and whose *The Truth About Geronimo* is a classic of Western history, wrote of him that he was "a thoroughly vicious, intractable, and treacherous man. His only redeeming traits were courage and determination. His word, no matter how earnestly pledged, was worthless." He acquired a position in his tribe because of his dubious talents as a medicine man; but when he tried to seize the tribal leadership, on the death of the legitimate chief, only thirty warriors would follow him. What brought him to prominence was his talent for talking, and when in the early 1880s General Crook, sent back to the Southwest to quench the last embers of Indian resistance, wanted an Apache go-between,

Naiche (left) and Geronimo at Fort Bowie, about 1885. (ARIZONA HISTORICAL SOCIETY)

Geronimo put himself forward. He helped Crook to bring the Chiricahuas, of whom only 500 were left, to the San Carlos reservation, where there was a year's uneasy peace.

Gordon C. Baldwin believes that Crook made a mistake in trying to make the Apache take up farming, instead of herding, which would have been more natural to them. Certainly it was a mistake to order Geronimo to disgorge the horses and cattle that he had stolen on his way to San Carlos. In any case, it was foolish to settle Apache of different bands on the same reservation; many of them hated each other as fiercely as they hated the white man. In May 1885, 144 Chiricahuas jumped the reservation, of whom 35 were warriors, the members of Geronimo's personal following. They were led by Geronimo, old Nana, who was crippled with rheumatism, Mangas, son of Mangas Coloradas, and Naiche, son of Cochise. However, the other chiefs, disliking and fearing Geronimo, repudiated them, and kept three-quarters of the Chiricahuas at home at San Carlos.

For eight months, Geronimo and his 35 warriors went on a rampage. They killed for the sake of killing. They slaughtered 10 American soldiers, 73 American settlers and, according to the Mexican governor of Sonora, somewhere between 500 and 600 Mexicans. In January 1886, they were induced to discuss peace terms with "Gray Wolf," in person. They talked for three days, were photographed together, and all seemed at an end. Then an American whiskey peddler stole into camp and sold them liquor. Geronimo reeled away, with Naiche and 20 warriors—but Old Nana, Ulzana, and the others had had enough, and went back to San Carlos. Crook, already under attack from the professional Indian haters and Indian exploiters in Washington, resigned, and was replaced by General Nelson A. Miles.

Geronimo carried on his depredations with increased fury for another six months. The last phase was marked by senseless atrocities, as if Geronimo wanted to kill the entire white world, one by one. Sadly, he was providing the enemies of the Indian with the excuse they needed for the way they wanted to treat all Indians, everywhere. For half a year, two dozen Apache eluded twenty-five columns of American troops, lying in wait at every ranch house, waterhole, and way station. Heliographs winked on every mountaintop. The Mexican government gave Miles permission to send American troops across the border into Chihuahua and Sonora. Never in human history can twenty half-starved men, their ability to maneuver restricted by the presence of their women and children, have been the focus of such a manhunt. What finished them was the capture of their camp and baggage by an American flying column. A few days later, on June 6, 1886, Geronimo surrendered to Lieutenant Charles B. Gatewood, and on September 3rd was brought captive to General Miles. It was the end of aboriginal America.

Miles and his superiors then did a disgraceful thing. It was disgraceful not only because it was cruel in itself, but because such things ought not to have been done by white men—by men, that is, who prided themselves on their alleged superiority, as civilized and educated men, over their opponents. People who aspire to lofty standards automatically impose on themselves the requirement of living up to them. Now, at Miles' orders, the Chiricahuas—all 500 of them—men, women, and children—were jammed like cattle into railroad cars and deported to military prisons. And the prisons were in Florida. There might have been some justification for deporting or shooting Geronimo and his warriors, on the spot, after their recent abominable spree: but the Apache who had kept their word, and who had remained peacefully at San Carlos, were deported too. So were the Apache scouts, men who had actually served against Geronimo, including the two men who had recently led the Americans to Geronimo's camp. A number of Chiricahuas who had been called to Washington to receive silver medals from the President were arrested as they left the White House, and packed off to Florida with the rest.

In Florida, the Apache males were segregated in one camp, their children and womenfolk in another. Enforced separation, homesickness, the flat landscape and wet climate, quickly began to take their toll, as their captors had intended. Eventually, some politician suffered a twinge of conscience. In 1887, the Apache were moved to a military prison in Alabama. In 1894, reduced

Apache Gan Dancers at Beaver Creek, Arizona.

now to four hundred, they were transferred again, this time to Fort Sill in Oklahoma. They stayed there for nineteen years, and it was at Fort Sill, in 1909, that Geronimo died. His last years were pitiful. He was exhibited like a freak in the St. Louis and Omaha expositions, and was carried in the cavalcade of the presidential inauguration in 1905, like a Gaul in a Roman procession. He would have done better to have died rifle in hand, in the Gila, a generation earlier.

It was not until 1913 that those Chiricahuas who wished to return to the Southwest were allowed, after twenty-seven years, to do so. Most of them had grown accustomed to existence at Fort Sill, and only 187 made the final journey. Some of them went to the San Carlos or White Mountain reservations in Arizona, some to the Mescalero reservation in New Mexico. There, the Western, Jicarilla, and Mescalero Apache had escaped some of the worst trials experienced by the Chiricahua, though they too had been badly harried. The Mescalero were transferred no less than eight times from one location in New Mexico to another, before they were permitted to settle down in a spot which the Anglo felt he had no use for. For once, the Anglo had made an error: he had presented to the Mescalero the glorious high hill country around Cloud-croft and Ruidoso which, while it may not be good for farming, and possesses no important minerals, is excellent for grazing cattle and sheep, for horse wrangling, and for winter sports. It is only thirty miles across and twenty miles deep, but the heart lifts at the sight of the alpine meadows alive with remudas of fine horses. If the Apache were indifferent horsemen a century ago, they are certainly so no longer. The Mescalero, too, run a skiing facility, on the slopes of the Sierra Blanca, and operate gift shops where they sell Indian handicrafts—mostly the work of other tribes, for they have never acquired the artistic abilities of the Navajo or Pueblo Indian, though they have shown themselves highly practical in other directions.

The 1,500 to 2,000 people on the Mescalero reservation have serious problems. Half the population are under fifteen; the birthrate is too high, in spite of an infant mortality rate of almost 10 percent; the average life expectancy is around forty; more than half the work force is unemployed; most houses are substandard and without adequate sanitation; less than 10 percent of the people have completed high school; and there is the usual problem with alcohol. Yet the tribe is well led, in spite of its past dislocations, and the outlook for the future is distinctly hopeful. The 1,500 to 2,000 Jicarilla Apache, on their reservation in northwestern New Mexico, are similarly plagued with troubles, but are also energetic and forward-looking, and there is good reason to think that they too, in the long run, will make progress toward stability and prosperity. As for the Western Apache, on the much larger San Carlos and White Mountain reservations in Arizona, they now number no less than 8,000 to 10,000. In the past fifteen years they have proved increasingly vigorous, confident, and able to slough off the defeats inflicted on them a century ago. When all that primal fierceness has been rechanneled into productive enterprises, they will again be a potent factor in the life of the Southwest.

And yet . . . and yet . . . It is easy to write the glib phrase, "productive enterprises," by which one means, after all, chiefly the making of money. That was not what Indian life, either of the horse Indian or the sedentary Indian, was all about. In reconverting the Indian, in changing him from the unconscious to the conscious, from the Id to the Ego, the Anglo has denaturized him, as the Anglo has denaturized himself. The Indian showed that there was another way to live. It was the way the white man once lived himself; therefore the red man had to be punished for reminding the modern, socialized, urbanized American of what he had lost. Of course, the vicious, visceral mistreatment of the aborigine is not confined to the American. One could point equally to the depredations of certain of the English, French, German, Belgian, and other colonists throughout the globe in the nineteenth century, or to the things that Brazilian commercial interests are doing today to the natives in the forests of the Amazon. It was a process that began with the Industrial Revolution, with Big Business and Big Government, with the assumption by the apostles of Bigness that their way is the only way.

Consider what has gone. Consider what the Apache has given up. Con-

An Apache girl's Puberty Ceremony, Beaver Creek, Arizona.

sider what we ourselves have sacrificed. "It was a different world the Indian lived in," wrote Clark Wissler, writing over thirty years ago. "We spend our time on paved roads and cross streams on bridges. We have cleared away the forests, dried up the swamps and destroyed much of the interesting wildlife of the country. Much of the native flora has been swept away to make room for crops, meadows and golf courses. Surrounding ourselves by all sorts of mechanical aids, we have forgotten nature as the Indian knew it. He was at home in the forest; we are afraid. So much of our world is man-made that we think in terms of mechanics, a world which we manipulate and control. With the Indian it was different. He saw living creatures on every hand; he spied upon them until he knew their ways; he marveled at their skill in eluding him, their humanlike ways and his inability to communicate with them. He felt the forest as a living thing; the trees were to him almost as persons, and the winds were the breath of some great unseen supernatural. When the storm clouds rolled, the thunder pealed, the tornado crashed through the trees, he felt the presence of powers upon the highest level of creative and destructive force. As he walked abroad, he felt himself in the presence of living things conscious of his existence, who could speak to him, if they chose, and at any time change his fortunes for good or ill. To them he turned for guidance and wisdom."

Oh yes, we have surrendered much—Indian and white man together.

It would not be right to end a chapter on the Indian of the Southwest without at least a passing glance at the Comanche and the Ute. If one feels a tendency to oversentimentalize the Indian, the Comanche is an excellent corrective. He terrified the early settlers in the Southwest as thoroughly as the ruffianly crew of white gunfighters, whom I shall describe in another chapter. In fact, the Comanche were considered as much of a scourge by their fellow Indians as the gunfighters were by the white settlers.

If the Apache were the Visigoths of the Southwest, the Comanche were its Huns. A popular Anglo name for them was "the Cossacks of the Plains." We have noted that they were considered throughout America as the "horse Indians" par excellence, and no corner of the area was safe from their thundering invasions. With the Kiowa Apache, who were their neighbors to the north, they were the only Indians in the region who had ridden the great central ocean of grass and hunted the buffalo. It was their skill· in the chase that had perfected their horsemanship. Fortunately for the other tribes of the Southwest, sedentary and nomadic alike, by the time the Comanche came out of their original homeland in the Black Hills of Dakota, to settle in West Texas, the Spaniards and Anglos were already pushing and prodding at them from the westward. Their principal foes were the Spaniards, then the Mexicans, and ultimately the Texans, and between Comanche and Texan there grew up a special hatred. With the French, oddly enough, they had been on good and even affectionate terms, owing to the fact that the latter, thrusting westward from Louisiana, handled them cleverly and used them in their own struggle against the Spaniards. The French, coming into contact with them after the founding in 1724 of Fort d'Orléans, on the present site of St. Louis, Missouri, called them the Padoucas, which was the name they were called by the Sioux. Their own name for themselves was "Num," The People.

Until the middle of the nineteenth century, the Comanche were known to their Indian neighbors, who kept as far away from them as possible, as the

Snakes. With the Shoshone, the Ute, and the Kiowa, they formed the northern and easterly portion of the iron ring that prevented the early settlers from breaking out of the Rio Grande and the Pimería Alta, and which made existence irksome for the sedentary Indian. Even the Apache occasionally indulged in a little amateurish agriculture, hankering after some of the comforts of civilization; but the Comanche spurned such compromises. They were the Ironsides of the Indian scene. Unlike the Apache, who made themselves tigerish with *tiswin,* a liquor made of fermented corn, the Comanche were teetotalers; they did not need drink to stir themselves up. They also lacked the Apache taste for cunning and treachery, meeting their enemies, even the United States army, head on, in the open field, in straightforward combat. They were heartless and sanguinary, yet seldom committed the sadistic excesses for which the Apache were renowned. They would chop a man down, and carry off his wife and children, but they would not as a rule torture him or sentence him to a lingering death.

They had a low opinion of the Jicarilla, Mescalero, and Lipan Apache, with whom they disputed the enormous ranges of West Texas, in particular the Davis Mountains and the Big Bend. There was continuous fighting between the two peoples. Among themselves, they were more cohesive than the Apache, their subtribes larger, and when necessary they would coalesce into formidable units led by chiefs who wielded undisputed authority. They were also numerous, accounting for perhaps as much as a third of the 150,000 Indians who were thought to have existed in West Texas and the Southwest when the United States took them from Mexico. On the other hand, in spite of their regard for the French, they shunned the ways of the white man. They dressed simply and plainly, in strips of hide and leather; like the other tribes in the Southwest, they showed a deplorable absence of chic. In physique and appearance, they were not much more impressive than the Apache, and their camps, though sometimes extensive, were essentially transient. They lived in buffalo-hide tipis, with a flap of bearskin over the entrance, constructed round a central hearth. They were continually on the move, after the buffalo, or mounting raids. Apart from a passion for tobacco, their outlook was puritannical. Courteous to their women, except when they were unfaithful, in which case, like the Apache, they would slice off the ends of their noses, their deepest feelings seem to have been reserved for their horses. They amassed horses for their own sake, putting their mark on them by their custom of slitting their ears.

Their conservatism extended to their methods of hunting and waging war. They never took to muskets or rifles, but clung to the bow and arrow. With the bow, which they fashioned from orangewood, they were among the best performers in Indian America. They could gallop alongside a buffalo and shoot an arrow clean through it. They suspended their buffalo-hunting activities only during one part of the year, when they turned instead to hunting another prey—Mexicans. In the autumn, when the grass was high and the waterholes full, the shining of the big, blood-red September or "Mexican moon" summoned them southward. A vast number of Comanche, in a single column, would ride down from the Staked Plains, through the Castle Gap, across the Pecos, the Conchos, and the Rio Grande, into Mexico. Splitting into three columns, they would ravage the country as far as Chihuahua and Durango, while the Apache were similarly despoiling the country farther to the west.

It was a tragic time for northern Mexico. The great Comanche *razzias*, supplemented by minor platoons of Utes and Kiowas, began in the 1820s, when the Spaniards had departed, and went on until the 1870s. It was an agonizing half-century. The government in Mexico City, whose main efforts were concentrated on fighting the Texans and the French, was powerless. There were no troops to spare for New Mexico, whose governors were led into trying to make individual peace with the interlopers, on whatever terms the Indians would grant. During the 1830s and 1840s, the north of Mexico became virtually depopulated. The mines and haciendas were abandoned. The Spaniards had struggled heroically to push the frontier north of Durango —now Durango was once again the front line, a frightened and demoralized city.

The Mexicans were not saved by their own exertions. They were saved by a situation which developed in West Texas and the Southwest in the 1860s and 1870s, and which came to demand the total attention of the Comanche. The white buffalo hunters came flooding on to the Plains, systematically decimating the buffalo. Their methods were diametrically opposed to those of the Indian. When the Indian went hunting, he generally did so in a spirit of moderation. He killed only as many animals as were necessary, and ate or utilized every scrap of them. Not so the white man. It seems unbelievable, but the numbers of the buffalo declined from an estimated 100 million in 1860 to 1,000 in 1900. It seems equally unbelievable that most of the damage was done in four years, between the opening of the eastern market for hides in 1870, and its closure in 1874, when there were no animals left to hunt. It is paying the buffalo hunters a compliment to call them huntsmen at all. Buffalo, with their bad eyesight, poor sense of smell, and nonexistent sense of self-preservation, were sitting-targets. No more skill or courage was required to kill them than clubbing seals or firing explosive charges into whales. Legions of white riffraff, armed with monstrous "buffalo guns," flocked to the Plains, where even the most cowardly and inept of them could shoot two hundred of the great helpless beasts between sunup and sundown.

The buffalo crisis served to throw up a last great Comanche leader. Quanah Parker, an Indian of singular gravity and good looks, was born about

1845, into the Quahadi Comanche, reputedly the most warlike of all the tribal bands. His father, Nokoni, was its chief, his mother, the chief's principal wife, was Cynthia Ann Parker, a white woman who had been carried off at the age of ten from an East Texas settlement. Quanah was only in his late teens when Nokoni died, but such was his force of character that he was appointed head of the band, an unusual honor, since leadership among the Comanche did not ordinarily pass from father to son. Under the terms of the Medicine Lodge Treaty of 1867, the Comanche, Cheyenne, Arapaho, Kiowa, and Kiowa Apache had been granted reservations which were supposed to be inviolate. But the whites constantly invaded the tribal lands, and when the buffalo massacre began in 1870 the trickle became a flood. The Indians could not ignore a threat to their very means of subsistence. Quanah Parker collected together several hundred Comanche, Kiowa, Cheyenne, and Kiowa Apache, and in June 1874 attacked a gang of thirty buffalo hunters holed up in an old trading post at Adobe Walls, near the junction of Bent's Creek and the Canadian River. The hunters had something more taxing to fire at than a herd of docile behemoths, but their enormous guns took their toll, and in three days of furious fighting the Indians, armed with bows and arrows, were only able to kill four of the white marauders. Then the army, under General Miles, moved into the Indian Territory, as the area was then designated, to take matters in hand. Within a year, the tribes were smashed, and their more intractable members dispatched by Miles to his prison camps in Florida.

Quanah Parker remained at large with his own band for a few months, but in the summer of 1875 he too rode in from the Staked Plains and surrendered. This wonderful man then demonstrated extraordinary qualities of intelligence and leadership. He faced the reality of the situation squarely and courageously, and instead of encouraging the Comanche, Kiowa, and Cheyenne to squander their vital energies in futile resistance, like the Chiricahua Apache, he formed them into a triple alliance and became its first leader. He was still only about thirty years old—but for thirty years more, until his death in 1911, he kept his people together, maintained their traditional culture and religion, and made many trips to Washington to act as their spokesman and to plead their cause. He became a legendary figure, and nearly a half-century after his death, in 1957, the mortal remains of Quanah Parker were reburied at Fort Sill, Oklahoma, with full military honors.

And so passed, at a hand-gallop, the brief but intense climacteric of the nomadic Indian. Some tribes bore up, under the events of the 1870s and 1880s, better than others. The sedentary Indians, dour and self-contained, managed in many instances to come through reasonably intact. But all Indians, horse and sedentary alike, except those in the pueblos, were relegated to the reservations. Today 400,000 of the nation's 550,000 Indians live on two hundred reservations, in twenty-six states. Seventy-five percent of them live in shacks, shelters, huts, or abandoned cars and buses. The same proportion haul their own water from pools, tanks, or rivers, often polluted. The Indian's average wage is $30 a week, compared with $130 for the white and black man. Unemployment runs over 40 percent for Indians, against 4 percent for the rest of the nation. In addition to syphilis, tuberculosis, and drunkenness, he suffers to an excessive degree from pneumonia, dysentery, trachoma, diseases of the bone and of the inner ear. Clearly, the Indian is literally the low man on the American totem pole.

There was no place for the Indian in the white man's scheme of things. He was an anomaly, an anachronism. The poorest and most underprivileged immigrant from Europe fitted into the emergent framework of modern America, sharing in the American ethos, wanting to be part of it. The white man and red man had nothing in common. Their life-styles were fundamentally opposed. The white man was Ego-directed, canny, provident, looking and building toward the future; the red man lived for the day, in the timeless present of the Id. He was not the material out of which a great nation-state and industrial complex could be built. His life was founded on alien imperatives. His existence was bound up with natural essences, with Nature itself, entities that must be ground out before the factories and power plants could arise.

Those Indians who had not succumbed to smallpox, tuberculosis, or the effects of drink, and had not been disposed of by the cavalry saber or the scalp-hunter's bullet, were driven on to the reservation, where it was confidently expected that they would quickly fade away. Indeed, they had been so battered during the last half of the nineteenth century that it seemed that they could never recover. Until the appointment of John Collier as Indian Commissioner, during the New Deal, it was official, explicit government policy that the customs, religion, and way of life of the Indian was to be suppressed and stamped out.

Collier, a wise and humane figure, singlehandedly changed most of that. He lifted the ban on Indian dress, ceremonial, and folkways, and by doing so restored to the Indian his individuality and sense of self-respect. Unfortunately, the Bureau of Indian Affairs, in spite of possessing many sympathetic and dedicated employees, has gone through several reactionary periods since Collier's time. As recently as the 1950s, President Eisenhower signed into law a number of repressive bills, and even today most Indians regard the Bureau with bitterness, and urge its abolition. It is unlikely, now, that the Bureau can relapse into the inhumane stance of pre-Collier days. The Indians have become too numerous and too vocal. They are still a disadvantaged minority, but it is no longer possible to dismiss them out of hand.

Much of the beauty and genius of Indian life, its better features, have been eroded; they are past recall. But something yet remains. And it still might happen that, when Americans begin to get over the Bigness Sickness, their fixation with Big Business, Big Oil, Big Politics, Big Crime, Big Everything, that they will begin to value those qualities of the Indian spirit which their forbears sought so hard to obliterate. It would be ironic if, somewhere in Grand Canyon Time, the Indian of the Southwest teaches the white man more valuable lessons than the paltry lessons the white man has tried to teach him.

NINE

THIS BOOK IS ABOUT the American Southwest: but the American Southwest is merely a part of a greater Southwest, the Southwest of the North American continent itself, which cuts down deep into Mexico. Nature takes no account of those four straight lines that the human hand has drawn across the map from the Colorado to the Rio Grande; and the Rio Grande, representing the international border from El Paso to the Gulf of Mexico, is in most places no more than a pathetic ditch across the barren expanse of the Chihuahua and Sonora deserts. The deserts pay no heed to the boundaries of the modern nation-states. The saguaros and Judas trees march along in unbroken battalions; the ocotillos are as crimson and prickly on Mexican soil as on American; the desert is as stony. Except at the recognized crossing-points, there are no fences or barbed wire barriers to tell you that you are in one country or the other. Why waste time building them? Smugglers or wetbacks are welcome to plod across the cactus-studded wastes. With bloody feet, they may eventually reach a main road, where they can easily be picked up by the police or the Border Patrol.

In the way that northwest Mexico and southwest America meld into each other geographically, so they do anthropologically. We have already noted the fluid manner in which, from earliest times, the tribes freely migrated northward and southward in the area; it was not a case of a steady human movement from the Pacific northwest down into the Americas, but of a constant churning and stirring about. The early hunters, and later the historic Indians, all had relatives or collaterals to the north and south of them, with whom they

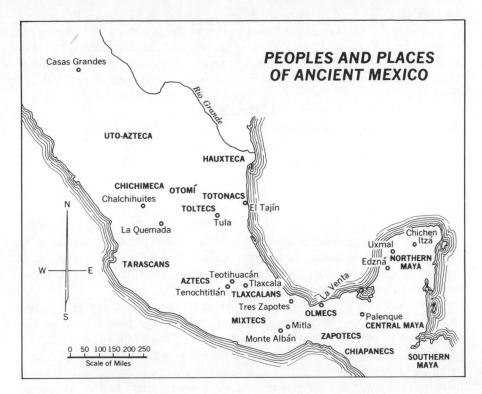

FIGURE 14

would link up in case of need. The Sandia-Folsom-Clovis complex, and particularly the Cochise and Hohokam cultures, had significant extensions into Mexico, while we have seen that such vital skills as growing maize and making pottery were of Mexican origin.

However, in Spanish times the tribes who inhabited northern Mexico were scarcely known to the peoples to the south, who regarded them as wild and barbarous. Durango, five hundred miles south of the present border, remained the most advanced bastion of New Spain until Chihuahua was founded in 1724. Father Kino had gone to Baja California and to the Pimería Alta to open up territories that were completely unmapped and virtually unexplored. The settlements between El Paso and Santa Fe were small havens in an uncharted sea.

Before Chihuahua was established, with the aim of shortening the gap between Durango and El Paso, the normal route to the north from Mexico City lay along the Pacific seaboard, west of the Sierra Madre occidental. As much of the journey as possible was done by ship, before moving inland from

❖ 191 ❖

the port of Culiacán. The northern tribes were feared. They hated outsiders, and were deadly shots with the bow and arrow. For the most part, they wore simple breechclouts, and lived on rats, snakes, and similar vermin, the diet favored by the Aztecs, whose homeland, Aztlán, lay somewhere among them. The number of tribes was bewildering. Around the shores of the Gulf of California, which until Father Kino crossed the Colorado was assumed to be a separate sea, dwelt the tribe called the Seris. Even today, the Seris are a shy folk, living largely on clams, mussels, crabs, and other shellfish which they gather on the beach. Their neighbors on the west side of the Sierra Madre were two fierce peoples, the Opata and the Yaqui, whom we have met before. East of them, on the other side of the Sierra Madre, in modern Chihuahua, were small groups of people, the Sumas, Mansos, and Janos, and two more bellicose tribes, the Conchos and the Tobosos. These were flanked to the east by the Lipan, Mescalero, and Kiowa Apache, who regarded northeastern Mexico as their stamping ground, though they were frequently required to share it with their hereditary enemy, the Comanche. All these Mexican tribes mainly belonged to the same far-flung Aztec-Tanoan family as the peoples of modern Arizona and New Mexico.

It is a remarkable tribute to the persuasive powers of the Jesuits and Franciscans that they were able to move freely among these remote people and convert so many of them to their own beliefs. The problems of verbal no less than vehicular communication were almost insurmountable. Even today, in Mexico, more than ninety distinct languages are spoken. All the tribes had their own tongues, and the priests who went among them had to start from scratch. Almost all these early missionaries compiled grammars and dictionaries of the native tongues that are invaluable to modern linguists. As in New Mexico, the history of the region was starred with serious revolts, sometimes against the missionaries, more often against the Spanish soldiers in the presidios. In the 1640s, the Conchos, Tobosos, and Sumas burned the Spanish settlements in Chihuahua, and the revolt of the Rio Grande pueblos under Popé in 1680 provoked a general rising throughout Nueva Biscaya. In 1695, even Father Kino's authority could not prevent the Pimas killing the priest at Caborca and attacking Magdalena. The Pimas, indeed, were in a constant state of unrest throughout the eighteenth century, and in 1751 they again murdered another priest at Caborca and repeated the act at Sonoita. The tiny people called the Tarahumare, who inhabit the depths of the Barranca del Cobre, in the way that the Havasupai live at the bottom of the Grand Canyon, were never reduced, and were in an almost permanent state of hostility. Today they live in amity with two young white missionaries who are translating the Bible for the first time into their language. Even Caborca is quiet now, a charming, sleepy town, affluent by Mexican standards, where on Good Friday one can join the procession that starts from the stately mission built on the foundation of Kino's adobe church. The townsfolk, in their best clothes, follow the priest in his purple vestments through the streets, behind a huge black cross carried by two boys. Periodically, the boys halt and hold the cross upright, the people kneel, the priest prays, the red-robed choir sings, the dogs bark, and the ice cream and lemonade vendors ply their cheerful trade. An innocent and peaceful scene, that would have pleased the heart of Father Kino.

While one entire phase of its culture reached the Southwest as a result of the Spanish conquest of New Spain, ultimately much of that culture had its roots in an older, pre-Cortésian stratum. I have visited most Mexican archaeological sites of consequence: and like most visitors to Mexico, at the beginning I was totally unprepared for what I saw. It is one thing to look at photographs of antiquities in books; it is another to see them on the ground, in their proper shape and size. The monuments of Greece are few, and largely broken up; those of Crete, elegant but small; those of Rome, generally cold and vulgar. Only the monuments of Egypt rival those of Mexico in number, scale, and individuality.

It is odd to reflect that, with the exception of the Olmec civilization at the beginning, and the Aztec civilization at its end, the great civilizations of Mexico rose and fell in a period of only one thousand years, roughly corresponding to the Dark Ages and Middle Ages in Europe. Odder still, nobody in any other part of the world had an inkling of the dramatic events that were occurring on the unknown shores of the Americas. And already, at the opening of the classic age, the civilizations of Mexico showed a taste for massiveness. I am compelled to speak not of "cultures," but of "civilizations." The word is apt. The Olmecs of southern Veracruz and Tabasco, the oldest of these great civilizations, erected in their swampy heartland huge conical clay temple-platforms, one hundred feet high, surrounded by elaborate ritual precincts. They seem to have been the seminal civilization of those that came later, and their so-called San Lorenzo phase can be dated long before 1000 B.C. They reached their peak about 500 to 300 B.C., when their monuments seem to have been drastically destroyed and their sites abandoned. The scowling Colossal Heads, eight to ten feet high, which are the most famous characteristic of their art, were buried deep in the ground, as if to banish them from man's sight. It has been suggested that the heads may have been, in fact, portraits of hated and tyrannical rulers. A series of these heads has been set up in a well-planned Olmec park at Villahermosa, capital of Tabasco, which is otherwise a sweaty, slovenly town, where you eat badly, sleep worse, and get bitten to death by mosquitoes and *jejenes*.

The Olmec park also features a number of altars or sacrificial stones showing a strange infant god, his Mongoloid face creased in what archaeologists call the "jaguar smile." He is nursed and tended by priests with robes and conical headdresses that are oddly Southeast Asian in appearance, though of course no connection whatever has ever been proved between ancient Asia

One of the Colossal Heads in the Olmec park, Villahermosa, Mexico. (PHOTO BY AUTHOR)

and Mexico, or between Europe and Mexico. These delicate, convoluted figures are also prominent at the great temple of Palenque, one of the westernmost of the Mayan temples, very close to the old Olmec territories; and by coupling this with the fact that the Olmecs invented systems of writing and arithmetic, which were to be such a vital feature of Mayan civilization, the influence of the Olmecs on the latter is easy to appreciate.

To the marvels of Mayan civilization I must, unfortunately, restrict myself to no more than a paragraph or two. It extended over an enormous area of southern Mexico and Central America, and many of its sites have scarcely been identified, let alone investigated. The Northern Maya inhabited the states of Campeche, Yucatán, and Quintana Roó; the Central Maya occupied the Petén and British Honduras; the Southern Maya the state of Chiapas, Guatemala, El Salvador, and Honduras. There are, of course, strong similarities between the sites of the three areas: but what must strike the visitor is their exuberant variety. Kabah is thirty miles from Uxmal, and Uxmal is eighty miles from Chichén Itzá; not great distances. But all three sites, belonging to the same complex, are different in aura and in architecture. You are in the presence of a cheerfully hybridizing imagination. And within the same area, with easy access to one another, are a score of other temple-complexes with their own quite distinctive appeal—Edzná, Labná, Sayil, Kabah, Dzibilchaltún, Tulúm. Every Mayan site possesses a similar repertoire of buildings—temples, ball courts, palaces, administrative offices, observatories, sacred wells: and the manner of their execution is always fresh and lively.

The Mayan sites are more accurately called temple-sites, not cities. They were not urban areas, but religious and political centers, immensely enlarged versions of the temples of Egypt, the monasteries of medieval Europe, or the Jesuit and Franciscan missions of the Southwest. They were at the same time schools, courts of law, agricultural and horticultural institutes. Most of them were vast, spreading out over miles of countryside. Unfortunately, the soil was poor: parched limestone in the north, tropical jungle in the center and south. Therefore, such expensive structures, the manifestation of some great compulsive dream or fantasy, eventually proved impossible to maintain. Sharply and suddenly, about A.D. 850, Mayan civilization collapsed as swiftly as it had mushroomed into existence about A.D. 300, less than six centuries earlier. What could have happened? We know that the Anasazi, in the American Southwest, were driven away from their cliff dwellings by prolonged

Edzná, a Mayan temple-complex, Yucatán, Mexico. (PHOTO BY AUTHOR)

drought. Drought may also have been partly responsible for the Mayan *débâcle,* though many other causes have been suggested: disease, war, revolution, earthquake, invasion by the Toltecs from the west. It seems very likely, since the Maya were, in the phrase of Michael D. Coe, "obsessed with war," that the innumerable theocratic states wore themselves out in fratricidal fighting, and were thus easy meat for the stern professional warriors from Tula, forerunners of the grim Aztecs. However, the secrets of Maya history, like the writing in which they are enshrined, remain largely indecipherable—although the work done on Mayan writing during the last twenty years, by such scholars as Knorozov, Berlin, and Tatiana Proskouriakoff, suggests that an important breakthrough may not, after all, be too far away.

In the case of the Olmecs, the great temple-sites of La Venta, Tres Zapotes, and San Lorenzo, though excavated, have long since gone back again to the Tabascan swamps; they do not dwarf and humiliate the wooden huts of the modern peasants. But in Yucatán, the temple-sites of the Maya are interspersed with the poverty-stricken villages of their present-day descendants. There are two million Mayan-speaking Indians still inhabiting the three classic areas, the largest American Indian bloc north of Peru. The Maya of Yucatán have always shown themselves to be fiercely independent. They resisted Cortés' former captain, Francisco de Montejo, whose palace still stands in Mérida, the city he founded, when he subdued Yucatán with 380 men and 57 horses in the 1540s. He named it Mérida because, like Cortés and so many of the conquistadores, he was from Extremadura. Later, the Mayans resisted the Mexicans, with the help of British arms, in the long struggle for independence in the nineteenth century. Today they still nurture their separatist dreams. Mérida itself is one of the most attractive towns in modern Mexico, spacious and prosperous, but the *campesinos* in the hinterland are among the most destitute in the country. Almost their sole crop is *henequén,* or sisal, wrested from a fearsome cactus. It is a commodity for which world demand is shrinking. They are also the victims of *latifundia,* bound to estates owned by indifferent landlords who live elsewhere. They are forbidden to market their crops except through a state organization which they regard as oppressive and corrupt. They are ground down thoroughly by Big Landlords on one side and Big Government on the other. They survive on pride, resentment, and a handful of corn.

Gigantic as they are, even the temples of the Maya do not impress you by their bulk to the same extent as two other classic sites: Teotihuacán and Monte Albán. Teotihuacán, an hour's bus or taxi ride to the northeast of Mexico City, is a place of staggering dimensions. It extends over eight miles, and may have been the only true city, with a resident population, to have been created by any of the civilizations of Mexico. Its regularly laid-out streets may have accommodated 30,000 to 50,000 persons. Certainly, enormous

Plaza and Pyramid of the Moon, Teotihuacán, near Mexico City. (PHOTO BY AUTHOR)

numbers of people would have been needed to build such mammoth structures as the Pyramid of the Sun, the Pyramid of the Moon, the Avenue of the Dead, the Citadel, the numerous temples, and the palaces of the nobles. Teotihuacán was no doubt a slave state. It seems to have been to some degree Olmec-derived, and in turn it influenced the civilization of the Maya during the latter's formative stage. Then, about 600 B.C., after only three centuries of existence, when its great buildings were scarcely completed, it fell to fire and the sword, at the hands of barbarians. The destruction of such a place must have been a terrific and tragic spectacle: but the whole course of Mexican history, more than that of any other nation, in modern as well as in ancient times, has been little more than a succession of such bloody disasters.

Monte Albán was the capital of another great people, the Zapotecs. For over 1,000 years, from 300 B.C. until the holocaust that overtook all Mexico about A.D. 900, the Zapotecs led mainly peaceful and pastoral lives—by Mexican standards—in the inaccessible valleys of Oaxaca. Monte Albán is vast and sprawling, the buildings grandiose but gray-seeming. It lacks the totalitarian quality of Teotihuacán, but also has none of the sparkle of the Maya. It is true, of course, that some unpleasant things went on among the Maya, particularly when they eventually fell under the sway of the Toltecs: hearts were ripped out, skulls piled on the *tzompantli*, people thrown into the *cenotes*, or sacred wells. The players in the ceremonial ball games were decapitated—not the losers, as one might expect, but the winners, since the gods would be better pleased with the blood of the victors—an honor most sportsmen would decline. Yet the atmosphere of the Mayan sites is not at all depressing, unlike the ponderous vistas of Teotihuacán and Monte Albán. However, later in their history, at a nearby spot in the valley of Oaxaca, the Zapotecs, who then occupied more than two hundred villages, compensated for the gloominess of their great élite center by building the enchanting little temple-city of Mitla. The architecture of Mitla is joyful and elegant, a diminutive masterpiece, confirming that the Zapotecs were a less moodily aggressive people than most of the races of ancient Mexico. Ultimately, Mitla survived as the guardian of Zapotec traditions when the Zapotec empire had been taken over, only two or three centuries before Cortés, by their neighbors, the Mixtecs. Indeed, to this day Zapotec Indian ceremonials are still carried out annually at Mitla. Their conquerors, the Mixtecs, were another highly gifted and imaginative people, who buried their rulers in the subterranean tombs of Monte Albán that had housed the bones of the lords of the Zapotecs. From one of those tombs, known by the prosaic name of Tomb 7, came the wonderful treasure interred with the bodies of a Mixtec king and his ritually slaughtered courtiers. The discovery was the Mexican equivalent of the finds from the equally casually named Graves 4 and 5 at Mycenae. The objects of gold, silver, crystal, amber, and jet have the same splendid barbarity of conception and execution, and are fully equal to the Mycenaean standard. They are on display at the museum at Monte Albán, and are a high point of a visit to the agreeable town of Oaxaca, set in high, vertiginous country, ablaze with wild orchids and the wild crimson dahlia that is Mexico's national flower. The Mixtecs were capable soldiers, in addition to being excellent artists, and were one of the few peoples in southern Mexico to stand up to the Aztecs and actually inflict defeat upon them.

All the civilizations of Mexico were of necessity warlike, otherwise they could not have survived: and two of the later civilizations were outstandingly aggressive. These were the Aztec and the Toltec. For some reason, I find myself as much drawn to the Toltecs as I am repelled by the Aztecs. The Aztecs were the Mexican equivalent of the Waffen S.S.; the Toltecs, on the other hand, had the grace and the style of Samurai: there was order and beauty in their lives, as well as cruelty and bloodshed. They were regarded by their contemporaries and by those who came after them as aristocrats, whereas the Aztecs were never considered as anything but *arrivistes*. It was fashionable for all later peoples, including the Aztecs, who badly needed a pedigree, to claim descent from the Toltecs. It was an honor to link one's name with theirs. The Aztecs represented the spirit of destruction; the Toltecs were innovators and culture-bringers.

Their capital, Tula, ancient Tollan, the Place of the Reeds, is situated at approximately the halfway point between Mexico City and the spacious, attractive city of Querétaro. In spite of its beauty and relative accessibility, I would guess that Tula, being slightly off the tourist route, is not much visited. A pity. It was at Querétaro, if I might make a slight diversion, that Juárez, an impassive Zapotec Indian from Oaxaca, finally ran down and defeated the Emperor Maximilian. Maximilian, and the two Mexican generals who were loyal to him to the end, were shot on the Cerro de las Campanas, a little grove of trees which is deceptively hard to find, although it is close to the modern four-lane highway between Mexico City and Querétaro. The townsfolk do not know, have forgotten, or think it impolitic to tell foreigners where it is situated. With their Mexican attitude to death, they certainly consider it very eccentric for a foreigner to spend so much energy tracking down the place where someone has been shot; shooting, after all, has been commonplace in Mexico.

The Cerro de las Campanas is a mournful spot, marked by a dispirited-looking funerary chapel which Juárez, who had rejected worldwide appeals for clemency, afterwards allowed the Emperor Franz Joseph to erect in memory of his younger brother. Juárez had sent the body home, more as a gesture of contempt than pity; and when the dead Archduke was being embalmed for the journey to Vienna, he visited the mortuary to inspect the remains. The embalmer had draped Maximilian's bowels and intestines round the corpse's face. Juárez looked at the dead man without expression, then remarked: "There you are, you see, I told you: he doesn't smell too bad." The Cerro seems a chilly place for the imperial dream to have come to an end. The palace at Chapultepec in Mexico City, which he built for his Empress and her Indian ladies-in-waiting, is equally cold and mournful. Maximilian was handsome, kindly, sincere, and idealistic; he was also vain, stubborn, and not very bright. He should have departed with the French, or have stolen away quietly, like the Portuguese Emperor of Brazil. But that would have robbed him of his tragic stature, for in spite of his faults—or because of them—he was a genuine tragic hero.

Tula—to return to my theme—is another difficult site to track down. You leave the motorway and find yourself in a maze of side roads. The countryside is white coated with flakes from nearby cement factories, drifting down on once-proud Tula. The city was savagely battered by the invaders who destroyed it, which was rather unusual in ancient Mexico; peoples who were conquered were killed, enslaved, or had their hearts torn out, but their cities were usually spared the worst sort of obliteration. But when Chichimec tribes from the north descended on the Toltecs for the last time, about 1150, they did their work so thoroughly that Tula was wiped off the map, and it was long thought that mighty Teotihuacán—it is a measure of their prestige—must have been their capital.

Ironically, the Toltecs themselves, like the Aztecs after them, were both of northern and Chichimec stock. The Chichimecs, who were typical of the barbarians who rose everywhere to power after the widespread collapse of 900, were an agglomeration of tribes of Uto-Aztecan descent, and therefore closely related to the tribes of the American Southwest. The early wave of Chichimecs quickly surmounted their lowly origins, and to the people of the south among whom they rose to power they became the Toltecs, "the Artificers," because of their outstanding architectural and artistic abilities. Tula, after it had been founded by Topíltzin, "Our Prince," the son of the warrior king Mixcóatl, "Cloud Serpent," about 970, must have been an exceedingly beautiful capital. Even today, with its clean lines and chaste execution, it is somehow reminiscent of Egypt; the buildings have the same air of poise and simplicity. The principal excavations have been in the area of the smaller of its two pyramids, the Pyramid of Quetzalcóatl. It was once surrounded by a palace complex whose spacious colonnaded halls were enhanced with magnificent colored friezes, some of which have miraculously survived, and is enclosed by a remarkable *coatepantli,* or serpent wall. Other features included a number of the well-known statues of reclining gods, holding a sacrificial tablet on their stomachs, called Chacmools. But the outstanding feature of Tula, as it exists today, is the group of colossal statues of Toltec warriors, backed by richly carved columns, which stand on top of the pyramid. They present one of the most striking sights to be seen in Mexico.

Originally, these statues and pillars supported the roof of a great palace that once existed at the foot of the pyramid. In 1960, they were carried up to its summit. It was an inspired idea. Climbing the ramp of the shapely, severe, five-stepped pyramid toward the quartet of eighteen-foot giants, you are filled with awe. They stand as straight and arrogant as guardsmen on parade, arrayed in ceremonial uniform, their faces stiff and stern, eyes front, chins in, shoulders back. Their heads are crowned with feathered helmets; in the lobes of their ears are enormous rectangular plugs; on their chests are breastplates in the shape of conventionalized birds or butterflies; their loincloths, belts, wristguards, anklets, and sandals are elaborately embroidered. In their right hands they clasp their spearthrowers, in their left a sheaf of darts, and slung on their backs are swords with edges of sharpened obsidian. These are the men who conquered Central America.

The badge that they wear is the feathered serpent, the emblem of the god Quetzalcóatl, the most mysterious and poetic of the gods of Mexico. His sinuous emblem is everywhere at Tula, taking pride of place above the coyotes, the jaguars, and the eagles. The Toltecs bore it with them to the remotest corners of Mexico. More, on one of the pillars behind the statues of the warriors can be seen the actual figure of the most famous king of the Toltecs, the founder and the high priest of Tollan, Ce Atl Topíltzin Quetzalcóatl. This was the Feathered Serpent himself. It gives you a strange feeling to rest your hand on that stone.

Quetzalcóatl was not only a god, he was a real historical personage. Topíltzin was the son of Mixcóatl, and although the cult of the Feathered Ser-

The Toltec warriors, Tula, Mexico. (PHOTO BY AUTHOR)

pent or Quetzalcóatl was probably in existence before he was born, he served it so faithfully and lived so extraordinary a life that he came to be identified and merged with it. He appears to have been a religious reformer, not unlike Akhenaton in Egypt, who set up the peaceful, humane cult of the serpent to counterbalance the cult of the ancient wargod, Tezcatlipoca, "Smoking Mirror." Tezcatlipoca was a reeking, bloodthirsty deity, patron of the military caste, who demanded offerings of hearts and skulls; not surprisingly, he became the object of special veneration among the Aztecs. Under the influence of Topíltzin's powerful personality, the Feathered Serpent was accepted first as the coequal, then the superior, of Smoking Mirror; but then the devotees of the latter staged a revolt, and Topíltzin Quetzalcóatl was driven out of Tollan. The actual date of his departure may be precisely stated as 987. The rivalry between the two gods, one the embodiment of light, the other of darkness, parallels the clash between the two great cosmic principles represented in ancient Persia, for example, by the eternal struggle between Ahura Mazda and Ahriman.

Accompanied by his sorrowing disciples, Topíltzin made his way eastward. In the mountain passes between the volcanoes of Popocatépetl and Iztaccíhuatl, three hundred miles from Tula, many of his retainers froze to death—a fate that would also overtake many of Cortés' soldiers, six hundred years later, during their weary marches through that inhospitable region. Finally, he reached the land of the Mayas, a full eight hundred miles from his

The pyramid at La Quemada, Zacatecas, Mexico. (PHOTO BY AUTHOR)

native city. There he was received with joy, and eventually died by immolating himself on a funeral pyre, wearing his turquoise mask and the quetzal feathers that were sacred to him. These quetzal plumes, which can be seen on the head-dress of the Toltec warriors, were the marvellously tinted and extravagantly long tail-feathers of the small, darting, glittering quetzal bird, its numbers now so depleted that it exists in only a few areas of Central America. It gives its name to the official currency of Guatemala, and can be seen on its coins and banknotes.

There was another version of Topíltzin Quetzalcóatl's end. In this, he was supposed to have sailed, on a raft of serpents, far away across the ocean to the fabled Tlapallan, the "Red Land." In both accounts, he became the Morning Star, or planet Venus, and was expected one day to return in glory to Mexico on the day of his own birthday, Ce Atl, "One Reed." By a truly uncanny coincidence, it was on exactly the day Ce Atl that the ships of Hernán Cortés, with their towering white sails, were first seen standing in to shore. More uncanny still, in face and physique Cortés closely resembled the traditional Mexican pictures and descriptions of Quetzalcóatl. No wonder Moctezuma was frightened and confused, and offered Cortés only a spasmodic resistance.

Once more the legendary account is rooted in fact. The chronicles of the Mayas record that, in 987, a foreign prince entered their land, conquering a part of it. In the Mayan tongue, Quetzalcóatl was called Kukulcán, "Feathered Serpent," and he was supposed to have settled at Chichén Itzá. And indeed, at

Chichén there is abundant evidence of the occupation and expansion of the site by Toltec invaders. No doubt these invaders were connected with the outcast army of Topíltzin Quetzalcóatl, who probably descended upon the coast of Yucatán by sea, from the vicinity of Veracruz. The typical Toltec porticos, columns, colossal statues, ball courts, skull racks, together with the unique Chacmools, appear at Chichén Itzá and other Mayan sites, embellished with the Feathered Serpent and the other tokens of the Toltec warrior-clans. It would appear that, after the collapse of the Mayan Empire, the Toltec overlords raised Yucatán to a last brief moment of glory before it relapsed into chaos. The situation was ripe for the appearance of Hernán Cortés and his vigorous lieutenants.

Quetzalcóatl and his legion were not the only column to fight their way free of Tula, shortly before or after the fall of the curtain. Quetzalcóatl went east, but other Toltec bands took a different direction, fanning out to all points of the compass. They reached the Pacific Coast, the Gulf of Mexico above Veracruz, Monte Albán and Mitla, and even the Southern Maya country. One of the earlier groups penetrated five hundred miles northwest of Tula, into the mountains of Zacatecas. There they settled down as warrior-farmers among the wild tribes of the frontier, much as the Hispanic pioneers would do three centuries later. The largest site of the Chalchihuites Culture, as it has come to be called, and which I mentioned briefly in an earlier chapter, is at La Quemada. It was crude, but sturdy, resembling a British Iron Age hill-fort. It has a large but coarsely constructed colonnaded hall, and a charming little pyramid, like the sub-Egyptian pyramids of Meroë in Nubia. It is worth seeing because almost nobody visits it, and you have the whole place to yourself. Mexico, indeed, is packed with hundreds of such sites, if you are willing to leave the tourist track.

The Chalchihuites people extended their chain of hill-forts almost as far north as Durango, deep into the country of the fierce Chichimecs, who had been both their ancestors and their destroyers. The Chichimeca, as the ancient Mexicans called them, were only one of a number of barbaric peoples, including the Teochichimeca, the Tamime, and Otomí, who had partly been roused by and had partly instigated the terrible disasters that rained down on Mexico about 900. Probably it was the Chalchihuites folk, planted athwart the eastern slopes of the Sierra Madre occidental, who brought a touch of the flamboyant cultures of southern Mexico to the placid Hohokam cultivators of Arizona. Until the creation of the Camino Real, the Sierra Madre route was the traditional road through the no-man's-land between central Mexico and the area that was to become the American Southwest.

Using the northerly outpost of Chalchihuites as a jumping-off point, Toltec traders pushed north to Arizona and the Rio Grande pueblos. Their journeys were infrequent; they could not have been expected to bring many of the culture traits of the exotic and martial south to the remote and peaceful peasants of the north. Nevertheless, Michael D. Coe assures us that "investigations have shown that the Chalchihuites culture was the intermediary between Toltec and Southwestern cultures like Hohokam. Suffice it to say that most of the more spectacular aspects of the late farming cultures of the United States have an ultimate Toltec ancestry."

Neither in his *Mexico* (1962), nor in his postscript to it (1967), however, does Coe mention the most—indeed the only—major archaeological site in the north of Mexico. Work on it had hardly commenced before the late 1950s. This is the huge and bewildering complex known as the Casas Grandes, situated in the Chihuahua Desert, 130 miles northwest of Chihuahua and 100 miles southwest of Ciudad Juárez. It was an enormous depot or staging-area for the Toltec caravans, and doubtless for the Aztec merchants who followed them. But it was more than that: influenced as much by the sober and industrious Hohokam to the north as by the volatile and colorful Toltec to the south, it developed into a real town, with plazas, three-story buildings, and an elaborate water supply. Indeed, the Casas Grandes people were probably relatives of the Salado people who built the Casa Grande, near Phoenix. However, its most intriguing features reveal a fantasy and extravagance more characteristic of the Toltecs. They include ball courts, pyramids, and a strange undulating structure, 450 feet long, that may be a sculptural representation of the Feathered Serpent. When Adolf Bandelier examined the Casas Grandes in the 1880s, there was nothing to be seen but an indecipherable group of mounds. Today, the area has been impeccably cleared, but is still enigmatic. By the local people it is called "Las Moctezumas," since, as I pointed out earlier, almost all antiquities in Mexico, as in the American Southwest, have become popularly associated with the Aztecs, although it was only the last of the classic Mexican civilizations. The modern Chicano nationalists in the Southwest go so far as to call their movement *Aztlán,* after the putative Aztec homeland in the north of Mexico, thus betraying a curious ignorance of the true nastiness of that particular people.

The part of Chihuahua in which the Casas Grandes is situated, incidentally, is today occupied by one of the world's most peaceful religious sects, the Mennonites. It is very curious to encounter these serious folk, of German origin and still German-speaking, in this remote spot. Both sexes wear Victorian costume, the men with beards and shovel hats, the women in long dresses. They are an earnest, innocent, timid people, Biblical fundamentalists who came to Mexico to escape persecution elsewhere. They left the United States when compulsory military service was introduced, and were welcomed south of the border because they are capable and hard-working farmers. They have rendered their allotted acres in one of Mexico's loneliest and least populated provinces exceptionally fertile and productive. Unfortunately, the Mexican authorities now seem inclined to withdraw from them their immunity from conscription, so their future is once again uncertain. It would seem that even in a lost valley in Mexico, miles from anywhere, a small, simple, laborious community cannot escape the meddling attentions of Big Brother. On the other hand, it must be said in favor of Mexico that so far she has avoided the insanity of most Latin-American countries, most of whom spend over 10 percent of their meager budgets on military hardware. Mexico expends less than 3 percent, three times less than any South American country. With twenty-two times the population of Uruguay, and ten times the area, she has less than three times the troops. A pity her example is not followed further south.

TEN

THE ETHNIC MIX of northern Mexico and the Southwest United States, on the eve of the American takeover, was rich and varied. On both sides of what would become the border, nomadic Indians, sedentary Indians, horse Indians, Spaniards, Spanish-Mexicans, were all inextricably mingled. Spanish rule over New Spain, New Mexico and the Pimería Alta had lasted for exactly three centuries; it left behind it a complex physical legacy: *peninsulares, criollos, mestizos,* and innumerable varieties of Indians.

Throughout the Spanish dominions, the acknowledged leaders of society were the *peninsulares,* the administrators and soldiers who came out from Spain, performed their tour of duty, and sailed home. Below them were the colonial aristocracy, the *criollos*—pure-blooded Spaniards, but born and living out their lives in the New World. Below these privileged castes came the *mestizos* or *ladinos.* Like their counterparts in British India, until they became numerous enough to be taken seriously they led an unenviable existence, despised and distrusted by those above them and by those beneath, but eventually establishing themselves as a middle-class. And finally there was the lowest and largest class of all, the Indians, with no one to care for their bodies and their souls except the Catholic priests, and sometimes not by them.

Later, in the old northern provinces, now sheared away by the United States, the Anglos would come to add their own diverse immigrant blood to the brew. Except in Texas, this would not occur in any significant degree until the 1860s and 1870s. Indeed, in the Southwest there had been an influx of Hispanic settlers into New Mexico which had brought their numbers up to

70,000 at the end of the Mexican era, as against only 10,000 Pueblo Indians. Until a century ago, the Hispanos were very much the dominant people in the Southwest. During the period 1830 to 1870, they gradually extended their holdings, despite the fact that the Apache had beaten them out of Arizona, being greatly helped by the remote and barren nature of the territory, and by the absorption of the Anglos in their Civil War. Texas, the more populous two-thirds of which belongs with the American South, and is therefore outside the scope of this book, was another matter. Aggressive Anglos, many of them criminals or *filibusteros,* had come west to settle in Tejas, as its Mexican rulers called it. George Sessions Perry, in *Texas: A World in Itself* (1942), quotes an early Texas settler as saying: "If you ask why a man has run away from the States and come to Texas, few persons feel insulted at such a question. They generally answer for some crime or other which they have committed; if they deny having committed any crime, or say they did not run away, they are generally looked upon rather suspiciously."

The Spaniards never exercised more than a tenuous hold over Texas, which they regarded merely as a buffer zone between New Mexico and the French. In New Mexico, on the other hand, they were strong enough, in spite of marauding Indians, to carry out their traditional policy of excluding foreigners. The only Americans to set foot on southwestern soil during the Spanish epoch were a few trappers and merchants, most of whom were summarily thrown into jail. When Lieutenant Zebulon Montgomery Pike, who has given his name to Pikes Peak in Colorado, entered the Rio Grande settlements in 1806, with a group of soldiers disguised as traders, he too was arrested, and sent downstream under guard through El Paso to Chihuahua. There he spent many weeks in captivity, while the suspicious authorities investigated his credentials. Evidently he was a charmer, for instead of being shot as a spy, he was courteously escorted back to the Rio Grande, and before he was expelled from Spanish soil was offered a large loan by the Commandant of Chihuahua. He left an entertaining account of his adventures in what, for an American of his time, was a totally unknown and unexplored region.

In the early 1830s, there were only about 5,000 Mexicans in the whole of Texas; yet 30,000 Anglo-Americans had already poured on to the rich farmlands in its east and center. The Mexican government, in its first throes of independence, distracted by constant coups d'état and the disruption of organized authority, tried at first to pretend that it was pleased by the influx of American go-getters into the province. But a swift confrontation was inevitable. Protestant Americans were not about to accept the sovereignty of Catholic Mexicans. Stephen F. Austin, the Father of Texas, after whom its capital is named, had been pressing the Mexican government for separate statehood and privileges for Texas as early as 1827. In 1834, after personally negotiating with Mexico's President, General Antonio López Santa Anna, he was arrested and clapped in solitary confinement in Mexico City's most noxious jail. He and his Texas colleagues, in their statehood conventions, had expressed alarm at the condition of civil war that had already begun in Mexico, and which would last with brief interruptions for almost a century. They were also antagonized by the antics of such figures as General Agustín de Iturbide, who crowned himself Emperor Agustín I, and was soon afterward shot. And then there was Santa Anna himself, a crazy and sinister clown, nine times president, whose exertions between 1836 and 1852 were to lose his country over half the territory bequeathed to her by Spain—though even now Mexico remains the eleventh largest country in the world, covering 760,000 square miles, larger than Britain, France, West Germany, Belgium, Spain, and Portugal combined. One can scarcely imagine what Mexico might have been today had it managed to hold on to its original territories.

Ironically, a principal stumbling-block between Texans and Mexicans was slavery. Mexicans, intoxicated by the revolutionary ideas they had borrowed from France and America, liked to make enthusiastic if hollow pronouncements in favor of freedom and the brotherhood of man. The Texans, including Stephen F. Austin, were slaveholders, and meant to remain so. This was one of the reasons, in addition to their rambunctious and combustible personality, that made Texans so unpopular in the north, and ultimately made their accession to the Union only possible as a result of the private intrigues of Andrew Jackson and his friend Sam Houston.

In the autumn of 1835, after two restless statehood conventions had roused the anger of Santa Anna, the Texans renounced the Mexican Constitution of 1824 and broke into open revolt. In spite of their bravery, and their accuracy with the long rifle, they were fearfully chastised. To the accompaniment of bands playing the *Degüello,* which signified "Cutthroat" or "No Quarter," Santa Anna killed and murdered 182 of them at the Alamo at San Antonio, in March 1836. He then captured and shot another 300 at Goliad, three weeks later. Everywhere his forces were successful. When he caught up with Sam Houston's exhausted little army at San Jacinto, on April 21, 1836, it seemed that Texan hopes of independence were about to be extinguished forever. But Houston, after all, was the protégé of Old Hickory, who had beaten the English fair and square at New Orleans, killing 2,000 and losing 20. He took Santa Anna by surprise at four o'clock in the morning, when it was barely light, and within half an hour the Alamo and Goliad were avenged; 1,260 out of 1,300 Mexicans were slaughtered, for a loss of 2 Texans killed and 23 wounded out of a total force of 783. Santa Anna, fleeing in the uniform of a private soldier, was captured ten miles from the battlefield. Brought back to camp, his identity was betrayed in a farcical scene. His fellow-soldiers, in spite of his furtive and frantic signals, insisted on leaping to attention, saluting, and shouting *Viva el General!* Sam Houston, who had himself been wounded, calmed him down with a dose of opium (Santa Anna was an addict), extracted from him an instrument of independence, and shipped him off to Veracruz. Twenty thousand Texans had wrested their freedom from nine million Mexicans, with no help from the United States. From April 1836, until its citizens, in face of the continuing Mexican threat, voted to join the Union in October 1845, Texas was a sovereign republic.

Santa Anna subsequently awarded himself $250,000 in back pay for the war against Texas. He was later to lose a leg in the "Pastry War," and had the limb buried with full military honors. Immensely popular with his countrymen, who are connoisseurs of failure, he was eventually exiled by Juárez. Eventually he died in his bed, bankrupt, in Mexico City in 1876, at the age of eighty-two. "The Almighty in His Wisdom," wrote Wilfrid Callcott, in his biography of this flamboyant and lamentable character, "had seen fit to bless this child of destiny with a marvelous personality, tremendous energy and a facile brain, but, for some inscrutable reason, had omitted the balance wheel and left him an opportunist."

It is amusing to recall that during those nine years the Texicans, as they were called, were often so disgusted with the half-hearted support they received from the United States that they were tempted to throw in their lot with Britain. They almost became subjects of Queen Victoria. It was actually the fear, deliberately nurtured by President Sam Houston, that Texas might become British that induced the Senate hurriedly to vote statehood for Texas in 1845. So, if matters had turned out differently, I might have been writing these lines on the soil of a British dominion, and the Governor of Texas might have been attending a Commonwealth Prime Minister's Conference.

Wily old Houston and cunning old Jackson had pulled off their coup. By nature I am a Jeffersonian, not a populist: but there is something about Jackson, some quality of manliness, that it is impossible not to admire. It is touching to recall that, when Houston heard that Jackson was dying at Nashville, he galloped seven hundred miles from Texas to Tennessee to see him. Visiting the Hermitage, it is easy to visualize Houston riding across the rough grass beneath the majestic elms, toward the high white portico—only to be told, as he threw himself from the saddle, that his friend had died an hour before.

One of his last acts, as President of Texas, was to sign a joint declaration with the United States that would grant Texas the status of an American territory. He knew that this would provoke Mexico into declaring war, which would in turn compel the United States to come to Texas' defense. It was the subsequent Mexican-American War, fought between March 1846 and September 1847, that not only yoked Texas to the Union, but brought beneath the American flag the whole of the West and the Southwest. In that conflict, the United States army was commanded by Zachary Taylor, a good plain soldier who, after he became president as a result of his efforts in Mexico, liked to graze his horse on the White House lawn. In the final stage of the campaign,

General Winfield Scott, "Old Fuss and Feathers," led the American troops into Mexico City, where he remained as a conqueror until the summer of 1848. As all Americans know, on Scott's staff were two officers named Lieutenant Ulysses S. Grant and Captain Robert E. Lee.

Scott brought no less than 43,000 American troops to Mexico City to enforce the Treaty of Guadalupe Hidalgo, named after the suburb where it was signed. It was ratified in May 1848, and was surely one of history's more momentous documents. For an honorarium of fifteen million dollars, the United States acquired possession of all of Mexico north of the Rio Grande—a slice of territory larger than the whole of Europe. At that, Mexico was lucky. President Polk and Secretary of State Buchanan declared that America should not have stopped at the Rio Grande, but should have gone on to draw the line at the Sierra Madre; while Jefferson Davis and the extremer Democrats called for the annexation of the entire northern half of Mexico. Other voices were raised to urge the taking over of the whole country. Winfield Scott maintained that two-fifths of the population of Mexico, weary of wars and civil wars, would have welcomed such a course. Polk and his party declared that "God ordained that Mexico should be an integral part of the Union," and foreshadowed the fate that was being prepared for the Indians of the Southwest by insisting that "The Mexicans are aboriginal Indians, and must share the destiny of their race—*extinction!*" The destiny of America, after this, its first imperialist venture, was now the Manifest Destiny that McKinley was later to enunciate. Only seventy years after independence, America was beginning to flex its muscles. Fortunately, wiser counsels, including that of Sam Houston himself, finally prevailed. Houston knew that Texas, and the United States, had a long period of ethnic and geographical ingestation ahead of them, without taking on the problems of Mexico.

The Texans, notwithstanding, had been showing a lively tendency to reach out and grab the whole of the Southwest, even before the Mexican-American War. In 1841, Mirabeau Buonaparte Lamar, who served as president between the two terms of Sam Houston, raised an expedition to cross the six-hundred-mile desert between the eastern Texas settlements and Santa Fe for the purpose of annexing the eastern half of New Mexico. After the victory of San Jacinto, Texas had laid claim, with typical modesty, to the whole length of the Rio Grande, from Colorado to the Gulf, as her natural boundary. For five years after independence, she had not felt strong enough to enforce her pretensions. Now, she thought, was the time not only to extend her sway, but to cut herself into the lucrative trade of Santa Fe. There, a group of American traders had insinuated themselves into residence under the patronage of Governor Armijo, a fat rascal to whom they paid a monstrous *mordida,* or "bite." Nevertheless, Armijo had the sense to leave them enough of their profits to make it worth their while to stay on. Naturally, they were terrified when they heard that the Texans were marching to their "rescue"; but they need not have worried. The 300 Texan volunteers had started too late in the season, underwent continuous losses of men and supplies, and arrived in New Mexico only to be rounded up like cattle. Armijo tortured and shot the leaders; the rest, at the orders of Santa Anna, were marched down the Rio Grande toward Mexico City. The commander of the escort was a sadistic brute who sabered the stragglers and cut off their ears. Fortunately, at El Paso they were taken beneath the wing of the commandant of the department of Chihuahua, a civilized and humane man. For three days, after five months of barbarous treatment, they were rested, bathed, and banqueted, and when they continued their march the general and the whole town turned out to wish them Godspeed. No wonder that the few of them who survived recalled with gratitude "the pleasant town or city of El Paso," with its "delightful situation in a quiet and secluded valley, its rippling artificial brooks, its shady streets, its teeming and luxurious vineyards, its dry, pure air and mild climate, and above all, its kind and hospitable inhabitants." The happy interlude was all too short. On reaching Mexico City, they were lodged in chains in its prisons. Mexican prisons are atrocious enough today; what they were like then, God only knows. Only a handful lived to receive the pardon of the capricious Presidente, and were allowed to crawl back like dogs to the United States.

The Santa Fe expedition was a total failure. Did it induce the Texans to abate one jot of their outrageous claims? Not in the least. In fact, being Texans, they pushed those claims all the harder. Only a minority proposed that Texas should face facts, retrench, and declare the Pecos to be its western boundary. The majority cried out for the Rio Grande, and nothing but the Rio Grande. The Rio Grande had always been their drive, their dream, the river which was interwoven with their consciousness and their destiny. For good measure, they now threw in the Arkansas River as well. In 1850, when they had been threatening Washington with war to make good their demands, the frontiers of Texas on the map in the Governor's office at Austin embraced the Oklahoma Panhandle, most of New Mexico, half of Colorado, and a sizable portion of Wyoming. It was the sort of behavior that had led a soldier to write home, toward the close of the Mexican-American War, that "Some one said that we ought to continue the war and whip the Mexicans until they consented to take back all of Texas." In 1850, however, the Senate called the Texans' bluff. The Texans were induced to accept more sensible boundaries, and were given $10 million as a solatium. It should be noted that even today, as a result of those early disputes, the western boundary of Texas is unrealistic. Texas ought indeed to end at the Pecos, and El Paso and the Big Bend country should be included in New Mexico, where they logically belong. El Paso, large and thriving city though it is, is too far from East Texas to feel a strong link with it, or to be treated as anything but a distant relative. It would make good sense to hive off West Texas and attach it to New Mexico, a poor state which would benefit economically from such a course. It is not, however, at all likely to happen.

The Santa Fe Trail, which bound New Mexico commercially to Missouri, was the route along which the Anglos had penetrated Mexican territory in the 1820s and 1830s. It was an important highway, the earliest of the great trails of the West. It ran from Santa Fe, through the Ratón Pass, across the Canadian, Cimarron, Arkansas, and Kansas rivers, past Fort Riley and Fort Leavenworth, to Missouri. It was roughly the track which Coronado had taken three centuries before, when he crossed the Staked Plains on the search for Cíbola. It was westward along the Santa Fe Trail that General Stephen Watts Kearny brought in two companies of the 1st Dragoons to occupy New Mexico during the Mexican-American War. He expected to encounter resistance in the high passes, but none materialized. He entered Santa Fe without a shot being fired, and on August 22, 1846, declared New Mexico part of the United States.

In fact, the nomadic Indians of the Southwest constituted a greater threat to the stability of the territory than the Mexicans, and Kearny was preparing to take action against them when he received orders to take the bulk of his Missourians, reinforced by the Mormon Battalion, to consolidate the seizure of California. This had already been virtually effected by Colonel Frémont and Commodore Stockton, and the dispatches containing the news of the event were being carried from California to Washington by Kit Carson. Kearny intercepted Carson on his way through New Mexico, and persuaded him to turn over the dispatches to another courier and act as his guide on the march to the Pacific. Carson, who preferred the West to Washington, agreed, and led Kearny and his men through the Glorieta Pass into Arizona, a route which would later become one of the principal highroads to Nevada and the West Coast.

To protect the Southwest, in the unlikely event of a Mexican counterattack, Kearny left behind him a scratch force under a cheerful and harddrinking backwoods lawyer, Colonel Alexander Doniphan. Doniphan, ordered to continue the campaign against the Indians, made his leisurely way with 500 infantry and 300 cavalry down the Rio Grande. Then he was suddenly instructed to hasten south, brush aside the screen of Mexican troops at El Paso, and join forces with an American army from the east in an assault on Chihuahua. He quickened his pace, left the Río Arriba behind him, and crossed the Jornada del Muerto. He had been joined by George Frederick Ruxton, one of those footloose Englishmen who were often encountered in the West at that date. Ruxton had been an officer in the British Army, and his first glimpse of Doniphan's brigade was a peep into hell. "No one," he wrote, "would have imagined this to have been a military encampment. The tents

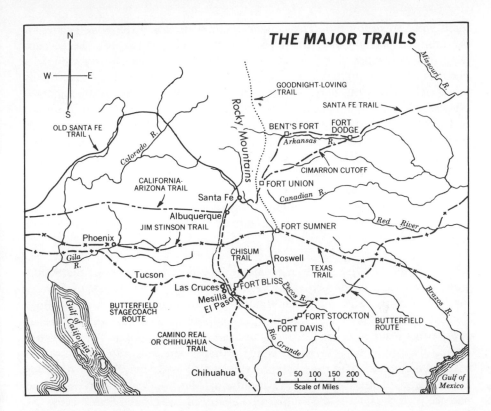

FIGURE 15

were in line, but there all uniformity ceased. The camp was strewed with the bones and offal of the cattle slaughtered for its supply. The men, unwashed and unshaven, were ragged and dirty, without uniforms, and dressed as, and how, they pleased. They were sitting in groups, playing at cards, and swearing and cursing, even at the officers if they interfered to stop it. Sentries, or a guard, although in an enemy's country, were voted unnecessary. Their mules and horses were straying over the country; in fact, the most total want of discipline was apparent in everything." Yet he readily agreed that "these very men were as full of fight as game cocks." Indeed, they proved it on the battlefield of Brazitos, forty-five miles north of El Paso, when they were challenged on Christmas Day by a well-found force of 1,100 Mexicans.

Doniphan was playing cards when the Mexicans closed in on him. The Mexican horsemen swung into line with grandiloquent shouts of *Libertad ó muerte!* Doniphan's order was more pragmatic: *"Prepare to squat!"* Squat they did: and when the Mexicans charged, the crouching tatterdemalions with the long rifles shot them out of the saddle. In moments the landscape was lit-

❖ 213 ❖

tered with Mexican dead. The Americans then broached the wine barrels in the captured enemy camp, and Doniphan returned to his cards. Three days later, he and his men were cordially received at El Paso, which they thought a gracious city after the pokey atmosphere of Santa Fe. There they gave themselves up to drinking, horse racing, wenching, and dancing "phandangoes." Nevertheless, in spite of hearing that the Indians at Taos had been in revolt, and had slaughtered the leading white people there, and that the army which they were supposed to meet at Chihuahua had never materialized, they voted unanimously to continue their campaign. On the last day of February 1847, Doniphan's little army, augmented by a few volunteers, defeated 4,100 Mexicans in a four-hour battle north of Chihuahua and took possession of the city. "Doniphan's March" was the only military action of the war in the Southwest; but it was gallant and high-spirited, and fully deserves its lively footnote in the history books.

With minor adjustments, the state and national boundaries of the Southwest were settled in the period between the signing of the Treaty of Guadalupe Hidalgo in 1848 and the middle of the American Civil War in 1863. Five years after Guadalupe Hidalgo, a complex negotiation with President Santa Anna resulted in the Gadsden Purchase of 1853; though as late as 1963, during the presidency of John Kennedy, there were still adjustments to be made to the boundary in the Chamizal area of El Paso, when the United States ceded a tract of 400 acres to the Republic of Mexico. In 1858, Washington had accepted the Gila as the southern boundary of the United States. Now the bankrupt Santa Anna was willing to sell, for $10 million, much of which he pocketed for himself, an additional piece of territory which would tidy up the border. The Americans had already appropriated the huge coppermines of Silver City and Santa Rita, but they jumped at the opportunity to acquire the rich farmlands of the Mesilla Valley, north of El Paso. The Purchase also included the town of Tucson. The treaty, negotiated by James Gadsden, a railway tycoon who was Minister to Mexico, was ratified in April 1854, and later that year United States troops entered Mesilla.

Mesilla is now a charming backwater, a tiny town with dirt streets, its pretty plaza dominated by a bandstand painted with the flags of Spain, Mexico, and America, and by the church of Saint Albino (whoever he may have been). It is like any small town in Mexico or Spain, and testifies to the universality and durability of Spanish culture. It was once an important agricultural and cattle center, though it has since been swallowed up by the city of Las Cruces—literally, "the Crossroads." During the 1850s, New Mexico was an enormous territory, comprising both New Mexico and Arizona; and the early Arizonans were naturally anxious to strike out on their own. It was therefore proposed that the two territories should be divided horizontally, New Mexico taking the upper half, and Arizona the lower, with its capital at Mesilla; but in 1863 Congress finally split the territories vertically, and gave them their present form.

What prompted Congress to act was the fact that the Confederacy had put into immediate operation a bold plan for seizing the Southwest. With only 250 Texas cavalrymen, Captain John Baylor captured El Paso and Mesilla in July 1861. He took the Union garrison at Mesilla prisoner and declared the town the capital of the Confederate Territory of Arizona. Congress woke up to the fact that the Southwest presented a strategic threat to the Union, providing as it did a wedge between the East and California. It was also a valuable source of supply, particularly of horses, for the Confederacy. Unfortunately, the United States military commander, General Canby, found himself outnumbered and poorly equipped. He abandoned all his strongholds in New Mexico, except for Fort Union, which guarded the Santa Fe Trail, deciding to concentrate his forces downriver at Fort Craig, below Socorro. There he would meet the Confederates and check their northward advance on Santa Fe.

The battle of Val Verde, which was actually the siege of Fort Craig, was fought between February 16 and February 21, 1862. Canby was severely mauled, but the Confederate leader, General Sibley, was unable to reduce the fort, and was unwilling to waste valuable time trying to do so. He marched his 3,700 Texans quickly upriver, taking Albuquerque and Santa Fe without any difficulty. But now, as he feared, the Union was sending reinforcements from the north. Colonel John Slough and 1,300 troops from Colorado entered New Mexico, to be challenged by Sibley as they came through the Glorieta Pass, fifteen miles above Santa Fe. Sibley was victorious, and beat the Unionists once more in a skirmish at Tijeras, and at another at Peralta two weeks later; but he never solved the problem of obtaining sufficient supplies; he had lost many of his wagons; and in mid-April he evacuated his troops from New Mexico while there was still time. He retired down the Rio Grande, sidestepped the unvanquished Union garrison at Fort Craig, and headed home for Texas. The North poured men into the territory to ensure that thereafter it would remain in Union hands. Fifteen hundred troops arrived from California to join those from Colorado, and another 5,000 were held in readiness at Fort Leavenworth.

To the east, in what is now the state of Arizona, Brigadier General James Carleton and his California column defeated a small Confederate remnant at a skirmish at Picacho Peak, north of Tucson, on April 15, 1862, and the town was occupied. Arizona was officially proclaimed United States territory on December 27, 1863, and the first meeting of its legislature took place at Prescott, which was also the site of the first governor's mansion.

There was no more Civil War activity in the Southwest, and the Union troops formed the nucleus of those that were to prosecute the Indian Wars that would rend the Southwest for the next twenty years.

ELEVEN

THE HISTORY OF THE SOUTHWEST during the half-century that elapsed between the end of the Spanish era and the aftermath of the American Civil War is inevitably confused. It was not until the late 1860s that the Anglos, previously discouraged by its isolation and by the Indians, began to permeate the area. The only exceptions were two specialist groups, the miners and the soldiers. Served by ill-defined wagon trails, both of them lived in extreme isolation, penned up behind their armed redoubts. After the discovery of gold and silver in California and Nevada, the bolder Texan and Kansan cattlemen also began to traverse the Southwest, bringing supplies to the mining camps and garrisons as a subsidiary to their main business of feeding the hordes of prospectors and settlers in the Far West.

Now that the 2,000 mile-long border between the United States and Mexico had been established, and the age-old traffic between the Southwest and Mexico had started to dwindle, an important shift of emphasis began to occur. Hitherto the lines of development had always been vertical, from south to north, up the Camino Real from Mexico City, Chihuahua, and El Paso into New Mexico, or up the Sierra Madre route into Arizona. From 1540 to 1848, this was the direction from which the soldiers, merchants, traders, missionaries, and Spanish and Mexican immigrants had flowed into the Southwest. Now the pattern changed. The lines began to realign themselves along an east-west axis. Instead of being the terminal provinces of Mexico, New Mexico and Arizona became intermediate territories of the United States, on the new highway between the Midwest and the Far West. The international boundary, the stagecoach routes, and the cattle trails, and eventually the railroad lines, would all run from east to west. El Paso would cease to be an intermediate stop on the Camino Real between Chihuahua and Santa Fe, and become a stop on the line that linked Fort Worth, El Paso, Phoenix, Yuma, and Los Angeles; Santa Fe would become a stop on the line that linked Independence, Las Vegas (New Mexico), Albuquerque, Flagstaff, and Los Angeles.

These creeping changes were not apparent at once. They were certainly not apparent to the Spanish-speaking element, which at this period was making what it took to be spectacular advances, later seen to be largely ephemeral. With the Pueblo Indians hunkered down in their villages, with the Plains Indians embarked on their death struggle with the American army, and with the Americans themselves embroiled in their Civil War, the Spanish-speaking New Mexicans expanded their agricultural and pastoral activities more widely than under Spanish or Mexican rule. True, many of them, particularly those in the Mesilla Valley after the Gadsden Purchase, refused to come to terms with the United States; instead, they retired to northern Mexico, where they formed the populations of what were eventually to become the teeming border towns. But many stayed on, including the wealthier families, who imagined that their security was guaranteed by the land grants given them by the Spanish and Mexican authorities, and which had been confirmed by the Treaty of Guadalupe Hidalgo. By the end of the century, however, the American courts had systematically stripped them of thirty-three million acres of land, snatched from them by the incoming Anglos. Their title was officially recognized only to a mere two million acres, for which the Anglos had found no use. Like the Navajo, the Apache, and the other Indians who had signed agreements with the Americans, they found that the word of the United States as embodied in such pacts was worthless. The land-grant dispute continues to this day, with the petitioners receiving no more satisfaction from the courts than they did eighty or ninety years ago.

The spearhead of Anglo colonization, in both New Mexico and Arizona, was provided by the miners. For 300 years it had been the lure of precious metals that had drawn men to the Southwest. The prosperity of Spain derived from her mining activities, and mining was as old as the Spanish Empire itself. Cabeza de Vaca, like most Spanish adventurers of the time, was an amateur prospector, and when he returned from his wanderings, in 1535, he inspired the Coronado expedition of 1540 by reason of his report of Cíbola with its "many signs of gold, antimony, iron, copper and other metals." Coronado's failure did not deter other treasure-seekers. The 170 unfortunates who accompanied Gaspar Castaño de Sosa—he who was exiled to China—to New Mexico, in 1590, were the inhabitants of a mining town in New León, hoping to make their fortunes by discovering mineral wealth. Juan de Oñate, *fundador* of New Mexico, armed himself before he set out in 1598 with a document that granted him exclusive mining rights.

The Spaniards pursued the business of mining in their northern territories with zeal, though it never yielded them the same benefits as in the organized and pacified provinces in Mexico. Most of their activities were concentrated in Sonora, in Father Kino's mission country, where in 1763 the famous *bolas de plata,* balls of silver, were found at Arizonac. During the 1850s, after the Hispano-Mexican departure, the Heintzelman mine at nearby Tubac was producing $100,000 of silver a year; but it fell into disuse, together with all the other mining enterprises in Arizona, when, in the chaos of the 1860s, the Chiricahua Apache and white renegades took over the southern half of Arizona. Activity in New Mexico was more sporadic, though a Spanish colonel had discovered the Santa Rita coppermines as early as 1800, and by 1804 six hundred men were employed there. Gold mining began throughout New Mexico in the late 1820s; but the Mexicans missed the opportunity to repeat the gold rush that had occurred in 1548 at Zacatecas because, exactly three hundred years later, they had signed the Treaty of Guadalupe Hidalgo and had surrendered California in the very month that John Marshall struck gold at Fort Sutter. They also lost the benefits of the gold that was found in Colorado, ten years later. The Colorado gold rush of 1858 soon petered out, but at its height it attracted 100,000 men to the diggings, and made several fortunes.

The Spaniards and Mexicans, however, had already made sizable discoveries of gold and other metals in California. These they had been able to exploit more steadily than the minerals of the Southwest. California was not only more fertile and less troubled by Indians but, once the sea route was properly established, it was more accessible. In the 1850s, thousands upon thousands of Mexicans poured into California to work in the mines for a dollar a day—a fortune by Mexican standards—going by sea, or taking the old De Anza Trail from Sonora and Tubac. The Americans of that epoch were without mining skills, and in California it was the Mexicans who carried out almost every phase of the work. After three centuries of experience, they were familiar with every type of technique, whether washing for gold in the placer mines, or in the "dry diggings." As late as 1870, three-quarters of the men in the mines of California and the Southwest were Mexicans. It was Mexicans who discovered for their Anglo bosses the *bonanzas,* or "rich lodes," including the famous Comstock Lode in Nevada.

Although many Mexican miners were skilled or semiskilled, others were no more than beasts of burden. During the Spanish and Mexican eras, and throughout the nineteenth and twentieth centuries in Mexico itself, not only convicts but innocent tribes of people were rounded up and sent to the mines. To the Indians of northern Mexico and the Southwest, the mines meant slavery and death. Mining has always been one of the unloveliest of human occupations, and its history in the Americas has been atrocious. The Pueblo Indians and Plains Indians were constantly on the watch for gangs of slavers, white or Indian, who kidnapped men and boys and sold them to the mines, which because of accident and disease always possessed an insatiable need for fresh labor. On the other hand, paradoxically, there were occasions when the Spanish-Mexican community and the sedentary Indians actually welcomed the presence of the miners in their midst. The mining camps, with their valuable equipment and their stock of firearms, drew the attention of the predatory Indians away from lesser targets, occupying them with battles and sieges which depleted their energy and resources. And as a result of this, the United States government, at a time when the population was reeling under hostile Indian attacks, was compelled to send in troops to act as the protectors of the white miners, the settlers, and the Pueblo Indians alike.

Between the end of the Mexican-American War and the end of the century, a network of forts was established throughout the Southwest. There were a score in New Mexico and a smaller number in Arizona, with outliers in Colorado and Utah. They were called "forts," since most of them had the palisades and watchtowers familiar from Western films; but most of them were temporary structures, few being occupied for more than ten years, and many for only four or five. Some, like Forts Marcy and Union, which sat athwart the Santa Fe Trail, or like Fort Bayard, that guarded the Santa Rita—Silver City mines, were occupied for as long as thirty or forty years; but the remainder were glorified camps, relocated in accordance with the progress of individual campaigns. The larger and more celebrated have in some cases been restored, or rebuilt for tourist purposes; but little is left of most of them. You stumble upon the vague stumps of adobe walls, a flattened and rusty tin can or two, a handful of blackened cartridge cases. The layout of the barrack-blocks and a faint trace of the paradeground are still discernible in the encroaching wastes of greasewood and lechuguilla. Ghostly bugles still reverberate. At Camp Ojo Caliente, at the end of a box canyon on the banks of a small creek, is the hole that once held the flagpole. It is a lonely, evocative spot; the shrubs, the ponderosas, the scarp of the hills, the creek, seem alive and alert around you. Here Victorio broke in during a night attack, killing eight men of the 9th Cavalry and running off forty-six of their horses; here Geronimo made one of his surrenders, and his 453 Apache were formed up to be taken on a three-week march to their reservation.

It would be a mistake, when you visit these ruined forts, only to picture sweating cavalrymen swinging to the saddle. The Indian Wars were fought not only by cavalry, but also the infantry, clumping along beside their mule-trains or horse-drawn wagons. The cavalry, however, was bound to be the main arm in warfare of that type, and most regular cavalry formations were sent to the Southwest at one time or another to be blooded or kept in trim. The 9th Cavalry, by the way, was an all-black regiment, though white-officered, and saw some hot action, particularly against the Mescalero Apache.

Cavalry or infantry, they had a tough time of it, and performed well,

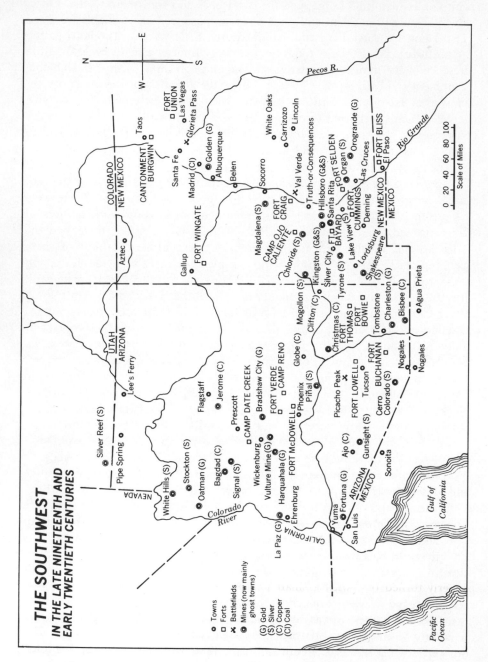

THE SOUTHWEST
IN THE LATE NINETEENTH AND
EARLY TWENTIETH CENTURIES

Legend:
- ○ Towns
- □ Forts
- ✕ Battlefields
- ◉ Mines (now mainly ghost towns)

(G) Gold
(S) Silver
(C) Copper
(Cl) Coal

Scale of Miles
0 20 40 60 80 100

FIGURE 16

The Queen Copper Mine, Bisbee, Arizona, 1880s. (ARIZONA HISTORICAL SOCIETY)

particularly in the years before the Civil War when they had to fight on the retreat. Totally without experience of that kind of terrain, there were 2,000 of them in that enormous area, to cope with 50,000 Indians, 20,000 of whom were hostile. It is not surprising that they could do little to protect the mines and settlements. After the Civil War, their numbers swelled; but so did their responsibilities. Had they been 200,000, instead of 2,000, they would still have had difficulty in fighting the aroused and confident Apache and Comanche on their native heath. The campaign they waged does not bulk large in the annals of serious warfare, but they were given a nasty job and they stuck to it. Nor were they a breezy, sloppy bunch like Doniphan's crowd. Photographs show them to have been dedicated professionals, thoroughly disciplined, properly turned out, with a smart paradeground manner. In the late 1860s and 1870s, the infantry wore the characteristic Civil War McDowell cap, or kepi, so called because it was taken from a French model; later it gave way to the more practical broad-brimmed campaign hat. They carried blanket-rolls and were armed with the Remington .44, then with the 1873 Springfield breach-loading 45–70, with bayonet. The cartridges were carried in the Mac-Keever cartridge box, then in the transverse "Prairie Belt," and finally in the

Mills web belt. The cavalry, mounted on the MacLellan saddle, an English pattern that was in use in the American army, with modifications, for a century, were outfitted for ceremonial occasions in dashing blue-trimmed dress uniforms, with shakos, or spiked helmets, that trailed garish plumes.

During the most intense phase of the Indian Wars, in the 1870s and 1880s, the number of mining towns the troops were called upon to assist trebled in number. A few camps were devoted to hunting for gold, but most of them now produced silver or copper, and toward the end of the century coal became paramount. Some of the richer finds were made by army officers or enlisted men who kept their eyes open—and their mouths shut—as they quartered the territory in pursuit of the Apache. When they were mustered out, they hurried back to stake their claim. The great copper mine at Bisbee, in the Dragoon Mountains, was only one of the mines to be discovered in this way. The silver mines are played out now, but many of the copper mines are still active, while the lead and zinc that was often found in natural association with them are being energetically extracted. Manganese, molybdenum, uranium, potash, helium, petroleum, and natural gas are all valuable resources of the Southwest today.

Rowdiest of all was the silver boom. Between 1875 and 1895, with a thundering upsurge in 1882, silver was supreme. At Lake Valley, between Las Cruces and Truth-or-Consequences, a prospector hit a vein that he sold for $100,000. Two days later its purchasers broke into a cavern, or vug, which they named the Bridal Chamber Vug, and discovered that it contained $3 million of the metal, some in pieces so large they had to be broken up before they could be taken out. Such finds were not uncommon.

The word "vug" is from the Cornish language, a separate Celtic tongue that died out a little over 200 years ago. On encountering the hard rock, it was customary to send to Cornwall for hard-rock specialists. The Cornish had been working copper mines for 3,000 years, since the Neolithic Age. It is odd to pass through towns in the American Southwest and see the characteristic Cornish names: Trelawney, Trevelyan, Trevithick, Trevanion. In Colorado I have eaten Cornish pasties, still called "pasties," though not "Cornish." With their short memories, the local people have forgotten the Cornish connection. Even the Trelawneys and Trevelyans had never heard of Bodmin or Truro. They do not know that their own names are Cornish, or where Cornwall is. Yet their cemeteries, and the cemeteries of ghost towns round about, are filled with the graves of "Cousin Jacks" who died underground, or coughing their lungs out far from their own dark moors. It is touching to see those weed-grown headstones and peeling wooden crosses. It makes one wonder if one's own fate will be like the English soldier, in Hardy's poem, who dies on the veld, the broad karoo:

> Yet portion of that unknown plain
> Will Hodge forever be,

His homely Northern breast and brain
Grow to some Southern tree,
And strange-eyed constellations reign
His stars eternally . . .

New Mexico is the classic hunting-ground for the collector of ghost towns. There must be upwards of seven hundred or eight hundred of them. Almost all of them were mining towns, though a few were stopping places or watering holes on the cattle trails, or wrong guesses about where the railroad would come through.

It is easy to form misconceptions about ghost towns. Most of them are small, just a house or two, occasionally a ruined store. There are not many left now, thanks to vandals and the elements, of the kind you see in the movies— long streets with boardwalks, with saloons whose batwing doors flap in the gritty wind. The big ones are the recent ones, and are less picturesque than they are unsettling, a vision of the world after the holocaust. They are usually coal towns, like Madrid, south of Santa Fe, which died in the 1930s, or Dawson, near Colfax, which died as recently as the 1950s. Their tumbledown houses, smashed pit gear, caved-in workings, neglected parks, and derelict football fields, offer a preview of the Rhondda Valley in a hundred years' time.

Most ghost towns with more than a broken handful of buildings are not, in any case, completely deserted. There is usually someone still living there— a store, a rundown gas station with antique pumps, a farmer using the barns or outhouses, squatters who are grateful for rent-free accommodation, an artist or two. These deprive the town of its dead atmosphere. Some citizens refused to leave when the crash came, others crept back later. A few ghost towns have been totally resurrected, where it has become economic to reopen the mines or sift through the dumps and tailings with modern machinery. Tyrone, between Deming and Silver City, was built by the Phelps Dodge Company, in 1910, as a replica of a town in Spain. The miners lived in luxurious little houses, and the railway station and public buildings glittered with mosaic tiles. It closed down in the slump of the 1920s, but even in decay it had an exotic air. Yet when I returned to it, after three years' absence, it had been entirely torn down, and a new town stood in its place. You cannot take ghost towns for granted.

Treasure-seekers, of course, have destroyed most towns. And in a land where raw materials are scarce, planks of good wood or other useful items are not likely to remain unused for long. Some towns have been entirely gutted; in others, the stores and houses have the appearance of bombed-out buildings after a raid; they have the same air of violated privacy, of family lives opened to the sky and to the gaze of strangers. There is even the same kind of debris: broken furniture, broken glass, broken dishes, broken hopes and broken dreams. You feel very close to the tragedies of ordinary people in ghost towns.

Ghost mining town, Madrid, New Mexico. (PHOTO BY AUTHOR)

Thou hast here no abiding city, thou art a pilgrim on the earth. All that work in the kitchen and the parlor, the dusting and scrubbing, the washing and ironing . . . all gone. The rooms where the Christmases were celebrated, where the wedding breakfasts were held, where the children grew up, where the coffins lay across two chairs, where love was made—all smashed, a trash-heap. *All things are taken from us, and become/Portions and parcels of the dreadful past.* Beyond the shattered windows, their frames eaten by the fire ants, lies the desert, vacant and gaping in the sunlight.

Some ghost towns, nonetheless, are not so melancholy as others. Lake View, where they found the Bridal Chamber Vug, is sad—an empty church and schoolhouse, ramshackle houses occupied by a few drifters and itinerant workers. Yet Hillsboro, only an hour away, is charming. The old jail still stands, its massive iron door hanging open, and you take pictures of your friends staring out through the bars. It is far smaller than the jails in the movies, but very solid. It had to be, because many notorious gunmen and rustlers were locked up in it, in the days when Hillsboro was in its prime. At that, they were fortunate, for in many towns the custom was to hold men for trial in a deep pit in the ground—primitive, but an easier way to guard them. Where two hundred people live now, seven thousand lived in Hillsboro in the high times of the 1870s and 1880s, when $10 million worth of silver was taken out of the ground in fifteen years. You can see the old workings the whole length of the valley through the Black Range, from Hillsboro to Kingston, and on to the mines of Santa Rita and Silver City. Kingston, with its three newspapers, its three churches, its unnumbered saloons and brothels, has entirely vanished, apart from the overgrown dumps and the cemetery. The latter contains the memorials of miners, pioneers, a lone Englishwoman, Indian scouts, Indian fighters, and soldiers killed in the Indian Wars. Mining and Indian attacks were synonymous with each other.

The graveyards last longer than the towns, as death is longer than life. One of the most interesting is at Shakespeare, three miles south of Lordsburg. Shakespeare had a population of three thousand in the 1880s, in spite of the fact that it began as the result of a fake diamond rush stimulated by means of salted stones. In its cemetery lie a pair of Wells Fargo riders killed by Indians, and a gambler called Russian Bill, an imposter who posed as a Russian prince (or was he a genuine one?) who was hanged in the dining room of the local hotel. He had stolen a horse. Unlike stealing cattle, this always tended to be a capital offense; a man's life, after all, could depend upon his horse. It was at Shakespeare that a man was once hanged for no specific crime, but simply because he was, as the court put it, "just a plain damn nuisance." In Boot Hill at Tombstone, an interesting little town in spite of being "gussied up" for the tourists, are the graves of many other plain damn nuisances, also the graves of two men whose memorial proclaims them to have been "hanged in error." Casual times. Pancho Villa, when he was once asked what he wanted to do with an awkward batch of prisoners, thought for a moment. "Let's shoot them," he said, "for the time being."

The town on the New Mexico border where Villa "invaded" the United States in 1916, with eight hundred of his men, is itself more or less a ghost town now, though it has a very satisfactory cantina. At Columbus, Villa killed eight civilians and seven troopers of the 13th Cavalry before, shot in the leg and leaving 250 of his men dead, he headed back to Mexico. Such were the talents of the much-touted peasant general. It is astonishing that Villa has been the subject of so much misplaced adulation; his military abilities were more or less confined to taking men, women and children off railway trains and machine-gunning them. It is not some impressive and noble figure like Emiliano Zapata, but Villa who has gone down to posterity as the embodiment of the civil war of 1917. Probably a brutal character must always be chosen to typify brutal events, like Michael Collins in similar circumstances in Ireland. Their cruelty is their recommendation, since the events themselves were cruel.

The cemetery at Shakespeare, like those of some other ghost towns, affords a surprise. It contains the graves of American soldiers killed in the Korean and Vietnam wars. Why? To tuck the casualties of those unpopular conflicts out of the public eye? A likelier explanation is that most of the dead soldiers were Mexican-Americans, since Arizona and New Mexico are poor states, and recruiting is always high in depressed areas. Like all Mexican-American graves, even though they are in ghost towns they are well-tended, decorated with photographs of the dead, and garlanded with plastic flowers.

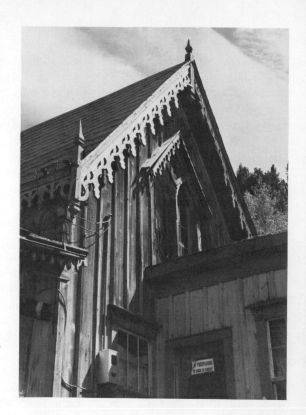

An ornate house in a Colorado
ghost town.

At Terlingua, a mercury mine in the Big Bend which went out of production
in the 1940s, there is a grave where a new stone cross has recently been erected
over a man who died in 1923. It took his family fifty years to save the money,
buy the cross, and hire a truck to transport it to that cemetery in the middle
of nowhere. At last, great-grandfather enjoys an honored resting-place.

TWELVE

IT WAS MINING that brought the first wave of Mexicans into the Southwest and California. It is worth emphasizing that, until that time, the Spanish-speaking element in the Southwest was Hispano or Mexican, not Chicano. The Chicanos, or Mexican-Americans, now outnumber the Hispanos, descendants of the original settlers of the Spanish era, by 100 to 1 in the Southwest, and 1,000 to 1 in the United States as a whole. The Hispano had the Southwest exclusively to himself until the mining boom began; and even the Mexican invasion of the 1870s and 1880s, for which the mining industry was responsible, was almost insignificant in comparison with the bracero incursions of the present century, which I shall describe later.

Mining brought Mexicans. It also brought wagon trains, stagecoach lines, and railroads. The military usually possessed their own wagon trains, but in the north of the area, based on Missouri, the wagon trade was soon organized on a professional basis by independent companies. Largest of these was Russell, Majors, and Waddell, which at a pinch could raise 5,000 wagons and 50,000 oxen to fulfill a major contract. The haulers also waxed rich on the Santa Fe and California trade. As in England, it was the common carriers who later bought the first motorbuses and created the country transport services.

The stagecoach came to the Southwest in 1849, as soon as the United States had assumed responsibility for the territory. The first line followed the well-worn track of the Santa Fe Trail, from Independence, Missouri, to Santa Fe. The fare was $250 one way, so stagecoach travel was not cheap. Service was once a month, though by the 1870s coaches were leaving daily. By the end of the 1870s, there were nearly forty separate stage-lines in New Mexico alone, most of them local and running between neighboring towns. The average fare was ten cents a mile, sometimes as high as twenty cents, and the coaches carried mail and packages to increase their profits. Payment was in advance: "No dead-head list," said the waybills, "cash up or no go." The best-known national line in the Southwest was the Butterfield Overland Mail, which superseded the short-lived San Antonio–San Diego Mail line in 1859, and linked Missouri with California until travel was interrupted by the Civil War. The Butterfield coaches started at St. Louis, swung south through the Ozarks, rattled through Fort Stockton, Fort Davis, El Paso, and Tucson, and passed south of Phoenix. They then crossed the Colorado River and ascended the California coastline as far as San Francisco. The trip took twenty-five days in good weather, and from San Antonio to Monterrey took eight to twelve days.

The word "rattled" is appropriate. The coaches flew along flat out, driven by expert and enthusiastic "reinsmen," and were provided with excellent mules or horses. Sometimes the horses were wild stock, which made the journey even livelier. The drivers kept up a high average speed, not only to cover the huge distances involved, but because of the danger from Indians and holdup artists. The time when the stagecoach flourished was the period when the Southwest swarmed with desperadoes of all kinds. Many coaches, particularly those that plied between mining towns, were lined with steel and provided with cavalry escorts.

The national lines maintained rough-and-ready stops every ten or fifteen miles. There the traveler could snatch a cup of muddy coffee and toy with a vile dish of "territorial beans" while the teams were changed, and in minutes he was whirled on again. Indian traders plied their trade there, and musicians serenaded the traveler; if a stop for the night was necessary, impromptu dances were sometimes held. A stagecoach journey was a wearing business, and for their drivers the companies deliberately recruited young men with strong nerves. They were kings of the road, with the panache of the English drivers described by Hazlitt or by De Quincey in his *English Mail Coach,* surging in and out of the main depots with much yelling and cracking of twenty-foot whips. But where the British drivers had only bad weather and boggy roads to contend with, the Americans had constant physical danger. In a four-month period, in 1867, the Post Office reported that Indians had stolen 350 horses, burned 12 stations, wrecked 3 coaches, and killed 13 employees. In the Southwest a few of these stagecoach stations are still standing, in forgotten valleys: a corral with a crude shed attached, where the passengers huddled and wondered what new peril and discomfort the next lap of the journey would bring.

At Santa Fe and other museums some of the original stagecoaches are preserved. Most of them are small, but beautifully made by the immensely skilled carpenters of that era. The usual complement was six passengers in-

Coach coming in! Arizona, 1880s. (ARIZONA HISTORICAL SOCIETY)

side and two or three in the cheaper seats on top; but the national coaches would sometimes accommodate an additional three people inside on a central bench. The biggest coach of all, the famous Modoc or Concord, made in New Hampshire, carried no less than eighteen passengers, nine inside and nine on top. Instead of springs, there were leather straps or "thoroughbraces," stretched fore-and-aft, which made the motion of the vehicle as violent as a ship at sea. Indeed, that was what a stagecoach was—a little ship, bobbing along on the great empty ocean of the plains.

One of the best descriptions of a stagecoach journey is contained in that incomparable book, Mark Twain's *Roughing It,* his account of his visit in 1861 to Nevada, where his brother had been appointed Territorial Secretary. He had just served for two weeks in the Confederate Army, and had been "exhausted by continual retreating." He describes the thunderstorms, the crossing of the rivers, the breakdowns, the occasions when the passengers had to get down and push, the fear when they were caught in the open as night fell and were lost. Here is his description of a night spent in that uncertain conveyance:

"As the sun went down and the evening chill came on, we made preparation for bed. We stirred up the hard leather letter-sacks, and the knotty canvas bags of printed matter (knotty and uneven because of projecting ends and corners of magazines, boxes and books). We stirred them up and redisposed them in such a way as to make our bed as level as possible. And we *did* improve it, too, though after all our work it had an upheaved and billowy look about it, like a little piece of a stormy sea. Next we hunted up our boots from odd nooks among the mail-bags where they had settled, and put them on. Then we got down our coats, vests, pantaloons and heavy woolen shirts, from the armloops where they had been swinging all day, and clothed ourselves in them—for, there being no ladies either at the stations or in the coach, and the weather being hot, we had looked to our comfort by stripping to our underclothing, at nine o'clock in the morning. All things being now ready, we stowed the uneasy Dictionary where it would lie as quiet as possible, and placed the water-canteen and pistols where we could find them in the dark. Then we smoked a final pipe, and swapped a final yarn; after which, we put the pipes, tobacco, and bag of coin in snug holes and caves among the mail-bags, and then fastened down the coach curtains all around and made the place as 'dark as the inside of a cow,' as the conductor phrased it in his picturesque way. It was certainly as dark as any place could be—nothing was even dimly visible in it. And finally, we rolled ourselves up like silkworms, each person in his own blanket, and sank peacefully to sleep.

"Whenever the stage stopped to change horses, we would wake up, and try to recollect where we were—and succeed—and in a minute or two the stage would be off again, and we likewise. We began to get into country, now, threaded here and there with little streams. These had high, steep banks on each side, and every time we flew down one bank and scrambled up the other, our party inside got mixed somewhat. First we would all be down in a pile at the forward end of the stage, nearly in a sitting posture, and in a second we would shoot to the other end, and stand on our heads. And we would sprawl and kick, too, and ward off ends and corners of mail-bags that came lumbering over us and about us: and as the dust rose from the tumult, we would all sneeze in chorus, and the majority of us would grumble, and probably say some hasty thing, like: 'Take your elbow out of my ribs!—can't you quit crowding?'

"Every time we avalanched from one end of the stage to the other, the Unabridged Dictionary would come too; and every time it came it damaged somebody. One trip it 'barked' the Secretary's elbow; the next it hurt me in the stomach, and the third it tilted Bemis's nose up till he could look down his nostrils—he said. The pistols and coin soon settled to the bottom, but the pipes, pipe-stems, tobacco, and canteens clattered and floundered after the

Dictionary every time it made an assault on us, and aided and abetted the book by spilling tobacco in our eyes, and water down our backs.

"Still, all things considered, it was a very comfortable night. It wore gradually away, and when at last a cold gray light was visible through the puckers and chinks in the curtains, we yawned and stretched with satisfaction, shed our cocoons, and felt that we had slept as much as was necessary. By and by, as the run rose up and warmed the world, we pulled off our clothes and got ready for breakfast. We were just pleasantly in time, for five minutes afterward the driver sent the weird music of his bugle winding over the grassy solitudes, and presently we detected a low hut or two in the distance. Then the rattling of the coach, the clatter of our six horses' hoofs, and the driver's crisp commands, awoke to a louder and stronger emphasis, and we went sweeping down on the station at our smartest speed. It was fascinating—that old Overland stage-coaching."

At the end, when he reached his destination, he experienced a pang of regret that the adventure and the camaraderie were over, and felt a justified sensation of a real accomplishment.

As with many such things in the United States, the heyday of the stagecoach was brief. Almost from the outset, the railroad began to build out along the main routes, and by the middle of the 1880s most stagecoaches were reduced to the role of ferry services for the railheads. A few lines survived as late as the present century, but only in the more inaccessible places. The railroads had started to appear in the Southwest as early as 1878, and by 1885 had laid down a complex network of lines (Figure 17). These lines, like the stagecoaches before them, followed the classic trails, pioneered by Indian, Spaniard, and mountainman. They are the routes followed today by the modern roads, just as European roads frequently follow the lines of roads laid down by the Romans. Traveling by early railroad, like traveling by stagecoach, was rugged. One of the most striking accounts of it is contained in Robert Louis Stevenson's *Across the Plains,* the second part of *The Amateur Immigrant,* his vivid narrative of the 6,000-mile journey which he made in 1879, to join Fanny Osbourne in California. The trip from New York to San Francisco took eleven days, was extremely unpleasant, and coupled with the second-class Atlantic crossing that preceded it can have done nothing to improve his already precarious state of health.

With the railroads, there was a preliminary period of bitter maneuvering for position. The Denver and Rio Grande Railroad, which nurtured great dreams, lost a tussle with the Union Pacific, and another to the Atchison, Topeka and Santa Fe. The latter finally cornered the northern route through the area, from California to the Middle West, with a minor branch dipping down the Rio Grande along the old Camino Real to link up at El Paso with the Mexican Central. The Southern Pacific, after making some small but vital trades with the Atchison, Topeka and Santa Fe, in order to rationalize

FIGURE 17

their individual strategies, lost no time in driving a parallel east-west route through the southern end of the territory, starting like its rival at Los Angeles and terminating at New Orleans. El Paso thus became an important junction for both the principal railroads. Already the home of Fort Bliss, the leading military establishment on the Mexican border, and today the largest single military installation in the United States, within a few years El Paso had mushroomed into one of the four "wide-open" cities of late nineteenth century America, together with New Orleans, Chicago, and San Francisco.

Although the great era of the railroads is over, it is still moving to lie awake at night, listening to the sad call of the Santa Fe. It drifts through the dark, over the city, from its distant tracks beside the Rio Grande. Arrivals and departures . . . An echo of a bruising past . . .

◈ 232 ◈

The mines brought the railways. The railways brought the Anglos.

In five hundred years, the Southwest has known at least five large-scale folk-migrations, of a type England has not experienced since the Norman Conquest. Indeed, American history reads like an account of the British Isles at the period when the Celt, the Saxon, the Viking, and the Norman were vying for supremacy. As I mentioned in an earlier chapter, it may be the destiny, as it is the instinct of America, not to settle down, but to ad lib its way through history. But, once more, we must remind ourselves that the country is young, a mere two hundred years old, and that we Europeans once went through what America is going through now. Ironically, Britain itself, after one thousand years, may be returning to something like the ethnic and political instability of the Dark Ages; so it is possible that the coming generation will witness a state of affairs in which America is slowing down and firming up, while sober old Britain is being shaken out of its Victorian mold and becoming more mutable.

The mind grows numb when contemplating all the incessant, monumental shifting around that is typical of America. Even today the American is an instinctive wanderer. Whereas the young European will quickly find a place to live and a job to do that will last him for the rest of his life, the young American will look forward to doing a dozen jobs in a dozen places before he is finished. American society is altogether more volatile. The leitmotif of this book has in fact been a succession of journeys. Everybody moves about: the individual, the family, the tribe, the race; on foot, on horseback, on mules, on travois, in carts, in wagons, in stagecoaches, in trains. It makes you feel tired to think of it. And consider the nature of the country they traveled through. An American today will drive five hundred or six hundred miles a day through the Southwest—but the Indian did it on foot, the pioneer did it in a wagon. What terrible compulsion do a great mass of human beings suffer from, that they cannot sit still in their own place, but roam constantly about, always unsatisfied? Perhaps we are talking about two principal categories of humanity: the Wanderers and the Stay-At-Homes. There are some lines of my fellow-countryman, Henry Vaughan, that I once appended to a novel:

> Man hath still either toyes or care;
> He hath no root, nor to one place is ty'd,
> But ever restless and irregular
>   About this earth doth run and ride.
> He knows he hath a home, but scarce knows where;
>   He says it is so far,
> That he hath quite forgot how to go there . . .

Life has certainly taught me, since I wrote *No Home But Heaven,* which of these two categories I myself belong to . . .

The Southwest has always known much restlessness and irregularity: but during the 1870s and 1880s it was given over to a positive frenzy of locomotion. If you had been crossing it by train, you could have looked out of the window and witnessed an entire landscape in movement. A stagecoach would be jolting along parallel to the tracks; a column of Apache prisoners, men, women, and children in arms, would be shambling back to the reservation under the eye of a squad of cavalry; a Wells Fargo messenger would be loping past with his mail-bags. You would see a mule or ox-train, the wagon master trotting anxiously up and down; a flock of sheep wheeling around its shepherd; a herd of cattle, 1,000 or 2,000 strong, trailing to distant Abilene or Dodge City; a file of Conestoga wagons creaking toward California. Your fellow passengers would all be members of the grand fraternity of the footloose: missionaries, doctors, artists, actors, engineers, carpetbaggers, snake-oil salesmen, gamblers, boosters, bunco-artists, pimps, prostitutes. And from the rear of the carriage would come the ribald shouts and rebel yells of soldiers going on leave, or cowboys coming back from a six-month drive, their traps and saddles piled up in the aisles.

For the '70s and '80s were the decades of the great cattle drives. Twenty years. A temporal fleabite. Yet there was a grandeur and recklessness about the undertaking that has forever made it memorable. This was America's heroic age: the age of the exploration and settlement of two-thirds of the continent, of the hammering through of the railroads, the heyday of the prospector and the cowboy. Its impact on the American consciousness has been out of all proportion to the amount of time it actually occupied. Because it is closer in time, and was so specifically American, it enjoys a more vivid existence in American minds than the colonial and revolutionary periods put together. The cowboy, the pioneer, the railroad man, the prospector—they were in themselves anything but glamorous figures. Yet what they did had a genuine glamour. They were true heroes, often tragic heroes, for they worked for tainted agencies pursuing tainted ends. They challenged nature, fate, the gods. They were risk-takers. And they were democrats: the American counterparts of the princes, prelates, knights, and barons around whom had coalesced the myths of other nations.

The cattle drives that are inseparable from the image of the American cowboy were mainly the product of Texan imagination and hardihood. They began in a haphazard fashion almost as soon as Texas became a republic. Along with their independence, the early Texans had inherited not only land, but hundreds of thousands of head of Hispano-Mexican cattle. Just as stray horses had escaped from the regular remudas to increase the stock of mustangs, so in the earlier days cattle had escaped from the regular herds to breed in the brush. The brush country of southeastern Texas was a paradise for these wild cattle, and the banks of the rivers that ran through the no-man's-land or the disputed territory between Texas and Mexico—particularly between the

Rio Grande and the Nueces—were teeming with stock. At their peak there may have numbered as many as three and four million. Raised in the *mesquitale,* or hard-scrabble country, they were not a pure or cosseted species, and their appearance and manners were uncouth. Frantz and Choate, in their book, *American Cowboy: The Myth and the Reality,* describe the Texas longhorn as "tall, bony, coarse-headed and coarse-haired, flat-sided, thin-flanked, sway-backed, big-eared, with tails dragging the ground and legs that belonged to a race horse." But the longhorn, with its magnificent spread of horns and its splendid spirit, was fitted as no other animal could be to the one-thousand-mile trek.

At first the Texans, far from bothering to round up such ridiculous, particolored creatures, rode into the *brasada* and shot them as game. Then, in the first impoverished years of independence, and when California was opened up and the mineral rush had started, the Texans began to take them more seriously. In the 1850s, when most cattle were shipped to California by sea, a few hardy Texans began to round up the longhorns, which were no one's property, and drive them through to the Pacific coast, dropping off some much-needed beef-on-the-hoof to the miners of Colorado, Utah, and Nevada. Not many of the early herds reached their destination. Trails had not been blazed; Indians ran off the stock; whole herds were lost and left to die in the desert. There was more profit in trailing cattle north to the Middle Western cities, or northeast to Pittsburgh, Philadelphia, or even New York.

The Civil War gave the cattle industry impetus. The armies needed fresh meat in enormous quantities, and arrangements had to be made to supply it. The American Civil War was the first modern war, in which both sides made use of railroads, and the cattlemen learned to employ this new mode of transport. However, the railroad system was still confined to the East. It had not yet reached the Deep South, let alone the Southwest, or the empty expanses of the central United States. Therefore Texas cattle had to be driven north to make connection with the rail terminals.

In the first year after the Civil War, a quarter of a million Texas cattle were driven north, in the care of those Texas war veterans who were the first generation of American cowboys. The owners expected an instant bonanza: but they ran immediately into two obstacles that had been encountered in the 1850s, but which now quickly attained major proportions. First, the war had created a crime wave that was peopling the West with penniless Southern soldiers, deserters, misfits, and opportunists of all kinds. They came together into gangs of crooks and rustlers who were a real menace in those first years after the war. The cowboys who brought the herds through in 1866 believed that when they had cleared the Indian country and reached Kansas and Missouri, they were safe. They were wrong. It was ten years before these pests were brought under control by the unreliable forces of law and order that were recruited to combat them. Many of the so-called lawmen, the sheriffs and deputy sheriffs, were poachers turned gamekeepers, needing little inducement to relapse to their native state.

The second obstacle was more obscure, but no less deadly. The Texas longhorn carried a tick which it picked up in the brasada, and which was as fatal to northern cattle as foot-and-mouth disease. The northern farmers had experienced "Texas fever" in the 1850s. Now they either drove the southern trailmen off their ranges on their own initiative, or hired desperadoes to do so. Sometimes a Texas herd was forced to wait for weeks on the open range, until the cold weather came and rendered the tick inactive, when the local cattlemen finally allowed the stranger to pass.

The year 1866 was so disastrous that it seemed the whole business of trailing might peter out. In 1867, only 35,000 animals went north. But in that very year the situation was suddenly turned around. A young Illinois cattleshipper, J. G. McCoy, after being rebuffed by two major railroads, managed to talk the small Hannibal and St. Joseph Railroad into building a livestock market in Kansas. Using rush tactics, he constructed the town of Abilene in sixty days, including a yard for three thousand cattle and a three-story hotel. In September 1867, a first consignment of twenty freighters carried cattle from Abilene to Chicago over the Hannibal and St. Joseph and Kansas Pacific railroads. Between 1867 and 1871, Abilene alone shipped out one and a half million head of cattle, and other livestock yards, such as Fort Dodge, Wichita, Ellsworth, and Newton, were hurriedly thrown up to cash in on the new boom. Soon, instead of being sent directly north, the lean steers were taken from the Kansas yards to be fattened up on the pastures of Nebraska and Wyoming, or even as far away as Montana, thus constituting another refinement of the whole process.

The animals in a herd were anywhere between four and fourteen years old. They were seldom the property of a single cattleman. Several owners would club together to form a herd and to hire professional cowboys. The trail boss commanded four or five dollars a day, while the standard rate of pay for the "waddies," as cowboys were called, because they chewed wads of tobacco, was one dollar a day. The herd was assembled, its characteristics were studied, and its natural lead-animals identified. Then it was taken swiftly away from its home pasture in marches of fifteen to twenty miles a day. After a week, it began to assume a manageable identity, and was allowed to fall into a more leisurely rhythm, covering thereafter about ten miles a day. This was the period of the great annual roundups and of the open range. The few farmers and squatters who had staked out claims under the varied Homestead Acts were allotted only small and uneconomical acreages, and were in no position to contest the passage of the herds and their retinues. The Indians were still a threat, but their power was on the wane, and the deserts and plains were free for all to roam in at will.

For the most part, the herds did not meander over uncharted country, but adhered to well-defined paths. The trails were not national highways: they were visible tracks, dusty roads scraped by millions of hoofs. When water or grass were deficient, detours were necessary, otherwise it made little sense to deviate into uncharted spaces. The trails mostly originated in Texas, and bore famous names: the Western, the Texas, the Northern, the Shawnee, the Bozeman, the Stimson, the Chisholm, the Goodnight-Loving. The Western or Texas trail started at San Antonio and San Angelo, ran northwest to Fort Sumner in New Mexico, then on to Abilene, a three-month journey. Fort Sumner was a busy center. To it ran the Stimson Trail, named after Jim Stimson, and it was the focus of the complex of trails named after Charlie Goodnight and Oliver Loving. Goodnight-Loving not only provided cattle for the northern depots, but supplied the mining and military camps of the entire Southwest. They utilized the Pecos Trail and extended it as far as Cheyenne, and established another route from Oklahoma to Santa Fe. The multifarious old Santa Fe Trail now did additional duty as a cattle trail, as did the old Camino Real, rechristened the El Paso or Chihuahua Trail. The Chisholm Trail, named after a half-breed Cherokee, Jesse Chisholm or Chisum, ran from Kansas to Roswell in New Mexico, and thence to Las Cruces, where it became one of the trails leaving the Rio Grande Valley for the West. Chisum, called the "Jinglebob King of the Pecos," from the style in which he cropped his cattle's ears, reigned over a ranch at Roswell that was 150-miles square, a fifth of the area of New Mexico. He was the usual mixture of the genial and ruthless, hiring professional killers (Billy the Kid among them) to kick out the farmers and small ranchers and anyone else who was opposed to him. His first headquarters was at the Bosque Redondo at Fort Sumner, where the Navajo had lain and suffered; and at his peak he owned some 80,000 head of cattle. Other westerly trails left the Rio Grande at Albuquerque and Socorro: but it should be noted that, in spite of its prominence in Western films and fiction, Arizona was primarily mining country, while the heart of the cowboy empire was Texas, Kansas, and New Mexico.

The order of march when trailing a herd was invariable. At dawn, the trail boss had already been scouting well in advance, making sure that the miles ahead were clear and the watering places adequate. If the herd had left the trail, he determined the direction it must take, either steering directly from landmark to landmark or using a compass. It was also common practice, when bedding down for the night, to point the shafts of the chuck wagon at the Big Dipper or some other prominent constellation, to give a rough course for the morrow.

In Western movies, the chuck wagon is usually seen trundling along in the rear of the herd. In fact, it would go on up the trail after breakfast, and again after the midday break, in order to be in position to give the men their meals. The cook was the first man up in the morning and the last to roll himself in his blankets at night, and he earned substantially more than the ordinary hands. All the same, he was usually an elderly, cantankerous man, his disposition soured by the banter and complaints of his companions. He seldom knew anything about horses or cattle, but had learned his trade in other places. Sometimes he was an ex-sailor, or a Chinese. His chuck wagon was a wonderful all-purpose vehicle which Charlie Goodnight is credited with adapting from an army original. It carried supplies, cooking implements, eating irons, bedrolls, blankets, saddles, tack, ropes, tarpaulins, branding irons, shovels, pickaxes, musical instruments, and such emergency items as splints, bandages, and a large pair of tweezers for pulling thorns and cactus spines out of various parts of a man's anatomy. It also carried a stock of stomach pills and indigestion powders, for the cook was also the doctor, frequently needing to prescribe correctives to the food he cooked over a fire of dried buffalo dung—a dreary *table d'hôte* of beans and bacon, sowbelly, cornbread and molasses, greasy stews, and grayish coffee.

When the herd started to move, at dawn, the riders took up their regular positions. The two most experienced rode "point"; behind them came the "swing" riders; then the "flank" riders; and finally, bringing up the rear, smothered in dust and misery, the "drag" riders. Together they moved the herd along at an even pace, making sure that it kept together without being bunched up, and watched for that ever-present danger, the stampede. Stampedes were usually caused when thirsty animals smelled water, and were often impossible to stop, even by shooting the leading steers. They could cost the men days of tedious roundup, not to mention deaths and broken bones. A particularly unpleasant break from routine came with the river crossings, which the direction of most of the trails, cutting as they did across the grain of the river systems, made inevitable. Coaxing two thousand stubborn steers and excited horses across the Colorado, the Brazos, the Canadian, the Arkansas, the Pecos, and the Red rivers was a tricky business, and cost the lives of many men.

Fortunately, the normal routine of the drive was not overexacting. The cattle were trailed for a few miles, allowed to graze for a few more, then trailed and grazed again, alternately. At noon they were watered and rested, then taken on till sundown, when they were driven into a compact circle and bedded down. The cowboy's work did not end at sundown, for there were four night watches to be kept, a vital task for which he used a special horse, his best horse, his "night horse," trained for that single purpose. Emergencies at night were infrequent, but when they happened they could be catastrophic. A cowboy might take as many as half a dozen horses with him on a long trail, and those he was not riding were kept together in a small separate herd watched over by the wrangler, or *remudero*. The wrangler was usually the youngest of the men, and the horses in his charge were known as the remuda, or the "cavvy" or "cavyard," from *caballado*.

What did the American "waddy" look like? What sort of a man was he?

It is difficult to generalize, even about his appearance. Sometimes he was a fancy dresser, sometimes his clothes were plain and serviceable. The stereotype, of course, is the Texas cowboy, his flamboyant getup influenced by the Mexican *vaquero* who was his predecessor. In more northerly areas, however, the cowboy was more likely to dress conservatively, in black broadcloth. Beginning at the top, his hat was patterned either on the Mexican sombrero or on the broad-brimmed hat worn by the military. Both were excellent headgear for fending off the glare of the sun. The more exaggerated hats, like the so-called ten-gallon hat, were spurious items foisted off on the public by Buffalo Bill Cody, whose Wild West Show would be responsible for creating a retrospective and totally exaggerated portrait of the cowboy. Around his neck was the familiar silk or cotton handkerchief, knotted behind. It was used as anything but a handkerchief (the fingers served for that), and saw service, according to one writer, as "a towel, personal or dish; bronc blind; tourniquet; pigging string; sling; water filter; ear muff; hot handle pad," and as a protection against the choking dust of the trail. It was usually as garish as the woolen or flannel shirt below it, though these high colors had a utilitarian purpose on the trail, where men needed to be visible to each other through the clouds of dust. Over his leather breeches were buckled the chaps, which were either leather or "angoras" of dogskin or bearskin, dyed black, white, or orange. The boots were high-heeled, armed with substantial spurs, and closed at the top to keep out stones, grit, and the all-pervading dust. To round off his outfit, the cowboy had an oilskin slicker or "fish" to keep out the rain, and often a big umbrella—unromantic, no doubt, but highly practical. You could always tell an old cowboy as much by his swollen, rheumatic hands and arthritic posture as by the convexity of his legs.

It would be impossible to describe in detail the innumerable types of spurs, saddles, bridles, cinches, stirrups, and other pieces of horse furniture which the cowboy used. There were hundreds of them, varying from man to man and district to district. It was a matter of personal taste. On the other hand, every cowboy without exception carried on his saddlehorn a *reata,* or lariat. It could be an expensive article of braided rawhide, or a length of cheap whale line, but it was an indispensable part of his equipment, and he knew how to use it. His guns, on the other hand, except for the rifle with which he shot game to vary the monotony of his diet, were almost entirely ornamental. A handgun may have been necessary in the turbulent '60s and '70s, but in the closing years of the century it merely rounded out the cowboy's romantic idea of himself, like an army officer's dress sword. In spite of the tall tales about Dodge City, the northern cowboys seldom carried guns, and jeered at the Texans for doing so. Guns were a Texas fad. On the trail they were carried in the chuck wagon, as they would have bounced so heavily on the hip that they would only have been a painful encumbrance. They were finally strapped on at the very end of the trip for the ceremonial entrance into Abilene or Wichita. In fact, it was just as well that their owners had little occasion to use them, except for a little innocent *feu de joie*. They were miserable weapons, and their possessors were mostly indifferent shots. The cowboys were lucky that the professional killers and gamblers who really knew how to shoot were mostly employed in killing each other, and contemptuous of ill-paid cowpunchers. It is also illusory to picture cowboys as mighty pugilists, wrecking saloons, throwing chairs at mirrors, jumping off bars, swinging from chandeliers, and disposing of everyone in sight with nifty left hooks and roundhouse rights. In actuality, they were as little given to fist-fighting as they were to bathing, shaving, or walking. After the hard months on the trail, they loved to charge into town and let things rip: but most of their behavior was sophomoric, a lot of noise and bragging and not much serious action, like undergraduates on Boat Race Night. When they sobered up, they meekly trooped out after the trail boss and paid for the damage.

Of course, guns are inseparable from the idea of the West, so a few lines must be devoted to them. In the first place, it should be recognized that three-quarters of the handguns used in the West were not the smooth, sleek objects of the movies, but big, bulbous affairs. It was more usual for a sheriff to crack a wrongdoer across the cheekbone with the butt or the thick barrel than to shoot him in the body. Sheriffs in the habit of shooting too many people were considered a menace, and requested to move on. Many guns, of course, were well-made—but it is hard to hit a target, even with a good handgun, at the best of times, and when shootouts occurred, they took place between pot-bellied, rancid-smelling, walrus-moustached opponents at point-blank range. There are few cases on record of men in the West being shot at a distance of more than a few feet; when it happened, it was a fluke, and an occasion for marveling. In any case, most of the victims were shot in the back, for it was sound practice to bushwhack and backshoot your man if you could, and only confront him face to face if it was absolutely unavoidable. Billy the Kid was shot by Pat Garrett when he was naked in bed, in the dark; Pat Garrett was shot when he had his trousers down, relieving himself by the side of the road; Jesse James was shot as he stood on a chair, hanging a picture. The ability to shoot quickly was regarded almost as miraculous as the ability to shoot straight. The guns weighed several pounds, were carried in clumsy holsters high on the hip, or simply stuck through the belt, and their action was ponderous and stiff. The quick-draw holsters which are seen in the movies are twentieth century fantasies; few gunmen experimented with such devices. Equally cinematic are such ploys as fanning the hammer, filing down the sear, and twirling guns around by the trigger guard—though, again, a few professional gunmen experimented with cutting away the trigger guard and other similar tricks. The probable result was that they shot themselves in the foot. Unlike the movies, the handguns of the West were loaded with real bullets.

A man did not strap one on until it was necessary, and when he did his knees knocked together.

The guns that made the westerners round-shouldered can be seen in a dozen museums. There was no need to dislocate your wrist by actually firing them, since merely pointing them would produce the requisite apprehension: it was like staring down the barrel of a howitzer. The popular caliber was the .45, the favorite make the Colt: Single Action, Double Action, Frontier, Bisley, Navy, Dragoon, or one of the countless models simply named after the year of manufacture. But every make and caliber were represented, from the heftiest models down to the handy little Remington over-and-under derringer that the gambler wore in a shoulder holster or stuck in his sleeve. The western rifle, on the other hand, was a much more artful and sophisticated object: accurate and delicate. The Winchester Model 1873, for example, was a beautifully balanced weapon that had nothing ornamental or frivolous about it. Rifles were serious items in a man's equipment; they were for use, not for show. Still, there is something about those brawny, swaggering handguns, with their blued steel and elaborate inlays, that is typical of the men who liked to wear them. Fortunately, in the case of both the guns and their owners, on the whole their bark was worse than their bite.

The cowboy was not an unduly aggressive or pugnacious person. His energies went into his work. He was used to loneliness and hardship, which made him reserved and melancholy. When he sat staring into the fire at night, his bones aching, a coarse blanket round his shoulders, the songs he sang or played on his guitar or harmonica were sad. He was keenly aware of his almost permanent separation from friends, wife, children, or sweetheart, and of his sacrifice of comfort and social advancement. The acrid and regretful tone of the old songs persists in the songs played by western radio stations today. It was a taxing existence, but it took a man to endure it. It brought him into contact with nature, with the sun, the soil, the wind, the rain, the stars, the night. It taught him what the Indian knew. It gave him an opportunity not granted to many men, and hardly ever to men who are rich, clever, and influential, to feel certain profound human emotions: comradeship, loyalty, courage, the practice of physical skills, the sense of a piece of work triumphantly carried through. He was a better man than many who thought themselves his betters. And he was the last *caballero,* the last man on horseback.

The great drives that were the apogee of his career lasted only eighteen years, from 1867 to the last drive in 1885. By that time the railways covered the country and made driving superfluous. Plumper and more docile breeds of cattle, Herefords, Shorthorns, and Anguses, could be raised closer to the railways and to market. The Texas longhorn, with its stringier meat, became obsolete (though today, thanks to preservation efforts in the 1920s and 1930s, there are over three hundred active longhorn breeders, and the breed is even making a mild commercial comeback). Worse, the range was becoming enclosed, like the common land of England after the Enclosure Acts. Cattlemen who possessed sufficient greed and muscle laid claim to ranches which were thirty or forty square miles in extent, monopolizing the grazing and water. They backed up their claims with guns, and with the hated "bob-wire," invented and patented by Joseph P. Glidden of De Kalb, Illinois, in 1874. A ton of wire built a three-strand fence two miles long, and in that year 10,000 pounds of wire were sold. In 1881, annual sales had risen to 10 million pounds, such had become the rapidity and relentlessness of the enclosure process. Glidden's Winner, made in Massachusetts by the I. L. Ellwood Company, became the most popular brand, followed by Baker Perfect (an ironic word to apply to barbed wire). Dozens of patterns were patented: Two-Barb, Four-Point, Telegraph Splice, Buckthorn, Flat, Split Diamond. This evil stuff contributed to the regrettable acquisitiveness and siege-mentality of the American rancher, over whose land you would be ill-advised to try to take the equivalent of an English Sunday stroll. In stringing up his acres, he strung up his nerves, until he is now for the most part only a mistrustful businessman, a factory farmer, a murderer of golden eagles.

The range wars that accompanied the coming of the wire reduced the cowboy from the status of line-rider to that of fence-rider; he was no longer a free agent but a protector of another man's property. They also brought a recrudescence of the violence of the post-Civil War years. Cattlemen fought with sheepmen, and both combined to run off the small farmer, burn his house, and terrify his family. There was no home for him on the range. Already in the 1870s such powerful organizations as the Northwest Texas Cattle Growers' Association and the Wyoming Stock Growers' Association had been formed, with increasing power to back up their decrees. To the army of cowboys turned enforcement officers were occasionally added hired toughs. All the same, we should try, of course, to understand the pressure of events, and to make a proportionate allowance. These were uneasy times. The Southwest had been in continuous ferment for over three hundred years, since the arrival of the Spaniard and the marauding Indians, and was no place for the soft or the irresolute. Frank Dobie coined a neat phrase to describe the hard-fisted westerner of the period. He called him: "A man suitable to the age he lived in." He was. He had every need to be tough and self-reliant. But perhaps the phrase begs the question, for there is a real moral difficulty here, and all historians of the period, except those who are crass and insensitive, have felt it. The times were difficult: but times are made by men: and did certain of those men have to make their times as difficult as they did? The cattle kings and the copper kings, hacking out their huge empires, behaved as callously as the oil kings who were to follow them. They did not present an edifying spectacle.

By the end of the century, then, the Anglo, in a bare fifty years, had overrun and become supreme in the Southwest. His rival, the Hispano, had come to the end of the delusive prosperity he had enjoyed between 1850 and 1870, when the Anglos had been largely occupied elsewhere. In New Mexico he was squeezed back toward the Rio Grande, surrounded by an iron ring of Anglos. Arizona became almost entirely Anglo country. Like the Indian, the Hispano was disinherited, allowed to survive only on the poorest and most unproductive soil. He had been superseded, as so many peoples have been superseded in the Southwest.

One does not know whether history, in its unfathomable way, might not be pickling a rod for the Anglo, too. Historians tend to write as if their last chapters represented the peak and inevitable crown of their story, as if evolution had risen to and had ended at that particular point. But a modern historian's last chapter is only, itself, intermediate, a transition.

And so, one day, the proud Anglo might suffer supersession in his turn, like the proud Spaniard. Only history knows by whom. The Russians? the Chinese? the Brazilians? the Venusians? All we know about history is that the unlikeliest events are the ones that are likeliest to happen. Who, twenty years ago, could have predicted that Saudi Arabia would become one of the most influential nations in the world? Could the Toltecs and Aztecs have foreseen that one day men would come three thousand miles across the ocean to crush them, and that their traditions and their very language would be snuffed out?

And yet, if such upheavals did not take place, what would future historians have to write about? . . .

I suppose that I ought to deal briefly with the gunmen and badmen of the Southwest. It is interesting to see the grave of John Wesley Hardin, in the Concordia cemetery in El Paso. It is interesting to stand in the square at Mesilla, outside the bar where Billy the Kid shot one of his twenty-six victims, or climb the stair in the courthouse at Lincoln where he killed a deputy sheriff with the man's own gun before riding off in leg-irons to Fort Sumner. You can put your finger in the bullet-hole: though it is scarcely the equivalent, after all, of putting one's finger in the bullet-hole on the staircase at Delft, where Balthazar Gérard shot down William the Silent.

It is right to harbor a liking for madcaps and misfits. It is proper to pay some attention to a group of men who were symptomatic of the ugly chaos of their times, and who became nostalgic symbols to their compatriots. It is simply rather sad that they were so inadequate to serve as any sort of symbol, and that nine-tenths of them, including the celebrated ones, were pitiful specimens of humanity.

A whole school of pseudoscholarship has grown up around them, although the hagiography of an earlier generation has gradually given way, following the fashion in more serious scholarship, to the practice of debunking and trying to put them in a more sensible perspective. Unhappily, there was little to "bunk" in the first place, and it would be foolish to devote to them the space which I have given to the conquistadors, the explorers, the missionaries, or the Indian chiefs—though some of them were vicious enough to resemble the more repellent type of Apache. It seems a shame that for every book written about Father Kino, there are two hundred or three hundred written about Billy the Kid. Such is the way of the world. The devil does have the best tunes.

It is not easy for an outsider to appreciate the American cult of the bad-man. The only historical badmen whom Europeans admire usually had a certain tattered grandeur about them. Perhaps the preoccupation with pirates in the last century comes closest to it. The Englishman delights in a juicy murder: but he does not make a hero of the murderer, as the American does of the gunman and the gangster. To find a Bonnie and Clyde in English literature you have to go back to *The Beggar's Opera*—and even that was offset by *Jonathan Wilde*. Europeans lack the tough-guy tradition in life and literature which is so central a feature in the United States.

It is a paradox, but while Europeans, who are highly individual and even eccentric as persons, will tamely hand over the conduct of their lives to the state, Americans, who are less individual and more homogeneous in a personal sense, distrust the state and love to see it defied. American heroes are outsiders and nonconformists; the Byron syndrome or Romantic hangover is even now not quite dead in the United States. The typical hero of the British detective story or thriller is a pawky Scotland Yard Inspector; even James Bond works for a government department; while Sherlock Holmes, Hercule Poirot, Lord Peter Wimsey and the others are all on the side of the Establishment. The American private-eye, on the other hand, is an outcast, a loner, a man whose code bears similarities to that of the cowboy. There are not many American novels extolling the CIA.

The Western badman—Hardin, Billy the Kid, Johnny Ringo, Curley Bill Brocius, Charlie Bowdre, Buckshot Roberts, Buckskin Frank Leslie, Ike Stockton and the rest—were deliberately upgraded in the popular imagination. In this they resembled the gangsters of the Prohibition era, as portrayed by Cagney, Bogart, and Robinson. Americans know perfectly well that it is only a convention, a charade, and that the gunmen and gangsters were in reality a low lot. They also know that private detectives are smelly little men who snoop at bedroom windows: yet they have been elevated into Sam Spades, Philip Marlowes, and Lew Archers. The process of ennobling the gunman must correspond to a deep psychological necessity.

The hard-boiled convention tells us an interesting thing about Americans: that they have little faith in their social system to regulate itself through official channels. They feel that an individual has to act for himself; they admire the man who bucks City Hall. The great private-eyes are sturdy individualists—which was how, perversely, the western badman gradually came to be viewed. Americans lumped them together with the cowboys, with whom they did not belong, as examples of the last free men: the final flourish of the frontier. When they passed from the scene, their mantle fell for a while on the gangsters of the '20s and '30s; but the latter were not able to wear it so long or so convincingly, since their brutishness was more evident. The famous Shootout at the O.K. Corral was actually as unsavory an episode as the St. Valentine's Day Massacre; but it was further off in time and space, and had pastoral overtones that made it easier to romanticize.

This ambivalence is rooted in the American psyche. These most conservative of people, terrified by the slightest sign of nonconformity, possess a sentimental spot for revolutionaries. Until they were disillusioned, they supported Fidel Castro, and are always disposed to regard foreign revolutionaries approvingly during the preliminary stages of an uprising. Hysterical where such home-grown terrorists as the Students for Democratic Action and the Symbionese Liberation Army are concerned, they cannot help sympathizing with the Irish Republican Army, though privately they know better. Conformists themselves, they have a hankering after nonconformity; they tend to support anyone who appears to be flouting authority—provided authority is not fundamentally threatened. This is why they like South American dictators—because they combine colorful uniforms and cloudy rhetoric about the Rights of Man with sound conservative instincts. Neither the western badmen nor the Cook County gangsters would have become popular if they had not been doomed from the start. Even the Mafia, a $200 billion a year business that used to be regarded indulgently as an example of an independent and enterprising spirit, is becoming unpopular as it grows gradually more immune and gorges itself on increasingly large segments of politics and the economy.

It is a sensible impulse to support the independent man, the outsider, in his struggle against the soulless forces of Big Government and Big Business. It is only unfortunate that the American seldom finds a suitable embodiment for such a man, and so often hits on inferior figures. Admittedly, genuine real-life heroes are not common: and the American always needs someone, besides actors and athletes, on whom to exercise his marked taste for hero-worship. Nor, indeed, are Americans the only people who are liable to make poor judgments when confronted with that most baneful figure of our age, the hooligan masquerading as an idealist. In spite of their colorful names, the Wild Bunch, the Dodge City Gang, and the Forty Thieves were not updated versions of Robin Hood and his Merry Men. It would be nice to feel that their actions in robbing banks and railroads actually represented a symbolic protest against the Big Business interests that were capturing the West; but in fact their exploits were selfish, commonplace and cowardly. They could not even carry out their enterprises with a certain wit, or a certain finesse, because they were mostly mental defectives. They were not honest cowboys, or industrious artisans down on their luck. They were not Ned Kellys or "Wild Colonial

Boys." They were drifters and grifters, recidivists and repeaters, the worst elements of frontier society. Many of them were dangerous drunks, and many insane. All were liable to commit violence for no reason at all. Allen James killed a man at the St. Nicholas Hotel in Las Vegas, New Mexico, because the man ordered eggs for breakfast. Jack Armstrong killed a barman in the same town over the price of a drink. Bill Daniels shot a twelve-year-old boy at Tucumcari who was standing in the road with his hands up.

With few exceptions, the Western badmen were regarded by their fellow citizens as "plain damn nuisances." Their deaths were greeted with acclaim. The atmosphere of terror evaporates swiftly when its causes vanish, as anyone knows who tries to explain the Hitler years to someone who did not experience them. It was the same with the western gunmen. The more capricious of them made life miserable for entire communities, who had hardships enough to contend with in the ordinary course of things. They lurked for days outside lonely houses, penning the inhabitants inside; or broke in and tortured them; or waylaid and beat them on their way to town. It is not surprising to learn that most of them were never tried, but were lynched or killed out of hand. It seems possible that there were more lynchings of bandits in the West in three decades than lynchings of blacks in the South in three centuries. Once the vigilantes took him, a bandit and his companions were usually treated to a "necktie party" in the nearest grove or barn. Shooting while attempting to escape was a popular remedy, and official hangings were always well attended, the best seats being assigned by printed invitation. The hangmen were not as skilled as they might have been, and it was sometimes necessary to hang a man several times. Black Jack Ketchum, who was hanged for "assaulting a railway train," literally lost his head: it came clean off as he dropped through the trap. Until 1890, the forces of law and order were unreliable, and it was possible for such men as Wyatt Earp, truly one of the most poisonous characters in the history of the West, to get themselves appointed town marshals. However, the situation began to improve as soon as bodies such as the Kansas Rangers and the Texas Rangers eventually came into existence. The brand of justice of the Texas Rangers was properly feared. They merited their boast: *"One riot, one Ranger."*

Life in the Southwest, for the pioneer Americans, was insecure and hazardous. What was more, the inhabitants of the small mining, cattle, and railway towns faced more substantial adversaries than a set of dim-witted gunfighters. The land companies, the ranchers, and the mining companies became increasingly heavy-handed as they expanded. They discouraged and ultimately drove out as many people as the drought and the desert. In 1890, there were only three towns in New Mexico with more than 2,000 people. Santa Fe was the most populous, with 6,000. In Arizona, Tucson headed the list with 3,000.

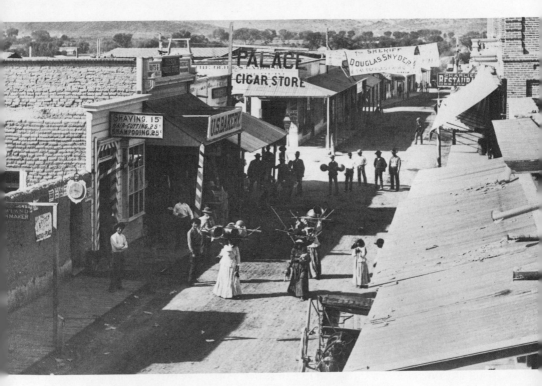

Congress Street, Tucson, 1880s. (ARIZONA HISTORICAL SOCIETY)

By 1930, the population of New Mexico had still not reached half a million, while Arizona was substantially smaller.

Yet the rigors of frontier life had their appeal; in fact, its rigor *was* its appeal. If you came to America to pioneer, it was to the West that you went to do it. You followed Horace Greeley's advice, or you rotted in the mills and sweatshops of the East and the Middle West. It was only as late as 1970 that the census showed that America had ceased to be predominantly rural, and had at last become mainly urban. Rural life suited the Americans. It gave them the opportunity to display in abundance those virtues which they admire, which they hold to be typically American, and which they still display to a high degree: the rural virtues of simplicity and neighborliness. They were comfortable in their old rural communities, in spite of the difficulties and drawbacks. Such communities fulfilled them, and they still cannot really adjust to the urban, let alone the imperial, role. At heart, they remain a race of countrymen.

The Southwestern pioneers had found space and freedom; whereas, little more than half a century after the Revolution, the Easterners were already beginning to suspect that something had gone wrong with the grand experiment. This is the central theme of the *Leatherstocking Tales,* written by James Fenimore Cooper between 1823 and 1841, and which, though technically "Eastern," set the pattern for the "Western." In *The Pioneers* (1823), Cooper already contrasts, less than a half century after the Revolution, the wholesome life and outlook of Natty Bumppo with the rigid code of Judge Marmaduke Temple. Owen Wister's classic *The Virginian* (1902) stated the conflict between traditional and modern America in a way that has become standard in the contemporary Western novel. Was American life, Americans were already asking themselves in the mid-nineteenth century, becoming coarse, mercenary and oppressive, even corrupt, a betrayal of the ideals of the Founding Fathers? Emerson thought so.

> 'Tis the day of the chattel,
> Web to weave, and corn to grind.
> THINGS are in the saddle,
> And ride mankind.

Thoreau said precisely the same thing: "We do not ride on the railway; it rides upon us."

Henry James, complaining of "loud longitudinal New York," had asked in his short story, *The Jolly Corner:* "How could any one—of any wit—insist on any one else's 'wanting' to live in New York?" A privileged soul, he could slip away eastward to more congenial climes. Less fortunate mortals escaped to the west—the Far West, or the Southwest. That was where those austere, primordial, and republican ideals could still be practiced, at least for a few decades longer.

Looking back on that toilsome era, most people who knew it felt that it had a lambent quality. Its burdens and its recompenses were poignantly eulogized by Willa Cather, who had been brought up in the prairie town of Red Cloud, in Nebraska. In such novels as *O Pioneers* and *My Antonia* she celebrated its frugal yet epic qualities. Yet in what is perhaps her most perfectly realized book, *A Lost Lady,* published in 1923, she was already looking back in a mood of resigned despair. "The Old West," she wrote, "had been settled by dreamers, great-hearted adventurers who were unpractical to the point of magnificence; a courteous brotherhood, strong in attack, but weak in defense, who could conquer but not hold. Now all the vast territory they had won was to be at the mercy of men who had never dared anything. They would drink up the mirage, dispel the morning freshness, root out the great brooding spirit of freedom, the generous, easy life of the great land holders. The space, the color, the princely carelessness of the pioneer they would destroy and cut up into profitable bits, as the match factory splinters the primeval forest."

In an essay, she asserted that "It all began to go wrong in 1922": but it seemed to many Americans that the blight had set in earlier than that. It was a feeling not confined to writers who were inhabitants of Willa Cather's plains and prairies. Robinson Jeffers, barricading himself on his flinty Pacific peninsula when still a young man, settled down to write such bitter poems as the famous *Shine, Perishing Republic;* and in his fine *Empire Builders,* Archibald MacLeish excoriated the commercial robber barons who had raped the West, the Harrimans, Vanderbilts, Morgans and Mellons who had "screwed her gaunt," and "fathered their bonds at her breasts till the blood ran from them," and looked back regretfully to those earlier days when the land was unpeopled and undeveloped.

Jackson had prevailed over Jefferson. The mercantile North had broken the aristocratic South; the Indian and the Hispano had been subjugated; the railway kings and the land barons had imposed their will. The great continent had been mapped; it was filling up; its limits were known.

America knew now what she was to be: a nation dedicated to Emerson's "THINGS": and she was not sure, in her heart, that she liked it. *Faute de mieux,* Americans sought to transfer their considerable enthusiasms from the Romance of the Great Outdoors to the Romance of the Machine, the Romance of Industry. It was not, and it could not be, the same thing. It was as Mark Twain wrote, in his *Life on the Mississippi:* "Now when I had mastered the language of this water, and had come to know every trifling feature that bordered the great river as familiarly as I knew the letters of the alphabet, I had made a valuable acquisition. But I had lost something, too. I had lost something that could never be restored to me while I lived. All the grace, the beauty, the poetry had gone out of the majestic river! All the value any feature of it had for me now was the amount of usefulness it could furnish toward compassing the safe piloting of a steamboat."

The circumstances in which America had been born had changed. The great epoch that had begotten and sustained the adventurous and energetic American character had petered out. The days were gone when you climbed on a raft and swirled down a vast dark river. It was a painful moment. Americans are always trying to recreate that epoch of ardor and advance: the New Frontier, the Great Society, the Peace Corps, Urban Renewal, the Space Program. Being people of great ability and vitality, they score striking achievements. But the New Frontier, or foreign wars, or overseas investments, or rebuilding the ghettos, can never possess the glamour of those youthful years, when everything was exciting and everything was possible. America had had her magic moment, her moment of springtime release, like Spain after the conquest of Granada. You cannot recapture your youth. America now has to subside, as Spain, France, and England have had to subside, into a decorous middle age. For a people that has worshipped youth more passionately than any nation since the Greeks, it is not an easy process; America is not a place where people grow old gracefully. But perhaps that too is part of the fascinating, even heroic appeal of America: its refusal to go gentle into the night, its rage against the dying of the light.

The glistening light over the land in the West and Southwest seemed as strong and hot as ever. And yet, in a subtle way, brightness had fallen from the air. The reign of the horseman had drawn to a close; it could not be replaced by the Model T.

The high horse was riderless.

THIRTEEN

In 1900, TWENTY YEARS after the Southwest had become the target of Anglo immigration, it still had only 350,000 people, about the population of a medium-sized modern city. By 1970, the population had increased tenfold, to just over 3 million, still an unimpressive figure in comparison with regions of comparable size. Arizona, it may be noted, with its 2 million people, has overtaken New Mexico, with slightly more than 1 million. This disparity will gradually increase, since projections show that Arizona will probably reach 2,700,000 by 1990, an increase of 30 percent, while New Mexico will reach 1,130,000, an increase of 2 percent. The startling rise in the population of Arizona, one of the steepest in the nation, is almost entirely explained by the burgeoning of the city of Phoenix, which has been growing for some years at a rate of 30,000 a year. Phoenix apart, the harshness of the environment can be expected to slow down growth in Arizona as it has done in New Mexico. As for Texas, its contribution to the population of the Southwest, in the shape of the city of El Paso, is also expected to increase, though with nothing like the surge of Phoenix, Tucson, or Albuquerque. The present population of the state of Texas as a whole is 11,700,000, and it is anticipated that it will become 13½ million in 1990, a growth of about 11 percent.

The Anglos entered the area mainly in a northerly direction, from the Middle West, with secondary influxes from Texas and California. The Texans settled in the Río Abajo and the south and west, while the Californians settled in the Río Arriba and northern Arizona. There, the Mormons sent a strong contingent, 10,000 strong, down from Utah, to proselytize as well as to colonize, and their influence on the life and manners of the region has been notable. We noted in the last chapter that a phalanx of Cornishmen had arrived to carry out specialist work in the mines; and Yugoslavs and Poles were recruited in the Eastern states and brought out en bloc for the same purpose. Among the other groups who made a contribution to the Southwest was a contingent of Jewish peddlers. They showed up in the 1880s and 1890s, driving donkey carts or pushing barrows, acquiring a clientele on the plains of the Southwest in the hard-driving way that their cousins were doing at the same time on the South African veld. A second body of Jews arrived during the 1930s and 1940s, entering the Southwest from Mexico. Refugees from Germany, they had gone to Mexico while awaiting visas for the United States under the quota system; but when they finally received their papers, they decided that there were better opportunities in the border states than farther north. Up from Mexico, too, came many of the Germans who were a part of that immense German migration to every corner of the Americas in the nineteenth century; but here, again, many Germans, Jewish or otherwise, took a fancy to Mexico, and settled there. Today, for instance, there is a sizable German colony in the city and the state of Chihuahua. In addition to Jews, a small but energetic contingent of Arabs has also established itself on the border. They too were peddlers and traders. They branched out from their traditional skill as sellers of carpets, in which they still specialize, into other enterprises; and one of the side effects of the Syrian and Lebanese presence is the existence of shops where Arabic foods are sold, a welcome addition to the American cuisine I shall be describing in my next chapter. The presence of Jews and Arabs in the same community, of course, produces a lively situation whenever the successive Middle Eastern wars occur. Of more distant Orientals, the Chinese and Japanese, there is a small sprinkling. A few Vietnamese, the wives of men serving or having served at Fort Bliss at El Paso, are in evidence, and the occasional Vietnamese restaurant, like the occasional Chinese, has come into existence. As for the blacks, although they are heavily concentrated in East Texas, they are not a significant factor in the ethnic mix of the Southwest. There are no more than 100,000 to 150,000 blacks in the entire region. Most of those who work or attend college in the Southwest appear to enjoy their life there, since they are not numerous enough to arouse prejudice or be the subject of traditional hostilities; though during the 1960s such hostilities seem to have relaxed almost everywhere. The blacks in the Southwest are in the situation of the West Indians in Britain forty years ago, before large numbers of Indians, Pakistanis, and Kenyans arrived and antagonisms started to spring up.

The Anglos, as we have seen, monopolized the leading positions in the mining, railroad, and other industries. They moved into or created the towns. In later years, however, the copper, coal, and railroad industries have declined, although the shortfall in jobs has been more than adequately made up by the expansion of military bases throughout the area. Fort Bliss remains an enormous installation, specializing in rocketry and acting as the instructional school for the NATO powers; and Holloman Air Force Base at Alamogordo is one of the main air force staging areas in the U.S. Alamogordo is also the center of the missile proving grounds at White Sands and the Tularosa Basin, while Los Alamos owes its existence to the requirements of atomic research. It has been calculated that between a quarter and a third of all the jobs in the Southwest are connected in some way with the military and atomic complexes, whose impact is felt in a multiplicity of ways. The excellence of southwestern universities in the fields of physics, chemistry, and mathematics has partially come about, for example, as a result of such activities; though the preeminence of the Southwest in the field of astronomy can be traced to less martial factors, such as its freedom from cloud and smog.

The Anglos occupied the lucrative and white-collar posts; the lesser posts and menial work was carried out by others. However, there were simply not enough Pueblo Indians or Hispanos to shoulder the burden. The Hispanos, in spite of the fact that they were losing ground, were a proud, rooted people, fighting a stubborn battle to cling on to what they had. The Pueblo Indians, too, were not the sort of people to be turned into casual labor; and it was equally inconceivable that the Navajo, Apache, Comanche, or other tribes could be turned into conventional wage earners. At that time, their sufferings had reduced their number, in any case, to under 50,000. Meinig writes: "As the result of the heavy impact of the Anglo conquest, the turn of the century was the nadir for Indian life in the Southwest. The demographic deformations and social disintegrations of several decades of warfare and relocation, disease, alcohol, and starvation were starkly apparent. Their reserved lands proved far from inviolable. Stockmen encroached at will across every border, railroads were given permission to build across reservations, and whole chunks of land had been taken away by abrupt decree, as in the contraction of the San Carlos Apache Reservation to release the mineral lands on either side around Clifton and Globe."

With the older ethnic strata unwilling or incapable of being transformed into a reservoir of labor, where were the Anglos to turn? They had not far to look. If the Hispanos, the Pueblo Indians, and horse Indians were in a sorry state, the *campesinos* of Mexico were in an even worse one. Between 1900 and 1930, 10 percent to 15 percent of the entire population of Mexico moved north across the Rio Grande, preferring semislavery in the United States to outright slavery in their own country. In that time, the number of Mexican immigrants into Texas, Arizona, New Mexico, and California jumped from 100,000 to 1,225,000.

These were the *cholos,* as they were then called, or the Chicanos, as they later became known, from the way in which they pronounced the *–xicano* in *Mexicano.* They were the latest, but doubtless not the last, of the great ethnic waves that have washed across the Southwest during this millennium. They were certainly the most pitiful. Their status was that of helots. Uprooted, illiterate, speaking no English, they were brought across the border, in defiance of the contract-labor laws, by *contrabandistas* or by *coyotes,* to whom they paid a fee of $15 to $20. The coyote then sold them to an *enganchista* or *papacito,* a labor contractor, for a dollar a head. Their wage, in the mines, on the railroad, in the citrus groves, in the cotton and beet fields, was twenty-five cents a day. Those enterprises were kept going by his labor. He not only built the railways in the Southwest, he provided 80 percent of the railway work force, living in railway boxcars that were shunted from one section of the line to another. For the most part, the cholo traveled no farther than the border states, but perhaps one in ten made his way farther north, as far as San Francisco or Chicago. It was a terrible life, in which the cholo was preyed upon and cheated at every turn by his overseers and employers. He was treated like cattle, often guarded by men with rifles to stop him running away, or marched through the streets between armed guards. Later, when the cholos began to settle down into regular work, they were permitted by their employers to buy their tarpaper shacks in the shantytowns of Texas and California. Thus they became the Chicano community which is now a key factor in western life.

In 1924, the government made an effort to tighten up the immigration acts. In that year the Border Patrol came into existence, to combat the coyotes and try to halt the flood of "wetbacks"—men who waded or swam across the Rio Grande. Regular programs, such as the ambitious bracero program, instituted during World War Two, were put in hand, and the Immigration Service was reinforced and introduced a system of "blue cards," or duly authorized work permits. Yet the tide of immigration has in no wise abated. Between 1971 and 1973, the Border Patrol reported that it had turned back or repatriated a total of 1,500,000 illegal immigrants. The statistic speaks eloquently about conditions that continue to prevail in Mexico.

The coyotes still run their lucrative business, with elaborate "underground railways" to take their clients quickly away from the overcrowded border to the labor markets of California and the Middle West. There, there are firms that will employ them, no questions asked, for a fraction of the union scale. Many Mexicans cross the border freelance, since the Rio Grande is no great barrier. However, since few of them speak any English, and would be at a loss in their new surroundings, the majority must rely on the expertise and contacts of the coyote. The coyote will collect as much as $200 or $300 a head for his human merchandise, in addition to whatever he can gouge out of the wetback. Sometimes, in default of finding his clients an employer, he will at least take them as far as Albuquerque or Tucson before abandoning them to their own devices; but sometimes he just unloads them as soon as they are across the border. The wetbacks themselves, of course, often have relatives in El Paso and other cities who will hide them and help them.

The coyote usually runs his consignments across the border at night, over shallow fords or unguarded crossings. It would be impossible, even by mobilizing the army, to watch every yard of the border, and the Border Patrol is a small force. The coyote brings the migrants over in trucks, packed tightly in the stifling darkness, often without food and water. Often there are tragic accidents; a truck is wrecked during a chase by the police or Border Patrol, or crashes, or drops off a cliff road. The trucks themselves are antiquated. Sometimes the coyote panics as he approaches a town or a roadblock. He ditches the truck and runs away, leaving its cargo locked up in the back. The Border Patrol has more than once discovered an abandoned vehicle with a load of Mexicans inside, dead from suffocation.

Some coyotes specialize in moving people across the main border crossings. They always select the busiest ones, at the busiest hours. There is a ready market for forged or stolen *micas,* the green cards in plasticized cases which are issued to legal migrants and Mexican day workers in the border cities. A coyote will have a collection of them. He will gather a group of clients together and give them each a mica, matching up the photograph as closely as possible to the physical appearance of its bogus bearer. The clients then cross at intervals during the morning rush, flashing the micas at the American customs man and relying on the fact that he will get only a momentary glimpse of them. Most Mexicans will look alike to him, in any case. The coyote will have crossed beforehand, with his own mica, and as his clients arrive on the American side, at a discreet distance from the barrier, he will take back the micas. It is an easy matter, if further insurance is needed, to slit the plastic covering of a stolen mica with a razor blade, insert a perfectly genuine photograph of the new owner, and reseal it with glue or a hot iron.

The single man or enterprising freelance has other alternatives. He can cross beneath a load of furniture, or fertilizer, or cement, or bricks, or vegetables, or pottery. He can hide on the roof of a big truck, or inside the paneling, or even cling on underneath, since the Americans do not use those mirrors mounted on wheels which the East Germans at the Berlin Wall push under the chassis. The trick is to cross at a peak hour, when crowds are returning to the United States from the Mexican restaurants, racetracks, and bullrings. At El Paso, there are something like forty million cars and trucks crossing the border a year; thus the authorities have no time to search every vehicle. Many Americans in El Paso have maids who are illegal aliens, and when these women need to return to Mexico, in the event of a family crisis or for a vacation, they are ferried backwards and forwards in the trunk of their employer's car. Often they lead pathetic existences in their El Paso households, for they dread the knock of the immigration officer on the door and seldom venture out.

One way or another, legal or not, the Chicano has become a major component in the life of California and the Southwest. His is the main contribution to the Southwest's growth and prosperity, for he does most of the manual work. Chicanos who become American citizens often retain much of the hatred of the American, and particularly the Texan, which is the legacy of the experiences of the past hundred years. The Chicanos as a whole live in the same poverty as the Hispanos, Indians, and the other groups who were despoiled and dispossessed by the Anglos. Nevertheless, it would be true to say that the position of the Chicanos has been immeasurably strengthened, like that of the Indians, blacks, and other disadvantaged groups, by the ferment over civil rights that characterized the 1960s. Their situation is not in many cases enviable, but seems to be improving. They enjoy a modicum of status, respect, understanding, and, above all, economic clout, that they certainly lacked a few years ago. It is still possible to exploit them, and instances of exploitation constantly occur, but it is by no means as easy to do so as in the past.

Many Mexicans, however, have no intention of trying to settle in the United States. They work in America solely for the money they can send back to their families in Mexico. They regard working in America as an unpleasant necessity, which they would avoid if there were any alternative. They find American life, for all its physical advantages, lacking in warmth, in love and leisure. As soon as they can, they hurry home to their villages south of the border. They prefer, whatever its drawbacks, the less exacting society of their own country.

In T. L. Peacock's *Headlong Hall*, one of the more eccentric members of Squire Headlong's house party produces the skull of Sir Christopher Wren. This steers the conversation toward the subject of architecture. "I contend," says Mr. Escot, the learned deteriorationist, "that the original unsophisticated man was by no means constructive. He lived in the open, under a tree." And after Squire Headlong proposes the inevitable bumper of Burgundy, Mr. Escot observes that "the propensity which has led man to building cities has proved the greatest curse of his existence."

American cities are not, by and large, places of beauty. They will have their outstanding buildings, and their clusters of neat and well-kept suburbs; but Americans are on the whole too busy to give much attention to aesthetics. As long as their homes, offices, places of business, and restaurants are clean and functional, they are more or less indifferent to their appearance. The principle of built-in obsolescence applies to American architecture as it applies in other things; buildings, too, are commodities. On the other hand, it is doubtful if the general standard of modern American architecture, in point of style and quality, is any worse than it is everywhere else in the modern world—which is to say, pretty bad.

The Southwest is fortunate among American regions in that, in spite of mining and military activities, there is an almost total absence of heavy industry. There are therefore few factory areas with their attendant slums, though there are plenty of those modern equivalents of slums (or which soon will be), the trailer-courts. The horrors of the Industrial Revolution have been largely avoided, and the region is also remarkable because it contains a palimpsest of architectural styles that correspond to its succession of cultures. Louisiana has its French architecture; Maryland and the Carolinas their British Colonial; but the Southwest presents a continuum of architectural styles from the days of the Hohokam-Anasazi up to the present. Its visual appeal consists not only of splendid natural scenery, but of a rich cultural mélange. There are cliff dwellings and adobe pueblos, Spanish colonial plazas and ranches, ghost towns and Navajo hogans. The adobe style of building has deep roots in the Southwest, and has inspired many of the modern architects in the area. The result is that cities which would quickly become disasters elsewhere in America grow up in the Southwest with individual and wholly charming features. Even a café or a motel can look agreeable, in spite of its makeshift materials, if it incorporates some of the attractive details that are native to the Southwest. The wide repertoire of styles often fires up the imagination of architects and builders whose work would be commonplace elsewhere. And the sun, of course, helps. Buildings which would look mediocre, or downright horrible, in the gray and rainy north, often look bearable, or at least not quite so offensive, when they are bathed in the mellowing rays of the southwestern sun. A bad climate brings out the worst in architecture.

The Southwest has also escaped becoming an eyesore because it is notably underpopulated. It is easier to put up with the junkiness of the urban scene when the cities are so few and far between. The cities of the Southwest do not clutter up the landscape. They could only come into existence at scattered intervals, wherever there were rivers, springs, artesian wells, or where the water table was high. The determining factor was water—and water is scarce in the Southwest. No water—no city.

Arizona, with an area of 114,000 square miles, has a population of 1,800,000; New Mexico, with 121,700 square miles, has an even smaller population, of just over 1 million. These two huge states possess only three large cities (Phoenix, Tucson, and Albuquerque), and only ten towns with a population of more than 15,000. In the West Texas portion of the Southwest, the only large city is El Paso, separated from its nearest neighbor to the east, Austin, by 600 miles of desert.

How, then, do these southwestern towns and cities appear to the eye of the tourist, the traveler, the European? What impression do they make? First and foremost, he must be struck by their isolation. The European driver, used to reading European road maps, is constantly making an elementary error that occurs because he keeps forgetting the difference in scale on the American map. He assumes blithely that it will take a few hours to drive across the map which has been supplied to him at the gas station; in fact it will take him as many days. He is simply not used to the scale or duration of such journeys. Even Americans are awed by the sense of immense distance, unbroken by towns, which typifies traveling through the Southwest. You reach its cities after a long hot slog across the blank desert, and when they rear up from the flat landscape you feel something of the relief that the Legionnaires felt when they caught sight of Sidi-bel-Abbès or Fort Zinderneuf.

Since they are welcome oases, caravan stops, watering holes, you are grateful for them. They seldom strike you as the torpid places they usually are. They have the sun; but that is about all they have. The only romantic thing about them are their names. Of Phoenix, far and away the largest of them, with a population which has almost reached the million mark, one visitor remarked: "After entering it, there is nothing to do but leave." In fact, leaving Phoenix is not easy. The modern city consists of what were once five separate towns, squatting around the same water supply. In course of time these towns—Phoenix, Tempe, Scottsdale, Glendale, and Mesa—became welded together, while two further townships—Avondale and Chandler—are now in the process of becoming absorbed. Like all southwestern cities, the emphasis is on single-story rather than two-, three-, or multiple-story buildings; and the single-story format takes up a great deal of land. The result is that Phoenix sprawls out between thirty-five and forty miles from north to south, and the same distance from east to west. Unless your business enables you to cross it on the interstate highway, driving through it takes an unconscionable time.

The city, like the phoenix, sprang virtually fully formed from the burning landscape. In 1864, it was a barnyard where the contractor to Fort McDowell kept his hay. There was no farming in the area until 1867, when the Swilling Irrigation Canal Company began operations. The railroad did not reach it until 1887, and it was only with the opening of the Roosevelt Dam, in 1911, that it started to grow. In 1926, when the arrival of the Southern Pacific Railway finally opened it up to the outer world, it still possessed only 30,000 people. Thereafter, particularly when the aircraft and other industries took root there in World War Two, the population has boomed until Phoenix and its satellites now possess an aggregate of over 500,000 people. It is the fastest growing city in the United States, the growth of its population seeming uncontrollable as fresh waves of settlers descend on it in search of sun, space and health, and to escape the pressures they encounter elsewhere. This is why the feathers of the phoenix now seem rather dowdy, and why the city gives you the impression of a cataract of cardboard and plasterboard, splattering in every direction, as if there was a gusher at its heart spewing out ephemeral houses, ephemeral factories, ephemeral stores, ephemeral shopping malls, ephemeral motels. It is a triumph of disposability, like the disposable sanitary towel.

By the law of averages, there are nuggets of serious architecture buried among the rubbish. Frank Lloyd Wright contributed to the Arizona State University, and there are several buildings and museums that merit attention. A redeeming touch is the presence of handsome date-palms, introduced from Egypt into Arizona and California about 1910. The enlightened exertions of the Office of Foreign Seed and Plant Introduction also brought into the Southwest, at that time, alfalfa from Turkey, cotton from Peru, soybeans from Japan, and new strains of grass and wheat from Hungary and Siberia.

On the northernmost outskirts of the city, on the slopes of the McDowell Mountains, stands what is surely the most interesting modern building, or rather complex of buildings, in the entire Southwest. This is Taliesin West, built over the course of many years, as time and funds were available, by Frank Lloyd Wright. It was mainly completed by 1938, and was the counterpart to Taliesin East, in the Middle West. Wright lived half the year in one palace, half in the other, shuttling like a potentate between them. It is now a place where architectural students are trained in the master's methods, and by the courtesy of his widow may be visited by the public. The great architect, proud of his Welsh blood, was fond of striking Celtic attitudes, and loved to play the aristocrat. His fellow countrymen found such poses distasteful; indeed, he was capable of laughing at them himself. But everything he was, and advocated, and believed in, achieves its supreme expression at Taliesin West.

Surprisingly, probably because of his fitful financial situation, the buildings are not at all grandiose. This is a palace—but a modest palace—an emperor's winter retreat. It is constructed of boulders taken from the surrounding mountains, hewn roughly to shape, and piled into walls constructed with a pronounced batter. The buildings—studios, community rooms, dining rooms, theater, concert hall, private apartments—are not lofty or pretentious; they flow into one another, full of unexpected corners and felicities. There are walks, patios, loggias, smothered with creepers and bougainvillea. The external wooden beams have been left undisguised, painted a dark magenta, a traditional and widespread color in the Southwest. The whole effect, in spite of the fact that the place is named after the sixth century Welsh bard who was Wright's inspiration, has none of the somber glitter of Welsh classic culture, but is Oriental in atmosphere. It could be a little lamasery, built somewhere on a sunny plateau in the highlands of Tibet. Inserted at intervals in the walls are Buddhist bas-reliefs which Wright brought back from his sojourn in the East, and clearly he sought to recreate something of the quietude and harmony of the monasteries he had visited in Japan. The Eastern atmosphere is enhanced by the fact that some of the students now resident there are Asian, and seem utterly at home. To spend an hour strolling about Taliesin West, sitting in a flower-draped arbor, listening to the splash of a fountain, is to experience a moment of peace and spiritual refreshment.

As he did with all his buildings, Wright placed on it his personal cipher. Set into a wall is a tile embellished with his device, a red square with a maze

Frank Lloyd Wright's Taliesin West, Phoenix, Arizona. (PHOTO BY AUTHOR)

motif. The building blends, according to his own precepts, and those of the Eastern masters by whom he was influenced, into the landscape. It is the same texture, the same hue. It is integral with Nature. And like much of Nature, unfortunately, it exists today under a threat. Slowly, a tangle of pipes, sewers, telephone poles and power lines is creeping toward it across the plain below. Wright fought unsuccessfully to make the city fathers of Phoenix divert, conceal, or at least bury these excrescences. They paid no heed, disliking a man who refused to conform, who was not cut from the common cloth. And lately the developers, the red-eyed scavengers of our society, have been casting glances toward the McDowell Mountains. Soon the cardboard gusher will start frothing out in the direction of Taliesin West, submerging what Wright created, sinking it beneath the weight of everything that Taliesin West was intended to defy.

Tucson, one hundred miles south of Phoenix, is a more immediately attractive and agreeable city, largely because it possesses the initial advantage of being less than half the size. It lies in a curve of the Catalina Mountains, one of the finest ranges in a state that possesses a wealth of fine ranges. From their foothills the coyotes call at nightfall. Eastward and westward, the city is flanked by the two halves of the Saguaro National Forest, whose Triffidlike growths march right into the suburbs. The saguaro, as I mentioned earlier, is the true indicator of the Sonora Desert, a columnar giant of odd but amiable appearance. In late spring, the citizens of Tucson are treated to the sight of its exquisite clusters of tiny, waxen, pale green flowers. Southwest of their city, on the Papago Indian reservation, they also have access to the Organ Pipe National Monument. The organ pipe has no columnar stem, and seldom exceeds twenty feet, but is striated like the saguaro and has a pale lavender flower that, like the moon-yellow blossoms of the Nightflowering Cereus, opens after dark to attract nocturnal insects and closes before the dawn. Also, to the west and northwest of Tucson, are extensive stands of the quaint Joshua Tree, which in spite of its blackened and hairy branches is actually another cactus, a yucca. Like the saguaro, organ pipe and other less spectacular cacti, its fruits, the product of a cream-white flower, are much sought after by birds and animals, and by Indians for making candy.

Tucson, unlike Phoenix, has Spanish ancestry. Father Kino built a chapel there, an extension of San Xavier del Bac, in 1700. It disappeared in the Indian troubles that desolated the parent church, and was not rebuilt until 1782. In 1776, the Spanish general, O'Conor, moved the Spanish presidio north from Tubac to Tucson, during the course of his astute and determined campaign against the Apache and Comanche. For two hundred years, it remained nothing more than a mud-walled compound. Surprisingly enough, Mexican troops were still manning it as late as 1856, three years after Tucson had become American soil after the signing of the Gadsden Treaty, but too soon for the incoming Americans to garrison that remotest part of the country. In 1860, however, its fortunes began to rally. It was formally renamed Fort Tucson, and became a stop on the Butterfield Line between Missouri and San Francisco. Like the other towns of the Southwest, it started to take on an air of permanency when the railroad arrived in 1880; and when the Central Pacific declined in the 1930s, and the interstate highway system started to take its place, Tucson was connected to the outside world by the excellent U.S. 80. With Phoenix, during World War Two it became an important center of Air Force and aerospace activity, and has since maintained a steady growth. In spite of the usual ravages inflicted by the city council and the chamber of commerce, it has managed to retain a fair proportion of its southwestern atmosphere. There are extensive stretches of whitewashed adobe; a mellow, old-established university; an imaginative zoo, called the Arizona Sonora Desert Museum, where the birds, animals, and reptiles are displayed as much as possible in their original habitat; and one of the colonies of artists and craftsmen whose presence is an integral and valuable part of life in the Southwest.

Unfortunately, Tucson also possesses another element, whose presence is not so valuable: the Mafia. In the past thirty years, organized crime has been filtering down into the Southwest from California and Nevada, as well as arriving from the East. The area is convenient for "washing" or "laundering" the huge profits from the Mafia's gambling operations in California, Reno, and Las Vegas, and offers a fresh field for investment in the apparently innocent businesses in which organized crime now puts its money. Naturally, the casinos and racetracks are almost all in Mafia hands, but the organization now tends to diversify in less obvious directions—construction, real estate, automobile dealership, supermarkets, and so on. Moreover, the Mafia is now being displaced in the big cities by the blacks and Puerto Ricans. The Italians have grown fat and prosperous, and are losing some of their taste for bloodshed. They yearn for respectability, seek to maintain a low profile, and send their sons into politics and the law. They only indulge in the more extreme forms of violence when absolutely necessary—though when it does become necessary, people are still clouted with baseball bats, or have their hands held on the railway line, or are dumped in the river with cement shoes. The Southwest, remote and little known, also makes an admirable vacation spot and retirement colony, and many a *capo mafioso* has a large estate in Phoenix or Tucson, while the surrounding desert is a handy place in which to bury his enemies or his mistakes. Latterly, the Mafia has also descended upon El Paso, both to control the drug traffic on the border and to keep an eye on the flood of money which it funnels into Mexico, with the acquiescence of Mexican politicians and entrepreneurs. When you visit Puerto Vallarta or Acapulco, you catch an immediate whiff of the Mafia. Some of the Watergate money, it will be remembered, was laundered through Mexico.

I wish I were justified in describing, at length, some of the peripheral cities of the Southwest—Las Vegas, Salt Lake City, Denver—which, though not technically within the boundaries of the area, are organically connected with it.

Las Vegas, of course, is the *reductio ad absurdum* of the American Dream, the grotesque embodiment of the more inane aspects of the Pursuit of Happiness. Probably all Americans have got a sliver of Las Vegas in their souls, just as all Englishmen have a bit of Blackpool. It is the spiritual, and sometimes the actual home of the Howard Hugheses, the Bernie Cornfields, the Robert Vescos, the Hugh Hefners. The satanic nature of the place communicates itself to you in Dantean fashion; you realize quickly that it is a city where everything goes, where no vice is not catered to, where everyone, including you, is meat on the hoof. At Las Vegas, there is complete toleration of human folly and wickedness, the toleration that exists in hell. It has the true Baudelairean, Beardsleyan quality, and like hell it operates at night. By day it resembles an empty nightclub, dingy and tatty, with the rips, rents, stuffing, and worn patches showing. When night comes, it puts on its cheap finery like a whore. It swells, quivers, palpates, ripens, splits open like a dark mephitic bloom. The devils who operate it crawl out from beneath their stones. The city envelops you with its infinite tawdriness; it gives you the feeling, which the damned must feel, that daylight will never come, the dawn will never rise. You are wrapped in a great soft warm suffocating mantle of evil.

One of the least complicated things to do in Las Vegas is to wander up and down the Strip, looking at the electric signs. These are works of art, a uniquely twentieth century art-form in which Americans excel. They have the joyous, innocent quality of fireworks, elaborate set pieces whirring and whooshing into the darkness. Before the fuel crisis led to their curtailment, giving the city the sorry look of hell without its flames, there were four million light bulbs and 125 miles of strip-lights in operation. My personal favorite, the sign at the Stardust Hotel, consumed $6,000 worth of electricity a month. In normal times, a specialized force of fifty men services the city's bulbs and neon lights.

You cannot stroll up and down the Strip forever. Like poisoned orchids, the casinos have been specifically designed to lure and trap you. All paths lead to the gambling rooms. You cannot eat, sleep, drink, see a show, or empty your bladder without passing through them. Like hell, they are painted and furnished in shades of dark red, which is the color that most influences people to become excited and reckless. They are crammed with roulette, blackjack, dice and card tables, and with battalions of one-armed bandits. They resound to the mournful murmur of the hunt for pleasure. The ceilings are two-way mirrors; the pit-bosses sit hunched like gargoyles on stepladders high above the crowd; the croupiers have the complexions of long-drowned corpses; the watchers who watch the watchers are themselves watched by watchers. This is—truly—hell.

However, a season in hell, when brief, can be fascinating. The casinos offer rich fare for students of hopelessness and despair. The compulsive gamblers who are on view there suffer, so the psychologists tell us, from a neurosis whose manifestations include hatred of parents and authority, sexual impotence, and suicide. Fortunately, most visitors to Las Vegas are not compulsive gamblers, but people who have merely been induced to have a flutter. For this, the worst odds are those given by the slot machines, which provide the most boring and inelegant way of losing your money; the best odds, and the most exciting spectacle, are to be had at the crap-tables, where the action can come alive like a painting by Bellows. My own taste is for roulette, despite the infamous American practice of having a double zero as well as the ordinary zero, giving the house an extra chance. But for a modest outlay, and if you keep your head, you can play roulette at Las Vegas for several hours and consume a fair amount of the house's sandwiches and liquor. The days when I employed elaborate systems—martingales, and so forth—are past. I divide my available stake money into equal proportions, and when I lose my nightly quota, or double it, I leave the table. If you manage to clean up at Las Vegas, by the way, be wary of elevators, lonely corridors and dark car-parks. Another tip: before you go, leave your rings, trinkets, and other personal valuables behind. You are in a place infested with crooks, with men and women who are broke and in trouble, and with drug addicts who must steal to feed their habit. And when you leave, remember Sodom and Gomorrah, and keep your eyes on the road.

Any more comical contrast to Las Vegas than Salt Lake City could not be imagined. True, the Mormons practiced polygamy, but so decorously that it could scarcely be considered sinful. Daguerreotypes show the Mormon patriarchs, surrounded by their womenfolk, looking preternaturally glum. Perhaps they were pondering the old saying about the punishment for bigamy being several mothers-in-law. I have noted how the Mormons spread throughout Arizona, and how they sent large numbers of their people to Mexico, where they could practice plural marriage and other articles of their faith without arousing local interference.

This was why they had made their trek to the West in the first place. Joseph Smith, the founder of the Church of the Latter-Day Saints, was born in New York State. There he experienced two separate visions, in the first of which he saw Christ, in the second an angel called Moroni (the golden angel on the spire of all Mormon temples), who revealed to him the existence of a sacred book written on leaves of gold. In 1830, after a further vision which was shared by his disciple, Oliver Cowdery, he published the Book of Mormon, then led his followers westward, in an attempt to escape from religious intolerance. They went to Ohio, on to Missouri, and then to Illinois, where in 1844 Joseph Smith and his brother were lynched by a drunken mob.

At that point, Brigham Young stepped forward to take charge of the situation. In 1846, the St. Peter of this remarkable sect brought his people through the mud of Iowa, and through the sickness and despair of a winter in Omaha. In July 1847, he reached the shores of the Great Salt Lake, where he is said to have declared: *"This is the Place."* The achievement was more memorable in that, en route, the Mormons had willingly detached five hundred of their youngest and strongest men to serve in a Mormon Battalion in the Mexican-American War, on behalf of a government that had savagely injured them.

The anabasis of Brigham Young and his pioneers calls to mind the Great Trek which the columns of Boers, under various leaders, made from the Cape to the Transvaal between 1835 and 1838. There is a Pioneers Statue in Salt Lake City, as there is a Voortrekker Memorial in Johannesburg. Both the Mormon and the Boer expeditions were attended by misery and death; yet the former was, if anything, the more striking. Many of its participants did not have wagons, or even horses, but made the entire transcontinental journey on foot, hauling their children and worldly goods in handcarts. The Mormons and the Boers still bear the marks of their early history. Both manifest a certain smugness, a sense of being set apart. They are both fundamentalists, obstinate and narrow-minded, but with a disconcerting if pawky kind of humor.

Both possess an unmistakable strength of will and character. Salt Lake City bears a curious resemblance to certain South African cities—Pretoria, for example—in the breadth of its main streets, which are designed to be wide enough so that spans of oxen could turn around. There is the same feeling of cleanliness, earnestness, and uplift, mingled with a touch of repressiveness (though the Saints, like Roman prelates, enjoy their comforts, and the Hotel Utah is one of the finest hotels in America).

Although the Mormons today claim three million adherents throughout the world, some of its own people in Utah, particularly the younger ones, find its tenets oppressive. Some have abandoned it, accusing its leaders of being hypocritical and dictatorial. The Mormons, like the Quakers, are shrewd and dedicated businessmen. This is a role which, like the Jews, they originally cultivated out of necessity, and which has now become second nature. Although Salt Lake City has a population of nearly 200,000, in its self-sufficiency and the common outlook of its inhabitants it would seem to fulfill, in modern terms, many of the requirements of the polis, which I praised earlier. From other accounts, it would appear to be organized more along the rigid lines of Calvin's Geneva. Every Mormon who lives there is bound into a closely meshed system. Below the First President and the General Officers of the Church sits the Council of the Twelve Apostles, then the First Council of the Seventy, the Patriarch, and the Presiding Bishopric. The young Mormon is steered systematically through the Primary Association, the Young Men's and Young Women's Mutual Improvement Association, the Sunday School Union, the Relief Society, and the Boy and Girl Scouts. The middle-aged and elderly Mormon is similarly slotted into a framework of benign but obligatory institutions. It is a kind of Freemasonry with teeth in it.

It all seems to possess more than a hint of the Brave New World. One wonders whether, like Dostoevsky's Grand Inquisitor, or Gide's St. Peter, Brigham Young did not build too well. Perhaps he, too, betrayed the simple message of his Master by constructing an iron machine. His portrait, surrounded by his boot-faced wives, can be seen in the Mormon Museum (and so—piquant object—can his bed). The representations of Joseph Smith, on the other hand, portray a slender, clean-shaven young man, in dress and appearance more like a Romantic poet than the founder of a severe orthodoxy. Somewhere along the way, the wild streak in Mormonism, the enthusiasm that characterized many of the American communes of the period, patterned as they were after Fourier and Robert Owen, succumbed to its own success, to the growth of the American business ethic. Oneida, for example, which also practiced polygamy, and enjoyed a similarly lively reputation, is now an institution for mass-producing tableware.

Indeed, there was much more than just a hint of the Romantic poet in Joseph Smith. He *was* a Romantic poet, a considerable one. In motels and hotels throughout Utah and the neighboring states, it is customary to find the

Book of Mormon, in addition to the Bible, beside your bed. It makes gripping, even hair-raising reading, and is well calculated to keep your light burning till the small hours. Whatever you might think of it from the religious point of view, and whatever you may feel about the likelihood of Joseph Smith finding it written on golden leaves, and translating it concealed from his scribe behind a curtain, it has the strange power of the more torrid productions of the Romantic era. It reminds you of Monk Lewis and Maturin; of Chatterton, who forged the medieval "Rowley Papers"; or of Macpherson, who masqueraded as "Ossian" in order to produce a resonant and unjustly neglected work. The Book of Mormon is a torrential farrago of Ossian (Napoleon's favorite writer), Edgar Allan Poe, and the more extravagant canvases of John Martin, Delacroix, and Géricault, mingled with the exaggerated antiquarianism of the eighteenth and early nineteenth centuries.

It is strange that a staid religion should owe its inception to such a lurid book. Mormonism seems to have experienced, as it settled down, a significant change. It was the same change that has taken place in American society at large, from revolutionary fervor to an intellectual conformity combined with an extreme technological inventiveness. In England, it corresponded to the change between the raffish vigor of the Georgians and the stuffiness and moral vanity of the Victorians. The Book of Mormon is an apocalyptic work, filled with visions of disaster and decay, and the early history of the Mormons is redolent of blood and mire. Yet, as you wander around Temple Square in Salt Lake City, you receive the impression of a sanitized, homogenized, lobotomized religion, from which the elements of suffering, martyrdom, and death—the fate of Jesus Christ and of Joseph Smith himself—have been banished. The sense of awe and mystery, inseparable from a real religion, have been excised in favor of the now obligatory upbeat ending. What remains is a Rotarian's creed, akin to the golfer's litany of Billy Graham. The Tabernacle, the Temple, the Assembly Hall and the other buildings in Temple Square have a peculiar Toytown appearance. After a while, you realize that you have seen them somewhere else in America: at Disneyland. History and religion have been dry-cleaned. Joseph Smith's crazy imagination has been tidied up. What remains is a religion without shadows, like a well-run bank. Joseph Smith's mad and magnificent poetry has been reduced to safe, pedestrian prose.

The corner of southern Colorado that contains the Black Canyon, the Great Sand Dunes, Mesa Verde, and Hovenweep, is rightly considered to belong to the Southwest. The cities of Colorado Springs and Denver, however, are more commonly thought of as being in the West. Yet, as far north as Denver, southern Colorado was saturated during the Spanish epoch with land-hungry and venturesome Hispanos, seeking their fortunes far to the north of the Río Arriba and Santa Fe. They came to constitute a distinct Spanish colony, with traditions of their own; and although their power and influence diminished during the late nineteenth century, when they lost their land-grants, their presence is still an integral part of the history and personality of the state, which owes its name to the *caballeros* of Francisco de Coronado.

Colorado Springs is a small gem of a city. It has a population of under 200,000, which makes it easy to drive around, to shop, and to park. It might be argued that between 100,000 and 200,000 is the optimum size for a modern city, a size at which it ought to be compulsively frozen, in spite of the lamentations of the land sharks. Colorado Springs, with the comely outline of Pike's Peak standing up ten miles to the west, is beautifully positioned. It lacks heavy industry, and in consequence its atmosphere is civilized and relaxed. At one time it was known as "Little London," and tea was taken at four o'clock, croquet was played on its well-kept lawns, and the Union Jack fluttered from many of its flagpoles. English people and English money had much to do with its inception. During the last century, the state of Colorado became a favored spot for British immigration, and Colorado Springs began as a resort for Americans and wealthy Europeans who had failed to find a cure for tuberculosis in Scotland or Switzerland. Several large sanatoria were built in the dry and sparkling air, some of them run by British staffs. The local cemeteries contain many graves of young Englishmen who, like the Cornish miners in New Mexico, died far from home. *Dulces moriens reminiscitur Argos.* "But who knows the fate of his bones, or how often he is to be buried? Who hath the Oracle of his ashes, or whether they are to be scattered?"

Colorado, together with Wyoming and Montana, contained ranches and estates, many vast in extent, owned by English magnates. Most were used as hunting preserves, enormous private coverts, but some were stocked or farmed in a serious fashion. At one time it seemed possible that the British presence in the American West might become comparable to that in the colonies and dominions; but the British never "took" in the West, as they did in Canada or Australia. A common ancestry, common history, and common tongue were not, in the long run, sufficient. Moreover, during the late nineteenth century and the early twentieth century, the British people and their role in the world were unpopular with every grade of American opinion. The agents and representatives of the English landowners had no scruples about short-changing and swindling them. The landowners realized that, to protect themselves, they would have to settle in Colorado permanently, or at least spend a great deal more time in the West. This they could or would not do, and one by one they sold up and departed. Nevertheless, an echo of the leisurely style of the English grandees still lingers in Colorado Springs.

Denver, further to the north, is a different proposition. It has a grand, metropolitan air. As the state capital, with a population of over 500,000, it is one of the most important cities in the West. It benefits from not being planned on the grid system, and its center is imposing, the buildings laid out with a refreshing irregularity. Unfortunately, the developers have done their deadly work on the outskirts, so the dignified center is spoiled by a scruffy setting. Once the rustic haunt of Kit Carson and his fellow *coureurs des bois*, Denver has now begun to pay one of the more obvious prices of bigness, in that its crime rate is one of the highest in America, and is rising steeply.

Albuquerque, which in 1850 had a population of less than 100, overtook Santa Fe to become the largest town in New Mexico when the railroad came through in the 1870s. By 1890, it had a population of some 5,000, and by 1930 had grown to 30,000. It has since expanded tenfold, thanks to its accessible, axial position. With over 250,000 people, it has soaked up a quarter of the population of the entire state. Like Denver, it is starting to suffer from the dire effects of bigness, and has proportionately the second largest crime rate in the United States. The only time in America I have ever had anything stolen from my car was in Albuquerque (though I had my luggage stolen from my hotel in Las Vegas). The city would naturally be subject, because of its situation, to interracial strains and rivalries, Anglo, Chicano, Hispano, Indian. But because of the mounting flabbiness which is the concomitant of bigness, it finds it hard to cope with them. When an explosive series of race riots broke out in the early 1970s, the authorities were neither prepared for them nor able to deal with them adequately.

The city, in fact, strikes me as possessing an uneasy atmosphere. I never

The annual Indian Market in the Plaza at Santa Fe. In the background is the palace of the governor.

Margaret Tafaya of Santa Clara Pueblo displays her famous polished blackware pottery in the Santa Fe Market.

enjoy staying there, though parts of it are tolerable. In the Old Town Plaza stands the pretty little church of San Felipe de Neri, which dates from 1706. Otherwise, apart from a scattering of adobe, the city is undistinguished, indeed poky and claustrophobic. As Gertrude Stein used to complain about Oakland, her birthplace, "there is no *there* there."

However, Albuquerque has it champions, and I do not wish to be unfair. It is a city where I have not had much luck. When I have been visiting it, or passing through, there have been rainstorms, hailstorms, snowstorms, or civil disturbances, or I have been trapped in traffic jams on its ring roads. There are certain places, as one has certain friends, with whom everything seems to go wrong. It may be like that with me and Albuquerque.

It has been the good fortune of Santa Fe, on the other hand, to remain small and to preserve its soul. It has taken a century to grow from 5,000 to 50,000, though the magnetic appeal of the Southwest, indicative of a dissatisfaction with the quality of life elsewhere, has operated in Santa Fe as in other cities. There are forecasts of an unhealthy increase to come. It has not escaped the attention of the cheap-jack developers, and its main approaches are the usual *viae dolorosae* of motels, gas stations, hamburger shacks, and rubber-chicken franchises. Yet, in the center of the city, all becomes transformed. The main plaza, except for modern shopfronts on two sides, is still recognizable as the terminus of the Camino Real. You have to be very unimaginative not to feel yourself linked, as you wander in the leafy patch of park, with that majestic square in Mexico City, the Zócalo, 1,500 miles away, and ultimately with the cobbled, arcaded Plaza Mayor in Madrid, dominated by the equestrian figure of Felipe III. The great-grandfather of the old gentlemen who snoozes on the white metal chair, and the great-great-grandfathers of those two young people holding hands, were citizens of Spain. Across the road, in the governor's palace, called in colonial times the *Palacio real,* the rulers of one of Spain's most distant provinces exercised command. There Don Diego José de Vargas ruled his polyglot fief, and there he spent three years in a dark cell. There, each summer since 1712, passes a procession held in his honor, carrying the figure of *La Conquistadora* from the cathedral to the Rosario Chapel, for a novena to be said for his soul.

The cathedral, a block away in Sena Plaza, stands on the spot where the original parish church was erected in 1610, the year in which construction began on the *Palacio real.* The church went through many vicissitudes, including destruction at the hands of Popé in 1680, before being finally demolished in 1869 to make way for St. Francis Cathedral. The cathedral was the work of Archbishop Jean Baptiste Lamy, "Archbishop Latour" of *Death Comes for the Archbishop,* and the struggle involved in its construction is movingly described in that book. Its dimensions, while imposing by the standards of the Southwest at that time, are modest in comparison with the cathedrals of the Archbishop's native country; its style is a gray and uninspired Romanesque. But it required a supreme act of faith and will to embark on such a structure in an era when materials were scarce, transport primitive, labor untrained, and Santa Fe itself comprised no more than 5,000 souls. The Cathedral of St. Francis now seems somewhat forlorn, reduced in size by the modern buildings around it; but unlike them, it was not thrown up casually, with ease and speed. It was built stone by painful stone, and is a fitting resting-place for the bones of its founder. Like Father Kino, he made wide and consuming journeys, and like Kino, in his mausoleum at Magdalena, when death came for him he had earned his rest. They had both wrought an enduring work in a hard land, and deserve their spacious memorials.

Santa Fe contains a wealth of streets, quarters, and buildings executed in adobe. Adobe is a simple medium, but one which is human and intimate, and which lends itself to almost endless variation. Many later buildings have also been built in this material, in order to remain in key with the ancient character of the city. Among the older buildings which should be visited are the Loretto Chapel, the San Miguel Mission, and the Barrio de Analco, and among the modern are the various museums, including those of Fine Arts, International Folk Art, and Navajo Ceremonial Art. Santa Fe is a center for the sale and manufacture of every kind of art and handicraft, Pueblo, Spanish, Mexican and Anglo, and contains some excellent bookshops. You can spend an instructive morning along the Canyon Road, watching the potters, glass-blowers, weavers, and other craftsmen plying their trade. There is always a busy, productive, happy atmosphere about Santa Fe. It possesses good hotels and restaurants, decorated in southwestern taste, which add to the general air of amenity. The city fathers, in their handouts, are fond of calling Santa Fe "The City Different," an excruciating example of a transferred epithet. Yet they are right: Santa Fe *is,* by American standards, "different" (that is, distinguishable from the others), and . . . *vive la différence!* . . . *viva la diferencia!* . . .

It is impossible to leave the subject of Santa Fe without mentioning the highlight of its cultural year, the focal point around which much of its life revolves. This is the Santa Fe Opera, which performs in July and August. It is housed in a building that stands on a ponderosa-studded hillside, a twenty-minute drive to the west of the city. The design is free-flowing and adobe-influenced, leaving the auditorium and the rear of the stage open to the surrounding landscape. As in a Greek amphitheater, you can experience great works of art in a natural setting. In addition to the standard repertoire, Santa Fe regularly mounts the operas of Stravinsky, Ravel, Hindemith, Berg, and other twentieth century masters. The *plein aire* atmosphere offers one an opportunity to hone a musical appetite that may have become slightly jaded in the opera houses of Europe.

FOURTEEN

I HAVE KEPT UNTIL LAST the city which, while its southwestern character is outwardly no more marked than that of Tucson or Santa Fe, by virtue of its situation on the Mexican border possesses its own distinct personality. This is El Paso. The fifth largest city in Texas, with a population of 325,000, El Paso is a sizable entity in itself; but it is actually a twin city, closely paired with the Mexican city of Ciudad Juárez, as Buda is with Pesth.

The population of Juárez was given in 1965 as 385,000. This would give El Paso–Juárez a combined population of 710,000, but in fact the figure for Juárez is almost certainly too low. It is impossible to carry out an accurate census in a country like Mexico, where much of the population is migratory, illiterate, or inaccessible. It has been fairly reliably estimated that the present population of Mexico, where the annual growth-rate is a startling 3.5 percent, will have doubled by the end of the century to over 100,000,000. The Mexican government, when served notice of the impending explosion, at first declined to introduce birth-control programs. Presumably it thought that numbers, illiteracy and poverty would render the rank-and-file docile. However, it has since grown apprehensive and tried to take matters in hand. It has realized that, in fact, overpopulation is deadly. The agricultural potential of Mexico, sterile in the north, oversaturated in the south, does not give rise to optimism. And the traditional savagery of agrarian revolts in Mexico can only send a shudder down the spines of Mexico's rulers.

With the population of Mexico soaring, the population of Juárez is soaring also. It is probably much closer to 700,000 than to 400,000. The border towns suck the peasants irresistibly from the interior, like Mexico City, which is surrounded by *colonias* of shacks made from wooden crates or gas cans, without sewage, light, water, or roads. Every month in Juárez there can be seen, rising higher and higher up the slopes of the Guadalupe Mountains, new clusters of *paracaidistas,* or parachutists, so named because they drop suddenly and unaccountably out of the sky. The Juárez council is doing what it can to cater for these new arrivals, drawn to an already gravid city by the proximity of the United States and the promises of urban life. This is no easy matter, given the climate of Mexican politics, though some of the burden is eased by the tourist traffic from El Paso, and the presence of a sizable job market there. Together, Juárez–El Paso represent a symbiotic organism approaching no less than 1,000,000 persons.

Until the close of the Mexican-American War, Juárez *was* El Paso del Norte. When the town was cut in half, and the north bank of the Rio Grande became American soil, the American segment tried out a number of names to signal its new identity; but eventually the Postmaster General firmly designated it "El Paso." There was continuing confusion until, following the death of Benito Juárez in 1872, in the middle of his fourth presidency, the Mexican half was renamed in his honor. On both sides of the river stand mission churches which served the previously undivided community. The oldest of them is the little church that Father García de San Francisco y Zúñiga named for the Virgin of Guadalupe in 1659. Today it has been literally taken under the wing of the cathedral in Juárez, a gloomy, frigid structure which like many Mexican cathedrals lost many of its ancient furnishings during the years of religious repression. The mission church, however, with its plaited roof over *vigas,* or tree-trunk beams, has the same atmosphere it possessed when Father García built it with the help of the Manso Indians. On the northern bank of the river, within the environs of the city of El Paso, or close to it, are three other mission churches, all heavily rebuilt or restored, but also retaining much of their original character. These are the Socorro, Ysleta, and San Elizario missions, built between 1682 and 1683 to bring spiritual and material aid to the confused population of New Mexico which had just been driven back on El Paso del Norte by Popé's revolt. Ysleta and Socorro are the oldest missions in the United States still in continuous use. They were already almost a century old before the first missions in California came into existence.

El Paso, then, is not only the oldest city in Texas, but the one with the most marked Hispanic and Mexican parentage. It could not disown this parentage even if it wanted to. In fact, it is learning, in an age of increasing dissatisfaction with uniformity, to take a pride in its *diferencia.* Of the eleven million Texans, 60 percent are white, 20 percent black, and 20 percent Mexican; but in El Paso the people of Hispano-Mexican blood number over 50 percent, while blacks are virtually nonexistent. With a community where half are English-speaking and half Spanish-speaking, there is simply no point in the kind of interracial hatred which has always been a feature of life in East Texas, where until a few years ago the motto was "The only good Mexican is a dead Mexican." There are, naturally, frictions between the two peoples, particularly since the Anglos possess most of the wealth and the lion's share of the good jobs; but a corrective ferment is constantly at work, and it is no longer relevant in El Paso to bother about whether someone has an English or a Spanish name or accent. The city represents, in fact, an absorbing laboratory experiment in interracial and international relations. At the University of Texas at El Paso, for example, built in an intriguing and highly attractive Bhutanese style, half the 10,000 students have Spanish names and are Spanish-speaking. It is therefore an exceedingly interesting and unusual institution, the only truly interracial university in the United States. With the exception of McGill and Laval universities in Quebec, it is the only such institution in the Americas.

Economically, El Paso is more dependent on Juárez than Juárez on El Paso. The Mexicans spend $50 million annually in the shops of El Paso, while the Anglos spend $20 million in Juárez. The two cities have no alternative to practicing good neighborliness. In El Paso, as throughout the Southwest, there are a number of Mexican-American ginger groups, ranging from the predominantly middle-class LULAC (League of United Latin-American Citizens) to the somewhat more radical student groups at the university. Texans, with their peculiar history, often overreact at any sign of supposed opposition; but the truth is that Mexican-Americans conduct their protests in a manner that seldom inclines to violence.

There is serious poverty and overcrowding in south El Paso, in the Spanish-speaking districts adjoining Juárez. However, they do not come close to the grimness of conditions in the poorer parts of the sister city, where the *barrios* resemble those in Mexico City which Oscar Lewis described in *The Children of Sánchez*. Spanish as well as English is spoken in El Paso, yet the city could not really be mistaken for anything but basically American. It is not characterized so much by adobe or adobe-inspired architecture, as by an architectural style based on a southern style. To cope with the influx from outside, now experienced by all southwestern cities, and with that part of the resident population that is continually bettering itself economically, the city also contains a rash of apartment complexes, often alarmingly eclectic in appearance.

As soon as you cross the Cordova or the Stanton Street Bridge, however, you are unmistakably in Latin America. The opaque, self-sufficient, Yankee-resistant nature of Spanish culture is immediately apparent. It is not that Juárez is Spanish-colonial in aspect; apart from Father García's church, nothing of that survives. Most of the city has the grimy, battered appearance of an English working-class district, the product of poverty everywhere. However, the omnipresence of the sun is a great concealer and consoler. Even Leeds or Manchester might be less gruesome if they had as much sunshine as Juárez. In the area of the town that is patronized by tourists, the central government, mindful of Tijuana, has commissioned a number of Mexico's best architects to build an ambitious shopping and museum complex. Tijuana has become such a cesspool that the government dare not risk the same fate overtaking an even larger border town, which also happens to be the main foreign point of entry into Mexico. Juárez has its seamy side, but it lacks the total loathsomeness of Tijuana.

The difference between El Paso and Juárez is signalled by such obvious things as buildings, clothes, the goods in the shops. There are also smaller and subtler indications: the difference in the smell of the cooking oil, in the smell of the gasoline, in the street smells, in the general healthy reek of a society not insanely sanitized and deodorized. A European visitor seldom has a feeling of being at home in an American town; he usually feels alien. But if you take him to Juárez, he perks up. Even if he speaks no Spanish, he feels on familiar ground. Juárez is like one of the less appetizing Mediterranean towns, and he will not be afraid of a little honest stink, a little genuine dirt.

The Spanish which they speak in Juárez and Mexico is not altogether, of course, the Spanish of Spain, although as I mentioned in my opening chapter, it has features of the Spanish of an earlier epoch, the Spanish of the sixteenth century. It is not simply the Mexican's hard nasal inflections, or his substitution of the *s* sound for the *th,* which is universal throughout Latin America, but of a wide range of grammar and vocabulary. The border Spanish of Juárez is as distinctive as the *pachuco* of the Mexican-Americans of California, of which it was an ancestor. In El Paso, the *tirilones,* or toughs, of the Chicano sections speak a *caló* or slang that has been compared by Professor Lurline Coltharp with the famous *germanía,* the argot spoken in Spain in the *Siglo de oro.* Teachers once treated American Spanish, with its individual character, as an inferior, bastard form of the imperial tongue. Whether it is "correct" or "incorrect" (and how many people speak any language "correctly"?) it is the tongue spoken by large numbers of people, who employ it easily and naturally. Fortunately, the older attitudes are growing more tolerant. The quest for linguistic conformity is being recognized as only another aspect of the cult of bigness.

I have no space to give examples of the more idiosyncratic examples of Chicano words, but some of the loan words are self-explanatory. Here are a few words I have culled from articles in *Studies in Language and Linguistics:* bil (bill); *bomper* (car bumper); *borlo* (wild party—English brawl); *bos* (boss); *carro* (car); *carrucha* (hot-red); *chanate* (coffee—Náhuatl origin); *chategón* (shotgun); *gaso, gasolín; grifa* (reefer, marijuana); *juila* (bicycle—English wheel); *keki* (cake); *lonche, lonchería, lonchear* (lunch, lunch place, eat lunch); *mein* (main street); *renta* (rent); *sitijól* (city-hall); *troco, troquero* (truck, trucker); *trale* (trailer).

Professor Ray Past, in an article in *Hispania,* culls an entertaining series of words from his endeavors on the golf course at the Club Campestre Juárez. He notes that the *golfista* takes his *bolsa* (bag), in which are his *maderas* (woods) and *fierros* (irons), and his *pichin güech* (pitching wedge), *san güech* (sand wedge), *chiper* and *pat* (putter). As his *cadi* watches, he puts his *bola* on the *tí* and aims down the *fargüey*, attempting to avoid a *juc* (hook), a *gancho* (slice) or a *puliada* (pull), and not to go *atabáns* (out of bounds). If he reaches the *grín* and executes a good *pat,* he may find that he has achieved a *par,* a *berdi,* a *bogui,* or an *águila* (eagle). If he is unfortunate, he can do no better than a *doble bogui,* which at the Club Campestre is referred to as a *zopilote* (a buzzard).

One of the more interesting Juárez loan words is *huachacarro* (watch-a-car-o), the man who guards your car against thieves when you shop, eat, or do business across the border. He wears a uniform, and has official status, but if you value your hubcaps you will give him a *cuala* (a quarter)—a *grande* (dollar) is too much—to do his duty. He is first cousin to the *velador,* the watchman, who will sit or lounge outside a private house to keep an eye on it, and who is roughly equivalent to the Spanish *sereno.* Juárez, more than most Mexican towns, is full of street people: beggars, cripples, sellers of smuggled American cigarettes, pimps, prostitutes, hustlers, and vendors of all kinds. Periodically, the central government is overcome by a bureaucratic hankering for tidiness, like that which led Mr. Butler to get the whores off the streets of London and out of sight in the 1950s. I doubt if their number has declined, if at all. It must be admitted, however, that the aim of the Mexican government is laudable, in that street life is in many respects wasteful and stultifying; but in a country as poor as Mexico it is bound to thrive, and efforts to sweep it away in the name of national dignity are bound to fail. The existence of street life, with its noise, movement, odor and variety, is another thing that makes Juárez different from American cities, and makes the European visitor feel at home. The American authorities have become even meaner than the British where allowing the beggar to beg, or the peddler to peddle, or the vendor to vend is concerned. In consequence, their streets are drab, and have lost the feeling of life.

Juárez is a free port. American citizens who cross the border are not asked for identification, and need no papers for their car. On return, they pass through American customs, though they are rarely subjected to an over-rigorous examination. Tourists bound for the interior are halted at a checkpoint two miles south of the city, on the road to Chihuahua; but in Juárez itself Americans are not subject to *papeleo,* or red tape (other nationalities do require visas). The fact is that Juárez cannot exist without its daily flood of visitors from El Paso. When the Nixon Administration virtually closed the border in 1972, with the expressed intention of putting pressure on the Mexican government to act more effectively against the drug traffic, Juárez started to strangle, and the operation had to be called off.

In Juárez, American visitors can buy liquor more cheaply than in the United States, and in greater variety. They can shop in the Mexican markets and supermarkets for items that are less costly than on the American side, and also find such commodities as fish, which is in short supply in El Paso. Mexican bread, hand-baked and free from chemicals, is another good buy. Above all, they can eat in the many excellent restaurants, where the menu is more varied and imaginative than in most American restaurants. El Paso, like the majority of American towns, is ill-supplied in that respect, whereas Juárez, reacting to sharp demand, possesses three or four times as many good eating-places as any comparable Mexican town. Only Mexico City contains more and better restaurants.

Mexican cookery is one of the world's most distinctive cuisines. Mexican dishes derive to some extent from pre-Columbian sources, and among the foodstuffs indigenous to Mexico are maize, sweet and white potatoes, squash, peanuts, the tomato, the chile, the avocado, the papaya, the zapote, and vanilla. The early Mexicans also domesticated the turkey, and fattened for consumption a small, fat, hairless dog which, when you put your hand on it, gives you a surprise, because it has an abnormally high body temperature. (I have not eaten one, because my English friends would not approve.) Then, of course there is chocolate, its name deriving from the Náhuatl word *chocolatl*. Bernal Díaz relates how fond of it the Emperor Moctezuma was, and how it was served to him frothed up with a special twirling stick, or *molinillo,* that you can still buy for a few pesos in all Mexican markets. It may in fact have been a drink reserved in former times for royalty and nobility, and cocoa beans were certainly used as a form of currency. The modern Mexicans flavor their chocolate with almond, egg, cinnamon, and sugar, and serve it to perfection.

In spite of this piquant list of ingredients, however, Mexican cookery rests on a peasant basis, and seldom reaches very great heights. The staple is ground maize, *masa,* in all its guises—a small portion of meat or vegetable encased in flour, or in a tortilla. It has been suggested that the dearth of meat, and thus of protein, was so severe in pre-Columbian times that the widespread cult of cannibalism was possibly a method of satisfying the craving for protein. Certainly maize is a wretchedly inadequate food, and it has been estimated by Mexican nutritionists that over 50 percent of all Mexicans are poorly nourished or actually undernourished. The method used to make such dull fare palatable, or to disguise the badness or toughness of whatever meat is available, is to have recourse to the all-pervading chile. The Mexicans are connoisseurs of chile, and there are at least twenty varieties, ranging from the large bell pepper and the ancho chile down to the wicked little yellow *cascabel,* or rattlesnake. When I was in the British Navy, I carried a little box of paprika round with me to sprinkle on the food, and it worked wonders. In time, people become addicted to chile as they do to paprika, sambal, or curry powder, other palliatives for bland or unpalatable food. However, chile has the unfortunate side effect of wearing a hole in the stomach, and in fact stomach trouble appears to be chronic in Mexico. Mexicans as a whole are neither healthy nor long-lived, and their diet and general eating habits must bear much of the responsibility for this.

It would be monotonous and imprudent for a non-Mexican to embark on a steady intake of tacos, tamales, chiles rellenos, chimichangas, and enchiladas, though all those can be delicious, as are the superb puff-pastry confections called sopaipillas and buñuelos. On the other hand, the occasional Mexican meal makes a welcome change, and many people develop a passion for Mexican food. As I have said, it is not *haute cuisine,* since independent Mexico never developed the aristocratic or high bourgeois culture needed to nurture that kind of skill. Nor did Mexico have civilized neighbors, and her European mentors, the Spaniards, were on the whole a Spartan and ascetic breed with little use for the pleasures of eating and drinking. If Maximilian and Carlotta had reigned longer, the picture might have altered, but the Mexicans showed no inclination to put up with French bayonets even for the sake of French cooking. Among the areas of Mexican culture where the French did make an impression, however, was in music. In Mexico City, as in New Orleans, they introduced the airs and dances of the day. The *mariachi* bands of Mexico, whose nucleus is the trumpet, fiddle and guitar, owe their name to the French word *mariage,* at which they were hired to perform during the French occupation. They imitated the music they picked up at French band concerts. Tunes reminiscent or borrowed from Rossini, Auber, Thomas, and Hérold are played over a brilliant and wayward Latin American accompaniment, while others are taken from the Spanish *zarzuela.*

On the other hand, the Mexicans have certainly put the world in their debt by the introduction of a novel drink, the *margarita,* invented by a Juárez barman. *Margarita* means pearl, and it is a pearl of a drink, enclosed inside a crust of salt on the wettened rim of the glass. Its ingredients are tequila and lemon juice, in equal amounts, with a dash of cointreau. Tequila, as most readers will know, is the fermented juice of the maguey cactus, and is named after a picturesque little town north of Guadalajara. At Tequila, the rows of the giant spiky gray-green *Agave tequilana,* with its saw-toothed leaves, march in a devil's vineyard across the hillside. When fully grown, the heart of the cactus is cut out, roasted, and fermented. Another fermented cactus juice is *mescal,* derived in similar fashion from other agaves, chiefly *Agave palmaris,* and sometimes bottled with the traditional *gusano,* or caterpillar, floating at the bottom; while the cheapest and most destructive of the cactus liquors, sold in booths and dram-shops, and responsible for much drunkenness and misery, is *pulque.* It is a fermented *aguamiel,* drained from the middle of the maguey (*Agave atrovirens*). The recognized Mexican treatment for hangovers, by the way, is *menudo,* or tripe, off which repentant revelers can be seen breakfasting in little neighborhood eating-places. Incidentally, I might mention that while Mexican wines are more mediocre than they ought to be, Mexican beers are absolutely first-class, and immeasurably better than their American counterparts, which have been pasteurized, vitaminized, and homogenized beyond any semblance of an honest beverage.

Besides the attractions of eating and drinking, El Pasoans and American tourists go to Juárez to visit the racetrack or the bullring. The racetrack is highly ornate, furbished with revolutionary murals, and offers both horse-racing and greyhound racing; but its function is the usual one of racetracks everywhere—that of transferring, more or less rapidly, the money from the pockets of the "patrons" into the pockets of the bookmakers. Something of the tortuous background of the Juárez track, opened in 1964, is told in Ovid Demaris' *Pozo del Mundo*—i.e. "Arsehole of the World"—an account of the seamier aspects of the Mexican-American border towns. To many people, bull-fighting is a cruel pursuit: but I wonder how many persons who frequent the Juárez and other racetracks ask themselves what happens to the horses when they are no longer fit to run? And do they realize that greyhounds which have ceased to earn a profit are promptly gassed or poisoned, in order to save the cost of their keep?

There are two bullrings in Juárez, a small rococolike ring downtown, and a huge one a mile away. The latter is one of the largest in a country of large rings. The Plaza Monumental in Mexico City holds 50,000 spectators, and is over twice the size of the Plaza Monumental in Madrid (23,000), which is also overshadowed by Mexico City's Plaza Nuevo Toreo (27,000). Mexico, with seven hundred bullrings, has almost as many rings as Spain, and features almost as many annual *corridas*. Bullfighting, in fact, was brought to the New World by the conquistadores, and is firmly established in several countries in Central and South America, in Guatemala, Colombia, Ecuador, Peru, and Venezuela, as well as being sporadically celebrated in others. The first corrida in Mexico took place on June 24, 1526, to mark the return of Hernán Cortés from his expedition to Honduras; and the official series of corridas dates from 1529. By the end of the sixteenth century, the first Mexican *ganaderías,* or ranches for breeding fighting bulls, had come into existence. The Atenco ganadería at Toluca, founded in the late 1550s by crossing Navarrese stock from Spain with native stock from Zalduendo, is said to be the oldest practicing ganadería in the world. José Maria de Cossío, in the latest edition of his magisterial *Los Toros* (1967), lists seventeen Mexican ganaderías bravas, and there are at least another fifteen of good reputation, and thirty of the second rank. Barnaby Conrad, in his *Encyclopaedia of Bullfighting,* lists eleven of the finest.

Bulls, of course, are the foundation of the *fiesta brava.* A bullfight can no more function without a good bull than a racing driver without a good car. Mexicans have a great knowledge and passion for the fighting bull, and their animals are on the whole smaller and more compact than Spanish bulls. You seldom see those gross, lethargic *catedrales,* or "cathedrals," that you see in Spanish rings. Mexican *reses bravas* are generally excellent: quick-footed, intelligent, and willing. So are Mexican *toreros,* though with a half-dozen exceptions, it would be hard, I think, to compare the present crop with their Spanish counterparts. In the past, of course, Mexico has produced many great matadors, including Rodolfo Gaona, Luis Freg (gored fifty-seven times, and five times given Extreme Unction), the Silvetis, Fermín Espinosa, Ricardo Torres, Hector Saucedo, Lorenzo Garza, and Andrés Blando. Carlos Arruza, of course, was one of the most complete toreros who ever lived, magnificent not only with the cape, the muleta, and the banderillas, but in his later years as a *rejoneador,* or mounted bullfighter. He was a great man as well as a great *diestro,* and the Spaniards gave him the Order of Benificencia. Ironically, like César Girón, the great Venezuelan, Arruza was killed in 1967 in a senseless road accident, in which he was not even driving.

Arruza notwithstanding, it seems to me, as an aficionado of some standing, that the present generation of Mexicans lack the quality of the Spaniards. It may be a matter of taste. The Mexicans traditionally belong to the feverish, eat-'em-alive school, bounding about the ring as though they meant to swallow the animal hoofs, tail, and all. There are fewer toreros in Mexico than there are in Spain, perhaps about 50 full matadors and 200 *novilleros,* as against 80 matadors and 1,000 novilleros in the metropolitan country. Comparatively few Mexicans make the journey to Spain to confirm their *alternativa,* and to compete with the best performers in front of discriminating audiences. But the real difference must lie in the national temperament of the toreros and in the tastes of the spectators. Of the visiting Spanish matadors, it was El Cordobés, with his acrobatics, who charmed the Juárez crowd; while Antonio Ordóñez puzzled and disappointed them. True, he had come out of retirement, was nursing himself for his resumed bout with Dominguín, and had no intention of dying in an obscure corner of the Americas; but he fought one of his bulls masterfully, with that blend of emotion and detachment which is the mark of the master. The Mexicans were bored. They did not comprehend the quiet art of the man who stands still, feet planted, tranquil, keeping the bull's muzzle glued in the cape and passing it with simple *naturales* and *derechazos.* The Mexicans are not satisfied unless the matador is leaping around, citing extravagantly, puffing out his chest and strutting about, executing fancy *mariposas, chicuelinas,* and *faroles;* or inviting the animal's charge on his knees, leaning his elbow between its horns, and taking the tip between his teeth. In Madrid, these antics would be greeted with ironic handclaps and derisive shouts of *"Música!"* Mexicans, with their *macho* philosophy, like to watch a man proving how brave he is, whereas Spaniards take it for granted that the man is brave in the first place. They deprecate flashiness and foolhardiness.

Where the Mexican matador, with his uninhibited approach, often scores is in the vehemence and sincerity with which he carries out the final act of the corrida, the killing of the bull. In earlier times, the last *suerte* was regarded as the culmination of the spectacle. The word *matador* means "he who gives death." It is commonly agreed that it was Juan Belmonte, in the late 1910s and 1920s, who downgraded the final act in favor of the work with the cape and muleta. Belmonte was a man of outstanding bravery, none braver, but he possessed physical handicaps that prevented him from being an outstanding killer. He therefore compensated in other directions. I have seen many honorable killers in Spanish rings in the past quarter century, but there have been very few consistent exponents of what should be the most solemn moment of the corrida. The finest of them was Jaime Ostos. He was regal, and he was tall, an almost indispensable requirement for adequate killing. The matador must lean in over the horn at the perilous moment when he is crossing his hands, cape in one hand and sword in the other. A short man is at an obvious disadvantage. Perhaps the Mexican toreros have never heard of Belmonte; in any event, Mexican spectators, with a fixation on death even greater than that of the Spaniards, await the death-blow with agonizing expectancy. They are not as indulgent as the modern Spaniard to the matador who, as long as he has satisfied them in other respects, can cheat them, and cheat himself, by flapping his cape in the bull's face as he slides around and sticks his sword in the side of its neck. I have watched the usual proportion of depressing kills in Mexico: but I have also seen toreros fling themselves at the animal, or even take it as it charges, *recibiendo,* and thrust the blade in straight and true—*hasta el puño*—up to the hilt.

Mexican matadors are handicapped by the slackness with which the spectacle is conducted. In Spain, when the minute hand touches the hour at which the fight is due to start, the trumpet rings out and the *paseo* begins. In Mexico, twenty or thirty minutes can tick away before the authorities have even taken their places. Nor does the *autoridad* conduct the proceedings with firmness and decision, as in Spain. Fights become sloppy, and the feeling of slackness is compounded by the fact that the senior matador, who should act as *maestro de lidia,* or director of the combat, seldom possesses sufficient experience or dramatic flair. In addition, the ugly but necessary part of the fight, the *suerte de varas,* is rendered even worse by the way in which the picadors are permitted to stab the bull at will. They are allowed to push it all over the ring, instead of working within strictly defined limits. The result is that as many promising bulls are ruined by being hit in the lungs or spine as there are in Spain. Finally, the *fiesta brava* at Juárez is too often spoiled by an element quite beyond the control of the matador—the wind. Juárez and El Paso are situated between high mountains, round which there are gusts and eddies even on the sunniest afternoons. Wind is as much the matador's enemy as the bull, and frightens him more. If the cloth is blown across his body while he is making a pass, he is done for. On such occasions, all but the most reckless Mexican—and many of them *are* reckless—will tend to dispatch a dangerous animal without any false heroics . . . and who can blame him?

I hope I do not sound ungrateful. Except for occasions in Mexico City or other Mexican cities, and six months in Spain, for the last seven years the corridas in Juárez have been, for me, "the only game in town." I have seen some very satisfactory encounters. In particular, I have twice witnessed Manolo Martínez, acting as sole matador, fight six bulls in an afternoon, the first time with bulls of San Martín, the second with bulls of Pastajé. He performed impressively both times, bringing back memories of the only previous occasion I saw this particular feat: by Antonio Bienvida, triumphantly, ten years earlier in Madrid.

Bullfighting, of course, is in a perennial state of decadence. The pundits shake their heads and assure us that the present spectacle is a travesty of what went before. In the past twenty years, bullfighting has undergone the horn-shaving scandal, the dilution of standards caused by catering to tourists, and the high cost of El Cordobés, who reduced bullfighting to a branch of show business ($50,000 per corrida). Now it faces the challenge of soccer, which exerts an ever greater appeal for the urban masses of Spain and Latin America. Soccer is a simpler activity, easier to follow, devoid of mystery and subtle emotion, perfectly suiting the character of a town-bred *lumpenproletariat*.

The fiesta brava was born in antiquity, in Crete and Iberia. It is rooted in an agrarian dispensation, in nature, though with numerous aristocratic grace notes. The bull represents the great, black, blind, careless, annihilating force of nature itself, which a man in his frailty, supplied with a few flimsy tools, must face with what courage and style he can. With increasing mechanization, and alienation from nature, the symbolic image of the bull must lose its power. The corrida de toros is another idiosyncratic activity that will succumb to the spreading blight of Bigness. Unless, happily, Bigness perishes before bullfighting.

Margaritas, mariachis, and corridas represent the sunnier side of Juárez. The dark side is prostitution, gangsterism, and crooked politics.

Juárez is, as I have said, immeasurably cleaner than Tijuana. All the same, prostitution is one of the city's most profitable industries—profitable, that is, for everybody but the prostitutes. The girls are sexual slaves, launched by their owners on their careers when they are fourteen or fifteen. They begin as call girls, or in the better brothels, then descend through the circles of their professional hell until they end, broken and used up, in filthy cribs. Their takings are shared out by the pimps, the gang bosses, the city politicians, and the state politicians; and finally, since anything of value in Mexico ends in the hands of the politicians in the capital, the whores' earnings help to run the government. Many of the girls are sold by their parents for pitiful sums, while others are literally kidnapped. I know an American who went to the railway station at Juárez to meet a sixteen-year-old girl who was coming to her as a maid from Monterey. When she arrived, she discovered that the girl had been driven away in a local taxi. A tenacious woman, she scattered banknotes around and managed to trace the driver. He had taken the girl to a downtown brothel, where the madam, following time-honored practice, had made her drunk and was preparing to send in a man to her. The girl would wake up the next morning and realize that she was ruined. Since losing one's virginity is a disaster in Latin-American countries, it would be impossible for her to return home; so she would resign herself to life as a prostitute. My American friend reached the scene, like the Seventh Cavalry, just in time, and dragged the comatose girl from a back bedroom. She then called the police who, simulating shock and distress for the benefit of the Gringo lady, beat the taxi driver unconscious in front of her eyes.

It is inevitable, since El Paso houses the biggest army base in the United States, that large-scale prostitution should flourish in Juárez. The trade formerly received a further boost from the quickie divorces that were practiced there. The formalities of the divorce took only thirty minutes to complete; but the travelers on the "Freedom Riders Special," as the incoming plane was called, usually elected to spend a night at a Juárez hotel to celebrate their liberation. Girls—or boys—were made available. Eventually, New York State, which provided the majority of the divorcées, changed its divorce laws, which rendered the procedure obsolete; at which time the Mexican government discovered that the racket had all along been an affront to its republican dignity, and officially closed it down.

Even with the loss of the divorce revenue, the profits from sin are not likely to run dry. There is, in addition, an activity as ancient as prostitution which yields its operators even higher dividends. This is smuggling. Smuggling is a way of life on the border, from the *coyote* with his human freight, the street arab with his stolen carton of cigarettes, to the professional "mule" driving over the frontier with $500,000 worth of heroin soldered into his gas tank. Drugs are, of course, the most profitable cargo. Mexican marijuana, mainly grown in the northern provinces, sells for $5 a kilo in Juárez. It fetches $200 in New York, if you can get it there. The American customs employs trained dogs to sniff it out, but enormous consignments, doused with Coca-Cola to lessen the smell, are still brought through. The customs relies less on dogs than on informers. Scarcely a week passes without a naive young American, who is sure he can make a fortune, being caught at the bridge with several bricks of marijuana hidden in the panels or tires of his truck or camper. He had bought the stuff from a dealer in Juárez who, after taking his money, promptly called the American customs to tell them the lad was on his way. Thus the dealer not only makes the sale, but collects a bounty too. Or else the "grass" which the youngster has bought turns out to be just that—*grass*.

Heroin, being less bulky, can be taken across the bridge more readily. The smaller carriers put it in balloons or condoms which they swallow or insert in their anus. A better method is to take a packet under the chassis or bumper of a parked car belonging to a visitor from El Paso. When he drives back across the bridge, all that is necessary is to follow him to his house or apartment and pick a time to remove the package. But the Mafia and their Mexican contacts, who control the heroin business, seldom bother to use the international bridge. They are not dealing in petty amounts. A kilo of 80 percent or 90 percent pure heroin costs $10,000 in Mexico and fetches $500,000 in the United States, by the time it has been cut a dozen times with sugar or milk powder. The big operators seldom concern themselves with the sweat and harassment of the border. Their bases are sited well back from the frontier, in the cities of Hermosillo, Chihuahua, or Monterey. They take their consignments to the coast, where they are put aboard small craft bound for San Diego, Los Angeles, or Galveston. Often, according to the American Coast Guard, private yachts and power boats are hijacked, and the crew and passengers dumped overboard. At the end of the cruise, the merchandise is dropped at prearranged marks, or taken into crowded marinas. Or else it is flown across the border, to a disused airfield or a suitable spot in the desert in West Texas, New Mexico, or Arizona. Sometimes the aircraft will make a quick landing on a road, where a car will be waiting for it. In August 1974, police intercepted a cargo of 13,000 tons of marijuana that had been flown from Colombia in an old transport plane to a disused airport near Atlanta. Such traffic is virtually impossible to stop. Clearly, only a fractional amount of the drugs smuggled into the United States each year , is seized by the police. The only leads the authorities can hope for, in this as in most other types of crime, is from tip-offs, either from common informers, or stemming from gang rivalries. The mortality rate among informers is high, as the number of bodies fished out of the Rio Grande attests.

However, the mortality rate throughout all Mexico, one way or another, is high. Mexico is a high-risk country. The drug producers and drug smugglers flourish because crime in Mexico is a respectable, or at least a respected, profession. Its practitioners have *palanca,* or political influence. They are protected by *pezgordos,* or big fish, and are pezgordos themselves. And in Mexico you cannot be a pezgordo unless you enjoy the favor of the ruling party, the PRI, whose name means the Party of Institutionalized Revolution.

Mexico and Russia both had their revolutions in 1917; and there is an odd similarity between the way both countries are now run. In both, there is the pretense of democracy, of socialism, of encouraging a certain measure of opposition. In both, the Party is absolutely supreme, and no one can aspire to wealth or position without joining it and becoming an *apparatchik.* There is no future outside the PRI; there is a bright one within it. Promising recruits are sought out in high school and university, mainly young opportunists with the gift of the gab. They are given scholarships, special privileges, and comfortable government jobs. Eventually one of them will hew his way through the party ranks to become president.

The Party controls all facets of Mexican life. It selects occupants for every important post in the central government, the trade unions, the cultural institutions, the law, the professions, the armed forces, the provincial administration, the newspapers and television. Officially Marxist and atheist, like the Party in Russia, it has reached a *concordat* with the Church, which it manipulates for its own ends. It rigs the elections. Since it was founded, in 1929, by General Plutarco Calles, the self-styled Maximum Chief of the Revolution, it has never been challenged. Occasionally, deliberately or through an oversight, a member of the opposition party, PAN, the Party for National Action, is allowed to win a seat or two. Life is then made difficult for him, and if he is a mayor or state governor the central government will starve him of funds to make him look inept. You have to be brave to belong to, or to vote for, PAN.

In my book on Cortés, I wrote with guarded approbation of the PRI. On reflection, I think I went too far. Like the Party in Russia, it trades on the fact that it is certainly an improvement on what went before. By making an alliance with Big Business, the PRI has improved the standard of living of many Mexicans, and the standard of living of many politicians. Nobody could help applauding the cessation of murder, bloodshed, and civil war which the Party has brought about, even if in many respects it is the peace of the graveyard. But the Party is an unlovely thing: Big Government personified, a cruel and unyielding dictatorship rendered more nauseating by its humanitarian protestations. It produces almost as many spouters as the British Socialist Party. In 1973, President Echeverría, leader of a country where great numbers of people are illiterate, starving, and without shoes, elected to present to the Club of Rome a Charter of Economic Rights. He was the man who, in 1968, when the students had rioted in Mexico City on the eve of the Olympic Games, called out the tanks and shot down 400 of them.

I have lived for some years in Franco's Spain. I have no great affection for the regime, although, like most Spaniards, I feel a grudging admiration for the hard-headed old Gallegan who could make even Hitler respect his siesta. But I would far rather live in Franco's Spain than in the Mexico of Echeverría. There is corruption in Franco's regime; but the law of *mordida,* of "the bite," is not paramount in Spain as it is in Mexico. Mexico functions almost entirely, from top to bottom, by means of bribes, fixes, and wire-pulling. Many Mexican civil servants and policemen are paid practically nothing, and are expected to create a salary for themselves by means of graft. The customs at Juárez are manned on a rotation basis by officers from all parts of

Mexico, so that every member of the service can get his chance to sop up the gravy. When a revolution becomes institutionalized to that extent, and encourages its citizens to prey on one another, it is oppressive and debilitating.

What saves the Spaniards is that, though they live under a dictatorship, they are by nature more democratic than most *soi-disant* democrats. Spaniards treat each other with as much openness and frankness as Americans, which is an enormous compliment. There are masters and servants in Spain; there are dirty and menial jobs; but there is no caste system. No Spaniard thinks less of himself because he digs a ditch, cooks your food, or brings it to your table. Every Spaniard knows that intrinsically he is as good as every other Spaniard. He is not demeaned by poverty; poverty is an inconvenience, not an obscure moral punishment. It would never occur to the poorest Spaniard, doing the most miserable job, not to look his fellows straight in the face. In Spain, apart from a few foolish *señoritos,* I have never seen a rich man behave arrogantly toward a poor man. In Mexico, the rich behave toward the poor, the educated toward the uneducated, the light-skinned toward the *Indios,* in the way the South Africans are supposed to behave toward the Bantu. A wealthy Mexican, who may be a very pleasant fellow in El Paso, cannot keep the contempt and irritation out of his face as he snaps his fingers at a servant in Juárez.

It is not surprising that the poor in Mexico are starting to grow restless. In spite of savage countermeasures, the mountains of Mexico are once again beginning to swarm with outlaws and guerrillas, of every political stripe. The cities are becoming increasingly prone to bombings, kidnappings, and bank robberies. They will get worse.

But now, having touched tangentially on my impressions of the country which is the southern extension of the Southwest, I must move on, finally, to modern America.

Non licet omnibus adire Corinthum. "It is not given to every one to see America from a Greyhound bus." Or even from a vintage Mercedes.

One way or another, I have seen a fair amount of America in the past few years.

Then what do I, an Anglo-Welshman of peculiar views, make of it all? . . .

FIFTEEN

In RECENT YEARS, the older cultural layers of the Southwest have been heavily overlaid, and in some areas obliterated, by the culture of the Anglo which I have just been describing. They have been succumbing to the pervasive habits and standards of Middle America. The melting pot, like the mills of God, melts slowly, but it melts thoroughly. By now, most of the regional accents have been flattened into a generalized, indeterminate tone; and even though the older peoples of the Southwest and the older stratum of Anglos cling to many of their old traditions, they are bound to be affected by the widening uniformity of manners and outlook imparted by modern techniques of advertising, marketing, education, journalism, television, and the rest.

This new, intrusive outlook is that of the shallow but seductive culture of New York, and the other great cities. It began to impose itself on the Southwest no more than twenty to thirty years ago. Until that time, the Southwest, because of its inaccessibility and forbidding nature, was a backwater, as far as Anglo culture was concerned. The Anglos could not get to it. The automobile and the airplane reached it late, and the two states that are its heartland, New Mexico and Arizona, were both admitted to the Union only in 1912, the last states to do so until Hawaii and Alaska. Oklahoma, Kansas, Colorado, Utah, and Nevada all reached statehood before New Mexico and Arizona. It was only after World War Two that the Anglos suddenly became aware of the existence of the Southwest, and injected into it the bright and aggressive culture that they had developed elsewhere. It would probably not be facetious, in fact, to assert that Anglo culture could not root itself deeply in the Southwest until the spread of modern airconditioning.

It is this recent top-dressing of Anglo culture that I want to describe in my final pages. But the views which I shall express are necessarily subjective; another writer could not see modern American life in those terms at all. Every one brings his own attitudes and prejudices to the way he sees another country. What is more, I am a man approaching middle-age. I would certainly have reacted differently to America had I come here twenty years earlier; and it would have been a different America. In one's late forties, it is only too easy to become sentimental about the past, and to fall into the trap of becoming *laudator temporis acti*. All of us, in middle life, suspect that the world went wrong at some moment that coincided more or less with our own farewell to youth. One must be on guard against facile lamentation and hand-wringing. Yet I might urge two small points in my favor, as an independent witness. First, I have never been tainted with that distrust of America, or with the frank anti-Americanism, that one often finds in Europe. Secondly, when I am staying in one country for any length of time, I try to make a practice of not comparing it continually with another. Unless it is ruled by a Communist dictatorship, or some similar form of government—in which case I should in any case keep away from it—it is bound to display some features in which it will be superior to your own country, or the country you have just come from, and in other ways it will be inferior. You can expect some nice surprises, and some rude jolts. It is therefore only sensible to maintain an open frame of mind. No one is so maddening as a member of the "we-do-it-all-better-at-home" gang. Besides, it is an unsettling habit to keep looking over one's shoulder. On balance, I find that, for me, living in other people's countries has definite advantages. There is always the danger, of course, especially for a writer, that one's roots might dry up; on the other hand, you feel a calmness of outlook that comes from detaching yourself from the day-to-day irritations that afflict you in your own country whenever you open a newspaper or listen to the news. Of course, you have to take care that the insulation from such native annoyances does not degenerate into genuine isolation, or coldness of heart; but, as a clearer away of cant and cobwebs, living abroad has much to recommend it.

I must take care, therefore, to avoid reactionary comment and curmudgeonly grousing. It is easy to shake your graying locks, and tell yourself that the world is going to the blasted bowwows, and forget that out there, in the sunshine, the youthful and the vigorous are playing, making love, working, bringing up families, glorying in the world, and living contentedly in it. Nevertheless, I feel compelled to repeat that I feel that, in some fundamental way, all is not well with the societies that modern men have evolved for themselves. "Something is wrong with our bloody ships today." I would not go as far as Freud, who wrote in *Civilization and Its Discontents* that "I have endeavoured

to guard myself against the enthusiastic partiality which believes our civilization to be the most precious thing which we possess or could acquire, and
thinks it must inevitably lead us to undreamed-of heights of perfection. I can
at any rate listen without taking umbrage to those critics who aver that, when
one surveys the aims of civilization and the means it employs, one is bound to
conclude that the whole thing is not worth the effort, and that in the end it
can only produce a state of things which the individual will be unable to bear."

In 1929, Freud had good reason to feel something approaching despair.
He was writing at a time of economic anarchy worse even than ours; he had
watched the Austro-Hungarian Empire and the other great empires which had
brought the world into a rule collapse in the dust; in a few years he would
share the fate of millions of his fellow Europeans, and be forced into exile. He
lived through the First World War; mercifully he was spared the horrors of
the Second. Few people who experienced the terrors of the first half of our
century would have been willing to wager on the relative stability and common sense of the world today. The procession of gruesome events that started
on the Marne and the Aisne in 1914 continued without a break until the dropping of the bombs on Hiroshima and Nagasaki. Who, contemplating all those
upheavals, could have foreseen the comparative—I say the *comparative*—order
which is more or less the norm in our times? I am not forgetting Korea, the
Congo, Nigeria, Pakistan, Uganda, the Arab-Israeli struggles, Vietnam, and
the other wars that have occurred since the end of World War Two; nor do
I overlook the fact that during the 1960s two hundred separate coups d'état
took place; or that in only one year since 1945 has no British soldier been
killed in action. But granted this, and granted that the now crumbling *pax
atomica* is only a temporary sort of peace, it does seem to me that, as we enter
the last quarter of our century, we are in slightly better shape, despite the
economic and population crises, than the world would have dared hope for
thirty or forty years ago.

Having expressed this qualified note of optimism, I must nevertheless
repeat my original opinion: something, at bottom, is amiss with modern life
—though, of course, something is *always* amiss with life; it is the condition of
living. The activities of the historian and the archaeologist are not very highly
regarded by our society; but it is the historian and archaeologist who know
that human affairs could have shaped themselves at any given time in a different
manner from the way in which they did. They can see that at the decisive moments of history there were other options, other choices. They know that
human development is a haphazard business, in which there are as many
chances lost as chances taken. To most people, the point which we have now
reached was inevitable, simply because we have reached it; a simple philosophy
of *post hoc, ergo propter hoc*. This simplistic view, as I have tried to indicate
earlier, is particularly true of Americans, with their linear view of history. It
brings them a certain sense of satisfaction, but is also responsible for much of

their uncertainty and psychic tension. Since it is an American article of faith that the Republic must be close to, or at least within striking distance of perfection, the Republic's follies and failures arouse a sense of chronic dissatisfaction. Unlike Freud, I am not close to considering the whole of human history an unmitigated error, though I might agree with T. S. Eliot about "the immense panorama of futility and anarchy which is contemporary history," or much of it. But I certainly believe that, as it enters the Second Industrial Revolution, our Western society is marked by deep and ugly flaws; and since America is the world's leading industrial society, and the country where everything is taken to extremes, these flaws sometimes show up in their most startling form in the United States.

Of course many of these disagreeable traits manifested themselves in Europe before they did so in America. Certainly they are spreading to other continents as the rest of the world copies American and European models. But there is a growing feeling, both in Europe and in America, and elsewhere, that the way in which we live now and look like condemning ourselves to live in the immediate future may not be the only or the best way in which we could have lived. Not only the young people suspect this, but many of their elders also. Having endured the horrors of laissez faire capitalism, must we now move on to the overcompensations of overcollectivization, of socialism and communism? Is there no other way? Clearly our mode of life, even where it is blighted by socialism, is superior to the wooden coercion of communism; we may also claim, perhaps, that it is superior in several important respects to life as it is lived by many, though by no means all, modern Asians and Africans. But is that saying much? If our century is drawing to a close on the superficial level, in a fashion that gives some ground for hope, many people nevertheless feel increased misgivings about the nature of their society. Is the superficial level enough? Is merely being comfortable enough? Is a civilization which, whether capitalist or socialist, is based on the acquisition and deification of material objects, enough? Is it enough to possess a car, or two cars, a washing machine, a wallet filled with credit cards, an apartment in a highrise building? For billions of people living in wretchedness all over the world, these things are most certainly enough, more than enough. They would definitely seem so to most of the Indian and Spanish-speaking inhabitants of the American Southwest. Then why is it that, to so many people who possess them, they still do not represent, in spite of all the propaganda and the advertising slogans, the good and desirable life?

In America, at the present time, the feeling of a vague and unidentifiable dissatisfaction is very widespread. Could it be, one wonders in one's blacker moments, because the whole elaborate and glittering structure might be a commercial swindle, in the way socialism and communism are political swindles? Could it be because, despite its ease and convenience, such a life is actually only a form of slavery? The shackles are almost invisible; they do not chafe unduly; but they are shackles nonetheless, an affront to man's free spirit. For who owns that car, or that washing machine, or that apartment? Not the man himself. The banks own them, the insurance companies, ultimately the State. They are his only on credit, on sufferance. Every month he lops off a bit of his life and labor and mails it to the bank, or the credit card company, or the Government. He is in thrall; and there is no foreseeable end to it. The very people who own these institutions, who run these gigantic enterprises, despite their mountainous salaries are themselves in thrall, prisoners on the same treadmill. Was this, a man may ask himself in the dead watches of the night, was this the end for which a human being was intended by God, or by Nature? Was it for this that the Indian and Spanish-speaking peoples of the Southwest cast aside their ancient life styles—to become salesmen, insurance agents, bank clerks, civil servants? Is this the culmination of the grand experiment?

Behind all life in modern America is the thought that America, with 6 percent of the world's population, is using up 34 percent of the world's resources, without making a 34 percent contribution to the world's well-being. But before I probe this tender area, let me break off for a moment to speak of the positive aspects which, for me, far outweigh the negative ones of life in America.

The first and most obvious of these is the great good nature and generosity of spirit which characterizes Americans, the friendliness with which they still welcome, quite naturally, the stranger and the foreigner. This is a trait that was characteristic of an earlier America, and which has so far survived the onslaught of the Machine Age. To a European, this friendliness and generosity comes as both a surprise and a relief. And to an Englishman, used to *la morgue anglaise,* to the coolness, not to say coldness, of life in Britain, the warmth and immediacy of social relations in America are particularly welcome. Indeed, for a Briton, perhaps the most relaxing feature of American life is that one is automatically released from the tiresome class structure of Britain, from the snarling self-righteousness of both working and upper classes alike. Americans are altogether free from the suffocations of class; they accept people for what they are.

They are also free from another unpleasing trait of European society: pomposity. It is difficult to appreciate how stuffy Europeans tend to be, how prone to stand on their small distinctions, until you have lived in America for a while and breathed a larger air. And the general ease and approachability of Americans, which offends many Europeans, is attended by an almost complete lack of bitchiness and backbiting. Americans do try hard to like each other, to get on with each other, to see each other's good points. Sometimes this degenerates into blandness, naivety, and nice-guyishness, as when a Will Rogers made his fatuous assertion that he "never met a man he didn't like."

However, it is refreshing to enter such an atmosphere after the habitual wariness and suspicion of Europe, where a peculiar malice often governs the relations between individuals. And it is interesting to note that, although Americans share the natural love of gossip which is common to mankind, their gossip normally lacks the cutting edge of the gossip that one hears in other countries. This proclivity to think the best of one another is one of the secrets of their strength, in that unlike most Europeans, and certainly most Britons, they are actively eager to support and cooperate with one another. Cooperation comes as naturally to them as cantankerousness does to Europeans. Their openness with each other and with strangers also has another advantage: they are willing to acknowledge and to learn from their errors. They are not the sort of people who feel that the whole roof might fall in if they ever admitted that they made a mistake. Their flexibility is a noteworthy asset.

Finally, I must mention American good manners. You usually do not expect politeness and civility, of course, in swollen and frantic cities like New York or Chicago. The barbarity with which people treat each other in the world's big cities is one symptom among many of the complicated sickness of city life. But in the vast majority of communities throughout America, good manners are very much the rule, while Texan politeness is justly famous. I do not mean this to be a spinsterish observation, patting the boys and girls on the head for being nicely brought up; nor do I mean to imply that manners even in the larger cities in America or Europe are abominably crude, and that people stand on the street corners beating each other over the head. Nevertheless, outside the more unwieldy urban centers, Americans are remarkable for an affability of manner that is an extension of the general ease and openness of which I have spoken. A sour, dyspeptic, grouchy American is, at least in Texas and the Southwest, a distinct rarity. The ease and openness probably stem, at bottom, from the fact that America is still in many ways an underpopulated country, for all its staggering size, and that most of its people are not yet suffering from the nervous symptoms of overcrowding.

There is another aspect of American life, at least in the Southwest and similar regions, to which I would like to draw attention. This is its peacefulness. *Peacefulness?* Yet it is true, even though the statement runs counter to accepted opinion. In part this peacefulness, which like American good nature can also hover occasionally on the brink of passivity, derives from the fact that the Southwest and other rather similar areas are remote from the seats of power, and therefore lack the excitations of the major areas of population. El Paso is 2,000 miles away from New York and Washington, and almost 1,000 from Los Angeles; even its own state capital is 600 miles to the east, and Houston and Dallas further off still. As I pointed out in the last chapter, apart from El Paso, Phoenix, Tucson and Albuquerque, there are no large cities, and all of them are isolated from each other. It is hard to become hysterical over the events on the national scene when the places where they occur often seem almost as remote as if they were on Mars or Venus.

During my time in El Paso, the number of strikes, marches, counter-marches, and other disruptions of daily existence have been negligible, compared with what happens constantly in an English city of comparable size. As I said, it is all very peaceful. There seems to be a greater cohesion and civic discipline in America. I do not seek for a moment to gloss over the fearful incidence of crime in the United States. Statistics tell us that in 1970 there were 16,000 reported murders in America, and in that year there were 1,300 murders and 2,500 rapes committed in New York, against 120 murders and 7 rapes in London. However, most of those 16,000 were the usual spur-of-the-moment domestic homicides, largely taking place in the black or Puerto Rican communities. They were not the product of a criminal reign-of-terror, and there was a notable absence of bodies lying around in the gutters.

No less than 11,000 of these homicides were committed with firearms, and it seems obvious that, if guns were taken out of the hands of private citizens, the murder rate would sink to European proportions. At bottom, I insist, though my English friends will demur, that Americans are no more violent, and perhaps even less so, than people elsewhere. The Clockwork Orange syndrome is more typical of England. The number of annual traffic deaths in America, for example, runs between 55,000 and 60,000 a year—which is bad, of course, but proportionately no higher than in most other countries, and less than in many. Anyone who has driven widely in America will agree that Americans are, on the whole, excellent drivers, who by no means regard the automobile as a lethal weapon.

Why, then, their extraordinary addiction to shotguns and handguns? Handguns, after all, are ridiculous objects, which can only be used for shooting people, and have no other real purpose. They represent some childish and romantic notion that has got stuck in American heads, some folk memory of the prowess of the mountainmen with their Hawken rifles, of the frontier volunteers from Kentucky and Tennessee, of the Texas sharpshooters at Saltillo, and the Grass Fight. In twentieth century conditions, it is time such memories were laid to rest, deserving though they are of pride. Guns are satisfying virility symbols; but too many of them fall into the hands of idiots and maniacs. Can America continue to allow millions of its citizens to suffer from the outdated disease of Daniel Boone-itis or Hemingway-itis? Surely there is a better way to prove you are a man and an American than by going down to the local supermarket and buying a cheap pistol?

Nevertheless, I contend that it is self-evident that the average American is profoundly shocked by violence. The Calley affair was gruesome, and such things cannot be quantified; but it was surely small stuff compared to the masterpieces of those virtuosos of massacre, the Germans, the Russians, and the

Japanese. The Vietnam War was ghastly; but after six years its casualties hardly matched, in proportion, those of six days in the Congo, Indonesia, Nigeria, Sudan, Ceylon, or Madagascar. The assassinations of the Kennedys and Martin Luther King were shocking; but the world forgets that political assassinations occur everywhere. In England, a nineteenth-century Prime Minister was murdered by a lunatic; there were at least three attempts to assassinate Queen Victoria; one to assassinate Edward the Eighth; another to assassinate Princess Anne; and for all we know there have been attempts on the life of Queen Elizabeth. In any case, assassinations in democratic countries are an ironic compliment, testifying as they do to the openness of the social system and the willingness of royalty and government to mingle with the people. Unplanned assassinations seldom happen in Russia, whose leaders shuttle between their *dachas* and the Kremlin in bulletproof cars.

The point is that human life in America, even if you might get axed or potted by an angry spouse, is not held cheap. When three students at Kent State were shot dead, after a crowd had been spitting for an hour in the faces of a group of adolescent National Guardsmen, there was—and rightly—a tremendous outcry. In what other part of the world are the deaths of three students investigated so rigorously, or deplored so widely? In Japan? In Chile? In India? In Russia? I have already mentioned the massacre which took place in the Zócalo and at Tlaltelolco in Mexico City, at the time of the Olympic Games. Can one imagine what would have been said if the President of the United States had opened fire on the crowds outside the railings of the White House? It so happened that I was in Mexico when I read the news of the death of Martin Luther King. The Mexican papers pontificated about the "barbarousness" of American behavior. Rather rich, that, when you remember the persistent pattern of Mexican politics since 1819.

In imagination, and on celluloid, Americans are fascinated by violence, although they must appear to most outsiders as calm, almost placid citizens of an orderly and well-run country. A queer contradiction. Americans certainly *think* they are violent: but I believe that is largely a hangover from the old lawless times whose residual memory they cannot shake off. In reality, they are in a stage of psychological transition in which they are simultaneously paying lip-service to their past and trying to renounce it. The violence of their earlier history both attracts and repels them. Actually, they have long ceased to be wild and individualistic, as their grandfathers were. They are staid, conventional, rather timorous, and have an astounding dread of heterodox ideas. To tease them by indulging in the sort of conversational coat-tailing that is commonplace in Europe is to upset them dreadfully. They would love to think that what Toqueville wrote about them in 1835 was still true today: "The whole life of an American is passed like a game of chance, a revolutionary crisis, or a battle." There is still a grain of truth in it: but not more than a grain. The truth is that the modern American, particularly in Texas and the

Southwest, talks progressive, but he votes conservative. He assails Washington and all its works, but demands more than his share of federal money; indeed, the Southwest only exists at all thanks to federal spending on water projects, without which it would go back to the desert within a year. The Southwesterner flexes his muscles and goes into his old pioneer act; but when he creeps into the voting booth, he is a changed man. The modern American would like to shout and holler and crack his heels like Daniel Boone; but he must get up in the morning like everyone else, drive to the store or the office, and put in a solid eight hours earning enough money to pay the mortgage, the installment on his car, and for the braces on his daughter's teeth.

And in his soul, that is what he wants. The notion of the American spending his day in a revolutionary crisis or a battle is laughable. He hates revolutions; he hates battles. In spite of Paul Revere, Valley Forge, and the Continental Congress, and the homage he pays to them, he is the least revolutionary and least combative man in the world. He hates to fight. A child of revolution, the merest whisper of the word throws him into a panic. He thought hippies were revolutionaries. In European countries, George McGovern would scarcely have been regarded as mildly pink; in America, people talked about him as if he were a raving Bolshevik. Far from exporting revolution, this country born in revolution is on the whole a stabilizing and moderating force in the world. She has persuaded even the crackpots in Russia and China to calm down a little. For all the private arsenals, and the occasional shootouts, and the tomato ketchup in the movies, the world at large recognizes that fundamentally the American is a pacific and well-meaning soul.

Why *is* the American, so energetic in his outward appearance, nevertheless so timid and conventional in his inner life? Why does he fear any trace of genuine eccentricity or nonconformity? And why does he have such a dread of loneliness? Why, when you ask him if he would like to take a quiet evening stroll, does he bring along ninety-seven other people to accompany you? Why is he so frightened of sweet silence that he has to have Muzak wherever he goes? Why are his politics and his art almost devoid of theory or the profounder sort of originality? There is no space here to try to give a complete answer to such complex questions; but I would certainly place the facts of North American geography somewhere near the top of my list. As I wrote in my opening chapter, the modern American still feels the fear that his ancestors felt, when they left the cozy confines of Europe for a continent that was frightening in its extent and emptiness. The American still feels the touch of that old *horror vacui*. In the days when I used to fly from London to New York or Los Angeles, I was blasé about the country; but when I first had to drive across Texas in my Mercedes, and it took me three days, it made me begin to appreciate the scale of the natural setting and the smallness of the individual. Europeans too often overlook the sheer size of America.

SIXTEEN

THE AMERICAN, then, is a man caught between two worlds: the free, fizzy world that he imagines to be his past, and the regimented world he has constructed for himself, and to which he must now conform. Among the immediate reasons for the conventional cast of the modern American mind, I can very tentatively propose several. First, there is the leveling nature of much of American education. Americans want their educational system to be uniform, because they move about so constantly that it is sensible to be able to place one's children in a new school at the same grade as the one they have just left. They also base education on the principle of providing a fair education for the greatest number of people, rather than an élite education for a small group of the wealthy or gifted. Both these aims, given the sprawling size and ethnic complexity of America, are obviously sound. However, in practice the American school and university systems appear to have been designed by a demented German—and in fact much that is ponderous and heavy-handed in American life can be traced to the influence of the German immigration which took place into the United States in the last century. All American life has a distinct Teutonic tinge. In American schools, a child is put on a conveyor belt at the age of six, in the First Grade, and emerges twelve years later, at the age of eighteen, from the Twelfth Grade. The whole pattern is quite Prussian, and too cut-and-dried. In grade school and high school, the students follow precisely the same daily curriculum, day in and day out, and the only escape from the monotony is either to drop out of school or burn the place down. At college, the student is enmeshed in a web of "hours" and "requirements"

which make the average college resemble an automobile plant rather than a seat of learning. Students are processed rather than educated, and the acquisition of knowledge is made to appear less an adventure and a delight than a pitiless grind. The emphasis is not on the pursuit of enlightenment, but on staying the course. Since a college education consists in amassing the requisite number of "hours," and since collecting them can be done at any time, some men and women spend ten or fifteen years acquiring their degree; others leave college tottering and white-headed. There is a good deal to be said for the sudden-death European system: you go to college at eighteen and, unless you have a talent for research, you are finished at twenty-one—degree or no degree —and are ready to take your place in the world as a full-fledged adult.

If the conveyor belt character of education makes for dullness and orthodoxy, so does the environment in which the young American grows up and will live for the rest of his life. A few cities, such as New Orleans, Washington, San Francisco, Santa Fe, Denver, and Charleston, possess individuality. Most of the others are featureless, built on a grid system, their sections as interchangeable as if they were manufactured out of a child's construction kit. Their whimsical names, so evocative when one has never seen them, are often the only engaging thing about them. It is disillusioning to go to Truth-or-Consequences, to Laramie, or Cheyenne, and discover that they are merely segments of the same cardboard-and-plywood nightmare. If you were driven around blindfolded for three days, and dumped out of the car in the middle of an American city, unless the flora and the landscape were very distinctive you would find it difficult to tell if you were in Maryland or Indiana, Illinois or Oregon. Americans, in spite of their great qualities, are among the most aesthetically insensitive people on earth. Nature has provided them with an unrivalled landscape, and they have littered it with some of the ugliest cities mankind has ever built.

Again, there is a psychological reason for this. There is no doubt that Americans are fond of their shacklike cities, and approve of them being built in just this shoddy way. They are by nature a utilitarian people, exalting the practical over the beautiful. They have had to make a country from scratch, in less than two hundred years. Moreover, it is a comfort, when you are moving from one end of your huge country to the other, to be able to settle down in the same surroundings as those you have just left. It is a comfort to find the Exxon gas station on one corner, Kentucky Fried Chicken on another, Burger Chef on the third, Dairy Queen on the fourth. It is a comfort to drive seven hundred miles in a day and spend the night in a Holiday Inn or Travelodge absolutely identical, down to the last slab of plastic, to the one you slept in the night before. It makes nature seem more manageable: and as I said before, Americans are lonely in their huge country, and are frightened by it. It is curious that any group of South or Central American, Asian or European peasants should have been able to provide themselves with more attractive towns than the advanced American. Of course, there is another and simpler explanation of why Americans disfigure the countryside in the way they do: and that is commercial greed. Nature stands no chance when it becomes a question of the dollar. A developer can do more damage with his bulldozers in less time than the commander of a tank brigade.

In America, you can not only spend every night in identical surroundings: you can eat identical food. American women are superb cooks, but American cities lack good restaurants, and the regional dishes which provide the pleasure of dining in other countries are almost entirely lacking. There is, of course, a special cuisine in the Southwest, which I have described, and some big cities, such as San Francisco and New Orleans, have splendid restaurants. But most American eating-places (one cannot call them restaurants) stick to the same printed list of the same dishes. The typical meal consists of salad with a choice of three dressings (mass-produced and dispatched all over the United States in plastic containers); steak, with french fries or a baked potato; pie, with coffee. Steak, as in the Argentine, is a cult-object, an indicator of the national sense of well-being. More than the Dow Jones Index, the country is on the Steak Index. The steak habit goes back to the Civil War, when enormous amounts of it were fed to the troops of both sides, and when giant firms like Swift and Armour came into existence. Thus, after the Civil War, the great herds were built up, and the ranges became so overstocked that the price of steers fell to $5 a head.

Apart from steak, the range of meats and poultry eaten in America tends to be meager. Many kinds of meat and offal which are available elsewhere are unobtainable. Similarly, American fruit and vegetables tend to be tasteless, and practically everything comes out of a can, or is frozen. It is a healthful but unexciting regimen, represented at its most abysmal by the hamburger and the hot-dog, two of the most insipid comestibles ever devised.

One of the truly great pleasures and advantages of living in America, however, is to be able to drink American wines. It is becoming widely recognized that the best American wines are first-class, while the *vins ordinaires,* which are astonishingly inexpensive, far outrank most of their counterparts in Europe. American brandies are excellent, and the sherries of quite exceptional quality. You can drink your way backward and forward across America very contentedly.

But now, on the subject of drink, I really must ride one of my hobby-horses. I am now about to launch an attack on one of America's most revered institutions. The Presidency? The Supreme Court? The Congress? No. What, then? I am referring to—Coca-Cola. *Coca-Cola?* Why bother to dislike anything as harmless as Coca-Cola? You either like the taste of the stuff, or you don't. You can take it—or you can leave it. Yet, whenever I pass that blatant sign, whether in Texas or Timbuctu, I literally see red. And when I see and hear the advertisements for it, then, as the Americans say, I am fit to be tied.

"Next time you listen to a Beethoven Symphony," runs one of them, "listen with a Coke in your hand. It's the *REE-YUL* thing." Coca-Cola is *not* a "Ree-Yul Thing." What could there possibly be about this caramelized pap that merits comparison with Beethoven, or burgundy, or anything else that is a tribute to human taste and intelligence? "I'd like to buy the world a Coke and keep it compan-EE / I'd like to teach the world to sing / In perfect harmon-EE." Idealism and uplift, shamelessly combined with the profit-motive.

It is a pity that, to millions of people in the world, America *is* Coca-Cola. You will see its mark on a reed hut in Costa Rica, or a mud hut in the Sudan. It does seem regrettable that the making of this useless glop has been elevated to one of the major industries of the Western world. In scores of countries, the clinking trucks with the red eye on the side are rattling along the highways, carrying—what?—a load of colored water. When you wonder where some of that 34 percent of the world's resources is disappearing, think of those trucks.

One might think that this desire of Americans to squeeze themselves into a common, Coca-Cola sort of pattern would lower their vitality. Yet it does not. Americans are obviously one of the most energetic people in the world. Yet together with his formidable energy, his social cohesiveness, his Germanic thoroughness, the modern American displays a characteristic that seems quite out of key with those qualities, and which is hard to reconcile with them. For the American, who is in many ways such a solid and predictable fellow, nevertheless possesses what can only be called a remarkably short attention-span. It was Toqueville, again, who in his book on America pointed out that "the habit of inattention must be considered the greatest defect of the democratic system." I have already touched on the chopped-up nature of American education, where inside a monotonous syllabus students scramble for "hours" and "requirements"; and I have mentioned the temporary nature of American architecture, where people live in flimsy buildings that in the course of a few years will fall down, be blown down, or be torn down. America is a sort of gigantic transit-camp, which is why Europeans, with their irksome permanencies, often find it exhilarating to live in. It is the country of abandoned townships, of abandoned shops and houses.

The shortness of the American's attention-span applies also to personal relationships, and to marriage. In 1973 there were 725,000 divorces in America, and the chance of a marriage ending in divorce is now more than one in three, and will shortly become one in two. It is obvious what this means in terms of puzzled and distressed adults, and in numbers of insecure children. A large proportion of these divorces are undertaken on the spur of the moment, as a result of quarrels or misunderstandings that elsewhere are usually considered trivial and ephemeral. One wonders, too, about the basic soundness of that good old American custom, marrying one's childhood or high school sweetheart. Thousands of American girls marry at seventeen or eighteen, quickly realize they have made a mistake, and are divorced in their early or middle twenties, often with two or three children. There is nothing sadder than the spectacle of a young American divorcée struggling to bring up a clutch of children on her own.

Americans may also be said to possess a certain giddiness where their health is concerned. There is no need to labor the point about the time and money they spend on psychiatry. They also allow their surgeons to carve them up with the gusto of the surgeons of nineteenth century Edinburgh, who competed with one another to see who was quicker in lopping off a limb. The American Medical Association has stated that a third to a half of the operations performed in America are probably unnecessary. It is currently estimated that Americans swallow 8 billion pills a year, and in 1972 the President stated on television that the drug firms were manufacturing a yearly total of 5 billion doses of tranquilizers, 3 billion doses of amphetamines, and 5 billion doses of barbiturates. It has been said that one in three Americans regularly takes psychotropic drugs. There are other disturbing statistics. The number of reported cases of venereal disease, for example, runs at 275,000 a year; there are an estimated 6 million alcoholics; and there are over 325,000 known heroin addicts. Oddly enough, these figures may not testify so much to the sickness of American society as, paradoxically, to its vitality. Americans must indeed be a tough and vigorous breed to absorb such massive punishment and still stay alive.

The civilization of America is, in fact, a physical, muscular, combative, outgoing one. It is not intended for, or adjusted to, the private person, the introvert, the loner. Such people can suffer severely in American society. In such a predominantly athletic ambiance, it is not surprising that the phenomenon of the short attention-span should be nowhere more notable than in its physical activities, which are often symbolic of the inner nature of a society. In American football, for example, the game is broken up into a series of short, explosive, staccato plays. There is a game-plan to which the players adhere, but the overall appearance is not that of smooth, extended movements, but of a succession of sharp, jarring, convulsive clashes. It is intrusive to compare American football with European rugby or soccer. The European games are more fluid, more loosely organized, whereas the Americans, with that Teutonic desire for perfection, have developed their game into a marvellously intricate contest, a game of human chess, like the games that Frederick the Great played with his Grenadiers at Potsdam. In its ferocity, it resembles a miniature battle, a kind of masculine ordeal or ritual. Like all sports, one of its functions is to act as a safety-valve for deeper aggressions, and it commands an amazing following; each week the leading professional clubs attract a crowd numbering between 80,000 to 100,000, and would attract more if the stadiums were larger. It is certainly one of the cleverest, most riveting, most rigorous of all games.

It is reassuring that, with their enthusiasm for the martial evolutions of football, modern Americans possess so little liking for real warfare. Their enemies and detractors love to depict Americans as reeking, blood-soaked imperialists; but this is clearly nonsense. The Mylai massacre was carried out by a confused, inadequate boy, not by a trained automaton in the SS or NKVD. On the contrary, Americans are a decent, pacific people, not at all martial in the sense that the Germans, Russians, French, Spanish, Japanese, and English have been martial. Their attention-span in warfare is quite as short as it is in other matters. Except for the Civil War and Vietnam, American wars have been relatively brief. The War of Independence resulted in less than 3,500 killed in action on both sides; the War of 1812, though the British took a pounding at New Orleans (after peace had officially been declared), was a sideshow; the Mexican-American and Spanish-American wars were militarily negligible. Texas gained its independence for a loss of 750 men killed and wounded, including the 300 murdered at Goliad, and the Battle of San Jacinto was over in a matter of minutes. In World War One, American forces did not reach France until the summer of 1917; nor did they enter World War Two until December 1941. Their quick successes duped them as to the real nature of warfare, and it was not until Korea and Vietnam that they experienced an uneasy feeling that they might be getting out of their depth. In war, Americans tend to become bored easily; they like to pick up their marbles and go home when it suits them. They are civilians by temperament. Their sole field-commander of world stature since the days of Lee and Jackson was Douglas MacArthur, whose autocratic mien was resented. They are not attuned to the long haul; they could not have kept watch year after year at the outer limits of an empire, as the Romans and the British did; they would not have relished the incessant skirmishing on Hadrian's Wall or the Khyber Pass. After five years in Vietnam, the American army virtually disintegrated. The men were using drugs, refusing to mount patrols or to engage the enemy, and killing their officers and NCOs. This is hardly the portrait of a people brimming with martial ardor; it is the world of *The Good Soldier Schweik* and *Catch-22*. In 1971, there were 89,000 deserters from the American army in Vietnam, and even in the Marines the desertion rate had reached 59 men in 1,000; 194 men in 1,000 had gone absent without leave. In 1973, there were between 50,000 and 70,000 draft evaders living in Canada, and another 5,000 living in Sweden. One in ten of the military policemen guarding the American Embassy in Saigon were discovered to be heroin addicts, and the commander in chief's personal pilot was caught smuggling heroin back to the United States in his personal plane.

Of course, the Vietnam War became uniquely unpopular. In any case, all armies and navies have their troubles. In the past two centuries, the British, French, even the German armed forces have known large-scale mutinies. To Americans, however, any war of a sustained nature is likely to be unpopular. What Americans like is a rough-and-tumble, a Donnybrook; they are fighting-men, as distinct from soldiers. They prefer the scarlet epiphany of hand-to-hand combat to the disciplined tedium of strategy and tactics. Their military picture of themselves is that of Doniphan's army, advancing on the enemy cap askew, cigar in mouth, stripped to the waist. They love rowdy scraps like the Battle of the Horseshoe, Gonzalez, Goliad, or the Alamo. It was the image of the Alamo which reputedly haunted Lyndon Johnson, pathetically and absurdly, while he was engaged in a totally different kind of conflict in Southeast Asia.

Americans have no appetite for the slogging-matches, the Borodinos, Balaklavas, the Verduns. Their great-grandfathers did not leave Europe to become involved in senseless European-type butchery. They prefer to fight their battles on the baseball diamond and the football gridiron, where the action is short and sharp, and where no one gets killed. In the circumstances in which the world finds itself, is it really a reproach to a country that it lacks the military spirit? Surely the twentieth century has had enough of that? The only major drawback in the American attitude is that, their taste for warfare being minimal, their attention-span short, and their experience in Vietnam discouraging, they may be tempted, during a serious crisis, to opt for the easy way out. They may decide to use the atom bomb again, rather than face the protracted business of more conventional warfare.

I have saved, until last, my crowning example of the brief attention-span one encounters in American life: American TV and radio. Radio, an invaluable medium for disseminating music, opera, lectures, discussions, and educational programs, is an almost total write-off. Little is to be heard except the hyena voices of disc jockeys and hucksters, interspersed with rubbishy music and garbled newscasts. On TV, except in the gallant but restricted sphere of the Public Broadcasting Service, the programs are parceled out into grudging amounts of banal entertainment broken up by solid blocks of advertising. The advertisers entirely control the programs, which effectively ensures their puerility.

Fifty-five percent of these advertisements are devoted to bathroom matters. They represent the American people as a race of sweating, farting, itching, scratching, drooling, dribbling, defecating morons. American women, according to the advertising industry, possess smelly hair, smelly mouths, smelly feet, smelly armpits, and smelly vaginas; they wear smelly clothes, sleep with smelly men between smelly sheets, and cook in smelly kitchens in smelly houses. It would be interesting to try and decide when the Americans, the proud descendants of those muck-stained pioneers who broke the plains and deserts, parted company from their greatest poet, who declared in *A Song for Myself:*

> Divine I am inside and out, and I make holy whatever I
>   touch or am touch'd from,
> The scent of these arm-pits aroma finer than prayer . . .

It is extraordinary that no one feels affronted or disgusted by this intolerable parade of personal intimacies. The American preoccupation with bad odors is in fact very curious, and no doubt related to very complicated kinds of guilt; a sociologist might make much of it.

To give some idea of the present standard of American television, let me cite the fashion in which Marlowe's *Doctor Faustus* was presented in 1972 by ABC, one of the three major networks. It went as follows:

Introductory Commercial: Budweiser Beer

    (TITLES OF FILM)

Commercials: 1. Nestea
        2. Nescafe
        3. Oil Companies of America

    (SECTION OF FILM)

Commercials: 1. Schlitz (*"When you're outta Schlitz, you're outta beer"*)
        2. Breck Texturizing Shampoo (*"With protein"*)
        3. Coolray Polaroid Sunglasses (*"So you can see what you betta see"*)
        4. Movie Commercial (*Local cinema*)
        5. Executive Motors (*Local dealer*)
        6. Thomasville Furniture (*"That Thomasville look!"*)

    (SECTION OF FILM)

Commercials: 1. Clorox Bleach (*"For your children's diapers"*)
        2. Coca-Cola (*"Goodbye, Sugar, it was fun—but it was just one of those things"*)
        3. Chuck-Wagon Complete Four-Course Dinner for Dogs
        4. Franklin Optical (*"With three offices downtown"*)
        5. Northeast Furniture (*"Drive a little, save a lot"*)

    (SECTION OF FILM)

Commercials: 1. Lysol Spray Disinfectant
        2. Dial-Dry (*"Time-release antiperspirant formula"*)
        3. Coca-Cola (*"The uniqueness of Coke. You don't mess around with the real thing"*)
        4. Excedrin (*"For hours of relief when it hurts—and where it hurts"*)
        5. B and E Automotive (*Local dealer*)
        6. Movie Commercial (*Local cinema*)

7. Piggy-Bank Gasoline (*"Beautiful Free Thermo-Tumbler to Complement Any Table Setting"*)

(SECTION OF FILM)

Commercials: 1. Flying Insect Killer
2. Miller Hi-Life Beer
3. Vista Soft-and-Easy Wax
4. Pepto-Bismol (*"Soothes your stomach"*)

(SECTION OF FILM)

Commercials: 1. Ruffles Potato Chips (*"Rrrruffles!"*) ·
2. Lay's Potato Chips (*"Mini-Whizz Ring—It's Free!"*)
3. Buick Skylark (*"Get your hands on one now—while they last"*)
4. Lipton Iced Tea

Looks bad, doesn't it? . . . *Was this the face that launched a thousand ships?* . . . Cut to a can of dog food . . .

Beer, automobiles, aspirins, deodorants, gasoline, Coca-Cola, dog food, disinfectant, potato chips, shampoos, stomach powder. An unkind commentator would call it a grotesque summary of the typical preoccupations of American life. Large sections of American society have been totally brainwashed by the advertising industry, and there are even many thoughtful Americans who try to minimize the embarrassment which television causes them by pretending to be amused by the alleged cuteness of the commercials. A gallon of Pepto-Bismol cannot really prevent their stomachs from churning.

I have confessed that I have not succeeded in reconciling what is obviously well-ordered in American life with what is exaggerated and absurd. These characteristics can exist side by side in the same community, even in the same person. They are characteristics which Americans themselves cannot reconcile. It is possible that they proceed from a fundamental fissure in American life: the clash between a compulsive work-ethic on the one hand, and the pursuit of happiness on the other. On one side is the doctrine of justification by works; on the other, the determination to have a "fun time." A painful oscillation is set up as the urge toward progress and perfectibility vies with the desire to "let it all hang out." The idea of duty is at war with the pleasure principle. An overdeveloped Ego is locked in combat with a hyperactive Id. Americans are alternately dominated by one or the other, and cannot bring them into harmony. This is what may help to make them restless and keep them rushing about. It is a tendency that seems to be growing more pronounced. If you don't like your car, you change it; if you don't like your job, you change it; if you don't like your wife, you change her. There is some wisdom in this philosophy, but there is a question as to how far it can be taken.

The creed of the Pursuit of Happiness is held with genuine faith and fervor by Americans; they cling to it in spite of all setbacks and disappointments, and in spite of the fact that, as Mill pointed out long ago, in his *Essay on Liberty,* happiness is only a by-product of human activity, not an end-in-itself. Human beings may not be built for happiness; happiness may not be the true goal of their lives. However that may be, it explains why Americans deify youth. Youth is supposed to be the age at which people are at their happiest—although, for many young people, it is actually a time of muddle and misery. It also explains why middle-aged Americans sometimes swing to the other extreme and hate young people, because they are jealous of their youth and their alleged happiness, yet simultaneously envy and disapprove of their idleness. Furthermore, these psychological difficulties are aggravated by the fact that the concept of the Pursuit of Happiness has somehow got itself fused with the concept of the American Dream, and both have been projected from an unsatisfactory present into a hypothetically satisfactory future. Such an unrealistic attitude to life is bound to make for restlessness, just as the concept of the Great Red Dawn has made life miserable for the peoples of Communist Russia and Socialist England. Politicians know how to exploit our yearning for the perfect society, a yearning which is at bottom a regressive tendency to recapture the security of infancy and return to the Garden of Eden. They coin cynical labels for it. Kennedy had his "New Frontier," Lyndon Johnson his "Great Society" (a touch of Texas, there), and Harold Wilson his "Compassionate Society." Sooner or later, of course, their promises catch up with them; but such cant phrases can usually serve to win an election or two. Nevertheless, it is really astonishing that politicians still have the nerve to dish up this sort of thing to suffering humanity. Here is George McGovern, in the spring of 1972: "I am talking about declaring a new national goal: an end to poverty and pollution and racism; an end to the rot and decay of our cities; an end to undereducated and under-cared-for people. An end to it all by the end of this decade." George McGovern was going to abolish sin by 1980.

The bluebird of happiness flutters tantalizingly ahead, and the American flounders after it. However, there are times when this fluid, protean nature of American life, as I pointed out in an earlier chapter, is a positive advantage. It is, after all, more important to have goals than to reach them. American life is like no other, in that it exists in a perpetual state of change. It exists for change; it glories in it. Since it is not anchored in the past, it is not fettered by it. America began with a rush a mere two hundred years ago, ran headlong into the Industrial Revolution, and has maintained its momentum. It has no fixed traditions, because each new wave of immigrants was required to forget them—and *did* forget them, once they had two thousand miles of ocean between themselves and Europe. And since it was in a constant state of change, because its very essence was flux, it was in a unique position to profit from the turmoil of change and acceleration loosed on the world by the French and the Industrial revolutions. America has been able to ride the rough waves of our age more successfully than other societies because the people in the ship have not been looking back toward the land they left, or arguing about points of precedence among the passengers, or putting down mutinies among the crew. There has been a general sense of all being in the same boat.

On the other hand, this appetite for change, which enables Americans to sail confidently over dangerous reefs, has a noteworthy drawback. The traditions which other countries have inherited, and which sometimes hamper them and slow them up, also give them a sense of structure, of stability, a real if often restrictive code of ethics. Americans are not prone to the sadistic outbursts which Europeans indulge in two or three times a century: yet there is a breezy dishonesty about much of American political and economic life that may, sooner or later, sink the ship. There is no need to be too prim. There are sometimes advantages in living in countries which are moderately corrupt, though it is unpleasant to loiter in those which, although they may be otherwise attractive, manifest a total and systematic corruption, like many countries in modern Asia and the Americas. However, a judicious gratuity here and there does help to oil the wheels of the machines in which the politicians have enmeshed us.

The great mass of Americans, who are neither corrupt nor corruptible, are forced to live in a cancerous atmosphere of political and economic corruption. They know this, and are unhappy about it, but can do little to correct it. They are the sheep whom the politicians and the big businessmen shear. In his *Devil's Dictionary,* Ambrose Bierce wrote: "Politics: The conduct of public affairs for private advantage." What are Americans to say, when the Vice-President of the United States accepts money in brown paper envelopes in his own private office? What are they to say of the ITT and Milk Fund cases, or the secret contributions to the Committee to Re-elect the President? What are they to say when the Governor of Illinois, the author of a Presidential report on violence, and another on the riots at the 1968 Chicago Democratic Convention, is sent to jail for fraud? What are they to say when the staff of the Speaker of the House is found to have been infiltrated by the Mafia? What are they to say when a justice of the Supreme Court is forced to resign because he has been financially compromised? What are they to say about the multiple revelations of Watergate? Or what, to come nearer home, are the people of the Southwest to say about the Sharpstown Bank scandal that hit Texas in 1970, and which by the time it was finished had destroyed the reputations or had resulted in prison sentences for the Governor of America's second largest state, his party chairman, the Speaker of his House of Representatives, his Lieutenant Governor, his Treasurer, his Attorney General, and the Assistant Attorney General of the United States?

The law locks up both man and woman
Who steals the goose from off the common;
But lets the greater felon loose
Who steals the common from the goose . . .

The human story of the Southwest, like the story of every part of the globe, has been shot through with tragedy. The chapter through which it is now passing inevitably contains its tragic elements, like those that preceded it. As Robinson Jeffers wrote in *A Redeemer:*

Oh, as a rich man eats a forest for profit and a field
for vanity, so you came west and raped
The continent and brushed its people to death. Without
need, the weak skirmishing hunters, and without mercy.

It was an accident of history that the Anglo and the Spaniard, and the European in general, possessed an irresistible dynamic and an overriding technology. Isabella tells the judge, in *Measure for Measure: O! it is excellent /* *To have a giant's strength, but it is tyrannous / To use it like a giant.* In view of the giant strength that Europeans and their American counterparts have possessed for four centuries, it is remarkable that on the whole (with the exception of certain nations) they have tried to exercise it with a corresponding restraint.

Yet the history of the Southwest, this marvellous ethnographic laboratory, is not, as I have tried hard to show, entirely one of brutality and aggression, even in the European eras. And during the centuries when the Hohokam and Anasazi were in the ascendant, there seems to have been a generally mild and pacific interregnum. As for the Pueblo people, who are their descendants, they have also demonstrated that they much prefer peace, which is largely the art of minding one's own business and cultivating one's own garden, to war. But then, the Pueblo people are customarily regarded as primitive and backward, incapable of conceiving and manufacturing such wonders as the tank, submarine, and intercontinental missile. Of course, the Pueblo community is small, a factor that may have something to do with its artistic inventiveness and spiritual capacity. It has been my thesis that, in spite of the way in which the modern world is mesmerized by the idea of bigness, smallness is on the whole a more saving concept.

The Southwest, and the huge nation in which it is embedded, certainly possesses, as I have suggested in my last two chapters, its meed of problems and difficulties. Every age in the Southwest has brought its troubles: and it is because fresh troubles inevitably arise when others are being cleared up, because the very act of clearance actually appears to stimulate new ones, that I am no believer in progress, except in a very limited sense. Humanity will never get its equations right. But this does not mean that there is not a very great deal that is commendable about the modern Southwest, and about modern America—nor am I forgetting, when I say this, my earlier reservations about the fundamental nature of our society. I have indicated some of my reasons for liking and admiring America, and why I have enjoyed living in the Southwest and among Southwesterners.

The ills that assail modern America—dubious politicians, venal lawyers, slothful bureaucrats, unappeasable monopolists, untrammelled racketeers—afflict all other countries in the modern world, often to a much worse degree. With all their shortcomings, American politicians, lawyers, businessmen, and the rest remain more accountable to the public and are more accessible than their opposite numbers in Europe. Any American can easily imagine himself chatting on equal terms with his President, Senator or Congressman; European kings, queens, presidents, and prime ministers are seldom available for the man-in-the-street to talk to, and neither side would have much to say to each other if they were. One might have one's doubts about American leaders, but the gap that exists between leaders and led is smaller than in any other country I have visited. This testifies to the absence of caste among Americans, the existence of a sense of interrelationship, a more warm and family feeling. Fundamentally, I would deny the right of any man, even if he calls himself an elected representative of the people, to rule over another man and to impose his will on him. But if we must have governments, then on the whole I prefer the American brand to most others of which I have knowledge. It is more easygoing. I find American wheeler-dealers more amusing and less irksome than English idealogues. At their worst, they only want to steal your money; the English zealots want your soul.

Americans, with their whimsical historical and geographical perspectives, are fond of exaggerating their own importance and asserting that, in the famous phrase, "America is the last best hope of humanity." I daresay humanity will continue to stagger along, with or without the United States. But, in a difficult century, they have set a more or less consistent example of decency. In the hard times ahead, the world might be thankful for the qualities which Americans, in spite of defects and setbacks, demonstrably possess: energy, optimism, generosity, and the conviction, often betrayed but nonetheless firmly held, that men are brothers.

INDEX

Hopkins, Gerard Manley, 12
Horgan, Paul, 119, 122
Horse, 37, 114, 148–151, 154, 170,
185, 222, 234, 238, 239
Houston, Sam, 208–209, 210
Hovenweep, 60, 266
Hualapai, 47, 140–141, 171
Hudson, W. H., 150
Huxley, Aldous, 12, 89–91

I

Illegal immigration, 254
Indians, distribution of, in Southwest
and Mexico, 143–146
Indians, families and sub-families of,
144
Indians, in Southwest, 68, 70, 136–154,
206, 210, 236, 243, 249, 253
Indians, Plains, 84, 151, 217, 218,
253
Indians, Pueblo, see Pueblos and Pueblo
Indians
Indian Wars, 215, 219, 222
Isleta pueblo, 68, 82
Ixtaccíhuatl, 22, 201

J

Jackson, Andrew, 208, 209, 249
James, Henry, 248
James, Jesse, 240
Jumano Indians, 116–117, 136
Janos, 192
Java, 36
Jeffers, Robinson, 249, 307
Jefferson, Thomas, 209, 249
Jemez pueblo, 66, 68, 74, 118
Jesuits, 123, 127, 130, 142, 192, 195
Jews, 252
Jornada del Muerto, 22, 109, 110, 113,
133, 212
Joyce, James, 1
Juárez, Benito, 199, 209
Juárez, Ciudad, 7, 199, 204, 272–284
Jung, C. G., 5, 73, 76, 82, 88–89
Jutland, Battle of, 5

K

Kamia, 140
Kansas, 25, 106, 109, 112, 216, 235,
237
Kayenta, 60, 160
Kearney, General Stephen Watts, 159,
212
Keet Seel, 60
Kennedy, President John F., 214, 305
Keresan, 63, 82
Kidder, A. V., 66
Kingston, 224
Kino, Fr. Eusebio, 44, 123–127, 129,
130, 131, 172, 192, 193, 218, 244,
261, 270
Kiowa, 145, 172, 184, 185, 186, 187
Kivas, 48, 52–56, 60, 63–64, 73–74
Kluckhohn, Clyde, 3, 160
Koshares, 76, 78–80
Kroeber, A. L., 100
Kroeber, Theodora, 131
Kropotkin, Prince, 86, 91
Kuaua, see Coronado National Monu-
ment

L

Ladinos, 134, 206
La Farge, Oliver, 163–164
Laguana pueblo, 72, 82, 85, 118, 169
Lake Valley, 222, 224
Lamar, Napoleon Bonaparte, 210
Lamy, Archbishop, 270
Lanternari, Vittorio, 166, 167
La Quemada, 43, 203
La Salle, 118
Lascaux, 18, 38
Las Cruces, 214, 222
Las Humanas Indians, see Jumanos
Las Vegas (Nevada), 261, 262–264,
268
Las Vegas (New Mexico), 217, 246
Lawrence, D. H., 75–80, 90, 158, 171
Leakey, Louis, 36
Lee, General Robert E., 210
Lewis, Oscar, 274